AMERICAN INDIAN HISTORY

AMERICAN INDIAN HISTORY

Five Centuries of Conflict & Coexistence

Volume I
Conquest of a Continent, 1492–1783

Robert W. Venables

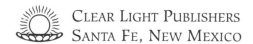 CLEAR LIGHT PUBLISHERS
SANTA FE, NEW MEXICO

*For my mother Florence Seldon Venables, my late father
Charles Ogden Venables, my spouse Sherry Baugher and
our son Brant, with love and gratitude for all your support
and encouragement.*

Copyright 2004 ©Robert W. Venables
Clear Light Publishing
823 Don Diego
Santa Fe, NM 87505
www.clearlightbooks.com

First Edition
10 9 8 7 6 5 4 3 2 1

Library of Congress Cataloging-in-Publication Data

Venables, Robert W.
  American Indian history: five centuries of conflict and coexistence /
by Robert W. Venables.— 1st ed.
    p. cm.
  Includes bibliographical references and index.
   ISBN 1-57416-074-5 (vol. I), ISBN 1-57416-076-1 (vol. II),
   ISBN 1-57416-077-X (set: vols I & II),
   1. Indians of North America—Government relations. 2. Indians of
North America—First contact with Europeans. 3. Indians, Treatment
of—North America—History. 4. Ethnic conflict—United States—History.
5. United States—Social conditions. 6. United States—Race relations.
7. United States—Politics and government. I. Title.
  E93 .V45 2003
  973.04'97—dc21
                            2002156507

Cover design by Marcia Keegan and Carol O'Shea
Cover images ©Culver Pictures, New York, NY: IND015 CP001 005 ("Visit of Pontiac and
the Indians to Major Gladwyn"), IND015 CP001 026 ("Treating with Indians in the Olden
Time"), IND002 CP001 030 ("Spanish Explorers Fighting Indians: Early"), IND018 CP001
022 ("Trading with the Indians"), IND005 CP001 126 ("They See a Lightning Flash, and
Hear a Roar.")
Interior design and typography by Carol O'Shea
Printed in the U.S.A.

Acknowledgments

Marcia Keegan and Harmon Houghton, the publishers of Clear Light, have continually provided moral and practical support, and I heartily thank them both. I am also very grateful that my editor, Barbara Kohl, provided such thorough and insightful advice on virtually every page. I would also like to thank the designer, Carol O'Shea, for all her fine work.

My parents, Florence and Charles Venables, inspired my initial love of history through their conversations, books and family travel. As an undergraduate at Northwestern University, I especially benefited from the insights and encouragement of Ray Allen Billington. During my graduate studies at Vanderbilt University, I deeply appreciated the thorough guidance of Douglas Edward Leach. His strong sense of ethics during the Civil Rights Movement of the 1960s significantly contributed to my moral development and political activism.

I owe a great debt to the many people of North America's First Nations who have helped me. I am especially grateful to Chief Irving Powless, Jr., of the Onondaga Nation, for giving me patient instructions for more than three decades. He, together with his wonderful wife, the late Helen Powless, always endeavored to increase my knowledge and the range of my thinking. I would also like to thank Professor Robert E. Powless (Oneida, Wisconsin) and his wife Linda for their three decades of friendship and encouragement. Oren Lyons (Onondaga) and John Mohawk (Seneca) have always been helpful, none more so than while I was writing of a chapter in their book *Exiled in the Land of the Free*. At Onondaga, I remain grateful for the support of Clan Mothers Audrey Shenandoah and Freida Jacques. Also at Onondaga, the late Leon Shenandoah, the late Chief Irving Powless, Sr., the late Chief Paul Waterman, and the late Alice Papineau all generously shared valuable lessons that I treasure. John Fadden (Mohawk) has always encouraged me when I needed it most, and I am also grateful to his father, Ray Fadden, for sharing his passionate interpretations of American Indian history with me when I was a teenager. I am also grateful for the guidance I have received from many friends at Akwesasne such as Chief Tom Porter, Chief Mike Mitchell, Chief Jake Swamp, Ernie Benedict, Salli Benedict, Doug George and Dr. Mary Arquette. I am grateful for all I learned among the Tonawanda Senecas, especially from the late Chief Corbett Sundown, the late Chief Bernie Parker, Ramona Charles and Darwin Hill. Rick Hill (Tuscarora) has demonstrated to me over the years how art, history and a sense of humor can be combined, and Peter Jemison (Seneca) has generously shared his extensive knowledge of both art and history. Joanne Shenandoah (Oneida) has encouraged me even as her wonderful music raises all of our spirits. Vine Deloria, Jr. (Standing Rock Sioux), has had an impact on my thinking since 1969, before I actually met him, and I am grateful for the few but significant times he has shared his thoughts with me in person. At the American Indian Community House, New York City's urban Indian center, I learned a great deal from Michael Bush (Mohawk) and Rosemary Richmond (Mohawk). Professor Angela Cavender Wilson (Dakota) and her father, Professor En Hidi Nazin (Chris) Mato Nunpa, have given me additional perspectives on comparative history, especially through their intensive studies of Dakota oral traditions, and I appreciate their friendship. Oscar Archiquette (Oneida, Wisconsin) passed away in 1971, but his instructions and insights remain vital to me.

At Cornell University, my constant mentor has been Kay WalkingStick (Cherokee), and I have gained wonderful insights through her art and our many conversations. I am grateful to the late Ron LaFrance (Mohawk), the former director of the Cornell American Indian Program, who increased my appreciation of the links between language and worldview. Stephen Fadden (Mohawk) provided many insights in the early 1990s when we team-taught American Indian studies courses at Cornell University to hundreds of students each semester. I also have enjoyed and benefited from the insights of undergraduate and graduate students at Cornell, especially those who were my teaching assistants.

Professor Laurence M. Hauptman, State University of New York at New Paltz, has been a solid friend and advisor for more than three decades. I owe a special debt of gratitude to another friend, Linda Rosekrans, who teaches Indian studies at the State University of New York at Cortland. She initially helped me teach and manage my large classes at Cornell. Then, because of her focus on English and literature, she generously agreed to retype most of this book into a computer—because I, having adopted computers rather late, composed all but the last chapters of this book on various typewriters. I would also like to thank the German journalist, Claus Biegert, for sharing his vast knowledge and network of contacts. Dr. Sally Roesch Wagner, with her vital research in women's history, has also remained a constant friend. Lawyers have been especially important in the development of my understanding of the complexity of Indian history, and thus I would especially like to thank Peter Hutchins, Anjali Choksi, Micha J. Menczer, Paul Williams and Joseph J. Heath for all their guidance.

Over many decades, I have benefited from the fine suggestions offered to me by colleagues at many universities and museums, but I would especially like to thank the staffs of the New York Historical Society and the libraries of Cornell University.

My spouse, Professor Sherene Baugher, continually provided me with insights and help in improving the book, and I have benefited tremendously from her long experience as an archaeologist whose ethical positions have encouraged First Nations to enlist her support on many occasions. Finally, I am deeply grateful for the unselfish love and patient support of both my son, Brant, and my spouse, Sherry—especially whenever I became frustrated with the book, various legal decisions in Canada and the United States, or life in general.

Table of Contents
Volume I

Introduction: Crowded Wilderness   VIII

I.   The Paradox of the Crowded Wilderness: Indians Discover Europeans, 1492–1566   1

II.   Old Confederations & New Resistance   36

III.   Thanksgiving's Children   74

IV.   Warriors & the Claims of Kings   114

V.   Trade & Land in the Contest for Empire   165

VI.   Retrospectives: Indian Impacts on Slavery and the Roles of Women in the Colonial Era   205

VII.   Betrayal "Christians Only Were Capable Of"   242

References   311

Index   320

Introduction: Crowded Wilderness

After Christopher Columbus and his crews arrived in 1492, American Indians saw their homelands increasingly crowded by Europeans who believed they were entering a wilderness. The "crowded wilderness" paradox lies at the heart of both the physical and spiritual conflicts that mark the last five hundred years of human history in the Western Hemisphere. No single moral logic has yet emerged from this crowded wilderness. Differing views continue to define concepts of America's cultural landscape—each person's sense of "the power of place" (Hayden 1997, xi, passim; Deloria 1991).

> "Calling the Indians Out"
> Trouble in our own land, crimes against the human soul
> far too large for any describing words to hold.
> Wynton Marsalis

"Calling the Indians Out" commemorates and evokes the spiritual and physical essence of all Indian people. Significantly, Wynton Marsalis, the classical and jazz trumpeter who is also one of America's most brilliant composers, placed this sacred remembrance at the very start of "Blood on the Fields," a jazz oratorio he created in 1994 that won the 1997 Pulitzer Prize for Music (Peterson 1997; Marsalis 1997). That an African American composer chose to address the conquest of Indian America at the very beginning of an oratorio that focuses on the issues of slavery speaks volumes about the darkest aspects of American history. Marsalis's jazz oratorio reminds us that much of American history is composed of repetitious cruelty. But his work is also a universal affirmation of how all humans who have been oppressed can endure by calling upon their spiritual faiths, their arts, and their survival strategies.

The histories of the United States and the entire Western Hemisphere demonstrate that warfare and slavery are not simply matters of cultural or racial confrontations. There is more than enough tragedy and irony to leave any student of history stunned. First, it is a fact that both American Indians and Africans suffered wars of conquest and subsequent enslavement due to European aggression. But it is also true that Africans sold other Africans into European colonial slavery, adding a moral complexity to the history of slavery and warfare in Africa—a circumstance Wynton Marsalis addresses in his oratorio. In comparison, the reader of this book will discover that while American

Indians and African Americans sometimes had much in common, they were also often on opposite sides, even to the point that many Indian individuals would eventually own African slaves.

"Crimes against the human soul"—Marsalis's words are applicable to all those morally complex aspects of human history wherever and whenever they may have occurred. Comparatively, many of the events detailed in this book are also a reflection of the darker sides that pervade all human history. Yet at the beginning of the twenty-first century, most of the people within the United States would rather define dark historic forces as they existed or still exist in other parts of the world, in Nazi Germany or in the Middle East for example, than to look to their own shores and recognize a parallel darkness. In fact, most citizens of the United States (and the other nations who have benefited from the conquest of the entire Western Hemisphere) have hardly begun to cope with the hemisphere's heritage of war and enslavement. Most citizens of the United States prefer a collective amnesia. As the Laguna Pueblo writer Leslie Marmon Silko notes sardonically: "In the United States, history goes back maybe two or three months" (Silko 1991). With the hope of removing at least a part of this collective amnesia, the events in this book will take the reader back to 1492 to witness some of the major events involved in the conquest of Indian America in what is now the United States.

As a result of the very complex history that defines the centuries since 1492, not one American Indian nation has full membership in the United Nations. This is an indication of how thorough the conquest of the entire Western Hemisphere has been. In contrast, there are Asian nations with full United Nations representation, reflecting religions and cultures of Asian origin. There are African nations with full representation, reflecting religions and cultures of African origin. And there are European nations with full representation, representing religions and cultures of European origin. Despite losing two twentieth-century world wars, Germans still have Germany. Jewish people have reasserted a homeland lost two thousand years ago, and Israel is represented in the United Nations. Lithuania, Latvia and Estonia are freed of the Soviet empire that once claimed them. Yet few North Americans would imagine, let alone encourage, the emergence of the Navajo Nation of the American Southwest from its bonds to empire—despite the fact that the Navajo Nation is larger (26,897 square miles) (Velarde Tiller 1996, 214) than Estonia (16,769 square miles), Latvia (25,190 square miles), or Lithuania (25,212 square miles) (Trumbull 2002, 600, 654, 660). Of course it just so happens that the Navajo

Nation is populated with fewer people, they are not white, and they don't happen to be primarily Christian. Instead of full membership in the world's "United Nations," the Navajo Nation and other First Nations of the Americas are relegated to the U.N. status of "nongovernmental organizations." They can only observe and comment on the proceedings of "recognized" nations (Quesenberry 1999, 103–104; Deloria and Lytle 1998, 241–42; *Akwesasne Notes* 1978, 5–6, 38–124).

The permanent occupation by non-Indian nations of what were once Indian lands has another significant implication: while there is a postcolonial history of Africa and a postcolonial history of Asia, a postcolonial history of the Western Hemisphere is not likely. The invaders' descendants and those who have benefited from their conquests now call Indian lands their own. These heirs of conquest will never return to their ancestors' homelands, and the First Nations will be forever surrounded.

In the United States alone, 98 percent of the land no longer belongs directly to Indian nations. Much of this land was transferred to the United States by treaties in exchange for a variety of guaranteed rights and promises. There are at least 395 Indian treaties sanctioned by surviving Indian nations and the U.S. federal government under its Constitution (Deloria and DeMallie 1999, 202–208). They are not just "Indians' treaties," that is, treaties that apply only to Indians. The obligations defined in these treaties lie with non-Indian U.S. citizens as well as with the members of particular Indian nations. Yet not one of these treaties is fully enforced, even though these treaties represent what were already the very cheapest—and simultaneously often the most fraudulent—land acquisitions in history. Under capitalism's rules of landlord rights and property law, American Indians should be the richest inhabitants of North America. Instead they are the poorest, and they are even poorer elsewhere in the Americas.

American Indians and invading Europeans had, and often still have, very different worldviews. Because of this, each Indian nation and each European nation defined events in irreconcilable terms. While the results and consequences of their conflicts were and remain one-sided, the history that brought all this about is multidimensional. That said, while the conflicts can be described and even understood intellectually, they remain difficult if not impossible to justify.

Chapter after chapter of this book details how the America of today was built on conquered and stolen land. A paramount fact emphasized in this book is that the invaders had no "rights," even under their own European international laws to begin the wars of invasion. What are often popularly described as "Indian wars" are actually "white wars." To justify these wars, the invaders created rights, such as the "right of discovery" and "right of conquest," pretending that these mental gymnastics were moral and sanctioned by their religious beliefs.

Cruel wars often led to cruel retaliations. While reading about all these conflicts, the reader might consider remembering that during all of these wars, the First Nations of the Americas were trying desperately to defend their families, their religions and their lands. Furthermore, the facts demonstrate that most of the cruelty was carried out by the invaders.

The conflicts described in this book were due in part to the invaders' greed, religious fanaticism and racism. But the reader will also discover that a major factor in these conflicts was a psychology of warfare all too common throughout human history. In fact, on all sides and in any conflict, including the history of Indian America after 1492, a psychology of warfare erupted within each combatant's existing philosophies, religions, cultures and social orders. To place the issue of warfare psychology in a perspective beyond the boundaries of American Indian history, it is useful to view the worst extremes of another American conflict of ferocious complexity, the Civil War, which raged from 1861 to 1865. The War Between the States created many extremes of hateful behavior and irrational propaganda by both sides. Those on both sides who held nobler sentiments could not diminish these attitudes, just as those on all sides, Indian and non-Indian alike, failed to temper the conflicts which followed 1492.

In 1930, William B. Hesseltine, a history professor at the University of Chattanooga, sought to understand the often ferocious passions engendered by the American Civil War by studying the horrific prison camps run by both the Union and Confederate sides. He applied his conclusions to human history in general, and they are certainly applicable to the conquest of America:

> Apparently an inevitable concomitant of armed warfare is the hatred engendered in the minds of the contestants by the conflict.... The attachment to an ideal, a cause, or a country, when such attachment calls for the sacrifice of security and life, blinds the person feeling that attachment to whatever virtue there may be in the opposing ideal, cause, or country. Seemingly, it becomes necessary for the supporters of

one cause to identify their entire personality with that cause, to identify their opponents with the opposing cause, and to hate the supporters of the enemy cause with a venom which counterbalances their devotion to their own (Hesseltine 1930, 172; cf. Horigan 2002).

Hesseltine also noted how an enemy's differences could be perceived as "sins."

Opponents appear to be defective in all principles....The enemy becomes a thing to be hated; he does not share the common virtues, and his peculiarities of speech, race, or culture become significant as points of difference or, better, sins of the greater magnitude (Hesseltine 1930, 172).

Attitudes held during wars, however, were just one factor in the conquest of Indian America because these attitudes were not forgotten during times of peace. Thus, while wars against First Nations were frequent, the reader will also realize how consistently the conquerors used periods of peace to manipulate and cheat Indian nations. In this sense, the unscrupulous events that followed each "peace" were at least as immoral as each war. The reader will also no doubt note that while all sides are involved in the brutality of war, only one side consistently broke each peace and each treaty throughout the centuries, throughout America.

The reader will also no doubt realize how often those who broke their declarations of peace did so at the same time they claimed to be devout followers of their particular religion. For example, when historian Roy W. Meyer described the Dakota nation's experience with whites who continually broke treaties in nineteenth-century Minnesota, he noted how the whites' behavior towards the Dakotas was not unique:

Many observers have noted the moral obliquity that seemingly afflicted white men in their dealings with Indians. Men justly respected for integrity and fairness in their relations with other white men saw nothing reprehensible about resorting to all manner of chicanery and equivocation when dealing with Indians (Meyer 1993, 77).

Sadly, throughout human world history, there exists the moral paradox of pious religious beliefs existing simultaneously alongside immoral actions.

John Ruskin defined this paradox in *The Stones of Venice*, published between 1851 and 1853. While Ruskin was describing the history of Venice, he could just as easily have been defining other eras of human history, including the European conquest of the Western Hemisphere after 1492:

> The most curious phenomenon in all Venetian history is the vitality of religion in private life, and its deadness in public policy (Ruskin [1851–1853] 2001, 9).

The reader will also encounter examples of how, in response to the invasions, American Indian leaders and nations sometimes compromised their own spiritual and moral beliefs in order to cope with or combat the invaders. For example, when Indian nations in the East made economic alliances with Europeans to trade furs or deerskins, the Indian nations purchased their survival by compromising their spiritual beliefs. These sacrificed beliefs included the concept that animals and all life forms had equal spiritual rights to survival on lands that the Creator had intended them to share. In some circumstances, Indian leaders determined that in order to fight the invaders, Indian nations had to resort to the strategies and tactics of the invaders, especially by centralizing resources and political authority to one leadership group or one leader. Still other Indians lost their bearings by consuming the invaders' alcohol. In all these ways and in many others as well, the centuries after 1492 corrupted everyone.

The reader may well ask why the warriors of the Indian nations all along the shores of the Western Hemisphere did not simply slaughter the European invaders before they had achieved a beachhead. Certainly they could have. And they certainly understood warfare. Warfare between American Indian nations—Indian versus Indian over trade or land—had occurred for centuries before 1492 (Schoolcraft 1975, 39–40). This warfare included wars of conquest and defense, as dramatically exemplified by the vast stockades and bastions at the Indian city of Cahokia in southern Illinois (Cahokia declined by 1300 A.D.) (Whiting Young and Fowler 2000, 248, 314; cf. Morgan 1980, 48–56). Thus there was no idyllic, peaceful America suddenly torn asunder by the European invaders. Furthermore, the reader will discover that warfare between Indian nations was ongoing when the Europeans arrived. Thus, the reactions of Indian nations to European arrival was in part based on perceived opportunities. The majority of Indian nations reacted to initial contact with Europeans by identifying the newcomers as potential allies and trading partners, counterbalancing the challenges of other Indian nations which had competed with them for trade or territory for centuries. Indian nations also initially perceived benefits through trade with the Europeans. These circumstances go far in explaining why Indians did not drive the first waves of Europeans back into the sea.

History after 1492 in what became the United States involved more than five hundred Indian nations, not just "the Indians." These eras also involve many distinct non-Indian nations as well—not just "the whites." Indian nations that had fought each other before 1492 continued to do so after 1492, often seeking a European colonial power as an ally in the post-1492 wars. The European colonial powers, as they fought amongst themselves in a hemisphere that belonged to someone else, also sought Indian nations as allies. Thus, no simple stereotype of conflict between oppressor and an oppressed exists. The reality of this history involves peoples of all races who often disagreed among themselves even as they challenged other nations and groups. No single race or group was completely heroic, and none was entirely villainous. With an abundance of causes, the tragedy of the result—the almost total subjugation of the aboriginal peoples on the continent—is all the more profound because of its complexity.

However "new" the Western Hemisphere may have appeared to the Europeans, the hemisphere was the "Old World" for the First Nations. Thus, while the starting point of this book is 1492, it is important to acknowledge that more than 95 percent of Indian history occurred before 1492. This 95 percent includes the northern areas of the United States and Canada that were finally made habitable when the so-called Wisconsin Glacier retreated in the centuries following 10,000 B.C. (Coe, Snow and Benson 1986, 28–29). Throughout the vast hemisphere that was not affected by glaciers, the origins of various First Nations each date far back in time. These "beginnings" of each First Nation's history are found in the origin accounts of each Indian nation. Each describes the spiritual forces that created the world in which each Indian nation would eventually flourish. To measure these origins in terms of years is irrelevant to American Indians who follow a traditional Indian religion, however interesting it may be to others. Thus, "how long"—however many tens of thousands of years—remains a matter of debate only among "scholars" (Wilford 1998, 2000; Dixon 1993; Fitzhugh and Crowell 1988, passim). While these origin accounts, whether by First Nations or scholars, are significant, they are beyond the scope of this book, as are all histories of First Nations prior to 1492.

The reader has perhaps already perceived that this book is sympathetic to the First Nations of the Americas. Is there another side to this history? Actually, this "other" side can be found in this book as well, in the quotes of those Europeans involved in the conquest. This other side reveals how determined Europeans were to seize the lands of other people, and how confident they were in believing that their "god" was on "their side." The debate among non-Indians over the ethics and methods of conquest are also presented, although those non-Indians who spoke in favor of Indian rights were always in the minority.

This book also attempts to define some of the debates and choices facing Indian people. They were often desperate to defend their homelands, and they fought accordingly. But they also had choices of trade agreements, military alliances and, above all, the choice to assimilate—to embrace willingly their conquerors' Christianity, social structure, political ideas, and/or economic structures. Assimilative choices weakened "tradition" and always subverted Indian independence. But for many Indians, survival meant turning away from tradition. The dilemma of making choices is a significant undercurrent throughout this book.

The reader may well ask whether the evidence in this book is intended to evoke feelings of guilt. If experienced, feelings of guilt are not one-sided. Should Indians feel guilty at having lost? Should non-Indians feel guilty at having won? While that decision is a personal choice, the intended purpose of this book is to create feelings of determined anger, not guilt. Determined anger will hopefully lead to reappraisals of responsibilities to the past as well as to the present and future.

The consequences of 1492 involve the entire Western Hemisphere, not just the First Nations lands now known as the United States. The reestablishment of justice is therefore an issue for all First Nations of the Americas. A part of this rebalancing of history will include the recognition by non-Indian governments of "aboriginal rights;" that is, rights that the First Nations exercised before the European invasions.

For those readers interested in the early twenty-first century's debate over globalization, the evidence presented in this book indicates how globalization began in 1492 as Western European concepts, economics and political systems engulfed half the world. By the beginning of the twenty-first century, throughout the hemisphere and particularly within the United States, the results of 1492 have been a globalization that has not emphasized pluralism. If pluralism is to mark the philosophies of globalization during the twenty-first century, the precedents of the post-1492 experiences in the Western Hemisphere will have to be reversed.

In the year 2000, the Seneca historian and philosopher John Mohawk summarized the moral choices facing the twenty-first century, not just within the Western Hemisphere but throughout the world:

> Some of history's darkest moments have occurred during times when people have been confronted with ideas they found enormously attractive. These powerfully attractive ideas propelled peoples into adventures that brought them into conflict with others. The result—whether the annihilation or near annihilation of the other or of themselves—have too often been tragic....
>
> The antidote to these kinds of movements is to defuse intolerance. ...To the degree a people or nation can be taught to respect the principles of pluralism and tolerance, the prospects of militias committing slaughters and armies participating in wholesale ethnic cleansing are dimmed. To the degree that pluralistic thinking is not respected or practiced such events await opportunity. To this, history is our witness. (Mohawk 2000b, 267)

Some of that history is described in this book.

CHAPTER I

The Paradox of the Crowded Wilderness
Indians Discover Europeans, 1492–1566

American Indians saw their homelands increasingly crowded by Europeans who believed they were entering a wilderness. Crowded wilderness: This paradox lies at the heart of both the physical and spiritual conflicts that mark the last five hundred years of human history in the Western Hemisphere. No single moral logic has yet emerged from this crowded wilderness.

Although there is a post-colonial Asia and a post-colonial Africa, a post-colonial America is unlikely. The descendants of the invaders and the governments that represent them are not planning to withdraw from any part of the Western Hemisphere. An example of just how thorough the conquest of the Americas has been is indicated by a simple fact: Not one American Indian nation has full membership in the United Nations.

American Indians and invading Europeans possessed very different worldviews. The specific details of each worldview held by each American Indian nation and each European nation were varied and complex. But one of the basic differences in overall philosophies was the nature of creation itself. The spiritual foundation of most American Indian nations was that the world was made up of interdependent and equal beings: Humans and all other beings had separate mortal functions but equal spiritual identities (what might be termed equal "souls"). In contrast, Europeans believed that only humans had souls. For Europeans, the world was a divinely ordained hierarchy—what might be termed "the Genesis pyramid." Humans, the only beings possessing souls, were atop this ecological pyramid. Beneath the humans were mortal beings who lacked souls and were thus objects or things intended for use by the superior humans. Because of the profound differences in worldviews, each Indian nation and each European nation defined events in irreconcilable terms. From a perspective in the twenty-first century, the conflicts that resulted can be described and they can even be understood intellectually, but they are difficult if not impossible to justify.

While bitterness and anger are understandable among surviving American Indians throughout the hemisphere, a basic philosophical principle that balances that bitterness and anger was articulated by the late Leon Shenandoah, an Onondaga Iroquois who was the Tadadaho of the Iroquois Six Nations Confederacy, the Haudenosaunee (People of the Longhouse). The Tadadaho's obligations are many, and include guiding the confederacy's council of chiefs in their deliberations. Chief Shenandoah, referring to all non-Indian inhabitants of the Americas, remarked to this author in 1979: "For some reason, the Creator has allowed you to stay. I don't know why. And I don't think you know why. But I do know that we will have to work it out together."

A premise of this book is that in order to "work it out together," we would do well to try to begin to sort out the complex and often dark history that followed 1492. The conquest of the Americas is the most important theme in Native American history. It is important in part because the conquest forever altered the positive themes in Indian history that had preceded 1492. The continued evolution of the incredible beauty of Mesoamerican, Andean and other Indian architectures was stilted if not halted after 1492. And of the thousands of flourishing Indian philosophies and religions, only a few survive, and none survive without the invaders' influences. There is no end to this list of endings.

For Europeans, the impacts of the conquest of the Indian Americas equal the impacts of the ancient conquests of the Roman Empire and the medieval Crusades. The last five centuries of conquest in the Americas share a common theme: the replacement of one people by another. Indeed, the magnitude of the conquest of the Americas may very likely make it the most important conquest in all of human history. For five centuries after 1492, a territory greater than the Roman or any other empire was subdued with a brutality whose magnitude equaled the continents at stake. The initial wars of conquest by Spain in Mexico (against the Aztecs) and in Peru (against the Incas) brought wealth that helped Europe seize the economic leadership of the world and hold it into the twentieth century. The Europeans, with Africans and Asians pressed into the struggle, repopulated great parts of the American continents and imposed new political orders that in turn asserted their independence from Europe. One part of the hemisphere, the United States, eventually challenged the older nations for world domination, a process that continues. The conquest of the Americas stands as the greatest chain of military and social events in history and will stand as such until waves of human settlers are launched into space—or until someone else in the universe makes the inhabitants of planet Earth the new Indians.

Hispaniola: The Four-Hundred-Year War with Europeans Begins

For the American Indians, the four hundred years' war began in 1493 when Taino Indians attacked Columbus's plundering soldiers on the island of Hispaniola. In what is now the United States, it ended in 1890 when the 7th Cavalry massacred more than two hundred Sioux at Wounded Knee, South Dakota. Isolated battles between Indians and non-Indians erupted thereafter throughout the hemisphere, but after 1890 wars as such were impossible, so dominant had non-Indians and their ideas become. North of Mexico, most Indian nations participated in the long struggle only for a few decades before succumbing to conquest, although some—such as the Haudenosaunee —were involved in resistance of one kind or another during all four centuries of open warfare. In the twentieth century, Indian peoples remain a significant factor in U.S. history as they work to ensure the survival of their own tribal identities and try to assert their sovereignty. Throughout the Western Hemisphere, Indian peoples face anti-Indian legislators who would have their views prevail in government. The four centuries of war are over, but the struggle to survive continues.

In North America, and in the interiors of Central and South America, it took the whites, with all their advanced weapons and technology, longer to conquer the Indians than it had taken the Romans to conquer the northern European nations fifteen hundred years before. By 1763, one of the most deter-mined European efforts at settlement, that of the English, was still bottled up within three hundred miles of the eastern coast (Cappon et al. 1976, 14–15). While economics and European rivalries played significant roles in this con-tainment, the determining factor was the tenacity of the various American Indian nations to stand against the encroaching whites. The success or failure of this tenacity was in part determined by what these Indian nations had devel-oped within their own cultures before 1492. In facing the Europeans, many Indian nations successfully tapped strengths and strategies they had developed long before Columbus. Thus Indian nations seldom played passive roles. And while Europeans may have perceived the Western Hemisphere as a "new" world, Indian nations took on the European challenge as a part of the continuum of their history, because while the invader may have been "new," Indian nations took their stands on "old" grounds—their homelands.

Indigenous civilizations in Mexico and Peru were overrun quickly because of Spanish audacity and smallpox, the latter being more important. Smallpox was brought from Europe and unintentionally spread among Indian peoples who had no immunity to the foreign epidemic.

Warfare against Indian peoples is a constant theme after 1492. And what war did not accomplish, alcohol and disease accomplished—and diseases caused far more deaths than war or alcohol. European diseases like smallpox and then African diseases such as yellow fever swept away whole Indian communities, frequently before non-Indians physically arrived in a locale. The diseases were carried inadvertently by the Indians themselves as the traveled along centuries-old trade routes. Non-Indians learned quickly that military and political pressures could be very effective against Native populations reeling from disease. Thus disease and war went hand in hand accented by libation after libation.

Despite the ravages of disease, the Indian peoples north of Mexico were able to withstand the first century of the white onslaught in part because the nations lacked the wealth of gold or other riches that acted as a magnet for Spanish conquistadors. Whenever the conquistadors found no riches and only determined resistance from Indian peoples, they departed—at least for a while.

Morality versus Economic Necessity (or Greed)

The exception was the Indian population itself, which a few Spanish freebooters raided for slaves to take back to Mexico or the Caribbean. Like the Vikings, the Spaniards had little capital backing their endeavors. In order to encourage exploration and conquest, the Spanish Crown could offer only a share of the spoils. Under the Spanish monarchs Ferdinand and Isabella, the Spanish had just captured Granada, the last Moslem center in Spain. Unemployed soldiers, together with adventurers who had not been able to participate in the war against the Moslems, eagerly accepted the new opportunity for glory in the Western Hemisphere.

A sense of moral obligation was not missing in these movements, but such a sentiment quickly subsided. In 1501, Ferdinand and Isabella attempted to direct the morality of their soldiers' conquests by issuing specific directions for treatment of the Indians. They ordered the new governor of Hispaniola,

Nicolas de Ovando, to convert the Indians to Christianity but to treat them well and to encourage the chiefs to report any injustices so that punishment could be meted out. All Indian wives, daughters and property that had been taken by force were to be returned to their communities, and although all Indians were to work for the Crown, they would receive fair wages. In order to ensure enforcement of these directives, no Spaniard was to live away from a settlement, where he could escape the scrutiny of the law. Had the king and queen been able to pay for all this government with funds raised in Spain, justice might have been established. But the monarchy depended on the wealth provided by the very men they were trying to regulate. If crimes against the Indians were committed, the monarchs could enforce the law only by arresting the men who were filling their treasury. Spanish conquest was therefore not a public or a national venture, but rather private enterprise licensed by the Crown. In order to attract private investment, the Crown ceded some of its moral control.

As the Indians of Hispaniola, Puerto Rico, Jamaica and Cuba were enslaved and robbed by the Spanish, the rest of Europe was aware of what was happening. More importantly, Europeans were aware of the moral issues involved. At the time of these conquests, debates arose regarding the justifications of Spanish actions. In 1510, debates at the University of Paris led a professor from Scotland, John Major, to defend the Spanish enslavement of the Indians by calling upon ideas of Aristotle. All Europe was undergoing the intellectual ferment of the Renaissance, and Renaissance scholars like Major were fond of quoting the classics to defend their arguments. Aristotle had stated that some people were naturally inferior, intended to be the servants of their superiors, and Major saw the Indians in that subordinate role. His views illustrate how, less than twenty years after Columbus's voyage, many Europeans had already placed the Indians within a stereotype that suited their own purposes or opinions.

On the Island of Hispaniola, a Franciscan friar named Antonio de Montesinos was convinced that Spanish policy was immoral. Addressing his Spanish congregation, he asked: "Are these Indians not men? Do they not have rational souls? Are you not obliged to love them as you love yourselves?" (Hanke 1959, 15; Hanke 1974, 4)

Most conquistadors did not agree with the revolutionary priest. But despite widespread support for Indian enslavement, the monarchy in 1512 felt a slight twinge of conscience and some rather minor legal protections were extended to Indians. Then, in 1513, the monarchy decided that perhaps the Indians were not being given a fair chance to submit peacefully to their superiors—Spanish slave catchers and armies of looters. To provide what the Spanish regarded as a legal basis for their conquests, the Crown ordered that a 1,000-word proclamation, the Requerimiento (Requirement), be read to the Indians before every battle to give the Indians the opportunity to surrender. Using this ethnocentric and self-serving document, Spanish commanders informed Indians that they represented the king and queen, "subduers of the barbarous nations." After four paragraphs explaining the history and rightful authority of the Christian church, the Pope and the Crown, the Indians were asked to ponder the statements carefully with as much time as necessary (in practice they were seldom given this privilege). If they accepted the sovereignty of the Church, the Pope and the Crown, they and their families would not be enslaved, and they would have a right to their own property and lands as subjects of the Spanish monarchy. If they refused, the conquistadors explained that they would make war "in all ways and manners that we can," enslave every warrior and his family, and seize all Indian property. Such cruel consequences, the Requerimiento emphasized to the Indians, "are your fault, and not that of their highnesses, or ours, or of these soldiers who come with us" (Gibson 1968, 58–60).

To make sure that the Requerimiento was being read before every battle or invasion, each Spanish commander was required to have its reading notarized. The document was indeed dutifully read, whether or not an interpreter was available. It was delivered from aboard ships too far from shore for the words to be heard and was even whispered so as not to spoil the approaching soldiers' chance to surprise an Indian community. The Requerimiento's reading was notarized faithfully and frequently, and Indians were slaughtered or enslaved ostensibly—legitimately, in the eyes of Spain—for having refused the Church, the Pope and the Spanish Crown.

In 1512–1513 the Crown established another precedent for Christianity in their New World. The Spaniards were convinced that the Indians were not accepting Christianity and civilization because they were by nature idle and lazy. Therefore Spain's most Christian monarch established the *encomienda*, a "humane" system for civilizing the Indians by which the Indians gave all their land, labor, and tribute to an entrepreneur (the *encomendero*). In exchange the entrepreneur provided the Indians with Christian instruction. The Indians had no choice, and they were distributed as the Spanish saw fit. The encomienda was forced labor in the name of Christian charity, but it was also an adapted extension of medieval Spain's warfare with the Moors, just as the Spanish conquest in the Western Hemisphere was a continuation of the war spirit that had overwhelmed the last Moslem stronghold in Spain at Granada in 1492. During the long medieval war with the Moors, the encomienda was often established over newly conquered areas, granted to a knight or other supporter of the war. In the Western Hemisphere, this policy of granting land to conquering soldiers, both in advance of and after a specific conquest, was continued until the nineteenth century by all non-Indian powers involved in the hemisphere's history, although only the Spanish included Indian labor with the granted lands (Gibson 1966, 50–58; Gibson 1968, 61–84).

The extent to which the Spanish Crown lost control of its loyal officials and soldiers was illustrated in 1519 when Fernando (Hernando) Cortés conquered Mexico with 508 men and 16 horses. He did so without the required license from the Crown. But when the new king, Charles V, learned of the vast amounts of gold Cortés and his conquistadors were seizing, the king not only forgave him but also made him governor of Mexico. Thus was Spanish law and order established on the mainland of North America.

Cortés was able to conquer the Aztecs because he gained the cooperation and alliance of Indian people such as the Tlaxcalans who were eager to see the Aztec Empire fall. But even these Spanish allies lost. Spanish government and Spanish religion placed a European elite in charge of a Spanish empire, which would forever alter the course of thousands of years of Mesoamerican Indian history. Perhaps the greatest loss was not political or social, but spiritual. Describing the conquest in all its manifestations, the following lines were written by an Aztec poet following the Spaniards' conquest of Aztec Mexico about the year 1523 (in Leon-Portillo 1962, 149).

> Nothing but flowers and songs of sorrow
> are left in Mexico and Tlatelolco,
> where once we saw warriors and wise men.
> We know it is true
> that we must perish,
> for we are mortal men.
> You, the Giver of Life,
> you have ordained it.
> We wander here and there
> in our desolate poverty.

We are mortal men.
We have seen bloodshed and pain
where once we saw beauty and valor.
We are crushed to the ground;
we lie in ruins.
There is nothing but grief and suffering
in Mexico and Tlatelolco
where once we saw beauty and valor.
Have you grown weary of your servants?
Are you angry with your servants,
O Giver of Life?

The last three lines define the most significant dilemma in American Indian history: Why had the spiritual forces to whom the Aztecs had been faithful not intervened? During the next five hundred years, variations of the question "Where was God?" would be continually asked in hundreds of Indian languages throughout the Western Hemisphere.

Many non-Indians chose to give a positive ethnocentric interpretation to this horrific question: These non-Indians would maintain—and often continue to maintain—that the "true" spiritual forces did indeed sanction the transformation of an Indian hemisphere into a non-Indian one. The roles of Divine Providence and Manifest Destiny are indeed significant philosophical issues, which still dominate the underlying thinking of all peoples of whatever race in the Western Hemisphere.

Ponce de León, Francisco Chicorana & the Spanish Colonization of Florida

While Cortés had been the first European conqueror to succeed on the North American mainland, he was by no means the first to try. In 1513, for example, Juan Ponce de León decided to explore the area he would name Florida. He had already conquered Puerto Rico, but at fifty-three he felt himself slowing down and was attracted by rumors of a fountain of youth lying to the Northwest on an island named Bimini. Apparently Indians fleeing in seagoing canoes had told of Spanish atrocities in the Caribbean, because groups of Calusa Indians twice attacked Ponce de León and his men and then tricked him into a meeting off the southern coast of Florida. While they beguiled him with tall tales of a chief named Carlos whose land to the north was filled with gold, the Indians massed canoes for an attack on the anchored ships. The Spanish discovered the plot too late. In two furious battles the Calusas nearly overwhelmed them, and the exhausted Spaniards were forced to withdraw to Puerto Rico.

Ponce de León intended to return to Florida in 1514, but he was ordered to crush rebelling Carib Indians in the Lesser Antilles. He did come back in 1521, but by this time the Calusa Indians living along the coast had experienced frequent Spanish slave raids. As his 200 men began to build houses for their projected colony, they were attacked, and Ponce de León was severely wounded. Forced to retreat with his men to Cuba, he died within a few days (Milanich 1995, 106–110; Bolton 1921, 5–11; Sauer 1971, 26–28, 35).

The Indians' stiff resistance to enslavement and the death of Ponce de León awakened the Spanish governor of Hispaniola, Don Diego Columbus, to the fact that if Florida were ever to be occupied by the Spanish, the slave raiders would have to stop antagonizing the Indians. Therefore, in the summer of 1521 when two Spaniards who were supposed to be exploring the southeastern coast returned instead with 150 Cusabo Indians from the Cape Fear River area of North Carolina to be sold into slavery, Don Diego ordered that all but one Indian be returned immediately.

Unfortunately, most died before the order could be enforced. The Indian retained was taught Spanish so that he could serve as a guide, and he was baptized Francisco Chicorana, Chicora being the name of his Cusabo homeland. Having been enslaved, Chicorana did not see any advantage to white civilization, and he was eager to return to his own people and way of life. But Lucas Vásquez de Ayllón, a superior judge on Hispaniola, instead took him to Spain to help persuade King Charles V to grant Ayllón permission to colonize the area. Chicorana realized that the more fantastic his story, the quicker he could go home. Soon he was enticing Spaniards with traditional Cusabo folk tales of white-skinned inhabitants who had brown hair down to their feet. These people had vast quantities of pearls, and they had domesticated deer, which supplied them with milk and cheese. They were ruled by a giant named Datha who had been grown by constantly softening and stretching his bones since childhood. Near this white race was an even more fantastic people who had tails almost twenty inches long. These tails were not flexible but, like those of alligators, were firm and strong. If these people wanted to sit down, they had to have a seat with a hole in it, or if they sat on the ground their comfort dictated that a deep hole be dug.

Perhaps Chicorana felt that of all the traditional stories he knew, he felt he had to include the ones about a *white* race in order to impress the Spaniards. Or perhaps white was the Cusabo color for witches. In any event, Chicorana was homesick for his own culture and wanted to go home. Because the Spaniards came from a medieval heritage abundant with stories of wild men and strangely shaped peoples and cultures, the stories Chicorana told had the desired effect. In 1523, Ayllón received permission from Charles v to colonize Florida and become its governor.

Charles v was experienced as a ruler both as King of Spain and as Emperor of the Holy Roman Empire, a far greater position incorporating much of Europe. He had devoted a great deal of effort and time trying to cope with Martin Luther's Protestant Reformation. Charles decided to try to infuse traditional Catholic morality into his kingdom abroad by means of the license to Ayllón. Charles insisted that Ayllón treat the Indians justly, never taking them as slaves or forcing them to work in any Spanish settlement. For the moment, Charles felt that the encomienda, with one race as the labor force and the other as management, had failed to achieve anything but profit and exploitation.

Finally, in July 1526, Ayllón, five hundred Spanish men and women, eighty-nine horses, three Dominican friars, numerous black slaves and Francisco Chicorana arrived at the Cape Fear River. Chicorana lost no time deserting the Spanish and disappearing into the wilderness to join his people. Ayllón decided to move south. He chose land near the mouth of the Pedee River to settle, and his colonists immediately began building the rude conglomeration of huts grandly known as San Miguel de Guadalupe. True to his orders, Ayllón did not use Indians as laborers. One of the friars with him on this venture was Antonio de Montesinos who had called for the reform of Spanish policy in 1511. Ayllón and Montesinos both believed that the Spaniards could be both ethical and imperialistic, but he discovered that the Spanish were not capable of sustaining a colony through their own labor and that of a few blacks. The Spaniards were not accustomed to doing much of the work themselves. Some fell sick, some starved. Ayllón himself died on October 18, 1526.

That same year, when the Spaniards pushed them to work harder, the black slaves revolted. It was the first black slave rebellion within the boundaries of the present United States, and it was successful. The general turmoil, including the burning of the home of the colony's temporary leader, encouraged an attack by nearby Indians. All this left the colonists' numbers devastated. In the preceding half year 350 had died, and in midwinter the remaining 150 sailed home to Hispaniola. The Spaniards had proved that they could not survive without forced Indian labor, and Charles v's moral experiment came to an end. Because the Spaniards could not subsist by their own toil, the encomienda continued. What continued in the lands surrounding the ruins of the colony can only be guessed at: Black slaves had successfully rebelled and had given nearby Indians the opportunity to strike their own blows. Were the blacks integrated into the local Indian towns? Whatever happened, the year 1526 reminds the present generation of how long Africans have resisted slavery within what is now the United States, and also that—in whatever ways unknown to history—Africans and Indians first shared a coastline they had both helped rid of Spanish oppressors (Sauer 1971, 69–76).

Florida Indians had to contend with still another expedition, this one under Panfilo de Narváez. Narváez landed 300 men at Tampa Bay on the Gulf or western side of Florida and almost immediately set out with one of his officers, Alvar Núnez Cabeza de Vaca, to find food. Accompanied by about forty-eight men, including a priest, they captured four Indians who led them to their town. The soldiers found some unripened corn, but the priest who was with them was more interested in the town burial ground. Like the Indians living along the East Coast as far north as Virginia, these Indians had wrapped their dead in deerskins painted with religious figures. The priest immediately decided this was idolatry and burned the deerskins—and the bodies. It was the first of many insults to the Indians by members of the expedition, and since the Indians already feared and hated the conquistadors because of slave raids along the coast, Narváez's entire expedition was soon under almost constant attack. The Indians were tall and muscular, and with their six-foot bows they could put an arrow through parts of the Spaniards' armor. Spaniards not only fell in battle, they were also picked off by Indian snipers as the conquistadors continued north, expecting to find a second Mexico City, called Apalache, filled with gold. The town was merely another village, and the Spaniards decided to turn toward the sea.

Vignette: Cabeza de Vaca's Odyssey

As the Spaniards marched south and west, they were again beset by Indians. Three hundred Spaniards had begun the expedition. Six months later, when they reached the Gulf Coast in September, there were 242. Constructing five barely seaworthy boats, they set off westward along the coast of Alabama. At the mouth of the Mississippi, the strong current and heavy winds swamped three of the boats. After further mishaps, including the death of Narváez, Indians found eighty survivors near Galveston Bay, Texas, and tried to keep them alive during the winter of 1528–1529. But by spring only fifteen remained, including Cabeza de Vaca.

The Indians hardly treated the Spaniards as white gods: They had been appalled to see live Spaniards eat dead Spaniards to keep from starving. Since the Spaniards seemed helpless without Indian aid, the Indians distributed them among various bands. Each one was made to work, which the Spaniards interpreted as being forced into slavery. Cabeza de Vaca resolved to escape and try to reach Mexico. With him was a black named Estevanico (Stephen Dorantes), a man who was already enslaved by the Spaniards. Estevanico, Cabeza de Vaca, and two other Spaniards served as traders between peoples. Cabeza de Vaca gained a reputation for being a great medicine man, and the Indians also respected Estevanico. Their journey along Indian trade routes is an indication of the Indian trade patterns that existed between the Mississippi Valley in the days of the mound builders and the Southwest. Late in 1534, while in northern Mexico, the wanderers learned from the O'odham (Pima) Indians that there were Spanish slave hunters nearby. Early in 1536, Cabeza de Vaca and Estevanico, accompanied by some of the Indians, went to meet the Spaniards. The Indians could not believe that Cabeza de Vaca and his companions were of the same nation as the twenty Spanish cavalrymen they finally found, because, as Cabeza de Vaca recorded, "we healed the sick, they [the slave hunters] killed the sound; ... we were not covetous of anything, ... the others had the only purpose to rob whomsoever they found" (Smith 1871, 186–87). The Indians proved to be right. As soon as the wanderers, escorted by a few of the slave hunters, were on their way to San Miguel Culiacan, Mexico, the rest of the Spanish cavalrymen captured many of the 600 Indians who had been with Cabeza de Vaca.

Cabeza de Vaca had suspected that this might happen, and he was glad when he discovered the mayor of the town agreed that these and indeed all Indians should be treated justly. The mayor had reasons of his own. Because the slave hunters had driven the Indians out of their towns and into the hills, the Indians' fields were not being cultivated and the fallow land was becoming barren or overgrown with trees. Food was needed to feed the Spanish, who could not survive like the exiled Indians, eating whatever they could find in the mountains. The mayor preferred to have the Indians work "voluntarily" under the Requirement. Cabeza de Vaca, after years of captivity and wandering with these Indians, understood their way of life and felt they could be dealt with peacefully. But it was also true that during his eight-year odyssey he had never given up his Spanish identity. Perhaps unconsciously, he slipped back into his old Spanish attitude almost immediately upon reaching his countrymen—an attitude of superiority. It could be salted with hate or contempt, it could be tempered with compassion, but it was always haughty. Cabeza de Vaca joined the mayor in helping to bring the Indians out of hiding in the hills and convince them that the Spanish wanted a serious talk with them. When a conference was finally arranged with fifteen chiefs, the mayor, with Cabeza de Vaca standing confidently at his side, had an interpreter translate the Requerimiento. The tenets of Christianity, Christian history, and the concepts of God, heaven, and hell were carefully explained to the Indians. If they would become Christians and "serve God in the way we required" (Smith 1871, 192), the Spaniards would treat them kindly. If not, the Indians would be enslaved and transported to other lands. The chiefs agreed to accept the Requerimiento, and many of their people finally became laborers for the Spanish and supplied them with food. In return, the conquistadors did not slaughter their children, and they did not transport their families to Spanish settlements farther south or to the Caribbean islands as slaves. Cabeza de Vaca was happy that so many of the Indians had been converted to Christianity. It was a comfortable feeling: He could know compassion and still retain his Spanish sense of superiority. What he had learned as a Spaniard was not replaced by what he might have learned from Indians with whom he had worked for nearly a decade.

Hernando de Soto in the Southeast

After landing at Tampa Bay, Florida, and moving inland, Hernando de Soto did what every other explorer had done: He seized local Indians to carry the Spaniards' packs. For four years his 600 men wandered looking for cities paved with gold, massacring hundreds of Indians as they went. Whenever the surviving Indians refused to carry the Spaniards' luggage they were forced into compliance by chains and collars. The Indians did not accept such treatment without a struggle, and there were many battles. Several times Indians determined to spare their people lured de Soto away from their territory by telling him there were wealthy cities just a few days away. After ten months, in March 1540, de Soto's expedition came across the Creek confederation of towns that stretched from Georgia to Alabama. Up to this point, all the Indians they had seen lived in dwellings of dried grass. But the Creeks, with a culture as yet uninfluenced by whites, lived in houses with clay walls and peaked, tile-like roofs made of cane. Near every home, another structure served as a kitchen. In colder areas, the Creeks had winter houses close to their summer ones. These winter homes were insulated with plaster inside and out and had only one small door; the house functioned like an oven, and occupants needed little clothing even during the coldest night. Status among the Creeks was demonstrated by the number of small, wood-planked storehouses, raised on four posts, which stood near their houses. The wealthier Creek homes also had porches. The Creeks wove blankets from the shredded interior bark of trees, and their tanned hides were dyed with such skill that a vermilion deerskin gave the same appearance as fine broadcloth.

The Portuguese chronicler of the expedition, "The Gentleman of Elvas," made one more observation about the Creeks: In addition to a bark-cloth cloak, "the men wear...a *bragueiro* of deer-skin, after the fashion of the woolen breech-cloth that was once the custom of Spain" (Smith 1866, 53; Clayton, Knight and Moore 1993, I, 76; cf. Hudson 1997). Had the Spaniards fully understood the implications of their own observations, the common humanity of Indians and Europeans would have been apparent without the declarations of monarchs and popes.

In the Creek town of Toa there was a ceremonial mound, for the Creeks continued some of the ceremonies and culture of the people they had conquered about 1200 A.D.: the mound builders, a complex agricultural society that survived in some parts of the south until the eighteenth century. The Creeks at Toa, however, had no gold and so de Soto continued his expedition. The next town he came to had been abandoned by the Indians, but the hungry Spaniards found a corn bin that they quickly emptied.

A month after leaving Toa, de Soto questioned four Indians whom the Spanish captured in the woods. Since they would tell him nothing, he had one burned at the stake. The other three then related that there was a town two days away. This town turned out to be governed by a woman whom de Soto had heard possessed fabulous wealth. The town, Cofitachique, was on the Savannah River in South Carolina, and it was also Creek. The woman turned out to be polite and generous, giving the perpetually hungry Spaniards many turkeys, but aside from 350 pounds of pearls, some of them intricately carved in the shapes of babies and birds, the Spaniards did not find the wealth they expected. The Spaniards inquired why there were so many abandoned towns, and the Indians reported that a plague had ravaged the area some years before. When the Spaniards found a dagger and beads of Spanish manufacture, the Indians explained that they had belonged to Spaniards who had landed on the coast many years ago—that is, Ayllón's ill-fated colony. It had undoubtedly been Ayllón's men who had inadvertently introduced the plague to the Indian towns.

De Soto was not content with the hospitality the chief had given his men. Her people told him that the town of Coosa to the north was the town of a more powerful chief, and so de Soto seized the chief and some of her people and forced them to guide him there. Through her influence, the chief could demand food for the Spaniards from Indians along the way. But she escaped when her captors relaxed their guard. The expedition finally reached Coosa, where the Spaniards were approached by the chief, who wore a mantle of marten fur and a plumed headdress. He was seated on a cushioned litter borne on the shoulders of his principal advisors. All around him attendants sang and played flutes. When he reached de Soto he welcomed the Spaniard. Messengers had informed the chief of the depredations committed by this invader, and the chief wisely had the Indians move out of their homes. He gave the Spaniards permission to live in the houses before the homes were simply seized, hoping this would keep his people safe. Still, the Spaniards kept the chief under a polite guard. His people decided to rescue him as soon as they removed their families from the vicinity, but the Spaniards pursued and caught them before they could get their wives and children to safety, and many men and women were brought back in chains. The chief was released as soon as the Spaniards passed through the Creek country, but except for a few minor chiefs other captives were kept for the rest of the expedition, "none returning to their country save some whose fortune it was to escape, laboring diligently to file off their irons at night; or, while on the march,...slip out of the way, observing the carelessness of those who had them in charge" (Smith 1866, 90).

Leaving Creek country, De Soto entered the domain of the Mobiles. The first major town he approached was that of one of the Mobiles' major rulers, Tascalusa, meaning "Black Warrior." Tascalusa and his people, like the Creeks, had retained some of the culture of the ancient mound builders, and when De Soto entered Tascalusa's town, the ruler, wearing a magnificent robe of brightly colored feathers, remained seated on a balcony atop a ceremonial mound at one end of the town square. De Soto climbed the mound and greeted Tascalusa, who sat on cushions and was surrounded by his advisors. One Indian held a red and white circular shade over the ruler's head to shield him from the sun. Tascalusa watched the Spaniards somewhat contemptuously and welcomed them formally without rising. The conquistador replied with a brief speech and their first meeting ended. Later de Soto demanded that Tascalusa give him a number of Mobiles to carry his luggage. Tascalusa scornfully replied that he was not accustomed to receiving orders, only issuing them, but that de Soto could obtain bearers in the next Mobile town, Mauilla, ruled by one of Tascalusa's vassals. To guarantee this, de Soto forced Tascalusa to accompany the expedition. Despite his captivity, Tascalusa retained his dignity along the march, his servant constantly shading him with a large fan of plumes.

When the Spaniards reached Mauilla, scouts warned them that it was a palisaded town that had been further strengthened, evidently as part of a plan to rescue the captured chief. Despite the fact that de Soto had been warned, the Mobiles tricked him into coming within the palisade, accompanied by Tascalusa and about fifty soldiers. Once inside the town, Tascalusa withdrew into a house guarded by many warriors with bows and informed de Soto that if he wanted to go in peace, he and his men would have to leave Mauilla immediately. When a passing chief refused to obey de Soto's command to come to him, one of de Soto's impetuous lieutenants yanked the marten fur mantle from the chief's back and slashed off the chief's arm with a cutlass. Instantly, warriors in the town fired volleys of arrows, killing five Spaniards. De Soto was badly wounded running from the town with his men. The Mobiles raced from the palisade to free the chained Indians de Soto had used as porters, giving them weapons so that they could join the battle. They also brought the Spaniards' goods into the palisade, including weapons, most of the pearls the Spaniards had collected, and most of the invaders' spare clothing. The Indians, knowing de Soto would mount an all-out attack on the town, convinced Tascalusa to escape. In the ensuing battle, the Indians fought valiantly, but the Spaniards stormed the palisade. To prevent the Indians from taking shelter in the houses, some of which had been loopholed for defense, the Spaniards set them afire and proceeded to wipe out every Mobile in the town. Twenty-five hundred Indians were killed. Eighteen of de Soto's men were killed and "one hundred and fifty Christians [Spaniards] had received seven hundred wounds from the arrow" (Smith 1866, 90). More than eighty Spaniards had already died of disease or in previous skirmishes, and de Soto's force was further weakened by the loss of many of their supplies, which were captured by the Indians and destroyed when the town was burned. Because their medicine had also been lost, the Spaniards dressed their wounds with fat stripped from the dead warriors.

After the battle of Mauilla, de Soto's fortunes declined. His reputation for cruelty preceded him to the country of the Chickasaws in northern Mississippi, where a Chickasaw chief attempted to trick him and wipe out his army. Feigning friendship for the Spaniard, the chief asked de Soto to help him defeat one of the vassal nations that had broken away from the chief's government. De Soto, with eighty infantrymen and thirty horsemen, joined two hundred Chickasaw warriors and went to the supposedly offending town. It had been burned and abandoned, and no opposition was in sight. De Soto rightly suspected the Chickasaws of dividing his forces in order to attack them, and he ordered his men to be alert. Unable to catch de Soto by surprise and aware that the main camp was also on the alert, the Indians did not carry off their planned attack. Instead the Spaniards lived with the Chickasaws for a few months without incident, although some of the conquistadors were guilty of looting.

In March 1541, de Soto decided to leave and he asked the chief for 200 men to carry his baggage. The chief answered that he would have them the next day. Suspecting a trick, de Soto warned his pickets to stand a very careful watch that night. Suddenly, at four in the morning, the Chickasaws rushed the conquistadors before the Spaniards knew what was happening. Men awoke and struggled out of the smoking houses bewildered and without their weapons and armor. The horses ran about wildly, but the Indians' fear of cavalry was so great that in the dark they mistook the horses to be mounted, and they fled before they could take advantage of the Spaniards' confusion. Only one Indian died in the attack, but the Chickasaws killed eleven Spaniards and another was so badly burned he died three days later. Fifty horses were killed and the Spaniards lost most of their weapons and clothing. Had the Indians attacked again immediately, they might have wiped out the conquistadors.

The Spaniards withdrew a few miles to an abandoned Chickasaw town where they made new lances, saddles and clothing. There, seven days after the first attack, the Chickasaws struck again, but this time the enemy was better prepared, and the attack failed. De Soto moved on, and when he came to an Alabama Indian fort made of palisaded logs he decided to capture the fort and face the Indians at once rather than risk being attacked from the rear at a later time. The Indians within the fort fought well, and when the conquistadors came so close to the fort that it appeared they would soon take it, the Alabama defenders withdrew. Only three Indians lost their lives, but fifteen Spaniards died of their wounds.

De Soto's men continued their march until they crossed the Mississippi. They also continued to enslave Indians to carry their burdens, but after the recent battles they could hardly be called glorious conquerors. The Spaniards had won most of their conflicts, but the price had been great and they were becoming desperate. From the beginning of the journey they had been unable to hunt enough of their own food even in forests filled with game, and they had often gone hungry until they found an Indian town to plunder. Now they were not only frequently hungry, they were without sufficient clothing and weapons, and after three long years they were nearing exhaustion. On May 21, 1542, de Soto died and his body was buried in the Mississippi because his officers wanted to prevent the Indians from learning that de Soto was not the immortal he had claimed to be. Of the 600 who began the expedition, only 311 finally reached Mexico after still another year of wandering. Their expedition was above all a testimony to the fact that, given even the slightest opportunity for profit, conquistadors were willing to break every directive of their church. In 1537, Pope Paul III had forbidden all Christians to enslave the Indians or seize their property. And he had also declared: "…[S]hould the contrary happen, it shall be null and of no effect" (Gibson 1968, 105).

Francisco Vázquez de Coronado in the Southwest

In 1540, the year after de Soto set out in the American Southeast, Francisco Vázquez de Coronado hoped to plunder fabulously wealthy Indians in the Southwest. His expedition lasted until 1542. Like de Soto he failed, and like de Soto he slaughtered hundreds of Indians along the way. His army included more than 300 soldiers, 1,000 Indian and black slaves and 800 Indian allies from Mexico. The Spanish had set the precedent of using Indians against other Indians in 1519–1521 when Cortés conquered the Aztecs. It was a precedent carried out during all four hundred years of the invaders' conquests of Indian homelands.

One incident during the winter of 1540–1541 illustrates Coronado's Indian policy. When Coronado's army reached the twelve multistoried towns of the Tiguex (Tiwa) Pueblos, they were greeted in friendship. The Spaniards demanded clothing. The Pueblos agreed but asked for time to gather the goods from the towns. The invaders could not wait. Cavalrymen rode into each town seizing whatever clothing they could find. Occasionally they literally stole it off the backs of protesting Indians. While the troops sojourned among the increasingly resentful Pueblos, one important Spanish officer saw a beautiful Pueblo woman at the town of Arenal and attempted (but evidently was unable) to rape her. When her indignant husband went to the Spanish camp and accused the officer, nothing was done. Unable to tolerate these affronts any longer, the Pueblos captured as many of the invaders' horses as they could and killed them within the palisades that stood around each town.

In December 1540, Coronado ordered the town of Arenal to be surrounded, seized, and all Pueblo defenders slaughtered. With the help of the Mexican Indian allies, the Spaniards broke through the walls into the lower apartments, aiding others who had climbed up onto some of the roofs. Seeing that the battle was lost, the Pueblos asked for and received quarter, and about 200 warriors surrendered. The Spanish commander of that battle, García López de Cárdenas, claimed later that he did not know that the warriors had surrendered voluntarily, that he believed them taken prisoner by force, and that Coronado had ordered that no warrior be taken alive. With this argument he later justified what he ordered done to the warriors. Enough stakes were erected to burn each one alive, but when the Indians "saw that the Spaniards were binding them and beginning to roast them, about a hundred men who were in the tent of Cárdenas began to struggle and defend themselves with what there was there and with the stakes they could seize. Our men who were on foot attacked the tent on all sides, so that there was great confusion around it, and then the horsemen chased those who escaped." The few warriors who were not killed "spread throughout the country the news that the strangers did not respect the peace they had made" (Hodge and Lewis 1907, 320).

By the beginning of 1541, Coronado had a full-scale war on his hands. The Tiguex Pueblos gathered into two large towns to defend themselves. Coronado himself supervised the siege of Moho (also called Tiguex), the larger of the two towns, trying several times to take it by storm, only to have his men driven back by arrows and showers of boulders. After weeks, the Indians' water supply had dwindled and they finally surrendered about 100 of their women and children on the guarantee that they would not be harmed. Nevertheless, the warriors and many of the women refused to surrender for they remembered the slaughter of most of the 200 prisoners, which proved the Spaniards "had no regard for friendship or their own word which they had pledged" (Hodge and Lewis 1907, 320). Finally, after resisting the Spaniards for fifty days, the Pueblo warriors, along with those women who had refused to leave earlier, tried to slip away early one morning. But the Spaniards caught them in the open and pursued them into the Rio Grande. Many drowned or were killed while swimming, and many of those who did reach the opposite bank were pursued the next day and brought back. Every survivor found by the Spaniards was enslaved, and similar treatment was given the other Pueblo town. America has made a national shrine out of the Alamo, the Texas mission-fortress that in 1836 held off the Mexican army for thirteen days, yet how many remember the pueblo of Moho?

Interregnum: Spanish Ethical Debates in the 1500s

While Cabeza de Vaca had wandered among the Indians, Francisco de Vitoria, a fellow Spaniard and a respected scholar at the University of Salamanca, had declared in 1532 that Indians were the rightful owners of the Western Hemisphere, even though, like children, they had to be supervised, and that it was not right to declare war on them simply because they refused to accept Catholicism. However, Vitoria also stated paradoxically that Spaniards had the right to live on Indian land, trade with the Indians, and preach Catholicism, and that if the Indians forcibly opposed any or all of these, they could be made subject through war. This concept, however paradoxical, was not unique to Vitoria. Its Christian foundations were medieval, especially in the Crusaders' wars against the Moslems. Its most famous if unexpected exponent in the 1500s was a predecessor of Vitoria, the English Renaissance philosopher Sir Thomas More who in *Utopia* noted the same rights of occupation and conquest. *Utopia*, which in the present day symbolizes an ideal state, was written in 1516 shortly after Nicolo Machiavelli wrote the notoriously brilliant guide to pragmatic, amoral politics, *The Prince* (1513). These books with such different reputations are indicative of the narrow spectrum of sixteenth-century mainstream politics, a spectrum that well-intentioned reformers of Indian policies would not be able to extend for five centuries. When any non-Indian government claimed the right to protect non-Indian property and citizens, any settlers who had been encouraged by a government to occupy Indian lands became pawns of expansion. During the next five centuries, if Indians attacked or even threatened settlers, non-Indian governments could always justify "protective" wars. And even when the Indians did not pose a threat, non-Indians could claim clear and present danger, conspiracy or even a lack of cooperation

to justify a declaration of war against Indian peoples. Non-Indians could usually be counted upon to believe anything about Indians, and the Indians themselves seldom had an opportunity to dispel such fictions.

As noted above, in 1537 Pope Paul III added a new element to the European
debate on ethics and the Indians. That year, he had issued a bull, *Sublimus
Deus,* declaring that the Devil had inspired many men to believe that the
Indians were "dumb brutes created for our service, pretending that they are
incapable of receiving the Catholic faith." But the pope affirmed "that the
Indians are truly men" and quite capable of understanding and accepting
Christianity. He therefore directed that all the Indians, "even though they be
outside the faith of Jesus Christ; ...may and should, freely and legitimately,
enjoy their liberty and the possession of their property; nor should they be in
any way enslaved; should the contrary happen, it shall be null and of no effect"
(Gibson 1968, 105). All these concepts had been stated before; in 1501, for
example, when Ferdinand and Isabella gave instructions to Governor Ovando
of Hispaniola. Like the 1501 order, the papal bull was ignored, and within
three years the Spanish launched two of their most significant expeditions
north of the Rio Grande: those of Hernando de Soto and Francisco Vásquez de
Coronado. Both conquistadors carried out their expeditions with a complete
disregard for the pope's instructions.

Although the conquistadors refused to comply with their monarchs and
pope's moral directives, many concerned Spaniards would not give up the hope
that someday the Indians would be treated justly. As early as 1511 a Dominican
friar, Antonio de Montesinos, preached two sermons in Hispaniola calling for
humane treatment of the Indians. When he went so far as to state that it was a
mortal sin to mistreat the Indians, King Ferdinand silenced him. Occasionally
priests refused sacraments to Spaniards who held Indian slaves, but most priests
viewed the Indians as heathens to be suppressed. One priest, however—
Bartolomé de Las Casas—soon emerged as the spokesman for reform. Although
Las Casas had himself owned slaves while a priest in Cuba, he was convinced by
1514 that the enslavement of the Indians was inconsistent with Christian values.
In 1519 he went to Barcelona to debate—in the presence of young Charles v—
with the Bishop of Darien over the right of the Spanish to enslave and perse-
cute the Indians. The bishop relied upon the same Aristotelian argument of the
natural inferiority of some men that John Major had advanced in 1510 to justify
Indian slavery. Las Casas countered with the argument that no classical philosophy was valid unless it agreed with the principles of Christianity. While no

judgment was made as to the merits of the differing opinions, Las Casas clearly affected the king's thinking, for in 1523 Charles ordered Ayllón, who was to occupy and govern Florida, to treat the Indians fairly. Still, there was a terrible irony in Las Casas' arguments. He felt that the black slaves brought from Africa seemed happy in their captivity, and therefore recommended that instead of enslaving the Indians, twelve blacks should be brought over to serve each Spaniard. It was not until about 1544 that Las Casas became opposed to black slavery.

By 1550 the Indians' situation was desperate. Millions throughout the hemisphere had been slaughtered, fallen victim to the white men's plagues, or had died in slave corrals, many refusing to work even when the Spaniards burned a few at the stake as an example to the others. The king's new laws of 1542 forbidding the enslavement of any more Indians and granting the Indians of Puerto Rico, Cuba and Hispaniola the same rights as the Spaniards there, were being ignored. Through the efforts of Las Casas and others, on April 16, 1550, Charles v finally suspended further military operations until the moral question of whether or not Spaniards had the right to enslave Indians could be firmly settled. Since the king suspected that his conquistadors would only ignore the suspension, he ordered a hearing convened in August 1550 before a Council of Fourteen at Valladolid in Spain. The council summoned Spain's two foremost authorities on the Indians, the scholar Juan Ginés de Sepúlveda and Las Casas, now a Dominican monk and seventy-six years old.

The Indians of Oaxaca and of Chiapas in Mexico, as well as Peruvian Indians, had already authorized Bartolomé de Las Casas to speak for them. These Native peoples of Mexico and Peru understood that the Spanish authorities would never listen to their own representatives, even the ones who had willingly converted to Christianity.

Sepúlveda maintained that by coming under the Spaniards' benevolent protection weaker Indian nations were protected from stronger ones, an argument used by whites until 1890. But Sepúlveda's main contention was that the Indian was inferior in culture, government, history, and civilization. He ignored the great Aztec and Inca artistic, architectural and governmental accomplishments that the Spaniards had encountered and destroyed, and he did so for an interesting reason: He had never been to the Western Hemisphere. His opinions were based entirely on accounts *he* judged accurate. In the firm confidence that is so often born of ignorance, Sepúlveda also stated that the Indians were the kind of inferiors Aristotle defined as being natural servants. Las Casas countered by asserting that the Indian way of life fulfilled every requirement Aristotle had set to define the good life in *Nicomachean Ethics*. He further insisted that the Indians were capable of understanding Christianity, and should be treated justly. No decision concerning the Indians' rights was ever made by the council, which dissolved itself in 1551. The popular Spanish opinion, however, was clear. In 1554 the Spanish town council of Mexico City, the richest city in the New World, voted to bestow on Sepúlveda jewels and clothing as an indication of their warm regard for his views.

The fact that no official Indian policy was forthcoming is significant not only for the Indians who continued to suffer. The 1550 debates are important because, like almost every other Indian affair until 1890, they revealed and reflected in microcosm the nature of the era as a whole. Charles v was the most powerful ruler in the world in 1550. His domain stretched from the Netherlands south through Germany to northern Italy, from Spain westward to North and South America and to the Philippines. Charles was a conscientious man, yet with all his power he could not settle the moral issue that conquest of parts of the Americas had presented. He was also at that time facing another moral issue in Europe, the Reformation. Martin Luther and religious revolutionaries like him were questioning the very foundations of the Catholic church. Germany, center of the Reformation turmoil, was part of the domain of Charles v's Holy Roman Empire. The failure of Charles v and the Catholic church to put Christian ethics into practice in the Americas was indicative of the moral laxity and weariness which, in Europe, caused men like Luther to challenge the Catholic church. Charles v was eventually defeated in his efforts to enforce his concept of ethics both in Europe and in the Western Hemisphere. He abdicated his throne in 1556 and retired to a monastery. There is a similar source of failure regarding both the immoral conquest of the Western Hemisphere and the revolution of the Protestant Reformation: The old order that claimed the position of moral leadership and was proved by events to be corrupt. There was a horrific ironic difference, however. The Reformation succeeded in forcing the peoples of Europe, whether they were Catholic or not, to examine their consciences, whereas the gold seized from Indian nations in the Western Hemisphere actually perpetuated the old order and its corruption.

During the 1550–1551 debate, Las Casas defended the Indians against Sepúlveda's accusation that the Spanish were morally obliged to conquer the Indians so that the practice of human sacrifices could be stopped. The issue raises an important dilemma for all ages: When should war be waged for moral purposes?

In examining this dilemma, Las Casas made two major points: that the Spanish were exceptionally cruel in their wars against Indians, and that greed seemed to be a prime Spanish motive rather than morality. But he went further than this. Las Casas presented an argument which would be regarded today as "relativist." He was a relativist because he tried to understand the Native perspective; he made comparisons to non-Indian history; and he justified his views by defining them within his own Catholic worldview. Las Casas detailed the arguments he used in his *In Defense of the Indians*, which he completed about 1552:

> Strabo [Greek historian, c. 63 B.C.–24 A.D.] reminds us that our own Spanish people, who reproach the poor Indian peoples for human sacrifice, used to sacrifice captives and their horses. He says that they forced some to live next to the Duero River in a Spartan manner. He continues:
>
> "Those [ancient Spaniards]...also practice divination with entrails, especially those of their captives...."
>
> Why, then, should it be thought that at the words of Christian soldiers, who exceed the barbarous peoples in their wicked deeds...the Indians ought to turn from a religion that has been accepted for many centuries, sanctioned by the laws of many rulers, and strengthened by the example of so many of their prudent men? As Chrysostom [Catholic saint, c. 347–407 A.D.] says, in matters that are sacred and of great importance and very difficult to give up they would be fickle and worthy of reproach and punishment if they put aside the many and great testimonies of such great authority and believe these soldiers in this matter, without being convinced by more probable reasons (which cannot be done in a short time) that the Christian religion is more worthy of belief.
>
> They should be ashamed who think to spread the gospel by the mailed fist. Men want to be taught, not forced. There is no way, however, for our religion to be taught in a short time to those who are as ignorant of our language as we are of their language and their religion, until those who prudently hold fast to these beliefs are convinced by reason. For, as we have said, there is no greater or more difficult step than for a man to abandon the religion he has once embraced....

Since, then, the pagans believe that the universal good and welfare of the whole state consists in sacrifice and immolation, that is, human victims, as we have proved elsewhere from Augustine, Chrysostom, and Valerius, it is not surprising that, when afflicted by needs, they sacrifice what in the judgment of all is most precious and pleasing to God, that is, men.... Titus Livy [Roman historian, c. 59 B.C.–17 A.D.] writes: "When their city was in very great danger, the Romans placated Mars by sacrificing a man and woman of Gaul and a Greek man and woman."

...We read in Judges, chapter 11, that Jephthah sacrificed his only daughter to God....

Even if the infamous deeds the Indians commit by human sacrifice and cannibalism can be stopped only by war, these practices should be passed over in silence and not corrected (or rather worsened) by war....

But if we cannot save and free all of them from death, certainly the interest of a great many is to be set ahead of the interest of the few, who can be saved only by the loss of a great many....

Shame, shame on those who in violation of Christ's law greedily lay waste to Indian realms, which are filled with innocent persons, like most rapacious wolves and ferocious thieves under the pretext of preaching the gospel!

...Do you want the ocean of all evils (that is, war) to surge against the pagans instead of Christ's meekness, which we ought to teach them? What do the heralds of the gospel have to do with armed robbers, who throw everything into confusion by fire and sword? What is there in common between Christ's instruction and these contrivances of frenzied men?

...So war against the Indians, which we call in Spanish conquistas, is evil and essentially anti-Christian. (Las Casas 1974, 224, 225, 238, 240–41, 245, 248, 297, 355)

Spaniards Return to Florida

By 1559, something other than gold brought Spanish soldiers back to Florida. In order to reach Spain from Mexico, Spanish galleons filled with gold had to pass through the Gulf of Mexico and then catch the Atlantic tradewinds off the east coast of Florida. Enemy ships, eager to plunder gold, could operate along the

Florida coast unless the Spaniards took firm hold of it. In addition, shipwrecked Spaniards were being executed by Indians who feared death or enslavement. Philip II, ruling Spain after his father's abdication, decided to establish one Spanish base at Pensacola along the gulf and another along the northeast coast. In 1559, fifteen hundred colonists, including Tlaxcalan Christian Indian farmers from Mexico and Coosa Creek women taken to Mexico by de Soto's men, landed at Pensacola. Soon a food shortage prompted the colony's leader, Tristán de Luna y Arellano, to send 300 men northward to the Creek town of Coosa, which de Soto had recorded as abundant with corn if not with gold. What the soldiers found illustrated the crushing effect of de Soto's attempted conquest just twenty years earlier. The town of Coosa had not yet recovered, and in the meantime Coosa had lost its status as the politically dominant town in the area. This collapse occurred in part because de Soto had forced well over a hundred Creeks to go with him as bearers. He had also taken their food. Another and perhaps more important cause of Coosa's decline was that while de Soto's men had departed, the European diseases they brought with them had not. Weakened by plagues, the people of Coosa and nearby towns allied with Coosa had been attacked by other Indian nations that once had owed them allegiance. When de Luna's soldiers arrived they found only a small village with untended fields. The Coosa chief requested that the Spaniards provide him with some forces so that the Coosa Creeks could seek revenge and reconquer the nearby Napochies, a Choctaw people. With 50 Spaniards—25 cavalrymen and an equal number of foot soldiers—300 Creek bowmen marched off to recapture past glory.

Eight war captains, each carrying a pole tipped with a bundle of white feathers, commanded eight different companies of warriors. These companies marched in a cross-shaped unit with two companies at each quadrant, the center of the cross being hollow. Such formal warfare impressed the Spanish: It was evident that these were not primitives. The Coosas' Napochie enemies were so decisively beaten with the help of the Spanish guns that they agreed to return to Creek vassalage. This marked the first time any Europeans had become deeply involved in the wars of one of the great Indian confederacies east of the Mississippi. In the future, other battles such as those of the Iroquois Confederacy (Haudenosaunee, the People of the Long House) in what is now New York state would be joined by European forces, and those battles would develop into wars of interlocking white-Indian empires, which in turn would help determine the continent's future (Swanton 1922, 230–39).

The French Arrive in Florida

Spanish King Philip II had to confront an increasingly energetic France. In 1562, red-bearded Frenchman Jean Ribaut, with 150 men in three ships, sailed from Le Havre to establish a colony on the northern coast of Florida. The colony was to be a haven for Huguenots—French Protestants—and also serve to establish France in the Western Hemisphere. Ribaut first landed on the northern bank of the St. John's River where he was received with great solemnity by the local Cusabo chief, whose attendants followed "with great silence and modestie: yea more then our men did." Ribaut treated the Cusabos with such respect that he was able to cross to the south bank and talk with a rival nation, probably Timucuas, without alienating either. The Indians Ribaut found, however, were hardly naive in viewing the whites, for they had encountered the Spanish. The only reason Ribaut was treated well was because, unlike the Spanish, he respected the Indians. Still, the Indians were cautious: Contact with the Spanish had left a vivid impression. When one Frenchman pointed to a warrior who had a collar of gold and silver adorned with a pearl the size of an acorn, the Indian quickly withdrew

> not for any feare that he had that they woulde have taken his Coller & Pearle from him for he would have given it them, for a looking glass or a knife: But that hee doubted lest they would have pulled him into the boate, & so by force have carried him away. (Hakluyt [1582] 1850, 105)

Continuing to another river, Ribaut found a Cusabo town of wooden houses with reed roofs, each house two feet off the ground on pillars which were brightly colored blue, red or yellow. At another landing, Ribaut took two Cusabo Indians on board, intending to take them back to France once he had settled his colonists. The two homesick Indians soon escaped over the side. Ribaut reacted not with anger but instead with the realization that the Indians had misunderstood his intentions. He resolved not to take any Indians with him until a future voyage, when the Indians had come to know him and to realize that he meant them no harm. Ribaut represented the new wave of Protestant thought in Europe that developed during the Reformation. In cases such as Ribaut's, the new faith seems initially to have infused its adherents with a firmer commitment to justice and compassion toward all men.

Ribaut was so successful with the Indians that when he left a colony of twenty-eight men at Port Royal in South Carolina, the Indians willingly provided them with food. When the French colony's crude log fort burned down the Indians helped rebuild it in twelve hours. Finally, when dissension broke out and the men decided to abandon the colony, the Indians helped them build the ship they needed to return to France.

In 1564, more French, later joined by Ribaut, returned and established a new settlement called Fort Caroline among the Timucua Indians on the St. John's River. The Spanish, fearing that the French would sail out of Fort Caroline and seize their galleons, established a garrison at St. Augustine in 1565, fortified a large Indian dwelling to use as a base, and prepared to attack. Only 35 miles separated the rival forts, and ironically the Spanish marched overland north toward the French at the same time Ribaut took his men southward by ship. Each force could conceivably have captured the other's fort, but Ribaut's fleet encountered a hurricane and was wrecked. The Spanish, guided by two Timucua Indians and a French prisoner, destroyed Fort Caroline and then hunted down the survivors of the hurricane. The Spanish then slaughtered a total of almost five hundred French Protestant prisoners, including Ribaut. But the Spanish spared about thirty French Catholics.

The clash between the French and Spanish for control of the Florida coast was the first international (not counting Indian nations) conflict fought on North American soil. Timucuas serving as scouts for the Spanish had ironically become involved in a battle to determine which European nation would dominate them. During the next 250 years they and those of their Native counterparts to the north and west would become increasingly embroiled in such conflicts.

About twenty of Ribaut's men managed to escape and make their way northward for at least 50 miles until they reached Guale (pronounced "wallie") Indian towns. Although the Guale Indians were traditional enemies of the Cusabos who had first befriended Ribaut, the French had managed to maintain good relations with both nations. With Ribaut out of the way, however, the Spanish soon began to dominate the Cusabos. When a war broke out between the Guales and the Orista Cusabo nation, the Guales, with the aid of the French refugees living among them, soon won an important victory over the Orista Cusabos by burning their main town.

In 1566, the Spanish persuaded the Guales to end the war. To enforce the peace, to lay firm claim to the Orista Cusabo country, and to make sure that the Oristas supplied the fort with enough food, the Spaniards erected Fort

Felipe and dispersed 150 troops to nearby towns. While the Guales did not betray the Frenchmen living among them, they were so impressed by the Spaniards' show of strength and were so convinced that a Catholic cross displayed to them had ended a drought, that they requested Christian missionaries be sent to them so they could learn the Spaniards' secret of power (Hakluyt [1582] 1850, 106–109; Sauer 1971, 199–203).

European-Indian Relations in the Northeast

While the Indians of the Southeast were enduring the continuous invasions and diseases of the Spaniards, the Indians far to the north along the St. Lawrence River valley and the coast along the Gulf of St. Lawrence were enjoying the best instead of the worst Europe had to offer: manufactured goods, traded to them primarily by the French (although it is possible that European goods including Italian beads made their way north from Indians in the Mississippi River valley or elsewhere in the south). Although European fishermen may have traded with Indians of the Gulf of St. Lawrence earlier, the influx of knives, hatchets, glass beads and cloth began in earnest with French explorer Jacques Cartier in 1534. Cartier came to Canada (a Huron word meaning "settlement") and the St. Lawrence River hoping to find a northwest passage to the Pacific and Indian kingdoms filled with gold. In 1534, he explored the Gulf of St. Lawrence. He encountered friendly Indians including Micmacs who were eager to trade their furs. Then Cartier came across some Iroquois under Chief Donnacona who were spending the summer on the coast. Cartier took two of Donnacona's sons, Taignoagny and Domagaia, back to France where they reported the existence of three Indian kingdoms in Canada. Each of these was centered around a dominant Indian town: Stadacona (there is no accurate translation of the word's meaning), their own home at what is now the city of Quebec; Hochelaga at what is now Montreal; and Saguenay, along the Saguenay River.

The following year Cartier was back in Canada. He sailed up the St. Lawrence to Stadacona. Cartier returned the two young Iroquois men to their homes. But to Cartier's disappointment, the town had no gold. When he told Chief Donnacona that he was going west, upriver toward Hochelaga, the Indians objected. The Stadaconans resented the possibility that the Hochelagans would share the presents Cartier was distributing. Nevertheless, Cartier continued up the St. Lawrence in longboats until he reached Hochelaga, where the Hochelagans nearly swamped the French with gifts, especially corn-bread, which they threw in heavy showers into Cartier's boats. (Hochelaga is an Iroquoian word for "at the beaver dam" and the word also served as the Iroquois name for the St. Lawrence River.) Hochelaga was an imposing town of fifty multi-family houses made of heavy bark set over arched wooden frames, each house about seventy-five feet long and twenty feet wide. The town was sur-rounded by three palisades of logs driven into the ground vertically, with the first and third tilted in toward the erect middle logs, and was further protected by two redoubts. Defenders could stand on a platform running around the inside of the walls and shoot arrows or hurl stones down upon attackers. Well-cultivated fields pushed back the perimeter of the forest. But there was no gold. Winter was approaching, so Cartier left the Hochelagans and sailed back to Stadacona. There he spent a terrible winter during which many of his men developed scurvy. The French knew no cure for this disease, but the Indians did. Given a tea brewed from the needles and bark of the hemlock, spruce or white pine, the patients recovered.

Chief Donnacona wanted to keep the French in Stadacona, but instead Cartier kidnapped him, his two sons and seven others, taking them to France. Extremely homesick at first, Donnacona told the French fantastic stories of Saguenay in hopes the French would take him home. He told the Europeans exactly what they wanted to hear. He discovered they valued rubies, and so he said rubies abounded in Saguenay. Yes, there were oranges, and cinnamon, and cloves. There were men who could fly like bats, and pygmies, and men who had only one leg. Like Francisco Chicorana in 1521, Donnacona emphasized that the most important people in Saguenay were white-skinned. Donnacona waited four years, during which time he and the other Indians were given feasts and honors. But European diseases took their toll. Before Donnacona could return to his homeland, he died, as did the other nine Indians who had been seized by Cartier.

In 1541, Cartier returned to the St. Lawrence. Searching for the fabled kingdom of Saguenay, he found iron ore he thought contained gold, and sailed back to France only to find he had brought back a shipment of iron as "fool's gold." The colonists he left behind under the Sieur de Roberval soon followed Cartier back to France, abandoning Canada to its original inhabitants.

The French, however, had made significant impacts upon the Indians, including what would become an ever-increasing desire for the manufactured goods of Europe. With the colonists gone, the Indians still had a source of supply, the European fishermen off the Grand Banks who came every summer. These fishermen—primarily Basque, Portuguese, English and French—would barter with the Indians while they dried their fish on the shore. During the 1550s, English fishermen began to force the French boats away from the best fishing areas, and in order to make up the difference in profit, the French began trading more seriously with the Indians. In exchange for blankets and metal goods such as knives, the Indians gave the French the beaver pelts needed to make the hats that were becoming stylish in Europe. By the 1560s, the French were trading vigorously all along the northeast coasts, especially around the Gulf of St. Lawrence and even up the river itself. Through these traders, epidemics again struck the Indians, but greed for the manufactured goods and jealousy that other Indian nations would obtain the goods were also spreading. Traditional rivalries were accentuated by these circumstances and soon became wars (Morison 1971, 339–463; Biggar 1924, 129, 306–11).

Perspective

In 1566, the moral crusader Bartolomé de Las Casas died at the age of ninety-two, ending a long life that included a career as a conquistador and later an impassioned reformer. The death of Las Casas symbolically marks the end of the early generations of Indians and Spanish contacts. Their cultural encounters and conflicts established the significant patterns of European-Indian relations that would dominate future centuries down to the present. That these patterns of history came primarily from the south—the Caribbean and Mesoamerica—was a continuation of the cultural rhythms of the Western Hemisphere, where major influences from Mesoamerica had influenced American Indians to the north of Mexico for thousands of years.

By 1566, some Indians had been the victims of the Europeans while other Indians had served with these conquerors as allies. Native peoples had suffered epidemic diseases. They had also realized the paradox of a trade with the Europeans that brought valued goods that both enhanced their daily lives and altered their indigenous cultures. By 1566, American Indian governments had realized the frustrations of negotiating with Europeans who only wanted to dominate rather than share the Indians' own homelands. American Indians had been exposed to white education and religion; a few had been integrated; many had been segregated in reserved areas, especially in the Caribbean islands; and millions had been exterminated.

By 1566 a powerful white government and a major white Christian religion had debated, defined and then failed to implement moral and legal solutions to the problems of its colonists' unbridled violence against Indians. The reason for these failures also became apparent (as perhaps it had been inevitable): Colonial expansion depended upon the support of private investment—a risk of lives and fortunes—and in exchange for this the government was willing to relinquish some of its theoretical control of its colonies. Five hundred years ago the Spanish government discovered that despite its ultimate aim of establishing justice, the military, victorious over the Moors in 1492, looked for continuing employment and opportunity and found it in the Western Hemisphere.

By 1566, Europeans had become involved in wars among themselves as well as against Indians for control of the hemisphere. French Protestant Huguenots had attempted to found a colony as a haven from religious persecution and had allied with Indians to fight the Spanish, who had Indian allies of their own.

Significantly, reformers such as Las Casas had emerged from among the colonists, demanding justice for the Indians. The Indians occasionally used these reformers to speak on their behalf, establishing another historical pattern. Las Casas, for example, had been asked by the Oaxaca Indians of Mexico to present their case. This Indian strategy was at least a successful delaying tactic, and it also led to the repeated historical circumstance of Indians appealing, through reformers, to the central government in the hope that the government would take action against its own citizens; a hope that always faltered, century after century, government after government.

Europeans at home and in the Americas were fully aware of the moral questions posed by their confrontations with the Indians. Sermons had been preached, books written, and the issues debated publicly. Variations on the same themes were to be repeated in every colony and on every frontier. Ironically, the Spaniards committed their worst atrocities at the height of their Christian zeal. The worst atrocities of the English, the French, the Dutch other Europeans, and the democratic citizens of the United States would come at the height of *their* zeal, be it religious or political.

By 1566, some American Indian nations were beginning to realize that the beings with whom they shared their various environments were being gradually replaced by European domesticated animals and crops, exemplified by the introduction of horses into Mexico by Cortés in 1519 and into the Southeast by Ayllón in 1526. But also by 1566, the Spaniards' introduction of Indian corn to

Spain had spread to other European nations such as France. These exchanges would forever alter American Indian environments and challenge those elements of their religious beliefs which were based on their relationships with the other beings of their environments. The Europeans would increasingly benefit from Indian native crops such as corn. Corn, unlike Indian gold that remained in the hands of the European elites, would enrich the lives of all Europeans, peasants and nobles alike.

By 1566, Indians north of the Rio Grande had taken the actions that would be the pattern other Indian nations would later follow. They had initially received the Europeans with kindness or, at the very least, respect. They had carefully considered and had often attempted to reject missionary efforts. They had adapted to the presence of Europeans among them by feeding them and by trading with them, eagerly adapting those aspects of European culture they saw as advantageous, primarily the manufactures they received in trade. They realized how Europeans could prove to be valuable allies in suppressing Indian rivals in order to make conquests of their own. But they had also become involved, as mercenaries or allies, in European contests for the Indians' own lands. When subservience or slavery could be resisted, Indians had rebelled, but even when the whites were driven away the respite was temporary, for Europeans always returned.

Two years before Las Casas died, he predicted the following: "Surely God will wreak his fury and anger against Spain some day for the unjust wars waged against the American Indians." (Hanke 1959, 84)

However, when Las Casas died in 1566, it was the Indians who were suffering from furies. European conquest was only one of these. Various diseases which the Europeans and their African slaves inadvertently introduced among the native inhabitants were as devastating. These diseases—smallpox, typhoid, influenza, syphilis, malaria, yellow fever, measles, diphtheria, mumps and other pestilences—would kill more Indians than all the weapons of battle. The impact and spread of these diseases were increased by the conditions under which Indians were enslaved or otherwise forced to work for the conquerors.

War, epidemics, enslavement and post-conquest living conditions were formidable and often lethal combinations. Although specific statistics are not available for sixteenth century Indian populations north of the Rio Grande, speculations based on documents, archaeological evidence and comparative studies indicates that war, conquest and diseases had overall impacts similar to the results evidenced by statistics for central Mexico. The scope of this level of catastrophe stuns the imagination: In central Mexico, 30 million Indians in 1519 had been reduced to three million in 1568.

This horrific trend continued until about 1900, when a recovery gradually began. By the twentieth century, Indian populations throughout the Americas had, within some wide variations, usually dropped at one time or another after 1492 in ratios of 25:1 or 20:1 (the higher figure in each ratio represents the pre-contact population density and the latter represents the population's nadir). The unseen enemies of disease could and did triumph over Indian peoples whether or not they raised weapons of war against the whites.

The following represents minimum estimates of what happened to American Indian populations during the last five centuries. Maximum estimates are in parentheses. In the statistics below, the term "American Indians" includes Aleuts and Inuits (Eskimos) whenever the statistics relate to Aleut and Inuit homelands (Dobyns 1983, 8–45; McNeill 1976, 203–204; Ramenofsky 1987, 1–21 and passim; Thornton 1987, 24–25, 30, 32, 36, 43, and passim; cf. Verano and Ubelaker 1992).

Western Hemisphere

1492: 72 million (112.5 million)   1990: 32 million

Central Mexico

1519: 30 million   1568: 3 million   1620: 1.6 million

North of Mexico

1492: 7 million (20 million)   1990: 2.5 million

United States except Alaska

1492: 5 million (15 million)   1900: 250,000   1990: 2 million

The problem with statistics regarding American Indians is that calculations have been controversial since the 1500s. In 1552, the Catholic priest Bartolomé de Las Casas declared that within the entire Western Hemisphere, a total of 50 million Indians had already perished in just more than a half century of Spanish invasion. Las Casas had been an eyewitness to some of this slaughter and to the depopulation caused by diseases inadvertently introduced by the Spanish. In his courageous protest of his own countrymen's "abominable cruelties, and detestable tyrannies," Las Casas asserted that five million had died in the Caribbean Islands and that forty-five million had died on the mainland (Las Casas 1656, 4–5).

Moreover, such statistics cannot reveal what Indian populations might have been if they had grown as did those of the rest of the world. But by comparison, between 1492 and the present day, the populations of each of the European nations increased between five and ten times. Thus, if American Indian populations had grown as much as European populations have since 1492, at least five times as many Indians would now be alive in every part of the Americas.

The debate over Indian population statistics has never ceased. But five hundred years after Columbus, in 1992, an American Indian point of view was eloquently expressed by Cherokee artist Kay WalkingStick (in Penney and Longfish 1994, 298–99). Referring to the Indian population north of Mexico, she asked:

> In 1492
> We were 20 million.
> Now we are 2 million.
> Where are the children?
> Where are the generations?
> Never born.

Where indeed? Events after 1566 would follow the patterns set before that year, generation after generation. By 1566, the continent north of Mexico was not yet a crowded wilderness, but the European transformation of America had begun.

CHAPTER II

Old Confederations & New Resistance

American Indians mounted their most successful resistance to the European invaders when they could make alliances with other Indian nations. Success was increased if the alliances, usually in the form of confederacies, had already been formed before the European invasions occurred. One of the most successful confederations formed prior to white contact was that of the Creeks in the Southeast. The Creek Confederacy was a continuation of one of the mound building cultures that had dominated the Southeast for almost a thousand years before the arrival of the Spaniards. As de Soto discovered, they could mobilize their own people and their neighbors with great success. Even though European diseases devastated them, they would reorganize and by the mid-1600s reestablish their vigor. Another example in the Southeast was the Powhatan Confederacy in the area of what is now Virginia. The Powhatan Confederacy, based on a political order in existence before 1492, increased its political reach around 1570 in response to Spanish incursions that brought changes and pressures throughout the Southeast.

Some of the Indian alliances and confederacies that had preceded European contact had ebbed or ceased to exist prior to European contact. Attempts to reestablish these ancient orders were exemplified by the Pueblos of the Southwest. For more than a thousand years, Pueblo agricultural communities had traded and created common cultural links throughout southern Utah and Colorado and northern Arizona and New Mexico. These Pueblo communities (known popularly today as the Anasazi) had been devastated by a severe drought that began in 1276 and lasted for a quarter century. Other factors added to these tensions, including occasional conflicts with the Apaches, the Navajos, the Utes and other neighboring Indian nations. The drought and other disruptions forced the Pueblos to abandon many of their communities and seek refuge among those Pueblos communities that could survive, primarily in what is now New Mexico and Arizona. When the Spaniards arrived in the 1500s, the Pueblos were still rebuilding their communities.

The Haudenosaunee (The Iroquois Confederacy of Five Nations)

The Iroquois Confederacy, also established prior to European contact, came to influence not only its Northeastern homeland, but eventually to affect Indian history into the Southeast and all the way to the Mississippi River. The confederacy was symbolized by the longhouse, the extended multi-family home found in all the towns, and the united people called themselves "Haudenosaunee," the people of the longhouse. Thus the multi-family longhouse also described the multinational confederacy. The founding of this famous league involved the combination of youthful inspiration (a young Huron, Deganawidah, known as the Peacemaker), the confidence of the women in the new movement (as represented by the female leader Jigonhsasee), and the mature judgments of the older generation (as represented by Hiawatha).

The era during which Deganawidah and Hiawatha ended Iroquois civil wars and united the Five Nations may have been as early as the 1100s. In the centuries prior to 1492, the increasing decline of the mound builder civilizations to the west of the Iroquois certainly must have shocked Iroquois trading and cultural life. The collapse of the neighboring nations on the Iroquois western and southern frontiers may have created the chaos that in turn led to wars among the Iroquois themselves. Whether this was a reason for the founding of the confederacy, the Haudenosaunee had long survived on the eastern periphery of far more populous Indian cultures. When the Europeans arrived, the Haudenosaunee took the diplomatic and trading skills they had developed with the peoples to the west of them and turned them one hundred and eighty degrees to the east. As a people on the periphery, no one surpassed the Haudenosaunee in their ability to survive as neighbors of far more powerful economies and larger populations (Mann and Fields 1997, 105–63; George-Kanentiio 2000, 25–28; Fenton 1998, 66–73; cf.: Beauchamp 1921; Wallace 1946; Emerson 1997; Thomas 1994).

Throughout the late 1500s and early 1600s, the league of the Haudenosaunee was beset with invasions, most notably by the Algonquins from the north, the Mahicans from the east, and the Susquehannas—another Iroquoian people—from the south. These invasions occurred while the Haudenosaunee were still adapting to the cultural and economic vacuums created by the gradual and continuing decline of the mound building civilizations to the west and south of them, a disintegration that had begun by the 1300s.

Into this already tumultuous Northeast marched the Frenchman Samuel de Champlain. He had arrived in the St. Lawrence in 1603, and in 1609 he decided to accompany an Algonquin and Huron war party of sixty warriors who intended to raid the territory of the Mohawk Nation, one of the members of the confederacy.

As they traveled south from the St. Lawrence toward the lakes today known as Lake Champlain and Lake George, the warriors often inquired at the start of the day if Champlain had dreamed the night before, because dreams were regarded as an insight into reality. Champlain had to reply honestly that he had not dreamed. But eventually one night, according to Champlain's own account:

> While sleeping, I dreamed I saw our enemies, the Iroquois, drowning in the lake near a mountain, within sight. When I expressed a wish to help them, our allies, the savages, told me we must let them all die, and that they were of no importance. When I awoke, they did not fail to ask me, as usual, if I had had a dream. I told them that I had, in fact, had a dream. This, upon being related, gave them so much confidence that they did not doubt any longer that good was going to happen to them. (de Champlain 1907, 163)

Upon learning this, his Indian allies were convinced that they would have a great victory. Like Champlain, many non-Indians during the next few hundred years would find themselves drawn into Native ways and perceptions at least momentarily, giving up various degrees of their European, African or Asian consciousness until some felt more comfortable among Indians than they did in their own culture.

Remarkably, the evening after Champlain's dream, the war party encountered a Mohawk force on an inlet of what is now Lake Champlain in the eastern Adirondack Mountains—as foretold in the dream, by a "lake near a mountain." The Mohawks, for their part, were on the way north to raid the Algonquins!

In a show of mutual, boastful chivalry, both sides agreed it was too late in the day to begin a battle. Each prepared for the next day's conflict with dancing and with defiant shouts of insults directed at the opposing war party. Champlain noticed that the Mohawks felled trees to erect a temporary fort using metal axes he believed they had obtained from warfare with the Algonquins, who had received them from the French.

The following day Champlain and his allies spread out near the Mohawk fort and waited. Champlain's two men with *arquebuses* (large-bore muskets) placed themselves on the flanks. Champlain accompanied the main body of Indians. At this point the Mohawks emerged from their fort, for they outnumbered Champlain's Indians three to one. The warriors wore armor made of quilted fiber reinforced with wooden staves, ample protection against arrows. But the Mohawks had evidently never seen a hostile white man before, or the power of gunpowder. An Algonquin war chief near Champlain explained that the three men striding in front of the main body were chiefs, easily identifiable by the three large plumes each wore over his forehead, secured by a headband. Champlain agreed to try to kill these men first. He loaded his musket with four small iron balls.

> Our men began to call me with loud cries; and, in order to give me a passage way, they opened in two parts, and put me at their head, where I marched some twenty paces in advance of the rest, until I was within about thirty paces of the enemy, who at once noticed me, and halting, gazed at me, as I did also at them. When I saw them making a move to fire at us, I rested my musket against my cheeks and aimed directly at one of the three chiefs. With the same shot, two fell to the ground; and one of their men was so wounded that he died some time after. (de Champlain 1907, 165)

Enthused at his shot, Champlain's allies let out such yells "that one could not have heard it thunder." Both sides released waves of arrows. Then one of Champlain's men fired his musket from the woods. This overwhelmed the Mohawks, and seeing two of their chiefs already dead, they fled into the woods. Champlain and his allies pursued them, and Champlain shot a few more as they retreated. Because the Algonquins and Hurons only numbered sixty men, they were not able to follow up their victory. Their mission, however—to humiliate the Mohawks—had been accomplished.

During the early 1600s the Haudenosaunee League of the Five Nations was constantly terrorized by war parties of Algonquins and Hurons. Occasionally the Haudenosaunee would launch counter raids, but this was seldom possible because of persistent attacks by the Susquehannas to the south and the Mahicans of the Hudson Valley to the east (in southern New England, the "Mohegans" were another Algonquin people who may have been related to the Mahicans). In 1614, the Mahicans in the Hudson Valley gained a tremendous advantage, for in that year Dutch fur traders built a small post, Fort Nassau, in the center of Mahican territory, near Albany, New York. With iron axes and the conceit of superiority that came from obtaining European goods, the Mahicans increased their harassment of the Haudenosaunee.

The enemies of the Haudenosaunee sensed the plight of the league. In 1615, the Susquehannas sent word north to the Algonquins and Hurons in Canada, proposing an alliance that would crush the Haudenosaunee forever. The Susquehannas also expressed an eagerness to open trade relations with the French in order to share the bounty of trade goods. The Susquehannas' circumstances indicate how all Indian nations had to take into account multiple interests on many fronts. The Susquehannas needed access to French goods because still other Indian rivals were already trading with the Dutch in New Amsterdam or with the English in Virginia. Negotiations soon led to an agreement to destroy the capital of the Haudenosaunee Confederacy at Onondaga. The Susquehannas agreed to send 500 warriors. Champlain volunteered his support and that of fourteen Frenchmen, most armed with the arquebuses. Surely this force would defeat the Haudenosaunee.

In early October 1615, Champlain and the Algonquin and Huron combined armies crossed Lake Ontario. They numbered between 2,000 to 2,500 warriors plus the Europeans as they headed toward Onondaga. On October 10, at three o'clock in the afternoon, they began the siege of the Haudenosaunee capital. The town was a stronger fortress than any Champlain had seen among the Indians of Canada, an indication that the Haudenosaunee had long experience defending themselves. A palisade of four interlaced, interlocking log walls surrounded the town. Each wall was thirty feet high, separated only by a system of gutters that could be filled with water to douse any fire set at the base of a wall. The four walls of interlacing logs were so tightly arranged that the gap between any two walls was not larger than six inches. Standing on platforms mounted behind and at the top of these walls, the Haudenosaunee were quite safe from arrows—and Champlain soon discovered that the walls were ample protection against French arquebuses. No wonder this and other Hauden-osaunee fortifications became known among the colonists as "castles"! The first day of siege ended with the Onondaga warriors defiant.

The next day began quietly. Then suddenly a towering log siege tower more than forty feet high lurched toward the Onondaga palisade, carried and pushed forward by two hundred warriors. It was a European siege tower constructed by Champlain and the Indians that Champlain called a "cavalier." They had man-aged to build this siege machine in four hours. Atop a supporting framework of logs was a walled platform the size of a small room. As soon as it was set down within twenty feet of the Onondaga wall, three Frenchmen climbed up with their arquebuses and began shooting down at the warriors along the parapets. At the same time, the Algonquins and Huron warriors charged, crouching behind small portable walls of logs called "mantelets," which they pushed in front of them—like the siege tower, the mantelets brought the techniques of European warfare along with the muskets and gunpowder.

At first, despite the murderous fire from the siege tower looming above them, the Onondaga warriors remained on the parapet, hurling stones and firing volleys arrows on the attackers below. However, the gunfire from the siege platform soon began to take a terrible toll, and the Onondagas aban-doned the parapet to take shelter in the buildings of the town, ready to shoot any attacker foolish enough to try to climb over the wall. At this point, instead of setting fire to the walls as Champlain had suggested, the Algonquin and Huron warriors dropped the firebrands they were carrying and began shooting arrows over the walls, screaming insults at the Onondagas. During the attackers' outburst, the Onondagas inside reorganized. Bowmen assembled where they could not be seen from the siege tower, and they sent volleys of arrows out through slits in the palisade or in perfect trajectories over the wall and into the ranks of the attackers. These volleys forced the Algonquin and Huron warriors to take the battle seriously once again, and they began lighting fires at the base of the walls. Because of the ingenious Haudenosaunee system of gutters, water was quickly poured between the walls to extinguish the flames. For three hours the battle continued. Gunfire from the siege tower could not stop the Onondagas from arching arrows over the walls and down onto the attackers. Although countless Onondagas had been wounded or killed, the Algonquins and Hurons were discouraged by their own losses that included the wounding of two important war chiefs. They decided to retreat into a temporary fort they had erected nearby.

The retreat of the Algonquin and Huron warriors dismayed Champlain, for he was accustomed to the discipline of European armies. "The chiefs have in fact no absolute control over their men, who are governed by their own will" (de Champlain 1907, 165), he recorded. But the real point was that the chiefs did not expect to have absolute control, for such control was impossible culturally. Indians did not have professional soldiers who were expendable. Each was a brother, father or husband with family responsibilities. In such circumstances, warriors could not be turned into cannon fodder in the European custom. The later colonial militias, with their own elected officers, were closer to the Indian model. This was true of almost all North American Indians, and it often prevented them from sustaining a war beyond an initial stage of enthusiasm. Although there were continuous intertribal wars, they usually consisted of brief battles. These relative short tests of the warriors' valor either accomplished an immediate victory for one side, or they were called off after one or both sides of warriors had proved their mettle. (The exception was when battles were being fought over territorial expansion.) This attitude put the Indians at a disadvantage when later confronted by whites committed to total war.

When the Indian army retreated from Onondaga to their fortified camp, Champlain convinced them to fight on for four more days in the hope that the warriors promised by the Susquehannas would arrive. Champlain was determined to win despite the fact that he could no longer directly participate because of arrow wounds in his knee and leg. The Indians pointed out that if any more of their warriors were severely wounded, it would be difficult to retreat while carrying them all. To Champlain, only future battles were to be considered. The Indians, however, regarded the return of the wounded to their homes more important than war.

A few skirmishes were carried on with the Onondagas, who daily emerged from their fortified town and challenged their opponents. On each of these occasions, Champlain sent some of his musketeers to help. As soon as these gunmen arrived, the Onondagas would retreat to their castle. The Onondagas became disgusted with the continual appearance of the French in the middle of a fight. They began to chide their enemies for depending on the whites to fight with them. They also berated the French, "saying in a persuasive manner that we should not interfere in their combats" (de Champlain 1907, 295). The Onondagas' will to hold their league's capital proved stronger than the Algonquin–Huron will to destroy it. Exactly one week after the siege had begun, the attackers retreated. Two days later the five hundred Susquehannas arrived at Onondaga, realized that they were too late, and retreated. Moreover, reinforcements for the Onondagas were on their way from the confederacy, and the retreating warriors counted themselves lucky that the Haudenosaunee had not discovered where their fleet of canoes was hidden along the banks of Lake Ontario. They paddled back to Canada, having failed in their campaign to destroy the Onondaga castle and deal a devastating blow to the Haudenosaunee. For the moment, the league had overcome another challenge to its existence.

The siege of the Onondaga castle proved to be a turning point in the history of the league. While other invasions of the confederacy's domain continued for more than a century, the Haudenosaunee increasingly took the offensive after 1615. Struggling valiantly, they believed that their survival demonstrated that the Master of Life had given them a special gift in the Good Tidings of Peace and Power. In the decades that followed, the Haudenosaunee began to emphasize the power promised in the Good Tidings. Having fought so long on the defensive, their successes eventually accumulated to become an offensive. Rather than just welcoming strangers into the protection of the teachings of Deganawidah, the idea evolved that they were appointed by the Master of Life to unite all Indians under their beneficent rule, a rule which would bring an end to all war through one law administered from Onondaga. While this may be a pattern seen throughout human history, in the seventeenth century Northeast it was an example of how the arrival of various Europeans and their new trade goods combined with old rivalries among Indian nations so that eventually everyone involved was corrupted by the interactive decisions all of them made.

The Southwest: Resistance at Acoma Pueblo

As the Haudenosaunee struggled for survival during the late 1500s and early 1600s, the Pueblos far away in the Southwest were again threatened by invaders. Devastated by the Spaniards' initial attacks and by new European diseases accidentally introduced by the Spaniards, the Pueblos had to decide whether to try to continue to reestablish the old order. The alternative was to accept the new order offered by the Spaniards. To some Pueblos who saw their traditional spiritual values already shattered by the drought of 1276 and other disasters, the new religion of the Spanish Catholics was attractive. For centuries before the 1276 drought, the Pueblo communities had demonstrated their devotion to traditional spiritual powers by building many ceremonial chambers ("kivas") within their communities. Yet the spiritual forces defined by Pueblo religion had failed to protect them from the drought and other challenges, and Pueblo communities had to be abandoned. While some Pueblo people were thus attracted to Spanish political order and Catholicism, other Pueblos believed that what was needed was more devotion—that their economic successes had corrupted their religious devotion and their collapse was their own fault. These Pueblos were determined to reestablish their regional systems of alliance to defeat the Spaniards.

After the invasion by Coronado in 1540, the Pueblos experienced a variety of white intruders, including missionary priests. These priests were part of an initial stage of white expansion, as missionaries would be for centuries to come. In 1581, the Tiguex Pueblos executed three Spanish priests who insulted their religion. The next year a Spanish expedition searching for gold and silver was suspiciously received and then resisted by an alliance of Keres Pueblos and Apaches. The Spaniards burned the Tiguex pueblo of Puaray and burned, garroted or shot to death about two dozen Tiguex captives before leaving in August 1583, taking Indian slaves with them. In 1590, about two hundred Spaniards on a plundering expedition robbed and killed some Pecos Indians after capturing the Pecos pueblo. In 1593, the Pueblos were again briefly beset by Spanish freebooters. Then, in 1598, an expedition under Juan de Oñate arrived that would seriously threaten the survival of Pueblo culture. This would motivate many of the Pueblos to focus on their traditions as they attempted to reinvigorate the political unity of the regional system that, before the drought of 1276, had been so effective.

Juan de Oñate, already one of the richest Spaniards in Mexico, led a wagon train northward with a total of one hundred and thirty colonist-soldiers, about the same number of Mexican Indian servants and slaves, some of the white colonists' wives and children and eight Franciscan priests. With them was a herd of seven thousand cattle. Leading an advance unit, Oñate had all of the Pueblo leaders he encountered swear allegiance to the Spanish king. Despite Pueblo protests, enough corn to load eighty pack animals was confiscated because Oñate's expedition had nearly run out of food. Oñate and his advance of soldiers finally halted at the Tewa pueblo of Ohke on the east side of the Rio Grande. Oñate renamed the town San Juan and proclaimed it to be the capital of his colony on July 11, 1598. On August 18, 1598, the rest of the Spanish colonists arrived and like the advance unit, moved in with the Ohke people and seized the apartments they desired most. The Spanish decided to praise God for all of this, and with Pueblos doing most of the work a church was erected and then dedicated on September 8. Another activity the Spaniards undertook was a ceremonial reenactment of their historic war with the Moslems back in Spain. In this elaborate ceremony, some Spaniards were dressed as Moorish soldiers to play the part of the enemy.

Oñate forced all nearby towns to supply him with laborers as well as with corn, beans, blankets, buckskins and other goods. In the meantime, priests spread out among the Pueblo towns. Now that the Pueblos had been set to work and Christianity fabricated, Oñate organized an expedition to establish Spanish authority throughout the Pueblo country and to search for gold, silver or salt deposits to bring his colony a fast profit. Traveling southward at first, he turned his men westward on October 23 at the pueblo of Puaray. Soon he arrived at the town of Acoma.

Acoma, one of the most visually spectacular of all the pueblos, was located 350 feet in the air, a city in the sky atop an awesome and forbidding mesa. One of the Sky City's leaders, Zutucapan, watched the approaching Spaniards with grave suspicion. He and other men from Acoma had visited Ohke, now the Spaniards' capital of San Juan. He was convinced that Spaniards were no more than parasites, offering nothing and demanding all. Zutucapan tried to convince his people to stand and fight. But his own twenty-year-old son Zutancalpo, an aged chief named Chumpo and a few other leaders were convinced that the Spaniards, whatever their intentions, were invincible. Despite the lack of consensus, Zutucapan and at least thirteen other men plotted to assassinate Oñate. Zutucapan and his supporters invited Oñate to see a great treasure supposedly hidden in one of the underground kivas. Once inside, Oñate would be killed. Oñate suspected a plot and diplomatically refused. Chumpo, Zutancalpo and other leaders took the opportunity to pledge the Acomas' allegiance to Spain and to Oñate.

Oñate and most of his army proceeded west towards the Zuni and Hopi pueblos. Behind him at Acoma, Zutucapan continued to try to convince his people that the Spaniards must be defeated lest they take over the entire area. Before he had time to organize nearby Pueblos into a more widespread resistance, however, circumstances turned in his favor. A detachment of about thirty of Oñate's best cavalrymen, under Juan de Zaldivar, stopped at Acoma on December 1, 1598, on their way to catch up to the main body of the Oñate expedition. The Spaniards demanded large amounts of corn, flour and blankets. On

December 4, Zaldivar and most of his men climbed the narrow and steep approach to the top of the Acoma mesa, leaving only a few at a camp and one below the mesa to tend the horses. After being given only a few of the goods they wanted, the Spaniards spread out among the Acoma apartments, demanding food and blankets, offering only a few trinkets and metal goods in return. The people protested the arrogance of the Spaniards' excessive demands. Then one soldier seized a turkey and a scuffle flared up. Some of the Spaniards mortally wounded one protester. The people of Acoma rallied and attacked their tormentors.

Both Acoma men and women fought, shooting arrows and throwing stones and other objects at the Spaniards. Ten Spaniards and two servants—one mulatto and one Mexican Indian—were killed. Zutucapan clubbed Zaldivar to death. Three surviving Spaniards scurried from the top of the mesa down the main trail, while five others faced certain death unless they risked tumbling and rolling for their lives off the top of the 350-foot–high mesa. They jumped, and amazingly four of the five survived. Joining the three who had already made their way down to the plain and the few who had been left to guard the horses, the Spaniards galloped away to spread word of the Acoma resistance.

Oñate dashed back to San Juan, and in a hurried council had his priests and officers declare the Acoma pueblo officially in revolt. This formality accomplished, Oñate sent Juan de Zaldivar's brother, Vicente, to exact a swift revenge. With seventy carefully chosen men, he arrived at the mesa on January 21, 1599, and called on Acoma to surrender. His reply came in showers of arrows and rocks, aimed by men and women atop the mesa. The Acomas shouted defiance and called out that after they killed the Spaniards they intended to exterminate the Tiguex and Zia Pueblos as well as fellow Keres Pueblos for reneging on their promises to help Acoma repel the Spanish invaders. Vicente de Zaldivar sent a dozen of his men secretly to the other side of the mesa while the main army prepared to storm up the primary trail. The dozen hoped to climb unnoticed to the top of the mesa and attack Acoma from the rear.

The men and women of Acoma were confident they could keep the Spaniards from taking their mesa by sending boulders and torrents of arrows and rocks down upon them. But because the Spaniards were heavily armored, they managed to climb their way slowly upward. In the meantime, the other twelve groped their way to the top of a cliff separated from the main part of the mesa by a narrow chasm. They stood alone for only a moment before swarms of warriors attacked them. The beleaguered Spaniards' gunfire enabled them, just barely, to hold their ground. The next day, with the Spaniards still at Acoma's rear, Vicente de Zaldivar led the rest of the men on a desperate charge up the main trail. They made it, and some set up two cannons that killed dozens of warriors, but the battle was far from over. The Pueblos retreated into their terraced town and fought all that day and part of the next. European rules of warfare dictated that a town taken by storm had no right to quarter, and the Spaniards progressed through the town slashing their steel blades at every man, woman and child they could find. Even those who had opposed resisting the Spaniards had fought them from the first day of battle. Zutucapan and his son Zutancalpo were killed and Acoma's defenders faced defeat. Rather than be taken by the Spaniards, Acomas killed each other or jumped off the mesa's highest cliffs in defiant despair. Of Acoma's approximately fifteen hundred inhabitants, six hundred were killed, chose suicide or were murdered by the Spaniards after they had surrendered. About five hundred women and children and seventy or eighty men who had surrendered were taken prisoner. Hundreds of others escaped.

Acoma's survivors were treated mercilessly. Oñate sentenced twenty-four warriors who were over twenty-five years of age to slavery for life—after the Spaniards chopped a foot off each of the warriors, as a reminder of the danger of resistance to Spanish will. Two Hopis seized along with the Acoma warriors had their right hands cut off and sent off to their mesa-top towns as a warning to the Hopi people not to entertain any plans of war. Other men and women were sentenced to twenty years of slavery. Oñate dealt with the children of Acoma as follows:

> All of the children under twelve years of age I declare free and innocent of the grave offenses for which I punish their parents. . . . I place the girls under the care of the father commissary, Fray Alonso Martinez, in order that he, as a Christian and qualified person, may distribute them in the kingdom and elsewhere in monasteries or other places where he thinks that they may attain the knowledge of God and the salvation of their souls.
>
> The boys under twelve years of age I entrust to Vicente de Zaldivar Mendoza, my sargento mayor, in order that they may attain the same goal. (Minge 1991, 14; cf.: Hammond and Rey 1953; Pérez de Villagrá 1933)

Under this sentence, seventy girls were taken to Mexico and distributed among various convents. As for the mesa-top town itself, Oñate ordered the Sky City of Acoma to be completely leveled. Almost immediately, the extreme cruelty of Oñate's sentences were debated in the colony and back in Mexico City, but for a decade the Spaniards would find it easier to debate than rebuke Oñate's actions.

The Spanish colony in New Mexico survived and grew only because it continued to exploit the nearby Pueblos for food and labor. Oñate's soldiers seized blankets literally off the backs of Pueblo women they encountered. They confiscated Pueblo food reserves so that when a drought came, famine broke out among the Indians. Pueblo women were so desperate to feed their families that they would follow the mounted soldiers who seized tributes of corn and pick up individual kernels that occasionally fell to the ground. Because of the colony's instability, it was reinforced from Mexico in 1608 and Oñate was replaced as governor. In 1610 the new governor moved the entire colony southward and established a new capital at Santa Fe. Only the Zunis and Hopis far to the west and northwest of Santa Fe remained free of Spanish domination.

Because Oñate and his henchman Zaldivar were now out of favor, their cruel deeds to the people of Acoma were finally dealt with by Spanish authorities in Mexico City. Spain's legal perspective can be measured in the so-called penalties imposed on both of them. Oñate was forever banished from New Mexico, and Zaldivar was banished from New Mexico for eight years. Each was fined and banished from living in the urban comforts of Mexico City—Oñate for four and Zaldivar for two years.

In contrast to these "punishments," former Acoma prisoners of war hobbled on one leg as they and their families remained slaves within an incomprehensible system of justice. Finally, during the 1620s when their twenty years of slavery ended, they moved back to reestablish their city in the sky, visited occasionally by a Spanish priest. Then, in 1629, the Spanish permanently assigned Father Juan Ramirez to Sky City. While he assisted in the rebuilding of the residences and was respected by many, he left a monument to his own beliefs and those of his Spanish masters: He directed the Acoma people in the building of a massive church, more than 100 feet long and 35 feet high, with walls nine feet thick at the base. Two towers flanking the front of the mission church emphasized the reality: This was not simply a church, it was a fortress of Spain.

The Southeast: Spanish Reliance on the Clergy

In the Southeast—in what today is Florida, Georgia, and South Carolina—the Spanish relied on a different kind of conquest. Rather than depending on military suppression, Spain depended upon the Catholic religious orders of Jesuits, Dominicans and Franciscans. Jesuit Juan Rogel, however, soon came to believe that the Devil had other plans. Rogel arrived among the Cusabos of South Carolina in 1569. He learned the Indian language in just six months so that he could explain the intricacies of his faith. But he might have done better to mystify them with the Latin Mass, because as soon as he began preaching in their language, the Indians decided that one of the sermon's main characters—the Devil—was quite like one of their favorite spirits. After all, this "Devil" of the Christians offered men strength and courage, and in their own language he sounded very helpful. This serious communication difficulty was further complicated by the fact that the Cusabos were split into many towns, each of which had three or four locations depending on the season. Rogel gave up in July 1570 and returned to Spanish headquarters at Santa Elena on the coast of South Carolina. But Rogel would soon be involved with Native peoples once again because of what occurred to fellow Jesuits to the north.

In September 1570, in what is now Virginia's Chesapeake Bay, eight of Rogel's Jesuit colleagues landed along what was perhaps the Rappahannock River. They were accompanied by the brother of a local chief, Luis, as he had been renamed, who had been kidnapped in 1559 or 1560 and taken to Mexico and Spain. When he was assigned to the eight Jesuit missionaries in Virginia, he convinced them to come without soldiers, for as the brother of the chief he could ensure their safety. However, when Luis and the Jesuits landed, they found his people decimated by a European plague that had struck sometime during the decade Luis was absent. Fields and towns had been abandoned, and the Indians were still weak. Not without reason, the people were fearful that the Jesuits might be bringing more disease. Furthermore, Luis, bitter that his own kidnapping and work with the Spanish had occurred while his relatives were dying of an epidemic disease, became convinced that the Jesuits were their enemies. In February 1571, Luis and his fellow warriors killed all eight priests, delivering some of the fatal blows with the Jesuits' own axes and knives. A Spanish expedition soon came looking for the priests. Arriving in the Chesapeake Bay, they saw Indians on the shore, some of whom were wearing the robes of the murdered Jesuits. The expedition returned to Florida but in 1572 the Spaniards set out to punish the Indians. The Spanish commander seized eight Indians and prepared to hang them from the yardarms of his ship. But Father Rogel, the Jesuit who had recently been among the Cusabos, was on board and intervened. Certainly Christianity dictated another course: The Indians should be converted; *then* they could be hanged! Rogel proceeded to convince the Indians of the merits of Christianity and the barbarities of their own way of life. Having done this, he watched the eight swung into the air where their lives—but not their souls—were abruptly terminated.

Rogel sailed to Havana, Cuba, where Indians were more cooperative after three generations of Spanish occupation. The Jesuits withdrew from the Atlantic coast that same year, 1572. Competition was keen among Catholic orders, however, and the Dominicans soon stepped onto the shores that the Jesuits had abandoned. The Dominicans had little success, except for the Timucua Indians around St. Augustine. They had been reduced in population by European epidemics accidentally introduced by the Spanish, and ironically they had to depend on Spanish guns to protect them from rival Indian nations. These rival Indian nations perceived the weakened state of the Timucua population as an opportunity to right ancient wrongs—and at the same time they understood the danger of the Timucuas' alliance with the Spanish invaders. Consequently, during the next two years, Dominican missionaries were killed as soon as they went inland. The Guale Indians of Georgia and South Carolina rose up against the Spaniards in 1573 and wiped out a detachment of fifteen soldiers. The Indians were doubly incensed: They resented the missionaries' attacks on their own culture and religion, and they were further angered every time Spanish soldiers marched into their towns to seize their corn and other food. Possibly the Indians were also turned against the Spanish by French corsairs who were trading along the coast.

In 1576, the Spanish officer left in command at Santa Elena (at the southernmost point of the coast of South Carolina) still had not learned to deal fairly with the Indians. He had recently executed two Cusabo warriors for no apparent reason except perhaps to intimidate the surrounding nations. At this point he ordered twenty-three men to march into a Cusabo town and seize enough corn to feed his garrison. The soldiers approached the selected town ready to fight if necessary. But the Indians seemed willing to supply the necessary food. The warriors, however, explained that the soldiers were frightening the women and children with the brightly glowing, cord-like matches that were attached to the hammers of sixteenth-century muskets—when the trigger was pulled, the glowing match came down into the gunpowder pan to fire the bullet. The warriors requested that the Spaniards put their matches out. When they did, they were slaughtered instantly, only one man managing to escape. Shortly afterward, nine other Spaniards on a scouting expedition were ambushed and killed. Spurred on by French advisors, two thousand Cusabo warriors finally attacked the Santa Elena presidio. Thirty-two more Spaniards lost their lives there, including three important officials. The Spaniards abandoned the fort and retreated to St. Augustine.

By the following year the Spaniards had returned and rebuilt their fort at Santa Elena. But twenty-seven soon died in various Cusabo ambushes. A punitive expedition was launched against the Cusabo town of Cosapoy and the invaders killed forty Indians. A few Frenchmen seized at Cosapoy were executed, for the Spanish believed them responsible for encouraging the Indians to fight. Three years of relative calm followed. In 1580, however, the nearby Guale Indian Confederacy went to war against the invaders. Again the Spaniards were forced to abandon the fort at Santa Elena. Although the fort was soon reestablished, the Guale Confederacy remained at war with the Spanish for thirteen more years. Finally, in 1593, twelve Franciscans managed to persuade each of the Guale towns to cease their attacks. The Franciscans then settled down, a few in each town, to promote their faith.

By this time there was a distinct difference between the Timucua Indians, who had lived under Spanish rule near St. Augustine for nearly thirty years, and the Guale and Cusabo Indians, who lived in Georgia and South Carolina. During the past decades, the priests had encouraged intermarriage to break down Indian culture, to instill the Catholic faith, and to help increase their own Spanish population. "Creoles"—Indians with some Spanish ancestry—were becoming common at St. Augustine as well as in parts of Georgia and South Carolina. At St. Augustine, a Timucua female chief married a Spanish soldier. Further north, among the Guales and Cusabos, Indian cultures remained strong despite the missionaries. The twelve Franciscans preaching there conceded that they could not transform Indian cultures. The Indians and most of the mixed-bloods carried on their religious ceremonies and dances. The warriors continued to wear their hair long, a custom the priests regarded as uncivilized but which the Indians felt symbolized their freedom. But to please the Spaniards, whom the Guales and Cusabos wanted to befriend, the Indians went through the motions of the Mass and even tolerated a few sincere converts among them. The Indians felt that the Catholic Church concentrated on the hereafter. The priests could have a part of that eternal domain as long as they remained out of temporal affairs.

But then in 1597, after four relatively peaceful years, the Franciscans decided that because they were not making a significant number of converts, they would attack Guale customs. One young Guale warrior named Juanillo particularly disturbed them. Juanillo wore his hair long and scorned the church. He publicly predicted to the Guale people that the priests among them would soon be followed by Spanish soldiers and settlers. He emphasized the importance of continuing Guale culture. As the son of the recently deceased chief, Juanillo was the likely successor to the leadership of the Guale Confederacy. The Franciscans had another candidate in mind, an old man named Don Francisco who was regarded by the priests as a sincere convert and whom they felt would willingly submit to Spanish rule and the imposition of Spanish culture. Pressuring the Guales, the Franciscans managed to get their candidate elected. But their success was short-lived.

Father Pedro Corpa was the primary instigator of Don Francisco's elevation to chief. On Sunday morning, 13 September 1597, he opened the door to his wooden chapel to prepare for the Mass. Juanillo and a few of his followers were waiting inside, and a club quickly ended the Franciscan's life. The next day Juanillo met with the chiefs of at least seven towns. He already had the allegiance of three others. Addressing the council, he warned that the Spaniards intended to destroy Guale traditions and customs. The Franciscans had already begun to interfere actively with Guale religious dances, ceremonies and holidays. They had begun suggesting with whom the Guale nation should or should not make war. They had attempted to change the marriage customs of the Guales, which allowed more than one wife under certain circumstances. Juanillo protested, "All they do is reprimand us, offend us, oppress us, preach to us, call us bad Christians and deprive us of the happiness that our ancestors enjoyed, in order that we may enter their heaven" (Lanning 1935, 85). He was tired of paying tribute to the Spaniards, of feeding them when he knew they would starve if left on their own. He also made an astute observation regarding Spanish policy. Since the Spanish would exact the same revenge for one Franciscan as they would for twelve, why not kill them all? Solemnly, the council had the head of Father Corpa severed and placed upon a pole as a symbol of resistance. Juanillo's most devoted supporter was old Don Francisco—the Franciscan candidate.

Within a week, half of the friars were dead. Another was sold into slavery to Indians further inland, and the others were alive only because they were among Spanish soldiers or among the few Indians who sided with the Spaniards because their chief was Juanillo's rival. A Spanish expedition burned towns and food reserves in retribution, but found only one Indian whom they garroted because he refused to show them the location of his town. What has become known as the Juanillo Revolt had begun. But in fact it was only a "revolt" from the Spaniards' perspective. Since the Spanish claimed sovereignty over the Guales, the Spaniards defined any resistance as a "rebellion" or revolt against legitimate authority. But from the Guales' point of view, the conflict was a war of an independent nation, not a revolt against a sovereign power. They were defending their nation and their homeland against invaders.

Juanillo gathered more support when the Cusabo Indians joined him. The Spaniards realized the grave threat this new alliance posed, and they evacuated all priests and civilians from South Carolina and Georgia to St. Augustine. One teenage boy taken back to St. Augustine was executed for having been present at the killing of one of the Franciscans, but the Spaniards could capture no one else. Perhaps as encouragement to his soldiers, the governor declared that any Guale Indian seized would immediately be enslaved—despite the fact that Spain had supposedly outlawed the enslavement of Indians in 1573. In 1600, the government in Spain nullified the governor's proclamation by citing the 1573 Spanish law. Instead, the governor set about totally destroying Guale cornfields and towns, hoping to starve the Indians into submission. At the same time he depended on the traditional rivalries of the Cusabos and Guales to break up the alliance. When a drought added to the Indians' difficulties, all but Juanillo's closest followers surrendered. In a benevolent mood the governor forgave them, reasoning that, unlike Spaniards, Indians could not be expected to judge right from wrong! In 1601, he persuaded the warriors of Guale, Cusabo and other nations to stamp out the last town held by Juanillo and Don Francisco. The well-stockaded town lay deep in the interior. Although the first attack failed, the town finally fell. Juanillo and Don Francisco were both killed during the last battle, and their scalps were sent back to St. Augustine. The four-year war was over.

The war's failure encouraged more Franciscans to attempt to spread their faith, and beginning in 1603 robed friars spread out even into the interior nations. By 1606, the Indian religions had been so undermined that the Bishop of Cuba made a visit to the Cusabo and Guale countries and baptized 2,453 Indians in ceremonies replete with beautiful vestments and golden vessels. But the Juanillo Revolt did succeed in stifling any desire on the part of Spanish colonists to settle and farm the area.

Interregnum: European Ethical Debates on Empire

The Spanish, long established in the Caribbean, had by the first decades of the 1600s established at least a presence in the North American Southeast and Southwest. Their methods, whether military force or religious conversion, were based on the same idea: The Indians were subjects and wards, not equal to the standards of Spanish civilization. The Spaniards' justification for empire was their self-proclaimed "right" of Columbus's "discovery." Most Spanish colonists regarded the Indians as their inferiors even as the Indians were also the second-class subjects of the same Crown. The status of "subjects" would place Indians in an untenable political position. As noted in the Requirement of 1512, the Spanish regarded any war begun by any Indian nation as a "rebellion" or "revolt" carried out by ungrateful subjects against Spain, which the Spanish regarded as the only legitimate political authority. What Indian people would view as wars to defend their homelands were seen by the Spanish as treason against Spain. Thus, for example, the war of the Guales led by Juanillo became known as the Juanillo Revolt, rather than a term such as the Guale War of Independence. This concept would continually be extended to newly encountered nations. But the Spanish conquest of the Americas never ceased to raise controversial questions among both Spaniards and Europeans in general.

In 1597, a Spanish historian, Antonio de Herrera, began to research and write the history of his nation's ventures in the Americas,

> so that foreign nations might know that these Catholic kings and their councilors have complied with the provisions of the papal bull [of 1537], and have not simply despoiled those lands, as some say. (de Herrera in Hanke 1951, 39)

Indeed, the Spaniards had made new efforts at reform, typified by the 1573 law outlawing the enslavement of Indians. It was this law that the governor of Florida had followed in 1600 when he pardoned most the Guales and Cusabos who had resisted Spanish expansion. However, while Philip II had declared in 1573 that the enslavement of Indians was illegal, he had added that if peaceful conversion to Catholicism failed, only the slightest force was to be used to bring the Indians to submission. The question, of course, was what constituted excessive force. Consequently, under this 1573 law the Spaniards continued to force the Indians in both the Southeast and the Southwest to grow food for them and perform other menial tasks. The ambiguity of the 1573 law is indicated by the fact that Philip decreed that the word "conquista" would no longer be used regarding the Indians. The proper word was now *pacificación*. There would be no difference, except perhaps in the minds of some legal scholars.

One of the most perceptive commentaries on the European invasion of the Americas was made by a Frenchman, Michel de Montaigne. Montaigne reflected on many subjects in his fascinating book, *Essays*, completed in 1588. (During the eighteenth-century Enlightenment, philosophers such as Voltaire would revive Montaigne's work.) Like many other Europeans Montaigne was intrigued with the implications of contact with the Indians and their "new" world because he believed such observations revealed, through contrast and comparison, as much about the nature of European society as they did of the Americas.

Despite his attempts at understanding the peoples of the Americas, Montaigne wrote, of course, from his own sixteenth-century philosophical point of view. Montaigne believed that the Europeans were the most advanced human society and had the superior heritage of Mediterranean and European civilizations. That said, his essays are interesting insights into the sensitive mind of one European who tried to see human circumstances relative to the cultural values that shaped them—a sensitivity not unlike that of his contemporary Bartolomé de Las Casas.

For example, Montaigne's essay "On Cannibals" dealt with Brazilian Indians whom he had interviewed in 1562 when the Indians visited Rouen, France, and also incorporated the observations of a white who had lived in their homeland for "ten or twelve years." Regarding these Brazilian Indians and their philosophical/religious beliefs, Montaigne wrote:

[T]hey [the Indians] have a way in their language of speaking of men as halves of one another—that they had noticed among us some men gorged to the full with things of every sort while their other halves were beggars at their doors, emaciated with hunger and poverty. They found it strange that these poverty-stricken halves should suffer such injustice, and that they did not take the others by the throat or set fire to their houses. (de Montaigne 1958, 119)

Would any other European nation do better than the Spaniards with regard to justice towards the Indians? The French record was as yet inconclusive. Would the English do any better? In 1576, in northeastern Canada at Hall Island (Resolution Island) off the larger Baffin Island, an English expedition under Martin Frobisher impudently claimed the Native lands for England. Some of the crew antagonized the local Inuit (Eskimo) people, and then opened fire on some Inuits in their kayaks. Frobisher took as hostage the only Inuit who seemed to want to trust the Englishmen. The Inuit hostage became ill and died of a lung disease in England shortly after the expedition's return.

Sir Francis Drake, who later would defeat Spain's Armada in the English Channel, sailed into a natural harbor along California's coast, perhaps San Francisco Bay, in 1579. Drake was on his way around the world, having stolen treasure from Spaniards who had previously stolen it from South American Indians. He reported that the California Indians were "a people of a tractable, freehand loving nature, without guile or treachery" (Drake [1628] 1854, 131). But he did not remain long enough to establish a pattern of what might be termed a sense of English justice.

Then, in 1584, Sir Walter Raleigh sent an expedition to reconnoiter the North Carolina–Virginia shoreline. The English found the Indians to be "most gentle, loving, and faithful, void of all guile, and treason, and such as lived after the manner of the golden age" (Barlowe 1955, 108). This same expedition brought back two Indians, Manteo and Wanchese, and the English treated them with great respect. Thomas Hariot, one of Raleigh's associates, carefully taught them English while learning a few Indian words himself. But the English thus far were only repeating Spanish experiences. English reports of the Indians' "loving nature" matched Columbus' first reports of the Indians. The Spanish had known, as the English now did, all the arguments in favor of a just Indian policy. And Indians had been treated well when brought back to Spain just as Manteo and Wanchese were now treated well in England. The proof would come only with long-term contact.

Early English Colonization Attempt: Roanoke

Although Sir Walter Raleigh never actually traveled to North America, he never doubted the rights of the English to subject the Indians to England's rule. But he also knew that it was an opportune time to demonstrate that the English were not going to act as the Spanish had. Raleigh sponsored a colony whose members landed on the North Carolina coast in July 1585. His Roanoke colony, as it became known, was begun just two years after Las Casas's *Very Brief Account of the Destruction of the Indies* was published in English as *The Spanish Colonie*. Publication of *The Spanish Colonie* was intended primarily to encourage English investment in colonization, not as a tract indicating mistakes the English could avoid in their relations with Indian nations. Its primary impact was as propaganda against Spain, England's unofficial enemy. At that time, Spain was attempting to suppress England's friendly neighbor, Holland, using cruel methods similar to those which Spain practiced in the Americas. Because Englishmen used the writings of Las Casas to show the barbarity of their Catholic foes, however, they also began pondering the rights of Indians. Sir Walter Raleigh often quoted Las Casas, and equitable treatment of the Indians was often accepted in theory as befitting the English sense of fair play.

When Raleigh's colonists sailed for North Carolina, Manteo and Wanchese accompanied them as translators and guides. Thomas Hariot, who had worked with these two Indians in England, also voyaged westward. The colonists were under the command Sir Richard Grenville and Ralph Lane. Once Thomas Hariot had landed and had encountered the North Carolina Indians, he wrote with genuine admiration that the Indians did very well with what they had, and given the limitations of their means and inventions, "they shewe excellence of wit" (Hariot [1588] 1955, 371). John White, an artist and a close associate of Hariot's, was assigned the task of visually recording, like a photographer of today, the Indians, their towns and the environment around them. The paintings that survive today—more than seventy—are among the best records of sixteenth-century Indians and their homelands. The humanists Hariot and White, however, were not in charge of the expedition.

Four days after the first encounter with the friendly Indians living near the Pamlico River on the North Carolina coast, an incident occurred that permanently shaped Indian–white relations there. On July 13, 1585, the English, evidently accompanied by their two translators Manteo and Wanchese, stopped briefly at the town of Aquaseogoc. They exchanged greetings with the Indians and were entertained by the leaders of the town. The English used a fine, valuable silver cup that night either during a toast or during a meal, and the cup was passed among both Indian and Englishman. When the English left Aquaseogoc, one of the Indians had the silver cup. It is possible that during their celebration one of the Englishmen offered the cup to him and he accepted it as a gift. The English did not miss the cup at first—perhaps alcohol had clouded everyone's memory—and they went on to another town, Secotan. The English were greeted with such friendship that John White was able to paint several of the people, views of the town, and views of at least one of their ceremonial dances. Three days later, however, as the English rowed their four small boats back to their ships, Grenville remembered that an Indian at Aquaseogoc had the cup. He ordered some of his men to go back and get it.

At Aquaseogoc, the Indians saw the boat coming toward them. The Indian who had the cup was told to give it back. Here again there may have been a misunderstanding in translation. The Indian refused and the townspeople fled their homes. Unable to retrieve the cup, the English burned the town and its cornfield to the ground, destroying the Indians' food supply for an entire year. Nearly two centuries later, Edmund Atkin of South Carolina submitted an official 1755 report to the British government's Board of Trade, outlining the history of Indian affairs. He explained:

> The early and long Series of Calamities and Distresses which Virginia Struggled under with them [the Indians] in its infancy was owing, (tho' no Historian hath made the Observation) to Sr. Richd Grenville's burning an Indian Town and Destroying their Corn in 1585, after a very hospitable Reception, in revenge for a Silver Cup stolen by an Indian, who did not know the difference of Value between that and a horn Spoon; which could not but shock their natural Ideas of Equity. (Atkin [1755] 1967, 38–39)

Grenville and Lane sailed further north until they came to Roanoke Island, North Carolina, where they established a colony. On August 25, 1585, Grenville sailed for home to gather reinforcements and supplies, leaving Lane in command. Relations with the Roanoacs and other nearby nations were at first amiable, although the English made no attempt to purchase from the Roanoacs the land they settled. The English occasionally entertained the Indians with clarions (small trumpets) and other instruments including a small organ, since the Indians enjoyed music. But all too often the English were like the Spanish: They expected the Indians to supply part of their food in exchange for nothing or perhaps a few metal goods. Of the two Indians who accompanied the colonists, the Croatoan Manteo remained loyal to the English, but the Roanoac Wanchese left the colonists to rejoin his people.

In the spring of 1586, Wingina, the chief of the Roanoacs, became so disgusted that he moved the people of the island town to a mainland town, Dasemunkepeuc. Wingina attempted to assemble one thousand to three thousand warriors from all nearby nations and even from Chesapeake Bay nations to drive off the hundred or so Englishmen. Wingina was so determined that he was even willing to hire mercenaries from nearby Indian towns, ironically using as payment copper he had received in trade from the English. As tensions increased, Lane finally decided that he had better attack Wingina before Wingina attacked him. On the night of May 31, Lane led his men in a surprise raid against Wingina and some of his army that had gathered on Roanoke Island. But when Indian sentries heard some of the English killing two unsuspecting warriors nearby, Lane had to call off his plan.

The next day Wingina agreed to talk peace and invited Lane into Dasemunkepeuc. Lane decided to use this opportunity to complete his original objective and assassinate Wingina: He gave orders that as soon as he spoke a certain phrase, his men were to open fire with their muskets and pistols. The Indians did not suspect a trick, nor is there any evidence they planned one of their own. At the chief's side were seven or eight advisors. Lane gave the signal; the soldiers opened fire at point-blank range. A pistol shot knocked Wingina to the ground, but he got up and ran. Another shot hit him in the buttocks, but he continued to run. One of Lane's Irish servants dashed into the forest after the wounded chief and emerged carrying Wingina's head.

The signal Lane had given to begin the murder was "Christ our victory" (Lane 1955, 287). Protestant Englishmen were no different from Catholic Spaniards. They murdered in the name of the Prince of Peace.

Later that month, on June 10, 1586, Sir Francis Drake arrived at Roanoke with a small fleet that had just burned St. Augustine. Drake had previously raided the island of Santo Domingo, and the town of Cartagena on the northern coast of South America. He brought from these two areas three hundred South American Indians and one hundred blacks whom he believed would make good slaves and servants for the Roanoke colonists.

Drake's attitude toward Indians had obviously become pragmatically European since his visit to the San Francisco Bay area in 1579.

The Indian response to the assassination of Wingina was a great alliance of former rivals. Lane and his men did not want to stay at Roanoke. So eager were they to leave that they could not even wait for three of their fellow Englishmen to return from the north, where they were perhaps negotiating with Indians along the Chesapeake Bay for land for a new settlement. These three men were never heard from again. They were the first of those who would become famous in history as Roanoke's "lost colonists." Nor has any record been found that indicates what became of the four hundred black and Indian slaves Drake brought to the island. On board his ships when Drake arrived at Roanoke, they were not recorded as arriving in England. It is unlikely that Drake would have freed these three hundred South American Indians and one hundred black slaves and permitted them to form their own settlements as best they could. More likely, they faced the same fate as the Jean Ribault's French Protestant Huguenots when they were taken prisoner in Florida by the Spanish in 1565: Their throats were slit. Whatever may have happened to them, these three hundred South American Indian slaves and one hundred black slaves became the second group in Roanoke's history of lost colonists.

A few weeks after Lane's hasty departure, Grenville returned from England. Surprised to find Roanoke abandoned, he left fifteen men to hold the claim of Sir Walter Raleigh and England. No other Englishman arrived until more than a year later, on July 22, 1587, when John White came back with about 113 men, women and children to establish a permanent colony. They discovered no trace of the men Grenville had left behind except a single skeleton. The English inquired among the friendly Croatoan Indians if they knew what had happened. Their story was ironic.

Thirty warriors had assembled from three Indian towns. Some were from Aquaseogoc, the town destroyed in 1585 for the silver cup. Some were from Dasemunkepeuc, the Roanoac town where Wingina had been assassinated. And some were from Secotan, where the English had been greeted with such open hospitality that John White had been able to paint so many views of Indian life and religious ceremonies. To complete the irony, one of their leaders was Wanchese who, while in England in the company of Thomas Hariot, had learned the English language and had taught his own language to Hariot. The thirty warriors approached eleven of the fifteen men near the colonists' house and asked for a parley. Two Englishmen came unarmed to meet two of the Indians, who were also supposed to be unarmed. But in a reverse reenactment of the betrayal of Wingina, one Indian embraced one of the two Englishmen while the other struck him fatally over the head with a wooden sword. The second Englishman escaped to his friends. After an hour-long battle that killed one man on each side, the Englishmen ran to the shore. They jumped into their large boat—probably a pinnace capable of being rowed or sailed with one small mast—and rowed out into the Roanoke sound. A quarter of a mile down the coast, they came across the four other Englishmen hunting oysters. Quickly these men scampered aboard. The thirteen men rowed south and vanished—the third group of lost colonists.

Despite the knowledge that the Roanoac Indians had driven off Grenville's men, and that he lost one of his own assistants to a Roanoac ambush, White wanted to establish peaceful relations with the Roanoacs and all their neighbors. He invited the Indians to make peace, giving them a time limit of one week. After the week passed, White decided to intimidate the Indians and at the same punish them for killing the Englishmen. On August 9, 1587, White and twenty-five men attacked Dasemunkepeuc. After wounding one Indian and sending others into panicked flight, White discovered that his victims were not Roanoacs but friendly Croatoans. The Croatoans had learned that the Roanoacs had abandoned their town but they were unaware of White's planned attack. The Croatoans had come to the abandoned town to loot whatever had been left behind. Manteo, the Croatoan who had aided the English since 1585, was at first angry with White, but he soon realized that White had no way of knowing that the Indians he attacked were Croatoans.

Unable to establish any communication with the Roanoacs, White christened the ever-loyal Manteo and titled him Lord of Roanoke and Dasemunkepeuc on August 13, 1587. As an English-style feudal "lord," he was also a subordinate to Queen Elizabeth i. While it is unlikely that Manteo was told how the English regarded the implications of this act, under English law this meant that all the Indian population and all the lands which the English chose to define as being under the control of Manteo were in turn subordinate to the English sovereign, Queen Elizabeth i, and to her governor, John White. Thus White could also now negotiate for land and supplies while legally regarding the Indians as subordinate to his authority. This legally erased, from the English point of view, the independence of all of the Indian peoples who were swept into this legal fine print. As far as the English were concerned, Manteo was now the legal representative of the Roanoacs, despite the fact that only the English had appointed him and despite the fact that he was a Croatoan, not a Roanoac. While such one-sided legal complexities may appear to be absurd, they remain at the foundation of the Indian policies of the United States today. This is because the United States claims to have inherited all the rights the English ever declared they possessed over any Indian nation they encountered—with absolutely no regard to the opinions of any of the Indian nations.

Once John White had done all he could to secure the tenure of his colonists at Roanoke, he sailed for England on August 27, 1587, in order to requisition supplies and reinforcements. He left behind about 112 colonists including his daughter Eleanor, her husband Ananias Dare, and his granddaughter Virginia Dare, born just nine days before his departure. Virginia Dare was the first English child born within what became the United States—born simultaneously with the Indian policy of English-speaking peoples that subordinated Indian rights and that would continue for more than four centuries.

White was prevented from immediately returning to America because most English ships were commandeered to resist the Spanish Armada that attempted to invade England in 1588. Although the Armada was defeated, the English feared that other armadas might have to be fought, and so no ships were available for a voyage back to Roanoke until 1590. Finally, on August 18, 1590, John White and some companions landed on Roanoke Island and approached the colony. White climbed atop a forested dune near the colony's stockade, noticing a tree with the letters "CRO" carved on it. Continuing on to the stockade, he saw that it was undamaged and that four small cannons remained within. The houses had been taken down and the grounds were overgrown. At the right side of the stockade's entrance, five feet from the ground on one of the main posts, the word "CROATOAN" was carved. Indian footprints were in the sand nearby, but no English voice called out a greeting. John White's daughter, granddaughter, and all the other colonists had vanished. The distress sign that White and the colonists had agreed upon before his departure—a Maltese cross—had not been carved over the inscriptions on the tree or the post, and there were no signs of violence. White interpreted the carved "CRO" and "CROATOAN" to indicate that the colonists had gone to the nearby island of their Indian friends. But no one ever found them, and even today no one knows what fate befell the fourth—and final—group of Roanoke's lost colonists.

Grenville's revenge for the missing silver cup and Lane's murder of Wingina led to considerable animosity on the part of the Indians. What had happened to English idealism regarding the Indians? Why had the English repeated Spanish mistakes? One answer is that despite their religious differences, the Spanish and English colonists had much in common. Many of the Spaniards were soldiers who, when confronting Indian nations, were quite willing to use the military expertise they had gained fighting the Moslems in Spain. Like the Spanish, the English were often dominated by their fighting instincts during their attempts at diplomacy with the Indians. Privateering shaped a part of their attitudes. One of the original purposes of the colony of Roanoke was to serve as a base from which privateers could plunder the Spanish ships sailing on the Gulf Stream. Thus, Grenville and Lane, on their way to settle Roanoke in 1585, had spent a month terrorizing Spanish shipping in the Caribbean.

In addition to their privateering experience, many English who came to Roanoke were veterans of European conflicts. Men like Grenville had also fought the Turks, the Moslem invaders of Eastern Europe (whose last siege of Vienna, for example, did not occur until 1683). Nor were the English novices in imperialism as they began their colonization adventures in America. Grenville, Lane and Roanoke's sponsor, Sir Walter Raleigh, had all participated in England's conquest and colonization of Ireland, where they seized lands from the Irish to create large feudal estates. Since the English had nothing but contempt for the Irish they subdued, it is not surprising that they would also be tempted to feel superior to the next people they attempted to conquer, the Indians. Another factor was the advice of the elder Richard Hakluyt, who told his fellow Englishmen in 1585 that the best way to handle the Indians, whom he had never encountered, was to impress them with English power but refrain from using it unless absolutely necessary. As with so many theories of deterrent strategy, the temptation to use that power became too great for the military leaders to resist.

Powhatan's Confederacy & the English in Jamestown

As the Indians near Roanoke struggled to understand the arrogant military nature of England's colonial leaders, an Indian leader named Powhatan (Wahunsonacock) was completing the organization of a confederacy to the north, in what is now Virginia. Powhatan's confederacy of between nine and thirteen thousand people consisted of thirty nations and two hundred towns, some of which had already repelled white intruders at least once, as in 1571 when they assassinated eight Spanish Jesuits. The Powhatan Confederacy was formed about 1570 and was an expansion of an earlier six-nation confederation. The exact reasons for the formation of Powhatan's league are not known. Powhatan's personal ambitions may have been reason enough. Spanish, English and other European slave raiders operating on the coast may have necessitated the creation of a defensive alliance. The introduction of European trade goods along the seaboard may have been a primary cause: Powhatan could have united nearby nations to ward off Indian invaders equipped with European goods, including metal axes. It is also possible that by obtaining his own European goods, Powhatan found himself able to bring other nations into submission. Spanish influence among nations further south may also have forced the Chesapeake Bay area Indians to unite, or perhaps the Susquehanna nation to the north threatened to oppress any nation without strong allies.

Whatever the reasons for its formation, Powhatan's confederacy was markedly different from that of the Haudenosaunee. Unlike the Haudenosaunee League at Onondaga, Powhatan's confederacy was based on intimidation rather than on voluntary cooperation. Powhatan demanded a heavy annual tribute in corn, animal skins, fish, venison or any other town product. By the 1580s, Powhatan had been told by his prophets that one day a nation would rise on the Chesapeake Bay and overthrow him, and in response he had conquered and nearly annihilated the nations there. Perhaps he had even considered the Roanoke colony a threat. But by the first years of the seventeenth century he felt secure, surrounded continuously by forty or fifty bodyguards as well as by numerous wives. Then, in 1607, three English ships sailed into the James River.

Powhatan was "a tall well-proportioned man, with a sour look, his head somewhat gray, his beard so thin that it seemeth none at all, His age near 60, of a very able and hardy body to endure any labour" (Smith [1612] 1910, 80). Although Powhatan had been warned by a prophesy that another nation would someday overpower him, it seemed absurd to consider the 105 Englishmen who settled at Jamestown as the genesis of that nation. Throughout the remainder of his life until he died in 1618, Powhatan watched these Englishmen. With inevitable regularity, the English would land and die of starvation, disease and incompetent leadership. At least four thousand English perished in the colony's first fifteen years (before March 1622) (Morton 1960, 14, 28, 88). A few English died in battle and ambush at the hands of Powhatan's warriors whenever the whites attempted to undermine the confederacy's strength by trading with its enemies, trying to take food by force or offending Indian people in other overt ways. But most perished without the intervention of the Powhatans.

Nevertheless, Powhatan feared the spreading of the European diseases that ravaged the white settlement. For example, six months after the first landing, only thirty-eight of the original 105 remained alive. Then, in 1609–1610, during the horror which the English themselves called the "starving time," some of the English were reduced to exhuming and eating the body of an Indian they had killed while another colonist murdered and ate his wife. By 1610, fewer than seventy were left of the previous year's five hundred. In 1616, despite further infusions of settlers, the Jamestown colony still numbered only 350. The reason so many perished was apparent to Powhatan from the beginning. Not only did the English bring with them terrible diseases, they were lazy and wanted only to find gold or other easy wealth. There were few wives and families. They did not plant enough corn and most were incompetent hunters. They stayed alive only because they bartered metal and clothing for food, and because some of Powhatan's more compassionate people brought the English corn as outright gifts.

The most important leader in early Jamestown was Captain John Smith, a man who was very much in keeping with the image of the first European colonial leaders. Smith had fought courageously against the Moslems in Eastern Europe. Thus, like Roanoke's Grenville and Lane before him and the Pilgrims' Myles Standish after him, Smith was a soldier for whom a temporary peace in Europe had brought unemployment. In fact, seven of the eight men to whom he reported—the charter members of the London Company—were military men. However, Smith made an effort to understand the Indians, and if half his observations of their society were unfavorable according to white standards, the other half were positive. He viewed the Indians as human beings with an average balance of foibles and strengths.

It was difficult for the other colonists to understand how they should approach the Indians, because back in England the Roanoke reports had preconditioned them to accept a stereotype that depicted all Indians as treacherous. Colonists clung to this negative image even when events disproved it. For instance, in 1607 Captain Christopher Newport reported paradoxically that Indians "are naturally given to treachery, howebeit we could not find it in our travel up the river, but rather a most kind and loving people" (Newport [1607] 1907, 377). The colonists' instructions follow:

In all Your Passages [explorations] you must have Great Care not to Offend the naturals [Indians] if You Can Eschew it and employ Some few of your Company to trade with them for Corn and all Other lasting Victuals if you [they?] have any and this your must Do before that they perceive you mean to plant among them.... (London Council [1606] 1969, 51–52)

Additional instructions warned the whites to be suspicious, never trusting the Indians as guides, never giving them guns, and above all never revealing the sickness or death of any Englishman, lest the Indians consider them weak. The whites gave a payment of copper to the Paspahegh Indians—one of Powhatan's subject nations living near Jamestown—for the land on which they built their fort, but only after the Paspaheghs and other Indians had demonstrated their resentment at the presumptuous English occupation by killing one white in an attack on the fort and by laying occasional siege to it. Powhatan's policy was to duplicate whatever English attitude was current: If arrogant, he countered with resistance; if friendly, with friendship. During times of peace he allowed corn to be sent to the colonists and tried to prevent antagonistic incidents. But Powhatan was also alert to any deception on the part of the colonists. In these ways both sides parried for position, each analyzing the other's moves to deter-mine future policy.

For example, during the summer of 1608 the colonists had become determined not to spend another winter as they had the previous one, starving and dying. It was clear that survival depended on the cooperation and food of the Indians, and a debate developed as to the best method of securing it. Most of the colonists wanted to crown Powhatan lord of the Indians—just as Manteo had been anointed in 1587 at Roanoke. Binding Powhatan through English feudal vows would make him obliged to come to their assistance, and if Powhatan then refused to do their bidding once he had been crowned, they could justify, in their own law, the right to use force. Captain John Smith, to his credit, opposed this ruse. Nevertheless, a copper crown made in England was shipped over to Jamestown and in the autumn of 1608, Powhatan was duly crowned. Although Powhatan accepted the crown, when he was asked to kneel in acceptance of the feudal vows, he demonstrated his own shrewdness by refusing. He thus received English acknowledgment of his power but gave nothing in return. Frustrated in their attempt to make Powhatan conform to their own English concept of government, the colonists and their London sponsors decided to circumvent Powhatan's leadership of his people.

Powhatan addressed Captain John Smith in 1609, outlining what was at stake in Virginia and trying to avert a conflict Powhatan feared might arise.

> Captain Smith, you may understand that I, having seene the death of all my people thrice, and not one living of those 3 generations but my selfe, I knowe the difference of peace and warre better then any in my Countrie. But now I am old, and ere long must die. My brethren, namely Opichapam, Opechankanough, and Kekataugh, my two sisters, and their two daughters, are distinctly each others successours. I wish their experiences no lesse then mine, and your love to them, no lesse than mine to you. . . . What will it availe you to take that perforce, you may quietly have with love, or to destroy them that provide you food? What can you get by war, when we can hide our provisions and flie to the woodes, whereby you must famish, by wronging us your friends? And whie are you thus jealous of our loves, seeing us unarmed, and both doe, and are willing still to feed you with that you cannot get but by our labours? Think you I am so simple not to knowe it is better to eate good meate, lie [lay down] well, and sleepe quietly with my women and children, laugh, and be merrie with you, have copper, hatchets, or what I want being your friend; then bee forced to flie from al, to lie cold in the woods, feed upon acrons roots and such trash, and be so hunted by you that I can neither rest eat nor sleepe, but my tired men must watch, and if a twig but breake, everie one crie, there comes Captaine Smith: then must I flie I knowe not whether, and thus with meserable feare end my miserable life, leaving my pleasures to such youths as you, which, through your rash unadvisednesse, may quickly as miserably end, for want of that you never knowe how to find? Let this therefore assure you of our loves, and everie yeare our friendly trade shall furnish you with corn; and now also if you would come in friendly manner to see us, and not thus with your gunnes and swords, as to invade your foes. (Simmonds [1612] 1907, 165–66)

In the meantime, across the Atlantic in London, on February 18, 1609, a book was published to encourage investment in Jamestown's sponsor, the London Company. Robert Johnson's *Nova Britannia* enticed prospective stockholders with the idea that every share might someday be worth five hundred acres of land. The London Company, already in financial straits, was offering land it did not own and could not afford to buy at a fair price—Indian land. Over the next decade the company became increasingly committed to issuing land dividends on its stock. The possibility of justice toward Indians decreased, for the company could never equitably pay the Indians for the vast lands promised to stockholders, even when the Indians were willing to sell.

Soon after *Nova Britannia*'s promise of lands became widely known, the company decided to break Powhatan's power. As a format, they specifically chose to duplicate Spain's suppressive and highly successful policy against the Incas of Peru. In the past, the Jamestown colonists had occasionally encouraged Powhatan's friendship by assisting him in his wars with Indian nations who had been his enemies long before the whites' arrival. Now, instead of helping Powhatan, the English decided to befriend his enemies in order to intimidate him. In addition, the company planned to exact a tribute in corn, skins and dye materials from each nation of Powhatan's confederacy, making them responsible to Jamestown's governor rather than to Powhatan. In order to undermine the confederacy's cultural unity, the company ordered the colony's leaders to discredit Powhatan's religious leaders. Most indicative of the new attitude toward Indian affairs, however, was the company's intention to demand a certain amount of weekly labor from the warriors of each nation, a policy that also duplicated Spanish practice. During the next few years, this policy of forced labor was carried out only sporadically, most successfully under Sir Thomas Dale from 1611 to 1616. The policy, of course, created a constant antagonism with the Indians—eventually enough to force them into war. Moreover, the policy revealed the Virginia colonists' refusal to labor in their own fields. Later, in 1619, the English would turn to African slaves, again following the Spanish example and the English plan of Sir Francis Drake at Roanoke in 1586.

Perspective

Just as a 1511 sermon by Antonio de Montesinos on the island of Hispaniola had criticized Spanish injustices toward the Indians and demanded reform, a 1609 sermon in London reminded the English of their moral obligations. That year, the Reverend Robert Gray of London gave his blessing to the Virginia colony but stated:

The first objection is, by what right or warrant we can enter into the land of these Savages, take away their rightful inheritance from them, and plant ourselves in their places, being unwronged or unprovoked by them. (Gray 1609, n.p.)

Gray then answered his own question by stating that the Indians would be willing to sell their lands if a fair price was offered. But the more convenient answer was put forth by the younger Richard Hakluyt in his introduction to *Virginia Richly Valued* in which he stated that,

[T]o handle them gently...will be without comparison the best: but if gentle polishing will not serve, then we shall not want hammerours and rough masons enough, I mean our old soldiers trained up in the Netherlands [against the Spanish], to square and prepare them to our Preachers hands. (Hakluyt 1609, [A4])

Once again, unemployed soldiers had prospects for work.

The English did not intend to resort to overwhelming force yet, however, because many colonists and company officials still hoped for harmonious Indian relations. Even those who wanted to use force were unable to, since there was insufficient manpower in the colony. In addition, trade with the Indians for furs and skins was somewhat profitable, and trade would be disrupted by tension or war.

In 1612, the secretary of the London Company, William Strachey, prepared Virginia's first code of laws, which included the death penalty for any Englishman stealing an Indian's property or taking an Indian's life. Yet by the next year, Strachey had completed a book justifying the confiscation of Indian land. The reason was that land had become even more important: In 1613 Jamestown had its first successful export of tobacco. Tobacco profits meant that more Indian land would be seized.

Strachey also wrote *Historie of Travaile into Virginia Britannia*, its best-known edition published in 1618. Strachey's history was based on his experiences in the colony during 1610 and 1611. He knew the Indians well enough to record an eight-hundred-word vocabulary, yet this intimate knowledge did not dissuade him from feeling that it was right that the English would eventually occupy the Indians' lands. He hoped that the English would pay for every square foot of soil and live in harmony with the Indians, but he also presented his justification for white occupation. He began with an idea adapted from Sir Thomas More's *Utopia* of 1516; the 1532 views of the Spaniard, Francisco de Vitoria; and English ideas set forth by Sir George Peckham in 1583. In brief, the English had an inalienable right to trade with anyone they pleased, including the Indians. Having explained that English trade gave them the right to be on Indian land, Strachey continued that because the land was sparsely settled, it would be wasteful of God's bounty if the English did not colonize it. Besides, if the English did not settle the Atlantic coast, the Spanish or the French would. Spanish or French colonization, he asserted, would be disastrous not only for the English but also for the Indians because they would be exposed to Catholicism. It was imperative to spread the Protestant faith.

Strachey proceeded with his imperialistic logic. Since the English had the right to trade and the right to settle, it was only logical that they had the right to defend what had become their property if they were attacked by Indians who refused to accept English Christianity. While Strachey's case thus far proved only what he wanted it to prove, he included a remarkable argument that provides insight into English customs as well as English justice. Strachey contended that colonizing among the Indians, even if such expansion became violent, was acceptable because it was like a father with his child "when he beats him to bring him to goodnesse." Strachey then added yet another analogy, an idea that already had wide currency in Britain and had even attracted adherents such as the artist John White after the failure of the Roanoke colony:

> Had not this violence and this injury been offered to us by the Romans ...who reduced the conquered parts of our barbarous land into provinces...[w]e might yet have lived overgrown satyrs, rude and untutored, wandering in the woods, dwelling in caves, and hunting for our dinners, as the wild beasts in the forests for their prey, prostituting our daughters to strangers, sacrificing our children to idols, nay, eating our own children. (Strachey [1618] 1849, 17–18)

England could now see its own past and present in relative terms, simultaneously proud of its historic resistance to the Roman imperialists while utilizing the consequences of their own defeat at the hands of the Roman invader to justify doing unto others what had been done to them, to their supposed eventual benefit.

While theories were discussed in absolute terms, life continued in the colony a mixture of good and evil. Powhatan resented English efforts to weaken his power, and he and his people chafed at occasional forced labor and the demands for corn. But all the Indians were eager to obtain trade goods that the English offered in exchange for furs and deerskins. The English trade goods included copper knives, hatchets, cloth, hoes, beads and scissors. Since the English numbered only 350 in 1616, they were usually tolerated, with only sporadic violence and death on both sides.

English colonial life was not without its diversions. An incident involving Pocahontas—in legend, supposedly responsible for saving John Smith's life in 1607—reveals a flirtatious personality not burdened with the European concept of "original sin." Pocahontas, if the record is to believed, had a remarkable way of attracting the attention of the men in the fort. About 1610, Pocahontas was described as

> ...a well featured, but wanton young girl, Powhatan's daughter, sometimes resorting to our fort, of the age then of eleven or twelve years, to get the boys forth with her into the market place [of Jamestown], and make them wheel [cartwheel], falling on their hands, turning up their heels upwards, whom she would follow and wheel so her self, naked as she was, all the fort over. (Strachey [1618] 1849, 65)

This uninhibited young lady was later captured during a tense confrontation between the English and the Indians in 1613 and brought back to Jamestown as a hostage. But the following year she married John Rolfe, who had just made his first successful export of tobacco to England. Their diplomatic marriage restored peace. Pocahontas was a convert to Christianity who believed fervently that the religion of her people and Christianity were compatible, and that an enduring peace was possible. In 1616, to encourage interest in the colony and to raise funds to provide a Christian education to Indian youth, Pocahontas traveled to England with her husband and ten other Indians. In 1617, just before she was to return to her homeland, she died in England of smallpox. One consequence of her visit was the creation in 1618 of an endowment sponsored by King James I and the Anglican church to set up a college in Virginia to educate the Indians. In 1620, Captain George Thorpe was put in charge of supervising the endowment, which had become tangled in a mass of bureaucratic confusion and misuse. Thorpe valiantly struggled to befriend the

Indians he sincerely wished to serve. The foremost object of his endeavor was Opechancanough, a brother of Powhatan who had succeeded the chief after his death in 1618. Thorpe built Opechancanough a timbered English house complete with a door and a lock. Opechancanough was so pleased and intrigued that he reportedly stood in front of his new home, repeatedly locking and unlocking his door. Perhaps he was using that fascination as a time to think. Perhaps he understood that the hinges and locks of the door were more than a curious English invention. His people stood upon a far more complex threshold, one that would determine whether two very different peoples could share the same home, the Indian homeland.

While Opechancanough may have only been amused with his door hinges and lock, he was clearly alarmed at the growth and direction of the Virginia colony. Between 1619 and 1622, 3,570 new colonists, including women and children, arrived to cut down his forests and plant more and more tobacco. Far more disastrously, however, the English colonists brought with them many fatal diseases such as smallpox. These diseases wiped out thousands of the English, and spread with at least an equal ferocity to the Powhatans. Because the English were too busy raising tobacco to raise their own food, they obtained corn, deer meat and other foods from the Indians through daily trade. This daily trade and other normal contacts between the two peoples carried the epidemics into the Indian towns with the same devastating effects. Friendship with the English was deadly.

For the English, the question now was whether the ideal of permanent, mutually beneficial relations, represented according to white values by Captain Thorpe's attempts to begin an Indian college, could continue while the tobacco economy expanded. In 1616, the London Company had promised fifty acres for every person brought to the colony, including women, children and indentured servants, the grant being made to the person who paid for the Atlantic voyage. This became known as the "headright" system. Historians have acknowledged it as a major factor in the establishment of a successful colony. Yet the headright system led to fraudulent purchase and outright seizure of Indian lands. In 1618, Governor Yeardley was authorized to distribute one hundred acres for each share held in the company, promising another one hundred acres when settlers occupied the first. By 1619, the headright system was extensively practiced. Opechancanough watched in anger as the English took more and more land and became increasingly abusive of his people.

As the headright system came into ever wider usage and tensions between Indian and white increased, the first House of Burgesses convened on July 30, 1619. Today, that historic meeting is hailed as the initial step toward modern democracy in North America. Twenty-two representatives met to debate colonial policy. All adult male inhabitants of the colony, English and non-English—Poles, for example—had the right to vote. Remarkably absent from these representatives, however, were the largest landowners in Virginia, the Indians. The year 1619 thus began a tradition of political exclusion that continued for centuries. The exclusion of Indian representation in the House of Burgesses imposed an ironic dual standard. The English demonstrated in the first House of Burgesses election that they were willing to accept other Europeans into their colony as equals. Furthermore, from the point of view of the English colonists, the Indians of the Powhatan Confederacy were legally regarded subjects of the English monarchy, especially after the ceremonious crowning of Powhatan in 1608. Yet for purposes of representation, no Indian "feudal lord" or other leader was invited to represent them. Then, in August of that same year, 1619, the Jamestown colonists purchased twenty African slaves from a Dutch trading vessel. The enslavement of Africans cannot have gone unnoticed among Opechancanough's people.

CHAPTER III

Thanksgiving's Children

In 1621, the Wampanoag Indians of Massachusetts shared a feast of thanksgiving with Pilgrim frontier settlers who had sailed westward from England. This feast was not the first thanksgiving on either side of the Atlantic. Native Americans had given thanks for their harvests for centuries. And in Britain, over the same centuries, the ancestors of the English Pilgrims had also given thanks for successful harvests. Yet the feast in 1621 has taken on the nature of a national myth within the United States, with the clear implication that what occurred that year *was* the first Thanksgiving. The myth ignores an even more important fact.

Fifty-four years later, the red and white children of those same celebrants went to war. Thanksgiving's children were intent on exterminating each other. Neither side succeeded in annihilating the other, but the English colonists emerged triumphant—thanking their God as they did so. While most non-Indian Americans are only familiar with the cooperative spirit of the 1621 thanksgiving feast, American Indians understand that the spirit of the original celebration ultimately failed. Thus Indians view the Thanksgiving celebration each November with a sense of irony, regret, remorse or bitterness.

Popular histories of the United States all too often ignore the fact that the most powerful indigenous nations—those of Mexico and Peru—had been conquered a century before the Pilgrims landed, and that the momentum of American frontier history had been shaped initially not by conquerors who spoke English, but by Spanish-speaking conquistadors. That the Pilgrims *knew* this Spanish history is also conveniently ignored. This is because history is almost always the verdict of the victor: For most citizens of the United States, history must begin at Jamestown and Plymouth, not Mexico City. Thus for the United States, the first Thanksgiving is a worthy and useful myth that also emphasizes how friendship had been sought and achieved by both the First Nations and English-speaking Europeans. Discussing the cruel conflict of Thanksgiving's children, on the other hand, is a tragic reminder of historic reality best omitted from parade commentaries, sermons and family prayers of grace around the turkey.

When the Pilgrims landed on Cape Cod in November 1620, they behaved as typical European invaders had throughout North America. On November 16, they looted large caches of corn belonging to the local Nauset Indians because they would have starved without the supplies they seized. They also dug up a Nauset burial ground but found nothing they coveted. Two weeks later, coming across a larger Nauset burial site, the Pilgrims unhesitatingly looted it and stole the contents they deemed valuable. In the large grave they disrupted, they discovered along with the body of a child the remains of a blond European sailor whom the Indians had honored with burial among their own people. Perhaps the shock of blond hair was what the Pilgrims needed to jar themselves back to their more customary morality, but more likely their grave robbing was brought to an end by the fact that they found no loot in this grave or in the others they probed. Shortly thereafter, however, others in the expedition found two wigwams and stole some Indian property. It is not surprising that eight days later the Nausets, perhaps after using the interim to organize their warriors, attacked the Pilgrim camp. But the Pilgrims' muskets drove them off without loss of life on either side. Thus the Pilgrims began their historic contribution to empire building and betrayal (Bradford and Winslow [1622] 1966, 1–11; cf.: Bradford and Winslow [1622] 1865, 15–34).

Why did the Pilgrims, in the "new world" to establish what they considered to be a more pious Christianity, commit such impious acts as stealing, looting and grave robbing, for which they might have been hanged in England? The answers lie partially in descriptions of Indians in contemporary European literature that the Pilgrims may have read before they left Holland and England. They were certainly aware of Las Casas's cry for justice for the Indians; his book had been available in an English edition since 1583, and in 1607, two years before the Pilgrims left England to seek a religious haven in Holland, a Dutch edition was published. More widely circulated than messages like Las Casas's, however, were tales of Indian attack and deceit at Roanoke and Virginia—stories that ignored any justification the attacking Indians may have had. Added to this was the declaration by numerous English explorers along the New England coast that the Indians were sinister savages likely to murder any

European. The explorers did not mention that some of the Indians' unfriendliness was because many whites kidnapped, enslaved or killed Indian people.

These accounts of Indian hostility convinced the Pilgrims they were entering a war zone. Furthermore, once the Indians had been established in the Pilgrim mind as "the greatest traitors of the world" as the younger Richard Hakluyt characterized them (Hakluyt 1609, A5), it was not difficult for them to treat the Indian's country and his person with contempt. As far as grave robbing was concerned, no less an Englishman than Hakluyt encouraged it in his *Virginia Richly Valued*, published in 1609. Hakluyt informed his countrymen of the wealth de Soto had found south of Virginia and suggested the English search likewise, stating that a

> very gainfull commoditie is, the huge quantitie of excellent perles.... The abundance whereof is reported to be such, that if they would have searched divers graves in townes thereabout, they might have laded many of their horses. (Hakluyt 1609, A3)

The implication was that Englishmen should turn up every Indian grave they found to see if it contained wealth—an activity the Pilgrims undertook even before they built their first home.

The grave robbing of the Pilgrims is recounted in the *Journall of the English Plantation at Plimoth*, published in London in 1622 and also known as Mourt's Relation. The account of the Pilgrims looting of the Nauset Indian graves on Cape Cod is remarkable for its clearly amoral, objective tone. But it also offers equally important insights into Nauset social and burial customs.

> The next morning we followed certain beaten paths and tracts of the *Indians* into the Woods, supposing they would have led us into some Town, or houses; after we had gone awhile, we light upon a very broad beaten path, well nigh two foot broad then we lighted all our Matches [in order to prepare to fire their muskets], and prepared ourselves, concluding we were near their dwellings, but in the end we found it to be only a path made to drive Deer in, when the *Indians* hunt, as we supposed; when we had marched five or six miles into the Woods, and could find no signs of any people, we returned again another way, and as we came into the plain ground, we found a place like a grave, but it was much bigger and longer than any we had yet seen. It was also cov-

ered with boards, so as we mused what it should be, and resolved to dig
it up, where we found, first a Mat, and under that a fair Bow, and there
another Mat, and under that a board about three quarters long, finely
carved and painted, with three tines [prongs], or broaches on the top,
like a Crowne; also between the Mats we found Bowls, Trays, Dishes,
and such like Trinkets; at length we came to a fair new Mat, and under
that two Bundles, the one bigger, the other less, we opened the greater
and found in it a great quantity of fine and perfect red Powder, and in
it the bones and skull of a man. The skull had fine yellow hair still on
it, and some of the flesh unconsumed; there was bound up with it a
knife, a pack-needle, and two or three old iron things. It was bound up
in a Sailors canvas Casacke [bag], and a pair of cloth breeches; the red
Powder was a kind of Embalmment, and yielded a strong, but no offensive smell; It was as fine as any flower. We opened the less bundle likewise, and found of the same Powder in it, and the bones and head of a
little child, about the legs, and other parts of it was bound strings, and
bracelets of fine white Beads; there was also by it a little Bow, about
three quarters long, and some other odd knacks; we brought sundry of
the prettiest things away with us, and covered the Corpses up again.
After this, we digged in sundry like places, but found no more Corn,
nor anything else but graves (Bradford and Winslow [1622] 1966, 11; cf.:
Bradford and Winslow. [1622] 1865, 15–34)

The elaborate nature of the grave indicated that the Nausets extended a high
degree of honor to the blond European who had died among them. It is very
probable that the European had also fathered the child, who was also buried
with ceremony. The sensitive placement of ceremonial and personal objects that
was evident in both burials indicated that the European had been adopted into
the Nauset nation. Since the New England coastal Indians were devastated by an
epidemic disease three years before the Pilgrims' arrival, it would be ironic if
this European, buried with such care, had been the person who carried the epidemic disease and accidentally brought devastation upon the very people who
had sheltered him. The body of the child was buried with strings and bracelets
of wampum. Sacred red powder had been placed upon both bodies.

After the looting, the Pilgrims moved off Cape Cod and settled on the mainland in December 1620. During the harsh New England winter, almost half of the
original 102 colonists died of disease. In February 1621, as the survivors built

shelters and prepared for spring planting, some of their tools were stolen by unseen Indians. The Pilgrims feared that an attack would follow. But on March 16, an Indian strode into their little settlement of huts and greeted them in broken English. Whatever the Pilgrims expected to find in America, it certainly was not an Indian who spoke English. Yet there before them stood Samoset, a Pemaquid chief from Maine. Samoset had been taken aboard an English exploring vessel as a guide because he had learned some English from Grand Banks fishermen, and he had been set ashore at Cape Cod just eight months before his appearance among the Pilgrims. Surely, the Pilgrims believed, Samoset's presence was a sign of encouragement from God. While his vocabulary was not extensive, he was able to inform the Pilgrims about nearby Indians. He promised to go back into the forest and bring a Wampanoag friend who not only spoke excellent English but also had recently returned from England.

Pilgrim-Native Peace Treaty

In a gesture of peace and friendship, Samoset soon came back to Plymouth in the company of five Wampanoag Indians who returned the stolen tools. Samoset went back into the countryside and was not seen for days. Then sixty Wampanoag warriors abruptly appeared at the edge of the forest. One of them explained to the Pilgrims, in English, that they came in peace as escorts to Massasoit, chief of the Wampanoags. The interpreter was the friend Samoset had promised: a Wampanoag warrior named Squanto. After formal greetings that included the blare of a Pilgrim trumpet to impress the Indians, Governor John Carver, Squanto and Massasoit arranged a treaty of peace, signed March 22, 1621, which lasted in its broadest outlines for half a century.

The treaty declared that the Wampanoags and Pilgrims would aid each other if either was attacked, a provision that benefited the Pilgrims, who were susceptible not only to attack by other Indian nations but also by European enemies. Just as important, however, the treaty gave Massasoit the ally he desperately needed in his struggle against the Narragansetts, a powerful Indian nation living to the west that may even have held the Wampanoags in vassalage at the time of the Pilgrims' arrival. Massasoit hoped as well to use the Pilgrim alliance in his conflicts with the Abnaki Indians (known also as the Tarrantines) who lived to the north. Massasoit's Wampanoags were especially vulnerable to intertribal warfare because they had been severely weakened by an epidemic unintentionally introduced by European fishermen and traders.

In 1616–1617, this plague wiped out at least one-third of the Indians living along the New England coast. In fact, the Pilgrims' Plymouth settlement was on the site of a Wampanoag town, Patuxet, which had been wiped out except for Squanto, who had been in England when the epidemic struck.

Evidently, the peace did not specifically define Massasoit as a feudal lord subordinate to the English monarchy. Massasoit was told that he and James I were to be friends and allies. The provisions indicated, however, that the English considered the Indians as subjects. Thus one provision of the treaty was decidedly to the Pilgrims' advantage. If an Indian was found guilty of stealing or of harming a colonist, he would be subject to English law, not Indian law. On the other hand, there was no provision for justice if a white was found guilty of harming an Indian: The only provision dealing with a white crime implied that any white would be tried by other whites under white law. These provisions reflected, even if they did not specifically state, the English concept of asserting sovereignty over Indian people and making them subjects. These provisions were one reason for the breakdown of the treaty a half century later, for the Wampanoags and other nations increasingly resented the enforcement of English statutes that did not always consider the much older Indian law and made little allowance for Indian traditions and customs (Bradford and Winslow [1622] 1865, 93–94).

Once the Pilgrims made peace with the Wampanoags, they wanted to form a similar bond of friendship with the Nausets, and they accomplished this by compensating that nation for their raiding of Nauset graves and the corn stolen the previous winter. As soon as Nauset friendship was secured, however, a faction within the Wampanoag nation challenged the Pilgrims. Its leader, Corbitant, did not approve of his nation's alliance with the English. Perhaps he saw the implications of both Indian and white being liable only to white law. He was certainly jealous of Squanto and two other Wampanoags who lived at Plymouth as interpreters. The Narragansetts, who were eager to destroy the English-Wampanoag alliance, encouraged Corbitant's frustration. Thus Corbitant and his nation's enemies, the Narragansetts, entered into an alliance of their own. The allies developed a plan. While the Narragansetts assassinated Massasoit, Corbitant was to seize the three Wampanoag interpreters at Plymouth. Massasoit would be dead, the English would be without "their tongue" (Bradford and Winslow [1622] 1865, 120), and Corbitant could assume leadership of all the Wampanoags or at least the independent leadership of his own village. The English, without Indian allies, could then be defeated easily.

The plan was not carried out. Massasoit was not assassinated, and although Corbitant seized Squanto and the two other interpreters, Hobomock and Tockamahamon, Hobomock broke away and warned the English. Immediately Myles Standish set out with fourteen Pilgrims to rescue the other two interpreters, with orders that if he found them already dead he was to return to Plymouth with the head of Corbitant. Fortunately for Corbitant, who was not in his village when Standish arrived, Squanto and Tockamahamon were still alive. Standish freed the two interpreters and left the village after warning the people that it would be a mistake for them to go to war. On September 13, 1621, Corbitant and eight other conspirators swore submission to James I.

The Pilgrims' handling of the entire episode impressed the Wampanoag chiefs who had opposed Corbitant. The Indians on Martha's Vineyard, evidently even before Corbitant surrendered, asked to be allowed to join the alliance. Local nations seemed quite ready to join this numerically small yet powerful new neighbor because the Pilgrims offered help against the dreaded Narragansetts.

The Thanksgiving Celebration

By late 1621, then, the Pilgrims had brought peace to the countryside. With their new Pilgrim allies, the Wampanoags and Nausets were secure as long as the Narragansetts did not choose to challenge the powerful muskets and cannon of the Pilgrims. Massasoit and his warriors celebrated this freedom from the Narragansetts with a feast and celebration lasting at least a week and hosted by the Pilgrims, who were themselves grateful that peace had allowed them to establish their homes and secure a bountiful harvest. Had no more whites entered Massachusetts, the situation would undoubtedly have remained harmonious. But other whites came, crowding the wilderness until the sons of these first Pilgrims would nearly exterminate the sons of the Wampanoags just fifty-four years after that first Thanksgiving.

The spirit of the first Thanksgiving did not long continue unchallenged. The Narragansetts, still the most powerful people, red or white, in the area, watched the Wampanoag-Pilgrim alliance with increasing apprehension. In January 1622 Pilgrim Governor William Bradford received a grim message from Canonicus, chief of the Narragansetts—a bundle of arrows bound together with the skin of a rattlesnake. As if there could be any doubt, Squanto confirmed it was a threat and a challenge that could not be ignored. Bradford wished to avoid a war. His colony was still too small to challenge this powerful nation, yet he could not afford to give the appearance of weakness. He decided to answer the Narragansetts in their own terms. He took the rattlesnake skin, stuffed it full of gunpowder and musketballs, and sent it back to the Narragansetts. That concluded the episode.

Bradford's brilliant diplomatic stratagem, which avoided immediate force of arms, could have been a precedent through the decades by the colony. But within four months, the Pilgrims gained a different kind of reputation. Squanto had been telling Indians that the Pilgrims kept a plague hidden under the storehouse floor in Plymouth, and that he knew how to persuade the Pilgrims to use it. After the terrible ravages of 1616–1617, the Indians viewed this message with great fear. One of the Indian interpreters, Hobomock, asked a Pilgrim if this were true. The Pilgrim answered, "No. But the God of the English had it in store: and could send it at his pleasure, to the destruction of his and our enemies" (Winslow [1624] 1897, 528). This attitude by the self-appointed chosen people was combined with, or perhaps even partially the result of, Pilgrim reaction to an event in far-off Virginia that would mark a turning point in Pilgrim-Indian relations.

A Decade of War Begins in Virginia

Opechancanough, chief of the Powhatan Confederacy, had watched the Virginia colony grow rapidly as tobacco plantations of hundreds of acres were encouraged under the London Company's direction. By 1622, 1,240 colonists were spread out on both sides of the meandering James River, some on lands that were purchased fairly and many on lands that were not. The white occupation was not entirely resented, however, because trade goods had enabled the confederation to grow stronger in prestige and to defeat traditional enemies to the west. The copper trade with the Indians living around the Great Lakes, at one time cut off from Virginia by enemy nations, was now open to Opechancanough's people. Thus the whites had helped to enable Powhatan and Opechancanough to sustain their powerful confederacy.

But Opechancanough became increasingly sensitive to the political and cultural imbalance created by the white settlements. Plans for a college existed and there were numerous attempts on the part of men such as George Thorpe to teach the Indians white ways at the expense of their Indian customs. Indians were frequently hired as servants or even enslaved, and although well-meaning white families adopted a few Indians, most whites treated the

Indians as inferiors. Opechancanough was not unwilling to accept the advantages of white technology. But the idea of the college, the missionary spirit among certain whites and the whites' general attitude of superiority spelled danger to the Indian way of life, particularly to Indian religion. Most Indians evidently doubted that the college would be of any benefit to their people, although they could easily see the potential dangers. The Indians' adoption of European ways would give the whites a tremendous advantage; the Indians would be stripped of their culture and be forced to deal only on white terms. In addition, hundreds of colonists arrived every year, then died by the hundreds from their strange European diseases, which subsequently spread and killed Indians. Could the Indian way of life survive if thousands of colonists spread an alien culture over their lands? Could it survive if colonists continued to spread disease? Above all, after fifteen years of settlement the colonists were still incapable of surviving without the Indians' constant supply of food, especially meat. The white population swelled and demanded more food, but the area in which the Indians could hunt remained largely the same. The eventual disappearance of wildlife would be inevitable if the Indians continued to meet the colonists' demands. In 1622, Opechancanough decided that the whites were no longer tolerable. They threatened his people's culture, land and food supply. They had to be exterminated.

The English suspected nothing. They believed that their relationship with the Indians was still mutually beneficial. On March 20, 1622, some of Opechancanough's warriors cheerfully guided a few Englishmen through the forest. But others sent home a young white man who was in one of their towns to learn their language, an ominous sign not recognized at the time. Ironically, a group of warriors on their way to plan war on the settlers borrowed some English boats to cross the James River.

On the evening of March 21, 1622, as was their custom, Opechancanough's warriors came through various settlements trading "Deere, Turkies, Fish, Fruits and other provisions" (Smith [1624] 1910, 573) to the colonists. Shortly after dawn the next morning, Good Friday, calls on customers were made again, but this time with a difference. The warriors were so familiar with the colonists' pattern of living that they knew where each group of colonists was likely to be. They looked for them in homes and fields, killing everyone they found, often with the colonists' own tools. In one incident, Opechancanough's warriors set a tobacco-curing barn afire and then rushed to the main house to tell the whites of the blaze. All but one of the colonists rushed out to fight the fire and were bristled with arrows and slain. Not even George Thorpe, in charge of setting up the Indian college but known among the Indians for his fair dealings, was spared. When a colonist could get to his musket, however, the Indians usually withdrew, so great was their fear of the whites' weapons. The fact that the colonists were spread out over the countryside saved a few, such as a family living in an area known as Martin's Hundred. Seventy-three of their neighbors—men, women and children—were killed, but this family lived in such an isolated area that they didn't learn of the attack for two days.

In this extremely well-coordinated Indian attack, which took place all across the countryside within a matter of hours, Opechancanough's warriors struck thirty-one locations stretching over seventy miles. Of the colony's total population of 1,240, at least 347 were killed immediately. Jamestown would have fallen easily had it not been for an Indian boy named Chanco who had been converted to Christianity and who worked for a white man, a Mr. Pace, who treated him as his son. The night before the attack, Chanco's brother came and told him that he must kill his white friend the next morning. After his brother left, Chanco revealed the entire plan to Pace, who immediately rowed down the James River and warned the town.

Despite their failure to capture Jamestown, Opechancanough's warriors had clearly demonstrated the might and unity of their confederation and almost destroyed the colony, despite its continual reinforcement by new colonists during the next months. At least five hundred additional colonists died of starvation and disease during the year following the attack because the colonists were so dependent upon Indian food supplies, now of course cut off and because the attack came during the spring, preventing the planting of the few fields the colonists did cultivate for food. Hundreds fled home to England. The situation was so desperate that in 1624 James I used the Indian attacks as an excuse to take over Virginia, the London Company's private enterprise, and make it into a royal colony run entirely at the discretion of the monarchy. Significantly, the English crown in subsequent decades often used the excuse of an Indian war to exert stronger royal control over the colonies, most notably in 1763 during Pontiac's War.

Following Opechancanough's initial attack, the Virginia colonists struck back in their own war of extermination, and battles continued sporadically for over a decade. The war would have ended sooner if the English had not decided that revenge and the conquest of territory were more important. In the spring of 1623 Opechancanough proposed peace, feeling that enough blood had been shed on both sides. The English pretended to agree and late in May sent thirteen men to a meeting on the Potomac River to which Opechancanough and other leaders were invited. During the meeting, the English proposed toasts to confirm the peace. Two hundred Indians died, poisoned by drinks the English had spiked. Fifty others were shot down. Going over the carnage, the English did not find Opechancanough's body—fortunately for his people, he had not attended the meeting.

A few whites regretted Opechancanough's war because it destroyed what they considered progress toward harmonious Indian-white relations. Plans for an Indian college, for example, perished with George Thorpe. But most whites, quick to overcome the shock of the first attack, welcomed the war as an opportunity to push the Indians off their lands. John Smith did not entirely agree with the majority, but he stated nevertheless that "now we have just cause to destroy them by all meanes possible: but I thinke it had beene much better it had never happened, for they have given us an hundred times as just occasions long agoe to subject them." Smith saw one result of the attack was "where before we were troubled in cleering the ground of great Timber, ... now we may take their owne plaine fields and Habitations, which are the pleasantest places in the Countrey" (Smith [1624] 1910, 578–79). Smith's words indicate that the Indians' well-cleared fields and towns, and not just their occupation of an area, were a major source of envy among the whites. A further comment by Smith reveals a white attitude that continues to the present day:

> [I]t is more easie to civilize them by conquest then faire meanes; for the one may be made at once, but their civilizing will require a long time and much industry.... What growing state was there ever in the world which had not the like? Rome grew by oppression....(Smith [1624] 1910, 579–80)

Oppression is certainly easier than diplomacy. But the 1622 attack did more than merely define future Indian policy in Virginia as one of conquest. It polarized the red and white races in the eyes of the whites, encouraging an already existent English colonial attitude of racial superiority. This sense of superiority was dependent in part upon white views of the Indian. But it was primarily sustained by the egocentric view of each white that, regardless of individual social status, a white had more in common with other whites than with any Indian. The whites perceived themselves to be members of a superior race and culture. White racial identification was also strong among the colonists because they felt insecure as immigrants. They also needed a justification for conquest. This conquest was more than just a military operation, because the white males were fighting to occupy Indian lands so that they could replace Indian families with their own families. Fear and hatred of Indians also enabled colonists to justify what they knew to be immoral activities. Another element of this mix was the bond of nationality—Englishman identifying with Englishman. This national identification played an important part in encouraging the growth of white racial association.

The Pilgrims Respond to War in Virginia

Overall, it was the whites' view of themselves more than their view of non-whites that gave the greatest force to their prejudice. They fortified this view with what they perceived to be differences with American Indians—differences such as religion—rather than recognizing what whites and Indians may have had in common, such as love of their families. The whites' attitude was so pervasive that whites would regard themselves as distinct from Indians, even when they legally defined the Indians as subjects of their own king and country. This firmer foundation for racism was a result of the 1622 attack. It gave those who were predisposed toward racism an excuse to discriminate openly. Nowhere was the increased racial feeling that resulted from the events of 1622 more evident than in Plymouth Colony, far to the north of Virginia, but suddenly close in common fear and common racial identity.

Upon hearing of Opechancanough's war, and because they also feared the Narragansetts, the Pilgrims erected a fort during the summer of 1622. The Pilgrims were no longer the only whites living along the shore of Massachusetts, however. In 1622 they had been joined by sixty not-so-pious Englishmen who established a ramshackle settlement, Wessagusett, near the Massachusetts Indians from whom they occasionally stole corn. They had not bothered to plant or harvest much for the coming winter, and as the Plymouth colonists were also low on food, the two white groups decided to go jointly to the Indians and trade for corn. The Massachusetts Indians had, at the suggestion of the Pilgrims, planted extra corn to sell to the whites, and they expected to receive the same rate they had gotten earlier from some of the Wessagusett settlers. Even though the Pilgrims were hungry, they decided that they could not make a profit at the Massachusetts' asking price, so they sailed south to take their trade to the Nauset Indians. The Nausets could not afford to spare any corn for the coming winter, and they protested when the Pilgrims proposed only a few trade goods as payment. They felt that if they were going to have to part with a precious food supply, the least the English could do was trade fairly for it. In exchange for enough corn and beans to fill twenty-eight barrels, the English finally gave the Nausets most of the trade goods they wanted, including what the Nausets prized most: metal hoes.

To supplement their diet during the ensuing winter, the Pilgrims were willing to eat acorns and whatever else they found in the forest, but the Wessagusett colonists quickly consumed their share of the beans and corn. Faced with starvation, the Wessagusett men began to sell their clothes and bedding to the Massachusetts in exchange for food. A few desperate whites even hired themselves out to the Indians as servants. Finally, some began to steal again, and even though Wessagusett officials hanged one man who was a perpetual thief, the Indians were not convinced that these whites should be tolerated. Added to these tensions were fatal diseases spread from the Wessagusett settlers to the families of the Massachusetts. The warriors finally decided to rid their homeland of the Wessagusett settler-parasites once and for all. Other Indians, including the Nausets and the Pausets, agreed, and because the Pilgrims had helped the Wessagusett colonists, it was decided to wipe them out as well. The Wampanoags were invited to join the alliance. Fate, however, came to the aid of the Pilgrims.

Massasoit, the chief of the Wampanoags, had always been friendly with the Pilgrims. More importantly, however, a Pilgrim had recently cured Massasoit when it seemed certain he was about to die. Massasoit felt bound to the Pilgrims, and refused to join the alliance. Instead, he informed Plymouth of the impending attack and suggested the Pilgrims assassinate the leaders. It was clear to the Pilgrims that the Wessagusett men were at grave fault for arousing the anger of the Massachusetts, Nausets, Pausets, and other Indians. They must also have realized that their joint expedition with the Wessagusett colonists to demand food from the Massachusetts had done its part to anger that nation. Fault for the crisis was clearly the white man's. The situation, however, was less volatile than the time the powerful Narragansett nation had sent the bunch of arrows bound with a rattlesnake skin to Plymouth. The nations now uniting were weak, and the plot had been discovered before its execution. Adroit diplomats would have restored harmony by chastising the Wessagusett settlers for stealing, making it clear to the angry Indians that the Pilgrims did not approve of their shiftless countrymen. Perhaps a show of Pilgrim military strength at this time would have impressed both the Wessagusett settlers and the Indian nations that the Pilgrims could back up their viewpoints. Because the Pilgrims had done their best to prevent violent outbreaks in previous crises, such a step might seem logical. However, the Pilgrims' attitude toward Indians had been altered by news of the surprise attack on Virginia.

Myles Standish and eight musket-bearing companions hurried by boat to the white settlement at Wessagusett. They pretended to be on a fur-trading expedition, but the Massachusetts were not fooled. They realized at once that their plot had been exposed and refused to come near Standish and his men. Negotiations seemed called for, and so late in March the chief of the Massachusetts, Witawamet, along with his eighteen-year-old brother and two warriors, came to Wessagusett. They evidently intended to tell Standish, who was still there with his men, that if he could persuade the Wessagusett colonists to stop stealing from Indian people, bloodshed could be avoided. Myles Standish, however, had already decided to substitute violence for negotiation. Once the Indians and whites had entered the building, the colonists bolted the door and killed Witawamet and the two warriors. The chief's brother was seized and hanged on the spot, and the English later killed three more warriors. Standish and his men returned to Plymouth with Witawamet's head and impaled the grisly trophy on one of the logs of the town's palisade. Not surprisingly, the Massachusetts retaliated by killing three Wessagusett men. The remaining Wessagusett whites decided to abandon their colony.

Despite the disbanding of the Wessagusett settlement, the Massachusetts nation was filled with terror by Standish's brutal murder of their chief, his brother and his warriors during a supposed peace mission. They were convinced that the Pilgrims would give them no quarter. The Massachusetts and their allies fled their fields and towns. The Pilgrims never attacked them, but because the Indians had not planted crops, many Indians died of starvation the following winter.

The murder of the chief revealed a dramatic change in the Pilgrims' attitude. The attack of Virginia had alarmed the Pilgrims to such an extent that they now overreacted to a crisis in their own colony. The Pilgrims did not view all Indian nations as dangerous, but Standish's action revealed that suddenly the Pilgrims—under separatist leaders who had rejected both England and Holland—found it possible to discover something in common with the disreputable Wessagusett settlers. Significantly, the Indians held no such common views of their race and did not therefore unite against the whites. Massasoit knew that the Wessagusett white men had committed grave crimes against the Indians, and he no doubt recognized that the Pilgrims were wrong in demanding food from the Massachusetts when that nation refused what was clearly an unfair exchange. Yet he regarded the Pilgrims as friends and he did not ally his people with other Indians. On the contrary, he had warned the Pilgrims.

Taking Witawamet's head back to Plymouth, the Pilgrims put it on a palisade, just as they would have done with traitors back in England. The Pilgrims thus demonstrated that they regarded the affair as an internal civil disturbance, not a clash between independent powers, for they believed that the Indians were under Pilgrim jurisdiction and law and were subjects of James I. Yet the Wessagusett white settlers were under this same law and king, and it is apparent that the Pilgrims did not make great efforts to stop the Wessagusett settlers from crimes against the Indians. At the same time, they took drastic actions against the Massachusetts, whose plan to attack the whites came only after they saw no other way to halt the whites' crimes against them.

Interregnum: The Pilgrims as God's Chosen

Standish's murders in 1623 impressed upon the Massachusetts and other small nations that it was foolhardy to challenge the English. They submitted to the tidal wave of 1,000 Puritan immigrants who came in 1630 under Governor John Winthrop of the Massachusetts Bay Colony. Soon, however, the Indians chafed at the constant influx of colonists, numbering 2,000 by 1632, primarily because other settlers wanted so much land. John Winthrop's Puritans were determined to treat the Indians with justice. But they were more determined to successfully establish their colony, which became a testimony to the Puritans' ability to interpret their own overriding interests as God's will. The friction with the Indians over land was soon settled, for the Puritans had brought with them a disease to which the Indians had no resistance: smallpox. Between fall 1633 and summer 1634, thousands of Indians perished in the worst epidemic since 1616–1617. The Puritans did what they could to nurse the nearby Indians, but at the same time they viewed the epidemic as an act of God clearing the countryside for his chosen people. On January 3, 1634, Governor Winthrop wrote:

[I]f God were not pleased with our inheriting these parts, why did he drive out the natives before us? And why dothe he still make roome for us, by deminishinge them as we increase? (Winthrop Papers 1938, 149)

The government recorder at Charlestown revealed another advantage to the smallpox devastation of the Indians.

By which awful and admirable dispensation it pleased God to make room for his people of the English nation . . . who, without this remarkable and terrible stroke of God upon the natives, would with much more difficulty have found room, and at a far greater charge have obtained and purchased land. (Anonymous 1846, 386–87)

Epidemic or no, the Puritans were fond of giving God the credit for special bargains wherever they were found. One man wrote, "God caused the Indians to help us with fish at very cheap rates" (Young [1731] 1846, 350). The Puritans also found that Indians would work for cheaper wages than fellow Englishmen, and that handsome profits could be made by buying furs from them.

By 1634 the Puritans had gained the upper hand in New England. They believed themselves to be the chosen of God and felt "Where there is a vacant place there is liberty for the son of *Adam* or *Noah* to come and inhabit, though they neither buy it, nor ask their leaves" (Cotton [1630] 1964, 103). Furthermore, as Governor Winthrop explained,

If we had not right to this land, yet our God hath right to it, and if he be pleased to give it us (takinge it from a people who had so long usurped upon him, and abused his Creatures) who shall control him or his terms? (Winthrop Papers 1938, 149)

The Puritans could ponder more than one hundred years of Spanish experience when they landed at Boston in 1630. A decade of Pilgrim Indian policy provided further examples. The opportunity for honorable treatment of the Indians appeared at the very start of the Massachusetts Bay experiment, for two moral crusaders appeared almost immediately: John Elliot and Roger Williams. These two men gave a high priority to the recognition of the Indians' rights. Even as Virginia's reform movement and the influence of Maryland's Jesuit missionaries under the Reverend Andrew White were cut short in the

1640s by Puritan political revolutions in Maryland and England, Elliot and Williams took those reforming trends even further. Unfortunately, their efforts did not have the full support of most New England colonists—although a few Puritans such as Thomas Mayhew, Jr., did their best in similar efforts.

Roger Williams arrived in Massachusetts in 1631 and almost immediately discerned the injustice of Puritan Indian policies. In 1633 Williams publicly denied the right of any European monarch, including England's Charles 1, to claim any Indian lands by the "right of discovery," which in European law allowed a monarch rights over all lands not occupied by Christians. Williams thereby denied that any king had the right to grant such lands to colonists. Land in America, including that being settled by the Puritans, could only be occupied after it had been purchased from the Indians, according to Williams. He also took a stand against the views of Governor John Winthrop. Winthrop believed that since the Indians did not settle all the land and "improve" it with farms and English-style frame houses, they had no legal right to it. Winthrop also believed that if the Indians were left enough land to live on in the European style, the rest of the land could rightfully be taken. Williams reminded his fellow Puritans that the Indians did indeed use all of the land, for they hunted everywhere, and that this possession was just as legal as that of rich nobles in Europe who set aside land exclusively for hunting.

Partly due to Williams's opinion on Indian rights, he was considered dangerous to the colony and was banished in 1635. Fleeing to Rhode Island, he carried on peaceful relations with the powerful Narragansetts, and he became useful to both red and white as an interpreter and intermediary. Despite Williams's rebellious stand against the Indian policy of Massachusetts Bay and his demonstration of a workable, ethical Indian policy in Rhode Island, his isolation in the latter colony put him outside the white political mainstream and away from the white population concentrations that ultimately determined Indian policy throughout New England. For example, after 1643 the Narragansett nation continued its occasionally violent conflict with the pro-Puritan Mohegans while trying to hold onto their entire homeland. The Narragansetts depended on the diplomatic maneuvers of one of their leaders, Canonicus. Canonicus sought to protect the Narragansetts by using English law against the Puritan colonists. On May 24, 1644, at the advice of a Rhode Island colonist, Samuel Gorton, Canonicus subjected his people directly to the English monarchy. Now if the Puritans threatened his people or their property, they would not only have to defy the

Narragansetts, they would have to challenge their own king. That the Narragansetts had surrendered their sovereignty as an independent nation was not explained to them. The matter, however, became moot, because other Puritans back in England were rebelling against Charles 1 in what became known in England as the Puritan Revolution. The revolution would lead to the beheading of Charles 1 in 1649.

European Land Hunger & Intertribal Conflict

Destruction of the Pequots

Two Indian nations in the region, however—the Narragansetts and the Pequots—still possessed a strength of determination that rivaled the Englishmen's. Fortunately for the Puritans, the two nations were archenemies and in 1634 were at war with one another, in the continuation of a conflict that had begun a generation or so before the Puritans arrived.

Many of the Pequots were originally from the upper Hudson River valley, but the pressures of the increasingly aggressive Haudenosaunee had pushed them into the area of eastern Connecticut. Like the English, they were recent invaders; in fact, Pequot is the Algonquin word for "destroyer." The Pequots dominated the nations of the Connecticut River valley, an area the English had coveted but could not obtain because the Pequots forbade their subject nations to sell. Suddenly, a rather far-fetched excuse arose for forcing the Pequots to allow land sales, and the Puritans seized it.

Captain John Stone of Virginia sailed forth from that southern colony with a shipload of cattle to sell in Boston. Along the way, he tried but failed to steal a Plymouth ship in the Dutch harbor of New Amsterdam (now New York City). When Stone arrived in New England, he attempted to stab the governor of the Plymouth Colony, and in Massachusetts Bay he was such a troublemaker that he was fined £100 and banned from Massachusetts Bay under penalty of death. Not the least chastened, Stone joined Captain Walter Norton and his rough crew of seven and sailed for the Connecticut River. They intended to trade with the Pequots and perhaps seize some of them to sell as slaves back in Virginia or the West Indies. Stone managed to capture two braves by enticing them on board his ship with offer of trade. But a group of the braves' friends observed Stone's actions, and as soon as Stone and his men came ashore, all the whites were killed and the two braves rescued.

A few Puritans felt that this was God's justice to an evil man. But many, enticed by the prospect of seizing Pequot land, saw this as an excuse to bring pressure on the Pequots. Suddenly, Stone and his fellow criminals were fellow Englishmen. Massachusetts Bay demanded that the Pequots turn over the warriors who had killed Stone and his men to be tried as murderers. The Pequots were already at war with the Narragansetts and with the Dutch, so they could not afford to fight a third opponent. They sent ambassadors to Massachusetts to ask for terms. The Pequot representatives explained that all but two of the warriors involved in the incident had died of smallpox, and that the chief who had led them had subsequently been killed by the Dutch. They agreed, however, in a treaty signed November 1, 1634, to give up the two warriors whenever the English wanted them. Furthermore, they promised as reparation to establish a fur trade, pay four hundred six-foot lengths of wampum (legal currency among the whites), forty beaver and thirty otter pelts, and most important to the Puritans, to allow the whites to buy land along the Connecticut River from Pequot subject nations.

The terms exacted by the Puritans were blatant in their opportunism: They collected a small fortune and valuable lands by posing as the righteous avengers of an unscrupulous lot whose captain had been banished from Massachusetts on pain of death. Moreover, the colonists who were killed were residents of another colony far to the south, and they died beyond Massachusetts's jurisdiction because warriors of the Pequot nation were intent on rescuing fellow Pequots who had been kidnapped!

The Pequots were unhappy about the treaty they had been forced to sign. Puritans came to buy land and settle at Hartford, and some trading was grudgingly carried on. But by 1636 the Pequots had paid only a part of the reparation, perhaps because their war with the Narragansetts, recently concluded (1634), and their ongoing war with the Dutch were so expensive. In addition, they had yet to turn over the two warriors who had participated in the killing of Stone and his men. Evidence indicates that the Pequots were also upset because they felt they had not been offered fair payment for their furs or corn by a profit-minded New England trader, John ("Mad Jack") Oldham. Oldham had a scoundrel's reputation even among the Pilgrim and Puritan leaders, but he served them well scouting out Indian lands for future expansion.

The Massachusetts Bay Colony decided to force the Pequots into compliance with the 1634 treaty or go to war. Before they could offer the Pequots the chance to settle the issue peacefully, however, another New England trader named John

Gallop sighted John Oldham's small ship off Block Island in the Long Island Sound, but could see only Indians on board. Gallop killed the surprised Indians and found John Oldham dead; later it was determined he was killed during a quarrel. Had the Block Island Indians been subjects of the Pequots, the Puritans could have moved with swift retribution, using Oldham's murder as an excuse. But the Block Island Indians were subjects of the Narragansetts, and the Puritans had to avoid a war that might bring the Narragansetts and the Pequots together as allies. Fortunately for the Puritans, the Narragansetts did not want war with the English. They forced the Block Island Indians to give them two white boys who were captured on the boat and taken ashore before Gallop's arrival, and the trade goods from Oldham's boat. After returning the boys and the trade goods to the Puritans, the Narragansetts explained that most of those who had killed Oldham had been killed by Gallop, but a few had left before Gallop's arrival. Those warriors had fled to the Pequots.

Massachusetts Bay decided that harsh justice was in order. John Endecott was ordered to kill all male Indians on Block Island and seize all the Block Island women and children who would probably then have been sold as servants or slaves. He was next to proceed to the Pequots and demand Oldham's refugee murderers. At the same time, Endecott was to obtain the two warriors who had helped kill Stone and his crew in 1634. Finally, a new reparation was to be assessed—a thousand fathoms of wampum, to be guaranteed by Pequot children held as hostages. If the Pequots refused, Endecott was to use force.

Endecott could only kill a few Block Island Indians, so he burned their cornfields and towns. Then he proceeded to Pequot territory. When he approached the main town at Pequot Harbor, the Indians met him with protestations of innocence. In an exchange perhaps hindered by translations tendered by Endecott's Massachusetts interpreter, the Pequots explained that their chiefs were visiting Long Island, that the killing of Stone in 1634 was not as it had seemed to the Puritans, and that they did not know the whereabouts of any of the murderers. Fearing the worst, the Pequots began to evacuate women and children from their town. They then asked that both sides lay down their arms for negotiations. Although there is no evidence to support Endecott's conclusion, he decided that the Pequots were not really interested in peace but were only trying to trick him. On order, Endecott's men fired a sudden volley at the Indians, killing or wounding a few. The rest fled, Endecott spent two days looting the Pequot town, and the Pequots found themselves in an unwanted war with the English.

The battles lasted from August 1636 to the end of 1637. At first the Pequots, under their chief, Sassacus, managed to hold their own and drive a number of colonists into the protection of forts. The Pequots often tortured white prisoners and they were not adverse to killing entire families, but neither were the whites. The outcome was inevitable, however, because the Pequots had few muskets and because they failed to convince the Narragansetts that the English would turn on them once the Pequots were out of the way. The Narragansetts chose to side with the English and so did every other nation in New England. Even the Pequots themselves were divided. In 1635–1636, a faction had broken away under Chief Uncas, and had taken a variation of the name they had had while on the Hudson River: Mohegans. Uncas and his Mohegans, along with some Narragansetts, joined the English and played a major role in the Puritan slaughter of more than 400 Pequot men, women and children surprised in their fort at Mystic, Connecticut on May 26, 1637. Only about seven Pequots escaped and seven or so others were captured, while only two Englishmen were killed and twenty wounded, and only a few of the Indians' allies were killed and perhaps fifty wounded. The governor of Plymouth, William Bradford, described the burning of the fort and the massacre of the Pequots:

> Those that escaped the fire were slain with the sword, some hewed to pieces, others run through with their rapiers, so as they were quickly dispatched and very few escaped. It was conceived they thus destroyed about 400 at this time. It was a fearful sight to see them thus frying in the fire and the streams of blood quenching the same, and as horrible was the stink and scent thereof; but the victory seemed a sweet sacrifice, and they gave the praise thereof to God, who had wrought so wonderfully for them, thus to enclose their enemies in their hands and give them so speedy a victory over so proud and insulting an enemy. (Morison 1952, 296)

Captain John Underhill, one of the English officers, added,

> [S]ometimes the Scripture declareth women and children must perish with their parents; some-time the case alters: but we will not dispute it now. We had sufficient light from the word of God for our proceedings. (Underhill [1638] n.d., 40; cf.: Orr 1897, 81 and Hauptman and Wherry 1990)

When the war finally ended, the Pequots had lost more than seven hundred people. The whites often shot defeated Pequot warriors rather than take them prisoner. Women and children were officially distributed among white soldiers to be their slaves. The English victory was so overwhelming that nearby Indians sent the Puritans the heads of any Pequot refugees they encountered rather than risk Puritan anger. The Mohawk Haudenosaunee of New York were so alarmed by reports or actual observations of English firepower that when the Pequot chief Sassacus and forty of his warriors sought refuge among the Mohawks they were executed, and Sassacus' scalp was sent to Hartford as a sign of the Mohawks' respect for English guns. On September 21, 1638, the surviving Pequots surrendered and their chiefs signed the Treaty of Hartford. They were stripped of their right to call themselves Pequots and forbidden to inhabit their former territory. Only 180 Pequot warriors remained, and they with their families were assigned as slaves to the Puritans' Indian allies. Eighty went to Uncas and the Mohegans, eighty to the Narragansetts, and twenty to the Niantics. Many of these Pequots did not continue as slaves but were adopted by the host nation, given homes and land, and allowed to call themselves Pequots. Nevertheless, under the treaty, the Mohegans and the Narragansetts agreed to pay the Puritans an annual tribute. This tribute paid for the labor the Pequots provided to the Mohegans and Narragansetts. The Mohegans and Narragansetts also agreed not to go to war with each other without the permission of the Puritans. Thus the English not only eliminated the powerful Pequot nation; they legally bound the Mohegans and the Narragansetts not to cause any trouble in the future. But the Puritans gained even more: They claimed the Pequot lands by right of conquest. Within four years, more than five thousand Puritans had settled on the Pequots' lands.

The Puritans and the Dutch in Indian Wars, 1638–1664

The Pequots had warned the Narragansetts that the Puritans would turn on them next, and they were soon proved right. The Puritans supported Uncas, whose numerically weaker Mohegans were willing friends. The more numerous Narragansetts found that Uncas and other Indians were telling the English that the Narragansetts were plotting an Indian alliance to massacre the whites, and Massachusetts Bay undertook preventive detention and the disarming of the leaders of suspect nations weaker than the Narragansetts. Partly in response to the rumors, the colonies of Massachusetts Bay, Plymouth,

Connecticut and New Haven decided to form the Confederation of New England on May 19, 1643, the English colonies' first attempt at unification. Shortly thereafter, Uncas declared that the Narragansetts had tried to assassinate him because of his friendship with the English. In a fury of frustration over Uncas's accusation, the Narragansetts finally attacked the Mohegans. Surprisingly, the Mohegans won the battle, and Uncas turned over the captured Narragansett chief, Miantonomo, to the Puritans. In September 1643 they decided to return Miantonomo to Uncas for execution, and Uncas's brother soon dispatched him with a hatchet.

The 1643 assassination of the Narragansett chief Miantonomo on the orders of the Puritans and Uncas continued to be an issue among the Narragansetts. After nearly a year of attempting to gain redress from the Mohegans, the Narragansetts complained about the matter to the Puritans' United Colonies (Confederation of New England). The United Colonies' decision denied the validity of the Narragansetts' claim that Uncas should either be brought to trial or that he should return a ransom paid by the Narragansetts for the safety of Miantonomo. In the spring of 1645, the frustrated Narragansetts attacked the Mohegans. The Mohegans would almost certainly have been conquered had Connecticut and New Haven troops not intervened. The colonial Puritans now threatened the Narragansetts with war if they did not cease their hostilities against the Mohegans. In addition to the conquest of valuable Narragansett land, the Puritans saw at least two other benefits to be gained by going to war, as set forth by Emmanuel Downing in an August 1645 letter to Plymouth's John Winthrop:

A war with the Narraganset is very considerable to this plantation, for I doubt whither it be not sin in Us having power in our hands to suffer them to maintain the worship of the devil, which their Paw wawes [Powwows or religious leaders] often do; secondly, If upon a Just war the lord should deliver them into our hands, we might easily have men, women and Children enough to exchange for Moors [black Africans], which will be more gainful pillage for us then we conceive, for I do not see how we can thrive untill we get into a stock of slaves. (Downing [1645] 1947, 38)

Roger Williams had just had Rhode Island sign a treaty of peace with the Narragansetts, demonstrating his disagreement with Puritan policy, and he made strong efforts on the Narragansetts' behalf. Nevertheless, the Narragansetts had to sign a treaty with the United Colonies on August 28, 1645, promising, among other stipulations, two thousand fathoms of wampum to pay for the white army that had been raised to fight them, and which would have been used if the treaty had not been made. In 1645 and again in 1648, the Narragansetts sought an alliance with the Mohawk Haudenosaunee against Uncas and the Mohegans. Both times the alliance failed to materialize. Henceforth, Puritan exploitation of the Narragansetts was unlikely to be hindered very much by the sincere but isolated Roger Williams.

John Eliot was more successful, at least from his own devoutly held perspective as a Christian missionary. He worked within Massachusetts Bay and demonstrated the possibilities of harmonious Indian-white relationships as the Puritan population engulfed the Indians. By modern standards one of his shortcomings was his insistence that the Indian should take up the Puritan lifestyle as well as religion: Indians were encouraged to cut their hair and move into English-style frame buildings. Eliot, like Las Casas before him and so many well-intentioned missionaries and reformers after him, believed that the whites had the right to determine what was best for Indians. But given his era, he did all that he could. After all, Eliot was the product of a culture that believed that man's relationship to the Supreme Being had to be Christian and that this Christian relationship was more important than any other aspect of life.

Eliot chose to work with small bands that were too weak to oppose the imposition of English culture. These bands had little influence on the sweeping events taking place primarily in Massachusetts, and primarily served to demonstrate what could be done if there were more missionaries and more money invested in converting the Indians.

Eliot, loved and respected by his fellow Puritans, actually succeeded as a teacher of whites as well as Indians. His ideas became models for social experimentation. By 1646 he was working to bring English civilization to the Indians. In 1649, thanks in no small part to Eliot, the Society for the Propagation of the Gospel in New England was founded in London with the purpose of financing missionaries. In 1663, Eliot published the culmination of more than a decade of labor, an Algonquin translation of the Bible, *Mamusse Wunneetupanatamwe Up-Biblum God*. But his greatest achievement was in helping to set up "praying Indian towns." These towns and others patterned on Eliot's model proved that the Indians, always the whites' equals by their own Indian standards, were also capable (according to white standards) of full equality in every aspect of white colonial life. The Indian town of Natick, Massachusetts, provided an excellent example.

In 1651, one hundred Massachusetts Indians (about twenty families) under chiefs Waban and Cutshamekin established an entire town on the Charles River just eighteen miles from Boston, after acquiring the land from the whites. They built their town on both sides of the river, connecting it with an eighty-foot-long wooden bridge. They erected a frame meeting house, and frame homes were added as fast as temporary shelters could be replaced. Frame barns and even fences dotted the town's landscape. The Indians even constructed their own fort and organized their own militia. Their children went to a school staffed by Indian teachers. It took almost a decade for the Indians to prove to white Puritan elders that some of them deserved full membership in the church, but by 1670 fifty of the growing population of 145 Indians in Natick were full members, quite an achievement considering the strictness of Puritan church membership requirements. The Indians elected their own officials in town meetings, and their preacher and church elders were all Indians. Indian adaptability was thus clearly demonstrated, indicating that if other Indians rejected white ways it was by choice, not lack of ability.

While the Indians at Natick and thirteen other praying Indian towns were proving in microcosm that Indians were able to undertake any aspect of white civilization they cared to adopt, the Puritans who lived nearby were proving in that same microcosm that no matter what the Indians accomplished, they would be treated as inferiors. For example, white citizens of the town of Marlboro greatly resented Christian Indians who owned 150 acres in their midst, and there was continual strife as the whites tried to infringe on the Indians' property rights. The praying Indians proved what all minorities in America were to learn from afar: The majority admires and encourages the efforts of minorities to achieve equality, but for those whites who live near the minority, resentment and jealousy dominate no matter how well the minority conforms to majority standards.

The Dutch: "To Kill Their Own Blood"

Early in 1643 in the Dutch colony of New Netherlands, Director (governor) William Kieft decided that the Algonquin Indian nations around New Amsterdam stood in the way of his colony's expansion (the Dutch had purchased Manhattan Island from local Indians in 1626). The Indians living in the lower Hudson River valley and on Long Island were of little use to him in supplying furs, since the Mohawk Haudenosaunee to the north provided all he needed in exchange for trade goods and muskets. In addition, local Indians cultivated land his farmers wanted. Kieft's opportunity came in February 1643 when Indians belonging to the Wappinger Confederacy north of Manhattan Island fled southward toward New Amsterdam after being attacked by musket-toting Mohawks (and perhaps by Mahican warriors subject to the Mohawks). The fleeing Indians came as close as they could to New Amsterdam, evidently in part because they had paid taxes to Kieft in exchange for the promise of protection by his soldiers. Kieft noted that the Indians were massed as they might never be again. By attacking them now he could catch them unawares. On the night of February 25, 1643, his men surrounded two camps, one at Corlaer's Hook on Manhattan Island and another at Pavonia in eastern New Jersey. The bands of soldiers killed a total of eighty Indian men women, and children and took their heads back to New Amsterdam. There one burly Dutch woman glee-fully booted some of the Indian heads down the street.

David de Vries was a prominent Dutch colonist who maintained reason-able and often friendly personal relations with the Indian people around him. He opposed going to war with the Indians. Shortly after the 1643 war had begun, de Vries found himself in a council with his former friends. De Vries recorded the protocol and the imagery of the council:

> The 4th of March, there came three Indians upon Long Island, with a small white flag, and called out [standing in what is now Brooklyn and calling across the East River] to the fort [on lower Manhattan]. Then Governor Willem Kieft asked who would go over to them. There was no one who was willing to do so, among all of them, except Jacob Olfersz and I, David Pietersz de Vries. We went to the three Indians. They told us that they came from their chief, who had sent them to know the cause why some of his Indians had been killed, who had never laid a straw in our way, and who had done us nothing but favors? We answered them that we did not know that any of their Indians were among them. They then said we must go and speak with their chief, who had fled seven leagues from there on the seacoast. We resolved to go with the Indians, for we believed that they were well disposed towards us two.
>
> At evening we arrived at Rechqua Akie [Rockaway], where we found the chief, who had only one eye, with two or three hundred Indians,

and about thirty houses. They led us into his house, and treated us to what they had, as oysters, and fish, which they catch there; told us we were tired, and must rest a little; they would early in the morning speak to us about the business upon which we had come there. During the night, I went out of the house, when there came an Indian to me, as the moon was shining, and told me I must come into his hut. I then went into his hut, and by the light saw he was an Indian, who lived half a league from my house at Vriessendael, with his squaws, who lived there with him, at which I was alarmed. Then he assured me, saying, that I was a good chief, and that I came to make Rancontyn Maruit; that is, in their language, to make a peace. I asked them how they came so far from their dwelling. They answered that they were out a hunting with these Indians, and had friends among them. I then returned to my comrade in the house of the chief. When the day began to dawn, we were awakened, and taken by an Indian, who led us into the woods about four hundred paces from the houses, and when we came there, sixteen chiefs were there of this Long Island, which is thirty leagues long. They placed us two by ourselves, and seated themselves around us, so that we sat within a ring. There was one among them who had a small bundle of sticks, and was the best speaker, who began his oration in Indian. He told how we [that is, all the Dutch] first came upon their coast; that we sometimes had no victuals; they gave us their Turkish beans and Turkish wheat [that is, Indian beans and corn], they helped us with oysters and fish to eat, and now for a reward we had killed their people. Then he laid down one of the sticks, which was one point. He related also that at the beginning of our voyaging there, we left our people behind with the goods to trade, until the ships should come back; they had preserved these people like the apple of their eye; yea, they had given them their daughters to sleep with, by whom they had begotten children, and there roved many an Indian who was begotten by a Swanneken [the local Algonquin word for "Dutch"], but our people had become so villainous as to kill their own blood. (Vries [1655] 1909, 229–31)

Although a meeting with Governor Kieft was later held, the resulting truce was brief, and the Dutch continued their war, killing even more of "their own blood." But Indian revenge was swift. Many Dutch farms and settlements were overrun and their inhabitants killed. The Dutch reported, however, that the Indians spared Dutch women and children. The warfare escalated. In 1644, according to Dutch records, Governor Kieft and many other Dutch colonists gathered for a public torture and execution of a male Hackensack prisoner of war. According to a Dutch record, Dutch soldiers skinned him alive, strip by strip, forcing him to swallow his own flesh. While he courageously sang his death song, the soldiers drug him down a street, "threw him down, and stuck his private parts, which they had cut off, into his mouth while he was still alive, and after that placed him on a mill-stone and beat his head off" (Melyn 1857, 258).

Kieft's plans of conquest were not matched by the colony's capability for war. The Dutch colony's total population was only about twelve hundred, including a mere sixty soldiers and some two hundred militiamen. Kieft hastily erected a log palisade along the northern limits of his tiny New Amsterdam. The military road that ran behind the palisade to supply any defenders has retained its name to the present day: Wall Street. (There is some evidence that the wall was not built until the *next* Indian war in 1655, but this wall may have been simply an improvement on an original.)

The Dutch colony survived because of two allies: New Englanders and Mohawks. Fifty New Englanders, including some veterans of the Pequot War, had settled there. Most prominent among them was John Underhill, one of the officers who led the Puritans' attack on the Pequot fort at Mystic in 1637. Underhill and his men with the aid of some Dutch soldiers killed five hundred Indians in one battle alone, and assured the subjugation of the nations living around New Amsterdam. Peace finally came in 1645, partly because the Mohawks, hoping to ensure the continuation of the lucrative fur trade with the Dutch, forced it upon the warring Indians.

Kieft was dismissed, and his replacement, Peter Stuyvesant, arrived in Manhattan on May 11, 1647. Dutch expansion accelerated. In 1655, local Indians, feeling the pressure and resenting Dutch trade with their Haudenosaunee enemies, tried to bluff the Dutch in New Amsterdam with a show of force that soon turned into a riot. Fighting with the whites broke out and the Indians found themselves embroiled in the Peach War, so called because the entire sequence of events had been sparked by a Dutch colonist who killed an Indian woman stealing peaches from his orchard. However, the Indians were too fragmented to fight a concerted war and the whites had technological advantages, so in 1657 the war sputtered to an end. The Dutch, aided by some Indian allies, fought two more major conflicts for land, called the Esopus Wars (1658–1660 and

1663–1664), against the Esopus nation about eighty-five miles north of New Amsterdam. By 1664, when the English sailed into New Amsterdam's harbor and captured the Dutch colony without resistance, the Dutch had completely subjugated the lower Hudson River Valley and eastern Long Island.

White Wars of Extermination, 1675 & 1676

For many of the eastern seaboard Indian nations, events during the seventeenth century culminated in white wars of extermination during 1675 and 1676. In Virginia, the Powhatan Confederacy had never fully recovered from the war they began in 1622, for the whites had fought them with a zeal inspired by the knowledge that Indian lands were the prize of victory. The whites ensured Indian deaths by starvation whenever they weren't able to kill the Indians outright by destroying the extensive Indian cornfields. The war was fought sporadically throughout the 1630s and by treaty was brought to a formal end in 1642, but in April 1644, Opechancanough, now an old man borne on a litter, led his people into battle once again. The wise chief had heard from some Englishmen about the bloody civil war then going on in England between King Charles 1 and the Puritan-inspired revolutionaries, and he decided to strike while the English could not afford to send help to Virginia. Opechancanough also took advantage of difficulties Maryland was having with the Susquehanna Indians, which made it impossible for that colony to aid Virginia, and it is possible that he even expected Maryland to offer him aid, so strong was the Maryland-Virginia rivalry. Opechancanough, hoping to stop white expansion and ensure the survival of the Powhatan way of life independent of the whites, won some initial victories, striking by surprise on April 18, 1644—tactics similar to those of 1622. Although the Powhatans were more successful than they had been in 1622, killing five hundred colonists, Virginia's population of eight thousand was better able to sustain this war. Opechancanough was captured, brought to Jamestown, and shot in the back by a vengeful soldier assigned to guard him. The war finally ended in October 1646 with a reservation north of the York River assigned to the Powhatans. In 1653, some of the Powhatan warriors were encouraged to take fifty specific acres of land apiece, with the right to hunt in areas not inhabited by whites. The Powhatans tried hard to adjust to the white man's domination. In 1656 they went so far as to send more than one hundred of their warriors with a white army to drive off a Siouan nation which appeared to threaten both the colonists and the Powhatans. This Siouan community had settled near the falls of the James River, and they probably came to the falls only to trade. Whatever the reason for their presence within the Powhatan sphere of influence, they were regarded as threats. However, through no fault of the Powhatans, the joint English-Powhatan expedition failed miserably.

The praying Indian towns of Wamesit and Nashob were weakened in the 1660s when they fought alongside non-Christian New England Indians in repelling Mohawk Haudenosaunee invaders from New York. Ironically, these actions played their part in defending the white frontier as well as Indian national borders. But the coming of what became known as King Philip's War in 1675 proved to be the greatest trial for Natick and the other praying Indian towns. The war in fact was the turning point for all the Indians surrounded by the New England colonists. There were many antagonisms and circumstances that forced Indians to war in 1675. Some were relatively minor. For example, had the Puritan colonists been confident that the non-Christian Indians were content and treated fairly before 1675, they would have allowed them to obtain muskets; they seldom did. The Puritans also forbade the Indians to purchase horses or large boats from colonial shipwrights, a policy hardly demonstrating faith in the effectiveness or justice of their own Indian policy.

In July 1675, some Doeg Indians were killed by Virginians because they had seized some hogs as payment for a debt owed to them by a frontier planter, Thomas Mathew. In retaliation, Doegs killed the planter's overseer, an Indian servant and his son. Continuing the pattern of vengeance, other frontiersmen killed ten Doegs and fourteen other Indians who turned out to be friendly Susquehannas. War followed, and frontiersmen led by a rabble-rouser named Nathaniel Bacon were encouraged by planters and land speculators to wipe out friendly as well as warring Indians. The slaughter ended in 1677 with the frontiersmen, planters and speculators in a position to reap huge profits from land grabs, and with the Powhatans, Susquehannas, Doegs and other local Indians reduced to desperate poverty. Ironically, Nathaniel Bacon and many of his followers had in the meantime extended the war against the Indians to rebel against the Virginia governor, William Berkeley, who sympathized with the Indians (Bacon's Rebellion). Bacon's followers were labeled rebels, and Virginia was restored to order by troops sent from England. Such political justice came too late for the Indian people.

In 1675–1676, New England brought upon itself an Indian war involving the two strongest Indian nations in the area: the Wampanoags and the

Narragansetts. The Indians' inspirational though not sole political leader was Metacomet, called King Philip by the whites. Philip was the son of Chief Massasoit, who had feasted with the Pilgrims on the first Thanksgiving in 1621. The Indian war in New England, called King Philip's War, was fought against a white society that proclaimed itself the bastion of true Christian practice, a city set upon a hill for the entire world to emulate.

Before 1675, some Indians had discovered ways in which they could survive among the whites. One in five became praying Indians. Others took up New England's expanding industry, whaling. But for the Indians who still held to traditional religion and culture, the growth of the white population was disastrous. By 1675, there were fifteen thousand Indians and seventy-five thousand whites in New England. Instead of heeding signs of increasing tensions, the Puritans acted more arrogantly. The New England colonies had always expected Indians to submit to Puritan law. In June 1675, King Philip and the Wampanoags were infuriated by the Plymouth Colony's conviction and hanging of three of their warriors for the January 1675 murder of an English-speaking Christian Indian from Natick, John Sassamon. Sassamon had been one of the few Indians ever to attend Harvard, and just before his death he had informed Plymouth Colony that the Wampanoags were organizing a war. Although an auxiliary Indian jury that supplemented the white jury and judge consented to the verdict of guilty, the Wampanoags were not convinced of the three warriors' guilt. The proud Wampanoag chief saw the executions as the most recent event in the continuing degradation of his people. Had the warriors been found guilty under Indian law, the sentence might have been exile or restitution to the relatives of the deceased. Under Indian law, the penalty might even have been execution, but it would have been a decision and punishment carried out by Indians.

The verdict and executions also cast suspicion on Philip. Was he really organizing for war? Whether or not Philip was planning a war before June 1675, he was forced by circumstances to lead one almost immediately thereafter. Beginning about June 19, some of Philip's young warriors looted recently abandoned white homes near their Wampanoag homeland. On June 23 a young white fatally shot one of these looters. The Wampanoags retaliated, and the conflict escalated to war. The white frontier reeled, and not even Boston was considered safe from attack. With careful diplomacy, the Puritans might have been able to keep the Narragansetts from joining Philip and the Wampanoags, because the Narragansetts stayed out of the initial hostilities.

However, the Puritans decided in December 1675 to assault the main Narragansett town, as the Narragansetts were moving this community into the safety of a swamp. Perhaps the Narragansetts were planning on armed neutrality and intended to remain aloof from the war inside the swamp. The Narragansetts in the swamp were not given the opportunity to declare their intentions or to negotiate, and the white army attacked. The sudden Puritan assault killed many warriors, old men, women and children; destroyed the town; and crippled the Narragansett nations, whose leaders such as Quinnapin, Pomham, Pessacus, Canonchet and a woman, Quaiapen, now had no choice but to join Philip. Among other nations to ally with Philip were the Nipmucks and the Pocumtucks. Two nations that had already joined a Wampanoag alliance, the Pocassets and the Sakonnets, remained loyal. Women led them both: Weetamoo led the Pocassets and Awashonks led the Sakonnets. Other Indian nations, unprovoked at the moment by the whites, chose not to go to war against the colonists; these Indians did not see a common interest among all Indian peoples, nor did they see a common danger in all whites. Uncas' Mohegans, longtime allies of the whites, also chose to fight alongside the Puritans, primarily because the Wampanoags and Narragansetts had been their enemies long before the white men arrived. Even some of the Pequots, descendants of the nation nearly exterminated by the whites in 1637, sided with the New England colonies, perhaps because they had learned the futility of opposing white muskets. In the case of the neutral Niantics, a branch of the Narragansetts under chief Ninigret, they too felt the whites were sure to be victorious and that it would be advantageous not to antagonize the winning side (Andrews 1915; Lincoln 1913; cf.: Lepore 1998).

Perspective

Perhaps the best example of the Puritans' failure to apply their own ideals occurred during the decades following the erection in 1656 of a large two-story building at Harvard College to house twenty Indian students. Having taken this first (segregated) step, the Puritans did not spend the time or the money necessary to prepare Indians to meet entrance standards, and so only about six Indians went to Harvard between 1656 and 1675, and only one of these graduated.

Law was another area in which Indians were not treated equally, although inequality was not as blatant as in the southern colonies. Indian legal codes, which New England Indians had developed over centuries, continued to be used by the New England Indian nations as long as issues of justice were between Indians of the same nation. But if a legal issue involved whites, the English imposed their own legal system. Under this white system, New England Indians could use white courts to sue whites for personal injuries or for damages done to their crops by the white men's stray cattle, and courts awarded many judgments to Indians; likewise, if a white was found guilty of murdering an Indian, he could be executed. However, the Puritans insisted upon determining sentences according to Biblical law, a law often more severe than Indian law. Furthermore, an Indian could not sit on a jury, and an Indian's testimony was not regarded by the white population as equal to a white man's despite occasional directions from governments and courts to the contrary. Concessions were few. For example, in 1673 a murder case in Rhode Island was tried in which the defendant was an Indian. Rhode Island's General Assembly—the most progressive of the New England colonies and influenced largely by Quakers—declared that instead of an all-white jury, six Indian men could sit on the jury with six whites. In that same year Rhode Island finally decided that an Indian's testimony was legally equal to that of a white. Although both the Pilgrim and the Puritan colonies soon concurred with Rhode Island in considering specific cases, equality under the law was not uniformly guaranteed.

There was also a vast difference between how Puritan courts sentenced white and Indian debtors and thieves. A white could be sentenced to a specific number of years of service to his creditor; if notorious he could be banished from a colony, still retaining his freedom; or in rare cases he could be sold as a servant within his colony or elsewhere, including the West Indies. An Indian, however, usually received more severe penalties for similar debts or larcenies, and if unable to pay even a small debt, the Indian could be legally sold into slavery in the West Indies, which usually ensured an early death. The proceeds of such a sale into slavery went to the creditor to pay off the debt. In 1634, in a typical debt case, a white man was sentenced by a Massachusetts court to servitude until he worked off a debt of four pounds sterling. Yet according to a Rhode Island law passed in 1659, Indian thieves who had stolen only the value of one English pound but were unable to pay it back could be sold into slavery for life—and Rhode Island was the *liberal* New England colony (Morris 1965a, 345–47; Vaughan 1965, 199, 206–207; Lauber 1913, 205–207; Jennings 1975, passim).

Regarding other crimes, very few Indian men molested white women, but the Puritan legal books are filled with cases of white men seducing or raping

Indian women. On the other hand, Indian abuse of alcohol constantly upset the Puritans and Pilgrims, to whom drunkenness demonstrated moral laxity. Indian drinking was due in some part to cultural background, which placed great importance on dreams: Indians found that the dreams induced by alcohol were quite pleasant and/or mystically revealing. Alcohol also provided an escape from the reality of the drastic changes brought by the English. Despite the Puritan abhorrence of Indian drunkenness, the Puritans could not, or would not, stop white men from trading alcohol to the Indians. Furthermore, although the New Englanders viewed Indian drunkenness as reflective of decadence, their own court records reveal white drunkenness, rape, sodomy and seduction, suggesting that Pilgrim and Puritan societies themselves were hardly models of moral health.

Puritan diplomacy was applied as unequally as its laws. For example, in 1643 the Puritans acted quickly against the Narragansetts when that nation attacked the Mohegans, and the Narragansett chief, Miantonomo, was turned over to the Mohegan chief Uncas to be executed. However, in later years when Uncas was the aggressor against these same Narragansetts, the Puritans did nothing to him, because the Mohegans were a smaller nation usually friendly to the English, whereas the Narragansetts were a strong and numerous people with an independent white policy.

New England's white governments tried but failed to keep the fur trade honest. By licensing only men of integrity to engage in the fur trade, the Puritans hoped to gain the respect of the Indian nations involved. But regulations were changed often as the whites experimented with different approaches. Indians could never be sure what to expect, while whites exploited loopholes and the fact that the trade was often carried out beyond the reach of the white legal system. The results were less than hoped for among Puritan officials, convenient and profitable for white traders, and frustrating for Indian people. Yet because the Indians wanted the European goods available through the fur trade, they put up with the frustrations. Furthermore, the fur trade reached its zenith about 1645 and then gradually declined. In its place the most important aspect of Indian-white relations became land.

Throughout the history of Indian-white relations, in all geographic areas and during all eras, a major harbinger of conflict were those points in time when whites changed their focus from trade to land. Whenever land and European settlement became more valuable and important than the fur or deerskin trades, Europeans and their Indian allies went to war with each other. A corollary to this was that the conquest of a local Indian people might also follow whenever a distant Indian ally of a European power became more useful as a trading partner than a local Indian nation. This was because the fur trade demanded large populations of fur-bearing animals whose numbers were usually diminished by hunting and European colonization, so that the fur trade continually moved farther into the interior and the lands of other Indian nations.

Whenever European expansion onto Indian lands occurred, several factors simultaneously jarred Indian nations. At first contact, sharing the land with the Europeans seemed reasonable. But whenever white populations expanded, Indians resented the shift from sharing their lands to losing so much of their territory. They also understandably resented what were usually fraudulent land transactions. Then there was the fact that white land expansion usually signaled a decline in the fur trade. This meant that just as several generations of Indians were becoming used to the adaptation of European goods, their abilities to accumulate those goods diminished. These types of frustration were all combined with an even greater loss: Indian environments were irrevocably altered. The American Indian religions and traditions that depended upon the interaction with this environment were altered, and the loss of traditional cultural values was sorely felt. Moreover, Indians who had been allied to the whites and/or had participated in the fur trade had helped bring about all of these changes.

The realization that these changes had altered and even corrupted Indian traditions, and the simultaneous realization that the Indians' ability to adapt had declined because of the decline of trade was a potent mix. Leaders could call for a return to tradition and a resistance to white expansion. Indian religious and political leaders also resented the missionary attempts to entice their people into a new religion, for the Indians' current societies were based on adapting traditional beliefs, not the wholesale adoption of new beliefs. The missionaries challenged the existing leadership no matter what the conditions, but when the existing Indian leadership no longer had the wherewithal to help their people adapt and change, they were especially threatened—and their followers could be increasingly attracted to a total adoption of white ways. Indian nations thus often went to war not because they were determined to maintain unchanging, static traditions, but because they were no longer able to adapt those traditions to the continuing expansion of white ways and white populations. Both before and after contact with Europeans, Indian nations had always changed, and always adapted. But when an Indian nation's ability to continue that adaptation was diminished, choices were few. They realized what they had lost in exchange for the white alliance and the white trade goods. The white trade goods, which the Indians had once found necessary, were now resented as a symbol of what they had given up and lost. Cut off abruptly from the future, they would call upon the past.

The land policies of the Puritans were often as regulated as the rest of their society. Unlike other colonists, Puritans were seldom guilty of getting a few Indians drunk and then having them sign deeds for vast amounts of land. Government officials carefully planned expansion in Puritan New England. Those colonists who wished to go onto "new" lands had to prove to Puritan elders their high moral character and agree to settle with other whites of equal character in towns laid out ahead of time. Usually, the land had to be purchased from the Indians, and on a very few occasions the Puritans paid for the same parcel two or three times, each time satisfying a different Indian or Indian group which claimed it.

Nevertheless, some Puritans simply occupied lands they wanted, without payment. In 1675 in a treaty with the Narragansetts, these unpaid-for lands were euphemistically defined as "quietly possessed" (Harris [1676] 1963, 95). And while most purchases were legal, they were hardly ever just. Double standards in economic policies make it impossible for the disadvantaged side to continue to adapt successfully. The Puritans always obtained land as inexpensively as possible, at rates that among whites would have been nothing short of fraud. Some historians have argued that at the particular time the Indians sold their lands they were often satisfied with the prices, even though they only received a minimum amount of metal hoes, cloth, kettles and other goods, for these goods were very valuable by Indian standards. Such an argument avoids the real issue. The injustice lay in the fact that the Puritans expected Indians to function according to the same legal standards as whites and to adjust their nations to the reality that the Puritans were their permanent neighbors. The Puritans were quick to belittle Indians for not living according to Puritan social standards, yet they conspired to make the Indian live according to a different and unequal economic standard. By 1675, most New England Indians sensed that they or their parents' generation had been cheated. They realized too late that the prices given them for their lands were not high enough to enable them to survive within the Puritan economic sphere. Another economic issue involved the strings and belts of elongated, tubular shell beads called wampum. For the first half of the seventeenth century, both Indians and whites used wampum interchangeably, alongside European currencies, as one of the area's legal currencies. But after 1650, bewildered Indians watched as their wampum was devalued unilaterally by the whites and was gradually replaced by metal coins and other specie.

The only way all New England Indians could have united was if they had become racists—not only racists with regard to non-Indians, but identifying themselves primarily on the basis of race. Such a racist identification was impossible, for it would have ignored the different cultures of each nation, and the rivalries that had existed long before the arrival of the English.

The fact remains, however, that of the fifteen thousand Indians in New England in 1675, about five thousand sided with the seventy-five thousand whites. Two thousand Indians remained neutral. Thus a total of about eight thousand Indians, or just over half the total New England Indian population, fought against the whites. Because only slightly more than half of the Indians in New England fought the whites in King Philip's War, the question persists: Just how oppressive was Puritan Indian policy if just over half of the Indian population resisted? Before percentages are used as indicators, however, it should be remembered that one hundred years later a much *smaller* percentage of whites—probably one-third—rebelled against England in the American Revolution. Today, U.S. history books and politicians certainly do not suggest that the Patriots overreacted and should have gone home. Perhaps if Philip had won and his people had written the history books, the war would be labeled, as the American Revolution so often is, a victory in defense of liberty. In this comparative context, it is noteworthy that when the decision for war was made, a greater percentage of Indian people put their lives on the line in 1675 than did Patriots in 1775.

While the Indians did not achieve unity among their various nations, the English colonists—who were supposedly all members of the same nation—did not present a united front either, another indication of how complicated all human beings and all human history is. Young men who preferred not to fight became New England's first substantial drafter resisters. At the leadership level, the governments of the New England colonies had difficulty agreeing on how to conduct the war (independent policy being especially strong in Rhode Island). And, most dramatically, on July 8, 1675, at the very beginning of the war, Connecticut faced war on a second front when Governor Edmund Andros of the English colony of New York, with two small ships and some soldiers, personally attempted to invade and occupy part of Connecticut. Andros was determined to use force to settle conflicting claims by New York and

Connecticut to some of the lands that lay between the Hudson and Connecticut Rivers.

King Philip's War was cruel for all sides. Atrocities carried out by all sides during the course of one battle or another numb the senses. For the briefest time, a victory by Philip and his allies seemed possible. During the war, the whites were poor wilderness fighters and were continually ambushed unless friendly Indians scouted for them. Starvation and the harsh winter of 1675–1676 weakened Philip's warriors and his allies more than Puritan military efforts did. Finally, on August 12, 1676, Philip and his main body of warriors were tracked down. Defeated and in flight, Philip was shot and killed by one of the whites' Indian allies. The war continued for another year in Maine, but for most of New England's Indians, the autumn of 1676 brought defeat.

Although the war was a military triumph for the whites, its results were not all advantageous to the colonists. Just as King James I had taken advantage of Virginia's weakness after the Indian attack of 1622 and had placed the colony under royal jurisdiction, Charles II in 1676 chose this time to send to New England a royal investigator, Edward Randolph. He confirmed that Massachusetts Bay was not obeying all the navigation acts nor was the colony allowing religious and other dissenters the rights they had been granted under English law. In other words, not even all whites could obtain equal justice in Puritan Massachusetts. Randolph's report criticized Puritan Indian policy and the Massachusetts Bay Colony's conduct of the war. His report was instrumental in leading, in 1684, to the abrogation of the Massachusetts Bay charter and the imposition of greater royal control, similar in circumstance and result to that imposed on Virginia in 1624 during the war with Opechancanough. Had the Massachusetts Bay colonists not fomented a war with the Indians, the colony might have been in a better position to resist royal pressure.

With few exceptions, during the war the red Christians fought alongside the white Christians. During this war, many New England whites identified a common and superior interest with all other whites. They labeled all red men as dangerous or at best untrustworthy, even when certain Indians were unmistakably friendly. Their governments failed utterly to protect the Christian Indians from white predators. The praying Indians, who numbered about twenty-five hundred in a total Indian population of fifteen thousand, associated their new religion with an obligation to be loyal to other Christians, and despite antagonisms from some whites, they were determined to remain loyal to the Bay colony. Job Nesutan, a Natick Indian who had helped John Eliot translate the Bible, gave his life in one of the first actions of the war. A detachment of fifty-two praying Indians fought more effectively than the English militia in that early engagement. Two whites sent by the government to investigate the loyalty of the Christian Indians at the praying Indian town of Natick testified to their steadfastness. Despite their courage in battle and overall loyalty, at least 500 praying Indians—men, women, and children—were placed in an overcrowded concentration camp on bleak Deer Island in Boston Harbor. They were forced to find most of their own food by gathering shellfish and clams at low tide. As soon as other praying Indians learned of their fate, many fled north and some even joined Philip. During the summer of 1676, the war was going badly for the Puritans. They needed Indian scouts, and they approached the men on Deer Island to ask for help. The Indians did better than become scouts. Leaving their wives and children on Deer Island, they formed a militia detachment, joined other praying Indians, and were credited with killing four hundred "enemy" Indians. After the war, all the praying Indians were released from Deer Island, only to discover that whites had confiscated most of their property. The Indians of Natick tried hard to reestablish their former lives. But by 1734 enough whites to elect a few white officials had moved into the town. By 1764 there was a white majority and finally, in 1781 during the American Revolution, the whites took over completely and incorporated Natick as a white town.

The fate of the Indians who resisted the Puritans was settled more quickly. The victorious whites dealt with the warriors and families who surrendered as rebels and traitors to the state, not as prisoners of war or the people of independent nations. At Boston and at Plymouth, captive Indian chiefs were executed. The English brought Philip's head to Plymouth and impaled it on a pole at the outskirts of the town. Moreover, the Puritans believed that the surviving Indian prisoners had forfeited all rights and could be sentenced to work for whites in New England for specific lengths of time, and that many could even be sold into slavery in the West Indies or elsewhere. Hundreds of Indian men, women and children, including Philip's wife and son, were sold into slavery and shipped to Virginia, Spain, Portugal, the Azores, the Spanish West Indies, Bermuda and the Mediterranean coasts, including Tangier. While Indians suffered the hell of enslavement, Puritans thanked God for the glorious Christian victory and moved onto the lands of the defeated nations (Leach 1966, 221–50).

A century after Martin Frobisher and his crews had fired upon Inuit (Eskimo) people, the English colonists all along the Atlantic coast had failed in conducting just Indian affairs, just as the Spanish and the Dutch had. When it came to dealing with Indian peoples, differences in the colonists' national backgrounds and religions proved insignificant. Indians died fighting Spanish, Dutch and English colonists. Clearly, the kinds of Christianity practiced by these Europeans lacked practical application to real world situations.

Ultimately Europeans of all Western faiths—including Jewish colonists who sold Indian slaves as enthusiastically as Christians—failed in their dealings with the Indians because both Christian and Jewish colonists were influenced in their thinking by Genesis 1: "And God said...let them have dominion over the fish of the sea, and over the fowl of the air, and over the cattle, and over all the earth, and over every creeping thing that creepeth upon the earth." All believed in a Genesis pyramid, with humans—especially European humans—at the top and all other beings below.

In contrast, Indian peoples throughout North America were confident that the Creator placed humans on earth to share nature's sustenance with all living things as spiritual equals. While each Indian nation's spirituality involved specific details and ceremonies unique to each nation, a major goal of most, if not all, Indian religions was to live in balance with nature. Dominion carried out by humans meant the loss of nature's order, a loss of balance. Dominion exerted by humans would have diminished the spiritual and temporal roles of the animals, trees and other beings who were meant to share the Creator's blessings equally with the Indians. The Indians could not accept the white man's concept of dominion and subjugation of nature, and the clash of the two concepts was perhaps the greatest cause of friction between red and white.

Tragically, by engaging in the fur trade, Indians contributed to their own dilemmas. They found themselves acting outside their traditional teachings. The praying Indians, in their own way, perceived this change. Believing that they could not alter the direction of history, they chose to adapt a religion that carried out the subordination of the natural world. The Indians who allied with Philip, on the other hand, possessed the hope that their cultures and religions could adapt without completely surrendering the thousands of years of culture and religion that had preceded the generation of 1676.

What neither the praying Indians nor the allies of Philip could have anticipated, however, was the ruthless peace that followed the war of Thanksgiving's children.

CHAPTER IV

Warriors & the Claims of Kings

American Indian religions and societies never existed in vacuums, and they were never static. American Indian nations had always traded with and learned from each other, and thus interactions with other peoples and their technologies had never been regarded as an automatic negative. When faced with the political crises caused by the invading Europeans, adaptation of European ideas and technologies continued.

In responding to the crises, some American Indian nations chose to ally with one European nation against another European nation. Some American Indian nations chose to go to war, or to rebel against Europeans who forced them into a European colonial system. Still other Native nations carved out positions of neutrality. Whatever the course of action—neutrality, war, or alliance—Native peoples never ceased to adapt, to alter their nation's policies and cultures. In short, they continued to grow, to mature, as all vibrant peoples must.

Regarding European technology, American Indians had adapted what they believed to be the best—or what was most necessary—from the very beginning. They incorporated what they wanted into their traditional cultures. Their objective in doing this was mistakenly interpreted by many colonial whites as a sign of their willingness to give up "primitive" ways in favor of white "civilization," whereas the Indians' real purpose was to retain, not surrender, the basis of their ways of life.

Whatever method or methods Indian nations finally chose, however, each finally had to confront white colonists whose policies and warfare during this period were increasingly determined by international events and the imperial claims of European kings.

Pueblo Uprisings in the Southwest

While Metacomet's (King Philip's) warriors desperately resisted New England whites in 1675 and southern Indians fought for their lives against Virginia frontiersmen the same year, the Pueblos of New Mexico were growing increasingly resentful of the near-century of Spanish occupation of their homeland. In 1650, some of the Pueblos—Tiwas, Keres and Jemez—had allied with Apaches in an unsuccessful war. During a severe drought lasting from 1667 to 1672, hundreds of Pueblos starved to death and the rest suffered greatly because the Spaniards demanded tributes that depleted the Pueblos' emergency food supply. In addition to depriving the Pueblos of needed food, the Spaniards failed to provide the military protection they had promised in return for Indian labor. Fierce Apache plunderers (themselves pressured by Comanche Indian expansion from the north) on traded or stolen Spanish horses raided Pueblo towns so frequently and caused so much devastation that the three pueblos had to be abandoned. An epidemic added to the Pueblos' woes. By 1675, the Tewa Pueblos were leading a revival of the traditional religion among all Pueblos in the hopes that good fortune would return if Pueblo spiritual harmony was restored. But Franciscan missionaries, backed by iron-fisted Spanish officials, continued to insist that the Pueblos discard their ancient religious beliefs and practices in favor of alien Catholicism.

In 1675, the Spaniards believed that the Pueblos used witchcraft to cause the death of between five and seven priests and three or four other Spaniards. Another Spanish priest claimed to have been bewitched by Pueblo medicine men. Since these Indian priests were the chief rivals of the missionaries as well as leaders of their people, the Spaniards set out to arrest a total of forty-seven of them. One hanged himself, three were hanged by the Spaniards and the rest were whipped, imprisoned and sentenced to slavery. Seventy Pueblo warriors soon appeared before the governor at Santa Fe, the Spanish capital of New Mexico, and demanded that he release the captives in exchange for ransom. The warriors threatened that otherwise they would instigate a war aimed at wiping out the Spaniards. If that failed, they would flee to the mountains and take their chances among the Apaches and Navajos rather than continue to live under Spanish domination. The Pueblos' two alternatives—war or flight—demonstrated the desperation of this agrarian people whose way of life was being eroded by the Spaniards. The governor knew that his colonists needed the Pueblos' labor and food and that he was already busy fighting one unsuccessful war with the Apaches. He prudently accepted the ransom and released the medicine men.

Popé's Rebellion, 1680

Among them was an energetic old Tewa medicine man at the San Juan pueblo named Popé. Popé realized that the Pueblos' common religious beliefs might provide the foundation for a permanent political confederation that had been previously hindered by the proud autonomy of each town. Unity could be achieved by striking at the common foe, the Spaniards. There were about thirty thousand Pueblos in the various towns along the northern Rio Grande and its tributaries, and only 2,350 Spaniards. Once united, the Pueblos would be irresistible. Popé decided that the first step in organizing Pueblo resistance was to weed out informers from among the Pueblos themselves. These informers were well paid by the Spaniards to betray Pueblo religious and political secrets. Popé accused his own son-in-law, Nicolas Bua, the Spaniards' puppet governor of San Juan pueblo, of being one of the informers. Bua was killed for his betrayal of his own people. Since this event was calculated to intimidate other informers, the Spanish quickly moved to reassert their power. Popé fled north to the Taos pueblo and hid in a kiva to elude Spanish investigators. While at Taos, Popé organized a resistance based on plans that had been discussed for years. Medicine men from surrounding pueblos, such as Catiti at Santo Domingo, responded enthusiastically. In the Taos kiva, Popé prayed and grew more certain that the time was right to attack. He set August 10 as the start of the war and sent a cord of maguey fibers to every pueblo, with knots tied along the cord to indicate the day of revolution. Knowing that some informers still existed—chiefs who had accepted both Christianity and bribes and who would surely warn their masters of the plot—Popé and the other leaders sent cords to them calling for an attack not on August 10, but later. As expected, Catholic priests living at the informants' pueblos soon sent word to Santa Fe that a revolt was planned for August 13.

What were Popé's thoughts as the time for war grew near? Jemez Pueblo historian Joe S. Sando spent decades during the twentieth century studying the Pueblos' oral traditions. Using these, he recreated an Enlish translation of what the oral traditions indicate Popé expressed to other pueblo leaders:

This is not the way of our people; however, we have been forced to the blinded path, and we can find no alternative. Our people do not approve of wars. But when such times do come upon us, the war chiefs can call us todefend out lands. Our people also exercise unlimited obedience to these leaders, who act under the religious leaders. It is the great duty of the people to abide by the decisions of these leaders. I can see no other possibility of escaping from the hand of the oppressor, and the deities know we have tried. I am fearful that the way we have just chosen will have to be the way. It is true that we respect the Kwan-Kus' (Spaniards') superior weapon power, but we also despise their unpolished manners. We know their weaknesses, and we must take advantage of them. (Sando 1998, 15)

At seven o'clock on the morning of August 10, 1680, a soldier galloped into Santa Fe. He reported to Governor Antonio de Otermín that the warriors of the Tesuque pueblo had appeared that morning in war paint, had killed the priest and a white trader stationed there, and were now marching toward the San Juan pueblo to unite with warriors from other pueblos against all Spaniards. For the rest of the day the governor received reports that pueblos all along the Rio Grande River basin—from Taos in the north, southward to Picuris, Santa Clara and other towns—were now at war. And at Acoma, the Sky City devastated by Oñate in 1599 and the site of Spain's great fortress church, the priest was killed by his parishioners, evidently thrown from atop the mesa. Every pueblo except those of the uninformed Piros to the south soon joined the war, and many Piros joined later. Together they killed every Spaniard they could find. Suddenly, at about nine o'clock on the morning of August 13, five hundred Tanos, Pecos, and San Marcos Keres warriors were sighted approaching Santa Fe itself. The governor had only fifty regular soldiers, many of whom had been drafted from Mexican prisons, but he soon organized an impromptu militia made up of Santa Fe's civilian colonists. Reconnoitering Spaniards saw a Tanos chief, who had been raised and educated in Santa Fe and who had been highly trusted by Otermín, "on horseback, wearing a sash of red taffeta which was recognized as being from the missal of the convent of Galisteo [a Tanos pueblo], and with harquebus [musket], sword, dagger, leather jacket and all the arms of the Spaniards" (Hackett 1942, I, 13). Otermín asked to see him and later recorded that:

[H]e came to where I was, and, since he was known . . . I asked him how it was that he had gone crazy too—being an Indian who spoke our language, was so intelligent and had lived all his life in the villa [Santa Fe] among the Spaniards, where I had placed such confidence in him—and was now coming as a leader of the Indian rebels. He replied to me that they had elected him as their captain, and that they were carrying two banners, one white and the other red, and that the white one signified peace and the red one war. Thus if we wished to choose the white it must be upon our agreeing to leave the country, and if we chose the red, we must perish....

On hearing this reply, I spoke to him very persuasively, to the effect that he and the rest of his followers were Catholic Christians, asking how they expected to live without the religious; and said that even though they had committed so many atrocities, still there was a remedy, for if they would return to obedience to his Majesty they would be pardoned; and that thus he should go back to his people and tell them in my name all that had been said to him, and persuade them to agree to it and to withdraw from where they were; and that he was to advise me of what they might reply. He came back from there after a short time, saying that his people asked that all classes of Indians who were in our power be given up to them, both those in the service of the Spaniards and those of the Mexican nation.... He demanded also that his wife and children [who lived in his house in Santa Fe] be given up to him, and likewise that all the Apache men and women whom the Spaniards had captured in war be turned over to them, inasmuch as some Apaches who were among them were asking for them. If these things were not done they would declare war immediately, and they were unwilling to leave the place where they were because they were awaiting the Taos, Pecurles and Teguas nations, with whose aid they would destroy us. (Hackett 1942, I, 98–99)

The governor ordered an attack. Against the guns and horses of the Spaniards, the warriors grudgingly gave way. The Indians took cover in the outskirts of Santa Fe in the homes of the Mexican Indians, and fought on with bows and arrows and a few captured muskets. By evening it looked as though they would be defeated, when hundreds of Pueblos abruptly came to their rescue after marching all day to join the fight. The Spaniards quickly retreated into Santa Fe. By Friday morning, August 16, Taos, Picuris, Jemez and Keres warriors had swelled to twenty-five hundred the Pueblo army that now charged the capital. By noon they were at the gates of the governor's palace in the plaza. The Spaniards rallied and cleared the plaza of warriors by nightfall, but the Pueblo army controlled most of the town. Knowing that they had to push the warriors entirely out of the town or die, the Spaniards charged again the next day. For hours a battle raged in the streets of Santa Fe as the Spanish horsemen and musketeers drove the Pueblos back. Finally the warriors gave up the town and retreated into the hills. The Spaniards claimed to have killed three hundred, thanks to their horses and guns. The forty-seven prisoners they took were shot to death. On August 21, Governor Otermín led the surviving Spaniards out of Santa Fe, southward toward present-day El Paso, Texas, and Mexico, for the moment returning New Mexico to the Pueblos. The Pueblo warriors allowed the Spaniards to escape. Their objective had been to rid their land of Spanish oppression, and no more Pueblo lives had to be sacrificed. As the Spanish governor and his people trudged toward El Paso, they passed pueblo after pueblo, all deserted. Men, women, children, old people—all had marched north to expel the Spaniards. More chilling were the fire-gutted ranches and dead Spaniards along their path of retreat. Behind Governor Otermín, 380 of New Mexico's 2,350 colonists lay dead, including twenty-one of the thirty-three missionary priests whose presence and demands that the Native peoples abandon their beliefs and traditions were particularly burdensome. With Otermín were many Pueblo captives, evidently including the wife and children of the Tanos chief who had led the first day of battle against Santa Fe. There were also some Christian Isleta and Piro Indians who, unlike the rest of the Isletas and Piros, had refused to join the Pueblo alliance and were now refugees like the whites.

The Pueblos had finally united, even though the Apaches, Navajos and Spaniards had each posed frequent challenges. The Pueblos had finally recovered the regional unity of their ancestors, the Anasazi, four hundred years after the terrible drought that had begun their ancestors' decline. The Pueblo people had overthrown almost a century of Spanish oppression. The Pueblo victors divided the Spanish goods left behind in Santa Fe and then returned to their towns. There, elaborate and solemn ceremonies using yucca suds cleansed every Pueblo who had been converted or baptized by the Spanish priests. The Spanish language was forbidden, and every Pueblo gave up his Christian name.

The incipient pan-Indian spirit of the 1680 war grew quickly. Early in 1681 many Apaches and Navajos previously hostile to the Pueblos made peace with them, undoubtedly to further intertribal trade. During 1680 and 1681, communications from the Pueblos and Apaches who had successfully fought the Spaniards inspired Athapascan Indian nations around El Paso also to attempt to drive out the whites. The Spaniards decided that the Pueblo homeland would have to be reconquered if the emerging pan-Indian movement was to be stifled. In late November 1681, Governor Otermín led an army of 146 Spaniards and 112 Indian allies, including some Christian Pueblos, into the country of the Piro Pueblos only to find all the Piro pueblos deserted—the Piros had fled north to the Tiwas in order to resist more effectively. Indications were that some of the Apaches remained hostile to the Pueblos, for a mounted band had looted one of the abandoned towns, and some animals from pueblos farther to the north had been stolen as well. Marching on, Otermín's army attacked the Tiwa pueblo of Isleta, which had played a minor role in the 1680 war. The Pueblos and Apaches soon organized armies of their own, a few of which were commanded by half-bloods. Mounted Pueblos and some Apaches, commanded by a Picuris Pueblo full-blood named Tupatu, cut behind the Spaniards as they conquered pueblos north of Isleta and asked the recently subdued Pueblos to join the partisans. The Spaniards feared the overwhelming numbers gathering in front of them and were wary lest Tupatu cut them off from the rear, and so Otermín retreated to El Paso in January 1682. The Spaniards had succeeded in leveling eight pueblos, including Isleta and Puaray, sacking three others, and carrying off 385 prisoners, but Indians still controlled their own homeland.

Otermín established a base for future conquest by setting up a new town south of the Pueblos, Isleta del Sur, where he was joined by Piro Indians who had fled with him in 1680. In 1688, the Spaniards renewed their northward invasion and massacred many of the Keres Pueblos living at Zia, but they dared not go any deeper into Pueblo lands. An expedition in 1689 also failed.

In 1681, at least some of the northern Pueblos had broken away and followed Tupatu, but Popé was reelected leader of these people during the invasion crisis of 1688. He died in 1690 but the Pueblos were soon faced with even greater problems. A few Apaches, so long a threat to the Pueblos, returned to mount even bolder raids now that not even one Spanish musket opposed them. At first, many Pueblos tried to trade with them as they were trading with other Apaches, for during the war the Pueblos had captured a commodity the Apaches especially desired—horses. The Pueblos traded these horses willingly, because they were primarily an agricultural people and had little use for them. These Apaches soon asked themselves why they should trade when they could steal. They intimidated the Pueblos, demanding tributes of corn, cotton cloth, cattle, horses and even Pueblo women. To make the Pueblos' dilemma even worse, the Keres and Pecos Pueblos began quarreling with the Tewa and Tanos

Pueblos. The hostile Apache bands then struck so hard at the Tanos that the latter had to abandon their homes and join other Pueblo towns. Various Apaches, Navajos and Utes allied with one of at least five Pueblo factions. These rivalries kept the Pueblo country in a swirl of rivalry, occasionally violent. This chaos was not based on broader national identities such as Pueblo or Apache but on local economic interests.

The Reconquest of the Pueblos & Intertribal Rivalries

Into this chaotic situation rode Diego de Vargas Zapata y Lujan with an army of Spaniards determined to reconquer the Pueblos for the glory of Spain and for the more practical reason of strengthening the Spaniards' Southwest claims against one of their white rivals, the French. The French, under such leaders as Rene Robert Cavelier, Sieur de la Salle, had already been active in the Mississippi River valley and the Texas coast. Furthermore, the Spaniards hoped that the Indian wars still rampant around El Paso could be stifled by conquering the Pueblos, who still served Indian peoples as symbols of successful anti-Spanish resistance. Beginning in 1692, Vargas slowly subdued the various Pueblos, executing all male prisoners of war unless the man's specific nation entirely submitted to Spanish rule. Many Indians, more desperate for their lives than for their freedom, welcomed the Spaniards, whom they hoped would aid their own particular Pueblo-Apache faction, and even aided the Spaniards in suppressing other Pueblos and Apaches. There were others, however, who preferred the hope of freedom and a continuation of their own traditions. Many rallied to Black Mesa and fought the Spaniards and their Pueblo allies for nine months before finally surrendering on September 8, 1694. Two years later a few Pueblo towns tried to spark another great war, but it failed. It had taken the Spaniards sixteen long years, but with the exception of the Hopis, the Pueblos were once again under Spanish rule.

The Indians, however, did not easily forget the years in which they had been free of the Spaniards. In the secrecy of their kivas they practiced their faith and kept their culture alive. The exhausted Spaniards did not make serious attempts to stop them. Thousands of Pueblos, however, were not satisfied with this. In the early 1700s, tired of Spanish oppression, several groups moved westward, some joining the Hopi Pueblos, others attaching their families to the Navajos. These thousands carried out the threat the Pueblos had made to the Spanish governor more than two decades earlier in 1675: If the Pueblos could not free themselves of Spanish domination, they would become refugees.

Those who fled turned out to be the fortunate ones. The Spanish policy of enslaving the Pueblos or making them work as near-slaves under the supervision of mission priests as well as ranchers resulted in a population decline of at least fifty percent between 1700 and 1750. However, promised Spanish protection materialized against the Comanches when they raided the Pueblos and the New Mexican Apaches and while these Comanches also pushed Plains Apaches into New Mexico. Of course, this military effort protected Spanish interests as well. The Spaniards' total economic exploitation of the mission system became so widespread and vital to the colony that any spiritual reason for the missions' existence was obscured. In 1767, as part of the secular upheaval accompanying the expulsion of the Jesuits from other parts of the Western Hemisphere, the Franciscan missions were secularized unless they were far from any Spanish settlement.

The Pueblos accepted Spanish sovereignty because the Spaniards tacitly permitted them to practice their religion as long as it did not become overtly political, although as late as 1733 the Spaniards were still trying a few Pueblos as witches for allegedly casting spells. With no alternative except extermination, the Pueblos adapted to the political sovereignty of the Spanish while continuing their cultural and spiritual independence. In order to protect their own homeland, Pueblos often allied with the Spaniards against other Indians. They even entered into the Spanish-French rivalry for North America. In 1720, for example, sixty Pueblos joined forty-two Spaniards in a march to Nebraska where they were defeated by Pawnees and Otos allied to nearby Frenchmen (Hotz 1970, 158, 172–234). Many Pueblo warriors fought in such expeditions as mercenaries, finding that military service provided an escape from poverty. Most important, the Pueblos as a people and a culture survived.

Indian Rebellion in the Southeast: European & Intertribal Rivalries

While defeat of the Pueblo revolution assured the continuation of Spain's empire in the American Southwest, no such assurances could be had in Florida and Georgia. The Guale Indians, who lived in southern Georgia and who had already gone to war against the Spanish invaders in the sixteenth century, never gave up their resistance. In 1645, the Guales rebelled against the demands for

tribute and free labor, and in 1647 the Spanish southeastern frontier was con-
vulsed in a revolution by Creeks, Yamasees and Chatots. The Spaniards retaliated
with the aid of the Apalachee Indians from Florida who had been thoroughly
intimidated and subdued during the previous century. Despite Spanish success
in crushing the wars, the southeastern frontier was vulnerable and invited further attacks by Yuchis, Creeks and Cherokees, beginning in 1655 and continuing
during the 1660s. The turning point on the Spanish frontier in Georgia, where
the attacks fell heaviest, came in 1670, but not only because of the Indians.

That year, taking advantage of Spanish weakness on the Georgia frontier,
Spanish expulsion from Jamaica in 1655, and the broader deterioration of
Spain as a European power, English entrepreneurs established Charles Town,
South Carolina (moved to its present location a decade later). In 1671, the
English colonists, with the support of small coastal nations, went to war
against the Kusso Indians and immediately discovered the profitability of
enslaving Indian captives, selling them to the West Indies, or keeping them for
personal exploitation. White land encroachments and unfair trading practices
increased the animosity of some nations. Then, in 1680, largely to obtain
Indian slaves, the white colonists, against the wishes of South Carolina's proprietary government, went to war with the Westo Indians (Chichumecoes).
The whites were aided by Savannah (Shawnee) Indians who were relative newcomers to the area. The Westos were defeated and enslaved by 1683, with remnants fleeing to the Creeks. The Westo War permanently weakened the
proprietary government and assured that what had begun in 1671 would now
evolve into a South Carolinian tradition: slavery.

Charleston (Charles Town) also traded with the various Indian nations
who were making war on the Spanish, exchanging guns and manufactured
goods for deerskins and other Indian goods. Armed with English muskets,
these nations intensified their attacks. The war, however, was not aimed solely
at the Spaniards. An English alliance gave the Indians an advantage over their
traditional enemies, the Guales. The Guales, many of whom had been converted by Spanish priests, drew closer to the Spanish out of necessity. In 1679
and 1680, the English mounted a direct attack against the Guales and
Spaniards. The English received the eager aid of Yuchis, Creeks, Cherokees and,
briefly, the Westos. The Guales fought hard, but Spanish policy, even in emer-
gencies, forbade the arming of Indians with muskets, an extreme disadvantage
against Indians equipped with firearms. By 1683, it was apparent to the Guales
that the Spaniards were letting them do most of the fighting. Most of their

towns had been ruined by invading Indians allied with the English, and the Spanish still refused to give them arms. Northern Guales rebelled in 1684 and then escaped to the protection of the English. The Spanish missions pulled back. In 1702, the remaining Guales saw that the Spanish used them merely as buffers against the English, and they too rebelled, rejoining their northern brothers and settling along the Savannah River. Weakened from decades of war, they prudently joined and were absorbed into the Yamasee nation. The few Guales who had remained with the Spanish withdrew into Spanish Florida.

The Spanish did not lightly accept the loss of an entire nation's allegiance to Spain and to the Catholic Church. With Spain embroiled in a broader European war, the War of the Spanish Succession (1702–1713), the Spanish in Florida launched an immediate counterattack in 1702 with the aid of nine hundred bow-and-arrow-bearing Apalachee Indians, planning to drive the English out of South Carolina. The Creek Indians, eager to continue an allegiance with the English because of lucrative trade goods, rallied five hundred warriors, many armed with muskets, and drove the Spanish and Apalachees back to Florida. During the winter of 1703–1704, a thousand Creeks aided by fifty English traders almost annihilated the Apalachee towns. Hundreds, perhaps a thousand, captured Apalachees were sold as slaves, the profit going to both the English and the Creeks. Several hundred other Apalachees were removed to lands on the Savannah River to become an English colonial protectorate. Despite the Spaniards' continued refusal to arm them, some Apalachees managed to hold their own until the Creeks retreated. The frontier settled into a kind of terrorized stability, as the Apalachees, the Creeks, the Spanish and the English were content for the moment to consolidate their positions (Swanton 1922, 89–121).

The Creek Confederacy: Experts in Diplomacy

One Indian nation had emerged supreme through all this: the Creek Confederacy. The Creeks combined a firm political expertise achieved long before white contact with the prestige and strength obtained through English guns and trade goods exchanged for deerskins, other produce and Indian enemies sold as slaves. They reestablished the might and influence their confederacy had forged before the Spaniard de Soto weakened them in 1540. The Creeks created a power structure that paralleled the Haudenosaunee dominance west of the Hudson River in New York. Although their power was dependent in its material aspects upon English trade goods, especially muskets and gunpowder, the Creeks were a shrewd and politically astute people who realized immediately the danger of becoming too closely allied with the English. The English, after all, could become just as oppressive to the Creeks as the Spanish had been to the Guales and Apalachees. The Creeks were determined to succeed in the new order brought about by the arrival of the English, and they knew that above all they had to remain independent.

As the Creeks carefully debated their foreign policy toward the whites, they had to consider still another force that had come into their political sphere. This force was the French, who had established a post at Mobile Bay in 1702. Creek policy thus had to adjust to include traditional Indian rivals such as Cherokees to the north and Apalachees to the south; hostile Spanish in Florida; eager English traders on the Atlantic coast at Charleston; and French on the Gulf Coast who were anxious to obtain Creek friendship in the hope of weakening Creek ties with the English. The Creeks spent the first two decades of the eighteenth century developing their policy. Like any nation they made countless mistakes during this development, and the English proved to be especially adept at taking advantage of those mistakes.

In 1711, while the slave-hunting Creeks were at war with the Apalachees and Spanish in Florida and the Choctaws and French in Mississippi, the English crushed the Tuscaroras in North Carolina. Some of the Tuscaroras, an Iroquoian-speaking nation, had fallen into heavy debt with English traders, who had then seized Tuscarora women and children as slaves to recover the debt. But all too often the whites seized Tuscarora land without even this excuse. The Tuscaroras resisted, and war began. The whites were aided by Yamasees and other Indians including the Cherokees, and together they seized as many Tuscaroras as possible for sale to English slave dealers. About 1714 the Tuscaroras who could escape fled north to the Haudenosaunee in New York. Eight years later, in 1722, they were admitted into the mighty confederacy as the sixth nation, and although they were never given direct voting privileges at the great council fire at Onondaga, the Oneidas agreed to represent them.

These circumstances were part of a complex series of wars and shifting alliances that are admittedly difficult to sort out. During 1712 the Creeks had made peace with the French and the Spanish and contemplated a policy of neutrality even toward their English trading friends. But in 1715 the English revealed that their true intention was to dominate, not coexist with, Indian peoples of the Southeast coast. The Yamasees suddenly found themselves hunted by English slave kidnappers and cheated by English traders just as the Tuscaroras had been. The irony of the Yamasees' increasing enslavement by the English was that the Yamasees had themselves been slave-hunters for the English during the past thirty years. In 1684, they had switched from the Spanish to the English side in order to escape the ravages of English-Indian attacks. They fought pro-Spanish Timucuas in 1685, sold Timucua captives to the English as slaves, and after 1711 had done the same to the Tuscaroras. Furthermore, the English justified their slave-taking among the Yamasees with the same reason they had used for the Tuscaroras: recompense for unpaid trade debts. Actually, tensions arose because of unscrupulous trade practices among the whites, which the South Carolina government usually failed to curtail. The Creeks, related to the Yamasees, encouraged resistance and may have organized an intertribal strategy. The French at Mobile urged the Creeks on.

The South Carolina government sent representatives to the Yamasees to record officially the Indians' grievances against the traders and to try to prevent war, but the Yamasees realized that whatever the Carolina government said, it knew of and condoned the slave trade. The Yamasees killed some of the white envoys on April 15, 1715, and a full-scale war against the English was underway. At the Creek town of Coweta, Brims, the emperor of the Lower Creeks and the man who may have organized intertribal strategy beforehand, now clearly took the leadership of the entire war. Shawnees joined the war near the Savannah River fall line, Santees, Congarees, Catawbas, and other small nations. The Choctaws, who were pro-French, joined their traditional foes the Creeks, and a very few Cherokees also fought the English. Brims and the Creeks tried to bring the Chickasaws in northern Mississippi and western Tennessee into the war by sending Creek warriors west to assassinate the English traders there. Although these Creeks killed some traders, the Chickasaws protected the surviving English traders and remained aloof from the conflict. The Chickasaws were not likely to become anti-English because they lived far from the pressures of expanding English settlement and because their enemies the Choctaws were pro-French. The Choctaws had sold many Chickasaws as slaves to the French who shipped them to the French West Indies. The Chickasaws depended upon the English for trade goods obtained in exchange for Chickasaw animal skins, salt, hickory nut oil and other Chickasaw produce. In addition, the Chickasaws traded Indian slaves they captured in wars with the nearby Choctaws, Acolapissas, Chawashas and Yazoos, and with such nations as the Cahokias of Illinois and the Caddoans west of the Mississippi.

In August 1715, Creeks and warriors of the Spanish-allied Apalachees under a Creek war chief, Chigelley, nearly overran Charleston. The Yamasees were then attacked by the English and forced to retreat to Florida where the Yamasees regrouped near the Spanish at St. Augustine in order to continue fighting the English. The Creeks appealed to the Cherokees to join them against the English, but traditional Creek-Cherokee enmity and the valuable trade between the Cherokees and the English prompted the Cherokees to hesitate and finally to side with the English. Soon, the Creeks were attacked by the English from the east and by the Cherokees from the north. Withdrawing whole towns westward to consolidate their position, the Creeks sought alliance with the French who had established posts along the Gulf Coast from Alabama to Mississippi in 1701 and 1702; they gave the French permission to build Fort Toulouse at the forks of the Coosa and Tallapoosa rivers. Numerous Creek envoys also went to Pensacola and then on to Mexico City to swear allegiance to the Spanish in exchange for their aid. But promised French and Spanish guns and material never came. Beginning in January 1717, the Creeks approached the English to discuss the advantages of making peace. The inability of the Spanish and French to supply them with guns or other aid forced the Creeks to make peace overtures that were welcomed by the war-weary English, whose economy, based at this time primarily on Indian and specifically Creek trade, was devastatingly depressed. The peace was encouraged among the Creeks by Brims's wife, Goa, who was interested both in ending the war and in reestablishing trade. Brims pledged the Creeks' desire for peace by giving his niece, Coosaponakeesa, the daughter of Brims's sister, in marriage to the half-blood son of Colonel John Musgrove, Johnny. By early November 1717, the Creeks and the English worked out a firm treaty guaranteeing trade at fixed rates so that traders would be less inclined to cheat the Creeks. However, in an all-too-typical provision which the English attempted to impose upon all Indian nations they contacted, English courts and law were to judge and punish not only Englishmen who committed crimes against the Indians, but also Indians who wronged Englishmen.

The Creeks wisely did not expect to depend solely on the treaty or English promises to ensure the future of the Creek Confederacy. Under their great leader Brims, they evolved a brilliant policy of neutrality, with four major emphases, to keep their nation intact in the midst of an increasingly English landscape. First, no new forts would be permitted to be built on Creek lands by any white nation or group, for the Creeks knew that forts could lead to further occupation by whichever Europeans built them, and that forts would invite invasion by one or both of the other European powers who were jealous of their rival's military presence on Creek land. Second, no Creek lands were to be used as a battleground in conflicts between rival white powers, because if any European power achieved victory in a battle fought on Creek land, the Creeks themselves would be the eventual losers. Third, the Creek nation was to be as independent from other Indian nations as it was from various white governments, for the Creeks saw other Indian nations either as outright enemies or as nations capable of pulling the Creeks into undesirable wars; the Creeks would stand in isolation, often avoiding opportunities to form an intertribal alliance to contain the whites in favor of their more certain and controllable separatism. Finally, all whites would be allowed to trade among the Creeks and to establish unfortified trading posts, as the Creeks hoped to keep their economic options open and promote competition among the whites. The Creeks realized that while they would probably have to depend primarily on English goods and guns if they were to continue as the most powerful nation in their locale, they could not afford to antagonize the Spanish or the French who might convince traditional Indian enemies of the Creeks to attempt to destroy the confederacy's power. Like most nations in all ages, the Creeks based their diplomacy on past experience rather than future possibilities, remembering both old intertribal rivalries and recent disastrous intertribal alliances. Unfortunately, while Creek diplomacy provided a plan for survival in the present generation, future generations of Creeks were to discover that the policy of neutrality would play into the hands of the more rapidly growing English colonies. In addition, the traditional independence of Creek town leaders would often upset attempts to put Creek diplomatic theory into action.

The English quickly profited from the Creeks' distrust of old enemies by encouraging the Cherokees to continue their attacks on Creek towns and then selling arms to both sides. When continuation of the war was assured by a renewed alliance between the Creeks and the Haudenosaunee of New York who were also at war with the Cherokees, the English continued to trade with all three nations. The Creeks understandably resented this two-faced English trading policy. Until the English ended arms sales to the enemy Cherokees, the Creeks refused to influence the Yamasees to end their war with the English.

Soon two factions arose within the Creek nation. The Upper Creeks who lived along the Coosa and Tallapoosa rivers in eastern Alabama wanted to force the Yamasees to make peace with the English in order to encourage better trade relations. The other faction, the Lower Creeks who lived along the Ocmulgee, Flint and Chattahoochee rivers in western Georgia, wanted to support the Yamasees until the English stopped trading with the Cherokees. The Lower Creeks, where Brims's influence was strongest, also desired to keep their nation aloof from the English and not entirely dependent on English trade goods so that they could continue a policy of neutrality with friendly relations toward all the neighboring whites—English, Spanish and French. As the years passed, what was already a complex situation became even more so, with the Creeks holding the balance of power between both white and Indian nations. In 1726, the English saw an opportunity to break the Creeks' pivotal power. The English instigated an attack against the Lower Creeks by five hundred Cherokees and Chickasaws armed with English weapons and carrying an English flag. During the attack, the invaders were ambushed and beaten back, the English flag was captured, and the Lower Creeks called for war against the English. The Upper Creeks needed English guns to fight those same Cherokees, however, and would not comply. While this invasion of the Lower Creek country did not bring about a Creek declaration of war against the English, the English themselves realized that the war they were promoting was likely to get out of hand, to England's detriment. Cherokees attacked one English trader traveling to the Creeks, and the English feared they would no longer be able to trade with either side.

In the past the English had kept the Creeks and Cherokees at war with each other, encouraging them to kill each other while Englishmen sold arms to both sides. But now the English ended both the Creek-Cherokee and the Yamasee wars by demonstrating the influence of their trade and their military potential. First, the English declared a trade embargo against Brims and his Lower Creeks because of Brims's support for the Yamasees. Second, they sent an expedition that destroyed a Yamasee town near Spanish St. Augustine. The expedition made the not-so-subtle point to Brims that the Spanish could no longer protect the Yamasees, and that continued friendship with the Yamasees and the Spanish might prove disastrous for the Creeks. Third, the English also persuaded the Cherokees to stop formal warfare with the Creeks, and finally in 1728 a general peace was arranged. Occasionally Creeks and Cherokees fought in raids, but outright war would not be fought again for ten years. Creek antagonism toward the English was smoothed over, and the Yamasees, resigned that the Lower Creeks no longer supported them, made peace with the English, ending the thirteen-year Yamasee War.

Brims died sometime between 1730 and 1733, his hopes for complete Creek independence outmaneuvered by the weight of English trade goods and English guns carefully manipulated by the whites among both his friends and his enemies. The Creeks were now economically tied to the vast English trading empire, largely because the French and the Spanish offered little. But Brims had left his people a tradition of political separatism, neutrality, and an open-door economic and friendship policy that they tried to perpetuate. Although he had been unable to keep the English from controlling Creek policy through the lever of trade goods and armaments, he had kept the Creeks intact as a confederacy during a very difficult period. Had Brims yielded to the English immediately, it is very likely that either the French or the Spanish would have retaliated by invading his country, or that the English would have felt free to expand and settle on his people's lands. Either prospect could have destroyed the Creek Confederacy. Brims and the Creeks had forced a stalemate upon the European powers vying for influence in the Southeast. What was clearly an English trading domain was not necessarily English in international politics, for the Creeks continued to talk and trade with the French in Louisiana and the Spanish in Florida. The Creeks would continue to hold the balance of power in the region until after mid-century. The English could not afford to antagonize them because of the profitable Creek-English trade and because the Creeks could always make good their threat to join the Spanish or the French. In the coming years the Creeks proved bent on survival—as Creeks, not as pawns or wards of Europeans. The longer the Creeks held back the Europeans, the longer they had to adjust their culture in preparation for the onslaught of settlers that all Indian people feared.

With the destruction of Yamasee towns near Spanish St. Augustine and previous similar experiences, Indians in the Southeast learned that a military alliance with the Spanish was useless because the Spanish were seldom able to protect their allies from enemy raids. From then on, the only Indians who became Spanish allies were those who had no choice, such as the Apalachees whose lands were directly occupied by the Spanish, or the Yamasees whose traditional Indian enemies were allied with the English. As for the English, they had a reputation for shrewd political moves but also for plentiful trade goods. The French reputation had not yet been determined. In 1729, a major event prompted many Southeastern Indians including the Creeks to view the French with alarm. In that year the Natchez Indians (who lived along the lower Mississippi River) rebelled against the French, who retaliated with a vengeance. The Natchez, primarily farmers who also produced the best pottery and weaving in the Southeast, were among the most respected Indians in the area because they had continued the culture of the great Mississippian Mound Builders who had flourished since at least 900 A.D. Neighboring nations considered the Natchez their cultural forbears and often visited them. The center of their capital was well known for two distinctive mounds, each topped by a building about thirty feet square. One mound and building was the home of the Great Sun, the religious and political leader of the Natchez. The other was a temple that housed the eternal fire of the Natchez, a fire that was to burn as long as the sun, worshipped as a great spiritual force by the people. The Great Sun was the sun's representative on earth, just as European kings were God's chosen rulers by "divine right." Here the parallel ends, however, because no son of a Great Sun could succeed his father.

French arrogance had caused the Natchez to go to war on earlier occasions. This time the French antagonized the Natchez by demanding that they abandon one of their towns to make way for French settlers. Joined by the Chickasaws of western Tennessee and Kentucky, the Natchez went to war, encouraged by English traders who hoped to make a profit from the gun trade and to weaken the French Mississippi Company that had settled Louisiana. The French used the Natchez war as an opportunity to solidify the support of the already pro-French Choctaw Indians who eagerly went to war against their traditional enemies, the Natchez and the Chickasaws. The French did not have enough soldiers to fight the Natchez on their own, and the Choctaws did most of the fighting. This war again proved the readiness of most Europeans, this time the French, to exploit the Indians' traditional rivalries and encourage them to eliminate one another. The Natchez were crushed by the Choctaws, most of them were slaughtered, and their traditional eternal flame was extinguished. A few escaped to the safety of the Chickasaw and Creek towns, but the Natchez disappeared as a distinct nation. The French ensured that end by selling 400 Natchez prisoners of war into slavery in Haiti. Among the 400 was the Great Sun (Swanton 1911, 45–257).

Creek Negotiations with the English: The Georgia Colony

The Creeks and many other Southeastern nations viewed the destruction of the Natchez with great alarm. The French reputation sank, and as a result the English in the Southeast gained some goodwill and were seen by many nations as a preferable alternative to the cruel French and the impotent Spanish. If the

English could avoid temptations such as cheating the Indians in trade, raping their women, and killing their people, they stood an excellent chance of peaceful coexistence. In 1733, it appeared that they would be able to accomplish that, for the very able and fair-minded James Oglethorpe arrived to establish the colony of Georgia. Although the treaty of 1717 forbade English settlement south of the Savannah River, the Creeks were willing to allow Oglethorpe to establish his settlement because they saw an opportunity to beat the English at their own game of "divide and conquer." The South Carolinians had always played the Creeks against the Cherokees to the profit of South Carolina. The Creeks now correctly analyzed Oglethorpe's colony as another source of English trade goods that would make the Creeks independent of South Carolina traders.

The Creeks did not intend Oglethorpe's settlers to have a foothold in Creek territory proper. Instead, they allowed Oglethorpe to negotiate with the Yamacraw band, former Creeks who had been expelled from the confederacy about 1728 for supporting the Yamasees in their war against the English. The Yamacraws were led by a chief named Tomochichi. Technically Tomochichi and his band were still Creeks and the confederacy promised to reinstate them if Tomochichi would grant Yamacraw lands to Oglethorpe on behalf of the Creek Confederacy. This Creek maneuver was typical of powerful nations, such as the Haudenosaunee in the North, who when faced with white demands for land gave away territory of their weakest subject nations to keep the whites away from their own lands. But Tomochichi was not the only Indian leader at the site—Yamacraw Bluff—where Oglethorpe wanted to establish the town later called Savannah. Mary Musgrove, or Coosaponakeesa, Brims's niece, lived here with her husband Johnny Musgrove, whom she had married as a Creek pledge of peace in 1717. Mary Musgrove welcomed Oglethorpe, for she knew that the arrival of new colonists would help the trading post she had established at Yamacraw Bluff to prosper. As it turned out, Tomochichi died before any significant disputes arose with the English. But Mary, as a representative of the entire Creek Confederacy, always made sure that the English observed Indian rights, and this led to many land disputes between the Creeks and those colonists eager to ignore the law.

Tomochichi, carrying eagle feathers that had been passed throughout the Creek Confederacy to signify unity of purpose, went to England with Oglethorpe in 1734 as an emissary of the Creek nation. After a meeting with King George II during which each pledged friendship to the other, Tomochichi was asked by the Earl of Egmont, a Georgia trustee, if he was impressed by the king's palace and England in general. Tomochichi replied that while the English had more material goods than the Creeks, the English were probably not any happier than Indians and that "the English lived worse than the Creeks who were a more innocent people" (Tomochichi [1734] 1967, 87). Before he returned to his homeland, Tomochichi explained that he was only uncomfortable around one man, the archbishop of Canterbury, who appeared to him to be a conjurer.

Oglethorpe and the trustees of the Georgia colony did their best to treat the Indians fairly. At the Creeks' request, they agreed to forbid the trading of rum to the Indians because traders cheated inebriated Indians easily. They also prohibited a particular fraud that Carolina traders from the north had perpetrated for years and which the Indians had continually complained about. The fraud depended upon the fact that deerskin prices were fixed per pound by treaty. The Carolina traders used a measuring weight of one-and-a-half pounds that they claimed to be one pound. The Georgia trustees also required traders to obtain Georgia trading licenses even if they already had licenses from South Carolina. Most traders angrily opposed these measures, and Georgia and South Carolina hotly disputed Indian trade rights. It might be expected that the Creeks welcomed this, for it set one white faction against another in much the same way that the whites had often pitted Indian against Indian. But a few Creek chiefs, who wanted to protect the bonuses they customarily received from Carolina traders, joined the traders in protesting the outlawing of the rum trade and dual licensing requirement. At the same time most Creek leaders favored the Georgia reforms, and the Creek nation split into factions paralleling those of the whites.

In 1736, a Christian missionary John Wesley arrived amidst this factionalism. Wesley would later found the Methodist Church. But in 1736 his goal was to bring Christianity to the Creeks. The Creeks had already been exposed to Spanish Catholicism, French Catholicism and several English versions of Christianity. He soon discovered that the Creeks had long since chosen to retain their old beliefs rather than take a chance on one of the Christian confusions presented by whites like Wesley. After a little more than a year, Wesley fortuitously discovered that God wanted him to return to England.

Another style of white proselytizing—political—found its way into the Creek Confederacy during 1738 as the French and Spanish each tried to entice the Creeks away from the English. The Spanish, feeling war was imminent with the English whether in Europe or in the colonies, were especially energetic.

Georgia's Oglethorpe, of course, wanted the Creeks on his side during any war with Spain, and he had an advantage over the French and the Spanish: one of his close friends was Chigelley, the regent for the late emperor Brims's young son Malatchi. Chigelley invited Oglethorpe to the capital of the confederacy, Coweta, where a great meeting was held during parts of July and August 1739. Upon his arrival in the town square, Oglethorpe was given the ceremonial black laxative drink of purification and then entertained with a great feast and an evening of Indian dancing. Chigelley and Oglethorpe reaffirmed all past treaties and Oglethorpe assured the Creeks that the English did not wish to expand any farther inland. Chigelley, however, made no offer of a Creek military alliance with the English because he greatly admired Brims's policy of neutrality, and he was determined to let the English fight their own wars. When Oglethorpe returned to Frederica, Georgia, he learned that England was indeed at war with Spain (The War of Jenkins's Ear) and he was very disappointed when Chigelley refused to send Creek warriors to help. Oglethorpe had to be content with a few dozen Creeks who lived near the Georgians and were willing to enter the war.

In the meantime, the French were working to end the Creek-Choctaw war, for it kept the Creeks dependent on English guns and prevented the French, who were friendly with the Choctaws, from creating harmonious relationships with the Creeks. In April 1740, the French invited Chigelley and Choctaw representatives to meet at Fort Toulouse. The French promised the Creeks rum and presents if they would make peace with the Choctaws. Chigelley was agreeable. The French commander at Fort Toulouse then asked the Creeks to demonstrate that they were not completely subservient to the English by looting an English trading post seven miles east of Fort Toulouse. Encouraged by Chigelley, about 200 Creeks rushed off toward the post, operated by John Spencer. However, many of the Creeks at Fort Toulouse disapproved and sent a warning ahead to The Wolf, the Creek chief who governed the lands upon which Spencer had built his post. The Wolf determined to protect Spencer's post against the approaching visitors. Dressed in the ceremonial feathers of authority and wearing war paint, he seated himself alone on Spencer's front porch, musket in hand. When the warriors broke into the clearing in front of the post, The Wolf pointed his musket at them ready to shoot the first warrior who approached too closely. Surprised and impressed by The Wolf's courage, the 200 returned to Fort Toulouse where the French commander refused to distribute the rum and presents. Since the Creeks would not break with the

English, he would not encourage peace between the Creeks and Choctaws. Chigelley went home to Coweta disgusted with the French and decidedly pro-English. The Creek-Choctaw war was renewed.

Although Chigelley left Fort Toulouse with fonder thoughts toward the English, Oglethorpe still could not obtain massive Creek military aid against the Spanish because the Creeks were too busy fighting the Cherokees and the Choctaws to the north. Since the English made a profit selling arms to both sides, they had not previously tried to end the war. With the beginning of the Spanish war in 1739, however, the English would have preferred to force an end to the Creek-Cherokee war in order to obtain Creek allies against the Spanish. But the trade-motivated English could not favor the Creeks in negotiations without alienating the Cherokees, and so they did nothing. The English learned once again, however, that selling arms to both sides in an Indian conflict had disadvantages when, in 1744, France declared war on England (The War of the Austrian Succession). Now the English not only needed the Creeks against the Spanish, they needed them to fight the French of Louisiana as well. Furthermore, they needed the Cherokees to fight the French in Canada. As long as Indians fought each other, they could not afford to spare warriors for the whites' wars. The Creeks held great debates as English, French, and Spanish emissaries tried to persuade them to go to war on their respective sides. As a result, they divided into factions and this, combined with the attempts of many Creeks to continue Brims' policy of neutrality, kept them from any commitment.

The Shawnee Proposal for Pan-Indian Unity

By 1745, although the European poweres were warring among themselves, the conflicts between Indian nations had weakened virtually every Indian nation while benefiting Europeans. The Shawnee Indians living along the Ohio River realized the eventual consequence of these conflicts. The victors would be the whites, whose constant immigration and/or powerful national resources would support them as Indian resources and populations declined. Beginning in 1745, the Shawnees began to promote new alliances among Indian nations. The Shawnees intended to create a new Indian unity, from the north to the south, which would be stronger than those regional alliances and confederacies that already existed, such as the networks of the Creek Confederacy and the Haudenosaunee. This Shawnee vision, which inspired many Indian people, would continue from 1745 until the dream died on northern and southern battlefields during the War of 1812.

In 1745, the Shawnees had a unique perspective on the frontier situation because some of their nation lived in the South, near and even among the Creeks, while others lived in the North. Neither the northern nor the southern Shawnees had the power of nations such as the Creeks, and so the Shawnees more readily realized Indian vulnerability. It did not matter whether the whites were French, Spanish or English—the Indians would be the losers. In February 1746, the Shawnees sent emissaries throughout the Mississippi Valley and the Southeast trying to convince Indians to give up their old rivalries and unite against the Europeans. The Indians' dependence on white trade goods, however, worked against the Shawnees' proposal (Corkran 1967, 118).

Perhaps Indian unity could have begun in the South, for in 1746 the Creeks and the Chickasaws managed to work out a peace with their long-time rivals, the Choctaws. However, it was also a peace advantageous to the French in Louisiana who still needed the Choctaws as allies and hoped to entice the Creeks to aid them as well. Just at this point, the French government far to the north in Canada sponsored a raid of northern Indians, including some Cherokees, against the Creeks. This forced the Creeks to forgo any negotiations with the French in Louisiana because they needed English guns to fight the northern Indians. The incident set back Shawnee hopes of intertribal unity, caused the Creeks to return to the English sphere of influence, and demonstrated that the French colonial governments in Louisiana and Canada were not following a coordinated Indian policy. Because the English colonies were unable to coordinate with one another, and because Indian nations were also criticized for failing to work together, the lack of unity between the North American French colonies is worth noting: this demonstrates how difficult it was for any European or Indian nation to create policies of unity.

With the Creeks once again tied closely to the English, the English took the opportunity of the Creek-Chickasaw-Choctaw peace to send English traders through Creek country to trade with the Choctaws. Late in 1747, some of the Choctaws, with English encouragement, were attacking their former French allies, threatening the main French post at Mobile, and fomenting a Choctaw civil war between pro-French and pro-English factions. When a European peace between England, France and France's ally, Spain, was signed at Aix-la-Chapelle in 1748, peace between the Europeans in the Southeast was also secured. However, intertribal wars, especially the Creek-Cherokee wars, continued to weaken the Indian nations while the white nations rested and became stronger.

With both England and France determined to dominate eastern North America, another war was imminent, and whenever it broke out, the Indians in the Southeast were still almost certain to be divided among themselves. While that factor was to the Indians' disadvantage, they also possessed certain advantages. It was actually the great intertribal rivalries, accentuated by the struggle to keep trade with the whites exclusively tribal, that had prolonged the conflict between France and Spain on the one hand and England on the other.

The Creeks, for example, had insisted on following their own eclectic policy that sometimes dictated ties with the English and sometimes friendship with the French and Spanish. Had the Creeks instead allied themselves firmly with one of the European powers, that power would have quickly dominated the Southeast. But the Creeks' policy, as independent as circumstances allowed, had the effect of keeping one European power from emerging supreme. Throughout the first half of the eighteenth century, the Creeks had in fact caused a stalemate in the Southeast, enabling them to adjust their way of life to the alien European intruders and to prevent their culture from being overwhelmed.

By 1750, the Creeks owned domestic fowl, hogs, cattle and horses, obtained primarily from the Spanish. Although the Creeks were still ardent hunters because of the lure of high profits from the deerskin trade, they had begun to farm their lands much more extensively. They continued their ancient cultural traditions, but they were now able to face the whites with an additional sophistication on the whites' own terms. Whichever European power would finally force the other whites out of the Southeast, the Creeks were in a position to survive. They could not be pushed aside easily, because they possessed an increasingly shrewd business sense that they had developed through the deerskin trade. This astuteness in turn assisted them in protecting their lands and property. The Creeks' survival thus far, however, had been at an extremely high price. Creek warriors had died in European-inspired wars, either between Indians or against other whites.

The Haudenosaunee Confederacy: Shift from Defensive to Offensive Diplomacy

Like the Creek Confederacy in the Southeast, the Haudenosaunee in the Northeast had also made impressive advances since the early 1600s. Faced with the choice of engaging in the northern fur trade or of perishing in the Huron-Algonquin attacks, the Haudenosaunee turned to the Dutch on the Hudson

River. But the Mahican nation dominated the northern Hudson River valley near Fort Orange (Albany) where the Dutch traded, and the Mahicans jealously resisted Haudenosaunee attempts to share that trade. Since Haudenosaunee survival depended on those Dutch goods, the Haudenosaunee declared war on the Mahicans and fought them until about 1677, just for the right to trade with the Dutch, and the English who supplanted them in 1664.

The Haudenosaunee had spent the first three decades of the 1600s fighting for their very existence by trying to repel invaders and at the same time obtain enough furs to trade for white goods. Yet in the history of almost every nation there comes a time when a defensive posture necessary to protect national freedom drifts almost unnoticed into a belligerent attitude of conquest and expansion. The Haudenosaunee underwent such a transition, shifting from defensive to offensive diplomacy and war during the 1640s, and the change shaped Haudenosaunee national history for 130 years, until the American Revolution.

The first advantage in the Haudenosaunee struggle against the Hurons and Algonquins was accidentally provided by the French, who unintentionally introduced a European plague into the Huron nation during the 1630s. Within a decade, that pestilence reduced the Hurons from a strong thirty thousand or thirty-five thousand to a greatly weakened fifteen or perhaps even ten thousand. Such a terrible loss—fifty percent of their population at the very least—might have prompted the Hurons to negotiate a peace with the Haudenosaunee. But French Jesuits prevented that peace. The Jesuits were certain that French success depended on division among the Indian nations and that a Huron-Haudenosaunee peace might allow the Dutch in New Amsterdam to obtain furs that would otherwise go to the French. Although the Hurons had been decimated by disease, the Haudenosaunee still had difficulty holding their own against Huron raiders who were joined by other French-allied Indians. In 1640, the Haudenosaunee again asked the Hurons for peace, and at first the Hurons responded favorably. But Jesuit missionaries, whom the Haudenosaunee called "the chief clerks of the fur trade" (Hunt 1940, 71), once again interfered and persuaded the Hurons to reject the Haudenosaunee peace plea. Moreover, the Haudenosaunee were desperate to find a new source of furs, for by 1640 they had trapped so many beaver and other fur-bearing animals in their homeland that the animals were nearly exterminated. Furs could be obtained in the northwest around all the Great Lakes and north to Hudson's Bay, but the Hurons controlled the trade in this vast area. The Haudenosaunee had no choice but to attempt to work their way into the Hurons' fur trading system. The Hurons' network was not simply an arrangement between Indian hunter and white trader. It was an extremely sophisticated economic organization and one that spawned a complex struggle over the trade routes into the lands around the Great Lakes.

The Hurons, who were part of the Iroquoian linguistic group, plus various Algonquin nations including the Ottawas and Nipissings, went west every year in great circular routes, hunting and/or trading furs in lands inhabited by other Algonquin nations. Since the fur-trading warriors could not also help their families at home raise food or hunt, they traded with two nations, the Petuns and the Neutrals, for corn and tobacco. The Petuns (an Iroquoian people) lived north of Lake Ontario and were noted for their corn. The Neutrals (or Attiwandaronks, of Iroquoian stock) lived just to the west of Lake Ontario and were especially famous for their tobacco. The Petuns and the Neutrals (the latter so called because they had remained neutral in the Haudenosaunee-Huron wars) would trade their crops to the Hurons and other fur-gathering warriors and receive in exchange some of the goods the warriors obtained when they sold furs to whites. The Haudenosaunee wished to be a part of this system. As their contribution, they offered the role of bargaining middlemen, because they were in a unique geographical position to play one white group—the French in Canada—against another—the Dutch, and later the English, in New York. This would enable all Indian nations to get the highest prices for their furs. The Haudenosaunee thus intended to make the eastern end of the distribution and sale of the furs as complete and sophisticated as the other end of the Indian economic system, the fur gathering, already was.

In 1641, the Haudenosaunee again asked for peace with the Hurons, but this time they went directly to the French, whom the Haudenosaunee now realized controlled the Hurons' decisions. The Haudenosaunee were especially anxious to work out a peace agreement, because the Dutch, aware that the Haudenosaunee were attacking Dutch-allied nations in the Hudson River valley, were temporarily refusing to sell them the muskets they needed for hunting and defense. The French insisted that the Haudenosaunee make peace entirely on French terms, a demand the Haudenosaunee rejected. The next year, 1642, the Haudenosaunee went to war against the Hurons in earnest by placing war parties on the Ottawa and St. Lawrence rivers, effectively blockading much of the Huron fur trade. In 1643, with the Dutch again providing the needed muskets, the Haudenosaunee continued to exert pressure on the Huron fur trading routes, continually sending out war parties to block the canoes bringing furs from as far away as Hudson's Bay to the north and Green Bay, Wisconsin, to the west. The Haudenosaunee blockade was extremely effective. By 1645, the situation of five years before had been completely reversed. This time it was the French who asked the Haudenosaunee for peace. The Haudenosaunee were especially confident now because they had also helped the Dutch successfully crush rivals in the lower Hudson.

At Three Rivers near Montreal in mid-July 1645, French, Hurons and Algonquins met in council with an Haudenosaunee delegation led by the great Mohawk orator, Kiotsaeton. As the Haudenosaunee had the upper hand, Kiotsaeton solemnly and graciously presented various wampum belts to his enemies, belts of beads that Kiotsaeton hoped would bind up all wounds, dry the tears of mourners and lift all the nations' canoes over rocky portages. With the thirteenth belt, Kiotsaeton opened the negotiations by reminding the Hurons that the Haudenosaunee had sought peace on many previous occasions. He noted that the Hurons always seemed willing only to change their minds suddenly. Kiotsaeton's implication was that the Hurons had become controlled by the French and that instead they should now follow their own best interests. Kiotsaeton then offered the Hurons peace in exchange for the Hurons' promise to bring all furs obtained in trade with the northwestern nations to the Haudenosaunee instead of to the French or the Algonquins (who lived closest to the French). The Haudenosaunee would then trade the furs to the Dutch and the French. The solution the Haudenosaunee offered was beneficial primarily to their side, but the Haudenosaunee were not begging this time—they were in control. The Hurons accepted.

The Haudenosaunee, demonstrating shrewd sophistication, approached the French in two secret meetings. They asked that the French make a peace that publicly acknowledged French support of the Algonquins, but which would secretly abandon them. It was the Haudenosaunee intention then to attack and exact revenge from the people who had oppressed them for decades. It was a maneuver as clever (or infamous) as any made in the halls of Europe. Shrewd diplomats themselves, the French, with the calculating concurrence of their Jesuit advisors, willingly agreed to abandon their Algonquin allies, but insisted that they had to continue to protect *Christian* Algonquins. How Haudenosaunee warriors were supposed to distinguish Christian from non-Christian Algonquins was not clarified, but the French corollary was accepted. The Haudenosaunee never did attack the Algonquins, despite the secret provisions in the peace treaty of 1645, because one of the Huron chiefs was married to an Algonquin woman, and an attack would have brought on a war with the Huron in-laws. It appeared, therefore, that the peace between the area's two most powerful peoples would end war on the fur-trading frontier. In September 1646, however, the Haudenosaunee discovered that the Hurons and the French had not intended to keep the treaty provisions. Instead of bringing the year's furs to the Haudenosaunee, the Hurons went directly to Montreal and traded eighty canoe-loads of furs to the French. It was the largest fur shipment thus far in the history of New France, and it clearly violated the peace treaty. The Haudenosaunee resumed their attacks, determined to share in the vast and profitable fur trade. Some of the Mohawks killed Father Isaac Jogues, a Jesuit who had come among them. As in previous wars, each of the five nations of the Haudenosaunee sent out its own independent war parties. There was hardly any coordination, for although Indian strategy generally included quick raids and the blockading of trade routes, it rarely called for all-out war to crush the enemy completely.

In 1648, despite the war, the Hurons made an immense profit from their annual fur fleet, and there was a possibility that the French and the Hurons would succeed in obtaining allies from the Susquehanna Indians, who had major towns near Chesapeake Bay to the south of the Haudenosaunee. Furthermore, the Onondagas appeared tempted to leave the league and join the French rather than continue to undergo the hardships of war. Hoping to use success in war to keep the Haudenosaunee united, the Seneca and Mohawk Haudenosaunee, perhaps along with other confederacy members, decided on a bold stroke. Gathering one thousand warriors for an attack in the middle of winter, a hitherto unimaginable feat, they marched north in the autumn of 1648 and hunted north of Lake Ontario all winter, planning to launch a surprise attack on the Hurons. Beginning on March 16, 1649, the combined Haudenosaunee army pounced. They burned two Huron towns and prepared to attack a third. But Huron warriors bravely counterattacked on March 17, and the town was preserved. The Haudenosaunee retreated on March 19, fearing a larger Huron counterattack. Overall, the Haudenosaunee lost two hundred men and the Hurons three hundred, so it was not an overwhelming victory from a statistical standpoint. But psychologically it was the most daring move any northern nation had ever made. How strong must the Haudenosaunee be if they dared to attack in winter with a thousand men! In panic, the Hurons abandoned fifteen of their towns by May 1, 1649. They had never seen war like this, and they expected the worst. About eight thousand camped near the French on Christian Island in Georgian Bay of Lake Huron.

Because the Hurons had decided to reduce their agricultural output in favor of the fur trade, they had obtained most of their food from other Indians. The Hurons were unprepared for the situation in which they found themselves, and the French did not exert themselves to help their Huron allies. The Hurons starved all during 1649. By March 1650, almost the entire nation— perhaps 10,000 Hurons—had died in twelve terrible months. In June, 500 survivors made their way to Quebec where today their descendants are the only major group of Indians still bearing the name Huron. Other Hurons did survive, however, and a few hundred were absorbed by neighboring nations; even the Haudenosaunee accepted some into full membership. Others fled far to the west to Green Bay, Wisconsin, where they found refuge among friendly Potawatomies, but the Hurons were finished as a major nation.

While the Haudenosaunee were immediately responsible for the end of the Hurons, it is the French who must bear the final responsibility. French Jesuits had time and time again persuaded the Hurons to continue fighting the Haudenosaunee. However, although they were allies of the Hurons, the French never gave them substantial military aid or protection. Even when the Hurons were starving, the French were unprepared to help, and the French took no extra measures to save their allies. Unable to back up their promises of the benefits of Huron alliance with the great monarchy of France, the French pursued a pattern of empire as disastrous to the Indians as any other European imperial effort in North America. The French would betray almost every one of the Indian nations that allied with them from 1649 to 1766. In that year, 1766, the Ottawa war chief Pontiac finally surrendered. The war he led against the British for three years was based in part on the expectation of French military aid that never materialized.

The Haudenosaunee invasion and devastation of the Huron towns marked their fateful transition from defensive wars to wars of conquest and expansion. On December 7, 1649, Haudenosaunee warriors struck St. Jean, a town of the Petuns or Tobacco Nation. Ironically the Petun warriors were all away from the town looking for the very Haudenosaunee column that suddenly attacked the defenseless town and destroyed it, dispersing, killing or capturing the women, children and old men. Two days later the Petun warriors returned. Overwhelmed with grief when they saw their town in ruins, without a word to one another the warriors sank to the ground and remained sitting, still and silent for half a day, distraught and ashamed that they were not present to defend their families against the Haudenosaunee. Then they gathered what survivors they could find and most marched north to join some of the Ottawas. Because the French still did nothing to stop the Haudenosaunee, both the Petuns and Ottawas decided to flee immediately westward until they came to Green Bay, where both nations joined the refugee Hurons and the local Potawatomies.

The Haudenosaunee next struck at the Neutrals. In the late autumn of 1650, they attacked and then dispersed or adopted one Neutral town of about sixteen hundred people, but the Neutrals took the war back into Haudenosaunee country by attacking a Seneca town on the Haudenosaunee frontier and killing at least two hundred. This victory could not counteract most Neutrals' great fear of the Haudenosaunee, whom they knew had crushed much greater nations than theirs. Seeing no help forthcoming from the French, the Neutrals dispersed. Some trekked southward to join the Catawba nation, an unfortunate choice, for in 1715 the Catawbas lost their battles against the English in the Yamasee War and about half the nation was sold by the English into West Indies slavery. Other Neutrals were adopted by the Haudenosaunee, who were always glad to have replacements for their own war losses. Many other Neutrals joined the refugee population at Green Bay, Wisconsin.

In 1653, the French and Haudenosaunee made peace, for the French wanted furs above all else and they had no qualms about getting them from Haudenosaunee who had just dispersed or killed France's Native allies. The French were willing to make peace because they saw the Haudenosaunee merely as another group of Indian fur suppliers. Just how opportunistic the French were willing to be was demonstrated one year after the treaty. In 1654, a Jesuit in residence at the Haudenosaunee capital at Onondaga, Father Simon Le Moyne, baptized one of the two Haudenosaunee captains of a twelve-hundred-man expedition, primarily Onondagas. The warriors were about to set out against the Eries, an Iroquoian-speaking nation that was not part of the confederacy, living south of Lake Erie. The fact that the Eries were allies of the French apparently did not bother the Jesuit. As for the war captain of the Onondagas, he regarded baptism as imbuing its recipients with the additional and special power of the French. Later, another Jesuit, Father Jean de Quen, recorded what the Haudenosaunee told him about the expedition:

Our Warriors entered that Country, remote though it was from Onnontague [Onondaga], before they were perceived. Their arrival spread such a panic, that Villages and dwellings were abandoned to the mercy of the Conqueror,—who, after burning everything, started in pursuit of the fugitives. The latter numbered from two to three thousand combatants, besides women and children. Finding themselves... closely followed, they resolved, after five days' flight, to build a fort of wood and there await the enemy, who numbered only twelve hundred. Accordingly, they intrenched themselves as well as they could. The enemy [Haudenosaunee] drew near, the two head Chiefs showing themselves in French costume, in order to frighten their opponents by the novelty of this attire. One of the two, who had been Baptized by Father le Moine and was very well instructed [in Catholicism], gently urged the besieged to capitulate, telling them that they would be destroyed if they allowed an assault. "The Master of life fights for us," said he; "you will be ruined if you resist him." "Who is this Master of our lives?" was the haughty reply of the Besieged. "We acknowledge none but our arms and hatchets." Thereupon, the assault was made and the palisade attacked on all sides; but the defense was as spirited as the attack, and the combat was a long one, great courage being displayed on both sides. The Besieging party made every effort to carry the place by storm, but in vain; they were killed as fast as they advanced. They hit on the plan of using their canoes . . . as shields; and, bearing these before them as protection, they reached the foot of the entrenchment. But it remained to scale the large stakes, or tree-trunks, of which it was built. Again they resorted to their canoes, using them as ladders for surmounting that sta[u]nch palisade. Their boldness so astonished the Besieged that, being already at the end of their munitions of war,—with which, especially with powder, they had been but poorly provided,— they resolved to flee. This was their ruin; for, after most of the first fugitives had been killed, the others were surrounded by the Onnontaguehronnons [Onondagas], who entered the fort and there wrought such carnage among the women and children, that blood was knee-deep in certain places. [The killing of women and children after the storm of a fortress was common practice throughout seventeenth-century Europe as well as Indian America.] Those who had escaped, wishing to retrieve their honor, after recovering their courage a little, returned, to the number of three hundred, to take the enemy by surprise while he was retiring and off his guard. The plan was good, but it was ill executed; for, frightened at the first cry...of the Onnontaguehronnons, they were entirely defeated. The Victors did not escape heavy losses—so great, indeed, that they were forced to remain two months in the enemy's country, burying their dead and caring for their wounded. (Thwaites 1899, 121–23)

The Haudenosaunee believed that the Master of life had inspired the founders of the Haudenosaunee, but the belief that "the Master of life fights for us" was also given impetus by the Judaic-Christian concept of the chosen people, stressed to the Haudenosaunee by the Jesuits. Many Haudenosaunee had promised that if the Jesuit-blessed war against the Eries went well, they would follow the French god, and they fulfilled this pledge until the French alienated them again. With the attack on the Eries, the Haudenosaunee had demonstrated what they had begun with the defeat of the Hurons in 1649: they were true empire builders complete with all empires' prime ingredient, the belief that the imperialist possesses the exclusive power of the supreme idea.

When compared to the European empires in North America, however, the Haudenosaunee empire builders were different. The Haudenosaunee conquered the Eries but did not destroy them, making them instead subjects of the Haudenosaunee by bringing them under the laws and protection of the confederacy in "foreign affairs," including trade with Europeans, but permitting the Eries—and any other nation that was adopted by the confederacy—to govern their own internal affairs, carry on their own customs, their own religion, their own language, and thus continue as a distinct people. Many Eries went to live on the upper Ohio River where they became known as Black Minquas, *minqua* meaning "rascal" or "bad man" in Algonquin. With the fur trade route to the immediate west secure, the Haudenosaunee looked forward to controlling the flow of furs to the French and to the Dutch, sending out their warriors to bring in canoe-loads of furs just as the Hurons had done before them. To their consternation and fury they discovered that while they were preparing to fight the Eries, persistent Huron refugees and Ottawas had returned from Green Bay in June 1654 with a flotilla of fur-laden canoes. The French were amazed, but quickly recovered and accepted the furs in trade. During the next year no fur fleet arrived, but in 1656 the Hurons and Ottawas managed once again to bring in furs. Not wanting a competitive market with the enterprising Dutch, the French gladly began working again with the Huron and Ottawa refugees, who could manage to get to only French posts. The French were quite willing to break the Haudenosaunee-French treaty of 1653 to prevent the furs from going to another, higher bidder.

In December, the Haudenosaunee sent twelve hundred warriors westward to Green Bay to surprise the refugees, who had expected such a move and escaped westward. The refugee Hurons, some becoming known as Wyandots, stayed on the move gathering furs. The Ottawas gradually made their way back to the river that bears their name in Canada to resume their trade with the French. The Petuns, also sometimes known as Wyandots, sought safety on Mackinac Island in northern Michigan. About seventeen hundred Ottawas and Hurons worked their way south so that by 1700 they were at Detroit. The Haudenosaunee still hoped the French would honor the treaty of 1653, and they allowed more Jesuits to come to Onondaga in 1656 in the hope that the French would give them control over the fur trade.

By 1657, there were sixty French near Onondaga and evidently they traded with the Haudenosaunee enough to encourage hopes for more. But by 1658, the Haudenosaunee realized the French still intended to trade primarily with the Haudenosaunee enemies to avoid competing with the Dutch. Furthermore, the Jesuit presence near Onondaga worked against Haudenosaunee unity. The Mohawks, who already had strong trading bonds with the Dutch, had lobbied for the Jesuit agents of the French trade to come among them instead of the Onondagas. The Mohawks perceived this a logical request if the confederacy was ever to play the Dutch off against the French for the best trade prices because it was the Mohawk towns that were closest to the Dutch, located at the confederacy's easternmost outlet of the fur trade. Dutch trade with Mohawks and French trade with Onondagas would surely disintegrate the Haudenosaunee, and both the Mohawks and the Senecas were painfully aware that ten years before the Onondagas had been tempted by the French to secede from the league. A Jesuit reported that a few Mohawks and Onondagas had been killed in an intra-confederacy skirmish over the issue. A friendly and bribed Haudenosaunee chief warned the French that the confederacy had decided against the French and that a war with French-allied Indians was likely to break out. The whites fled northeast to Montreal. The Haudenosaunee renewed their old blockading tactics, cutting off the fur trade along the Ottawa River and even laying siege to Montreal. But in 1662, one of their largest blockading armies in Canada was attacked and defeated by a coalition of western Indians, including Ojibwas, Ottawas and Nipissings, eager to break through to the French with their fur-laden canoes. Fate struck an even crueler blow to the Haudenosaunee that same year when a plague broke out in their towns.

War Between Haudenosaunee & Susquehanna Confederacies

Even worse, to the south of the Haudenosaunee, the mighty Susquehanna Confederacy, an Iroquoian people living in southern Pennsylvania and in the northern areas of the Chesapeake Bay, had launched a full-scale war against the Haudenosaunee as allies of the Hurons. The Hurons and other French-allied Indians also struck the Haudenosaunee from the north. The white rivals of the Dutch—the English in Maryland and the Swedes in their tiny colony on the Delaware River in Pennsylvania—encouraged the Susquehannas, hoping that they would be able to take over Haudenosaunee trade routes to the west and bring furs to the two colonies. The issue was further complicated by the fact that the Dutch, who supplied the Haudenosaunee, were at war with England and allied with France. When eight hundred Senecas tried to capture a walled Susquehanna town in May 1663, they discovered that Maryland had supplied it with cannon. The Susquehannas were so confident that when the Senecas sent in twenty-five negotiators (who may also have been spies), the Susquehannas burned them to death on scaffolds especially erected so they could be seen by the Haudenosaunee outside. The attackers prudently retreated.

The Senecas tried to open negotiations with the French so that they could obtain the munitions necessary to exact revenge, but the French refused. In 1663, Louis xiv made Canada a royal colony, removing it from private hands, because Haudenosaunee pressures were too great for private enterprise to meet successfully. To impress the Haudenosaunee with his authority, Louis sent his crack Carignan-Salieres Regiment to Canada and in 1666 launched it on two devastating expeditions into Haudenosaunee country. The Haudenosaunee sued for peace and accepted French terms in 1667. About four hundred Oneidas, Mohawks, other Haudenosaunee and even a few Mahicans and New England Indians were persuaded by the French to move to the St. Lawrence River valley between 1669 and 1680 and become Catholic subjects of France. The two mission towns established, Caughnawaga (Kahnawake) and the Mountain, symbolized the French success in demoralizing the Haudenosaunee and attempting to convince the Haudenosaunee that they could not continue independent of the French.

The Haudenosaunee were well aware of the threat to their unity and independence. The Haudenosaunee was, by its confederate nature, not centrally coordinated. Quite often in the past war parties from one nation would go out without the support of the other confederacy members. The Senecas, for example, did most of the fighting with the Susquehannas. The persistent

French threat to the confederacy, however, inspired the Haudenosaunee to unite behind the Senecas to strike decisively against the Susquehannas. Once again, as in 1649 and 1658, the Haudenosaunee would try to overcome internal dissension by rallying Haudenosaunee nationalism through a patriotic war. In 1673, the Haudenosaunee asked the French for aid against the Susquehannas, for the war was not going well. The governor of Canada, Louis de Buade, Count Frontenac, refused French support because a French official, the Intendant Jean Talon, had in the late 1660s finally discerned the real meaning of the Haudenosaunee wars: they were not battles among war-mongering primitives, they were instead complex struggles over the fur trade. The French decided not to back the Haudenosaunee because the confederacy was powerful enough to act independently in the fur trade, bringing furs to either the French or the English, who had in 1664 captured the colony of New York (except for a brief Dutch reconquest in 1673–1674). The French thought it more advisable to back weaker nations such as the Hurons and Ottawas, for those nations had no choice but to be dependent on the French.

When the French decided not to aid the Haudenosaunee against the Susquehannas, they were hoping the Haudenosaunee would be defeated. But the Haudenosaunee won. The Susquehannas were a very powerful people who had in the past proven their ability to play English, Dutch and Swedes off each other in the fur trade. Like the Haudenosaunee, the Susquehannas had never been conquered by any whites and were natural rivals of the Haudenosaunee in the struggle for Indian leadership along the English colonial frontier. This rivalry temporarily abated during the 1658–1662 period, when the Susquehannas and the Mohawk Haudenosaunee cooperated in imposing peace on smaller Indian nations along the Hudson River for the mutual benefit of an unhindered Dutch trade, but that interlude quickly ended. Until 1675, the Susquehannas successfully withstood Haudenosaunee invasion, but in that year their political independence collapsed entirely, primarily because of white international conflict.

Two years earlier, in 1673, the Dutch had reconquered New York and threatened to encourage an Haudenosaunee invasion of Maryland. Maryland had previously supported the Susquehannas, but now the colony ordered the entire nation to depart Pennsylvania and come under its territorial control. With this accomplished, the Maryland colony could ask the Haudenosaunee for peace and forestall the confederacy's threatened invasion. To complicate the matter further, Maryland wanted to expand into the Delaware Bay area claimed by the

Dutch and inhabited by the Susquehannas' tributary allies, the Delawares (Lenape). Maryland indicated to the Susquehannas the intention to declare war on them if they refused to relocate to the colony's territorial jurisdiction and allow her to occupy the Delaware Bay area. When the Dutch returned New York to England by the Treaty of Westminster on February 19, 1674, the possibility of a Dutch-sponsored Haudenosaunee invasion of Maryland was removed. Nevertheless, Maryland decided to continue its Susquehanna removal program and obtain a peace with the Haudenosaunee lest the long Haudenosaunee-Susquehanna war endanger Maryland's frontier claims and settlements. Maryland hoped to exploit a resident Susquehanna population dependent for its reservation land and trading economy on Maryland. The Susquehannas agreed sometime after June 1674 to move to Maryland, and in February 1675 showed up obediently with their families and property. The new royal governor of New York, Edmund Andros, proposed to resolve this highly complicated situation by working with the Haudenosaunee. In exchange for their help, he offered something they had never obtained from the French: the opportunity to forge an intertribal political stability to be dominated by the Haudenosaunee and sponsored by a white trading power.

The Haudenosaunee Choose Empire Over Pan-Indian Alliance

By June 1675, Governor Andros had established the basis for this stability by making peace with the Indians of the Hudson River valley, Long Island and New Jersey, as well as with the Delawares. Andros's efforts were abruptly endangered, however, when King Philip's War broke out in New England in June, and when the killings of Doeg and Susquehanna Indians in July by Virginia and Maryland frontiersmen set those frontiers aflame in what became known as Bacon's Rebellion. Governor Andros, like most English colonial officials up and down the Atlantic coast, was afraid that all the Indians from Canada to Virginia would unite against the English. Andros moved quickly and convinced the Mohawk Haudenosaunee to fight the rebelling Indians following King Philip. At about the same time Andros armed other Haudenosaunee, and these warriors struck at Susquehannas who were already fleeing unexpected white attacks from Virginia and Maryland frontiersmen.

The Haudenosaunee actions ended the possibility of a united Indian effort against the English colonies. (The Haudenosaunee, bent on their own supremacy, would refuse twice again to join what could have become a united Indian effort: in 1763 during Pontiac's War and in the 1790s, especially 1794, during the Miami Confederacy's war to defend Ohio.) By the summer of 1676 the Haudenosaunee were working closely with Andros to achieve Haudenosaunee political supremacy over eastern Indians—the Haudenosaunee because they were building an empire, and Andros because he hoped English trade goods could control the Haudenosaunee. The Mohawks invited the Susquehannas to flee white oppression, end the long-time Haudenosaunee-Susquehanna war and come under the protection of the Haudenosaunee. Most of the Susquehannas agreed, and many of these were adopted by the Mohawks and the Senecas. Many joined the Delawares, who in turn soon became Haudenosaunee subjects, some by choice and others by conquest. Other Susquehannas were not provided with choices: captured by white frontiersmen, they were sold into slavery in the West Indies.

By the spring of 1677, Andros and the Haudenosaunee were prepared for the final step in their grand design. Maryland sought peace with the Haudenosaunee and Andros arranged for both sides to meet in Albany. In July 1677, Maryland negotiators obtained the peace they desired, but the Mohawks, evidently speaking for the confederacy, made it quite clear to Maryland that the peace was secured because of the good efforts of Governor Andros. Andros had aided the Haudenosaunee in bringing the Susquehannas, the Delawares and the Mahicans under Haudenosaunee jurisdiction, later occasionally challenged but never overthrown.

The Mohawks explained to the Maryland negotiators that the Haudenosaunee with their new annexed nations were tied faithfully to Andros and New York, "for the Covenant that is betwixt the Governor General and us is Inviolable yea so strong that if the very thunder should break upon the Covenant Chain, it would not break it in Sunder" (Mohawk speech, August 6, 1677, in Leder 1956, 45–46). The Haudenosaunee and Andros based this "Covenant Chain" on Haudenosaunee tradition and on Dutch and French diplomatic precedents, and they had begun shaping it as early as August 1675. The Covenant Chain served as the basis for the Haudenosaunee-English diplomacy throughout the colonial period, as the English recognized that the Haudenosaunee comprised the most powerful nation in the colonies north of Virginia.

The Haudenosaunee had begun the seventeenth century on the defensive against French-allied Indian nations. Then in 1649 they defeated the Hurons.

At this point, the Haudenosaunee' defensive struggle gradually turned into an empire-building offensive. In the 1670s that empire was recognized and encouraged by a European trading power, the English. The Haudenosaunee, with English guns and trade goods, now had the opportunity to expand the confederacy's interests westward against the French and their Indian allies. In so doing, they would also serve the imperial interests of the English. During the long wars with the Hurons and other French allies, there was some question as to whether the Haudenosaunee would survive once the Haudenosaunee were secure from outside attack. Just when Haudenosaunee unity seemed lowest, when some members went willingly to live among the French on the St. Lawrence, the league had rallied, beaten the Susquehannas, and reversed the discouragement of the recent past. The Haudenosaunee now faced their prospects of survival with the support of the English, who could be depended on to have a much greater supply of trade goods, usually at cheaper prices than the French.

It was still possible for the Haudenosaunee to play the English against the French in trade relations, however. Along the Haudenosaunee western frontier, the English were dependent on the confederacy to represent their interests, because the English had almost no physical presence there. If the Haudenosaunee could occasionally obtain better prices from the French or could divide the fur trade between English and French, Haudenosaunee political integrity would be strengthened, because they would not be dependent upon just a single European nation for trade.

Because the Hurons, Ottawas and some Indians of the Great Lakes still held onto the French trade despite the power of the Haudenosaunee, the Haudenosaunees' logical source of new furs was the Ohio River valley that lay south of the lakes. They had already secured access into the eastern Ohio River valley with their dispersion of the Eries between 1654 and 1657. They had also made incursions into the western part of the valley and the area west of Lake Michigan, lands controlled by the Illinois nations of Illinois and Wisconsin, as early as 1655.

After 1670, and especially after the 1677 Albany Treaty, the Haudenosaunee decided to pursue trade domination more seriously. The French Indian allies—the Chippewas (Ojibwas or Anishinaabe), the Ottawas and the Hurons—had already gone to war against the Sioux west of Lake Michigan to secure that area to the French interests. In the meantime, French explorers such as Pere Jacques Marquette, a Jesuit, and Louis Joliet, a trader, scouted out the lands of the Illinois people. Peaceful Haudenosaunee fur traders were murdered at French instigation, embittering the Haudenosaunee since they still adhered to the French-Haudenosaunee peace of 1667.

When René Robert Cavelier, Sieur de la Salle, built the *Griffin*, a small, one-masted sailing ship, above Niagara Falls in Seneca Haudenosaunee country in early 1679, the Haudenosaunee knew he intended to use it to bring furs back from the West. La Salle's ship would undermine the Haudenosaunee position as middlemen-transporters of the fur trade. It seemed that the only way they would be able to share in the fur trade was by conquest. But to go to war against the French would be self-defeating because afterward the Haudeno-saunee still wanted to be able to play the French off against the English to obtain the best prices.

The Haudenosaunee solution was to try to conquer the Illinois and force them to use the Haudenosaunee as middlemen. In September 1680, five hun-dred Haudenosaunee warriors marched into the Illinois country and defeated them. Some Illinois fled westward, but many submitted to Haudenosaunee control with a promise of Haudenosaunee protection under their confed-eracy's rule of law—sheltering under the Great Tree of Peace. Thus, when Skidi Pawnees raided an Illinois town of Haudenosaunee subjects and then returned to their homes west of the Mississippi River, the Illinois demanded that the Haudenosaunee fulfill its promise of protection.

By 1680, there were three contesting empires in the Northeast: the French, the English and the Haudenosaunee. The French and the English claimed all the land from the Atlantic to the Pacific. The more realistic Haudenosaunee were content to stop at the Mississippi. But now a claim to the lands of one of those empires had been challenged by the Pawnees' attack. Would the Haudenosaunee back up the political system they were building on their fron-tier, or would theirs be, like the English and the French, an empire of paper claims? The answer came as Haudenosaunee warriors marched more than one thousand miles, crossed the Mississippi and completely destroyed one of the Skidi Pawnee towns. The warriors then sat back and waited, their very presence threatening other Pawnee towns. A team of Pawnee negotiators soon arrived, promising that the Pawnees would never cross the Mississippi to attack Haudenosaunee subjects again if the Haudenosaunee would stay east of the Mississippi. This was exactly what the Haudenosaunee wanted, and peace was arranged (Wissler 1966, 135–36).

The French and Their Allies in the West and Canada

Illinois Indians who chose to flee rather than become Haudenosaunee subjects accepted the protection of the French under La Salle. With the Frenchmen at this time were a number of New England Indians who had fled the English after King Philip's War in 1676. These Indian refugees hated the English and the Haudenosaunee alike because some Haudenosaunee, primarily Mohawks, had helped the English during the war. The refugees' leader, Nanagoucy, suggested to La Salle that they establish an Indian confederacy in the West to resist the Haudenosaunee. La Salle sent New England warriors, each with fifty beaver pelts as presents, to spread word of the proposed confederacy among nations around the western Great Lakes. By 1683, an intertribal settlement, Fort St. Louis of the Illinois (on the Illinois River in northern Illinois), had three hundred cabins around it inhabited by Illinois, Miami Illinois and Shawnee Indians. In addition, central Wisconsin Indians, fearing a Haudenosaunee invasion, had chosen to abandon their homes and join the confederacy at Fort St. Louis.

Despite French hopes, the western confederacy was never a total success, but Haudenosaunee conquest did stop with the subjugation of part of the Illinois: when the Haudenosaunee tried to capture Fort St. Louis in late March 1684, they failed. The Haudenosaunee finally decided that if necessary they would fight the French. In 1684, the Haudenosaunee accepted a promise of aid from New York's Governor Thomas Dongan in return for acknowledging English protection over their towns. By this date the French were in danger of losing their Indian allies because English goods were cheaper. The Ottawas, who had briefly considered deserting the French in 1670, were among the nations discussing the merits of becoming Haudenosaunee subjects in order to be sure of obtaining English trade goods.

Then in 1687, a combined French and Indian force of about three thousand, including at least one thousand French, invaded Seneca country and landed on the southern shores of Lake Ontario (Hunt 1940, 152–58). At the time the Haudenosaunee thought they were at peace, at least temporarily, with the French. But after a short skirmish, the Senecas saw they could not resist so powerful an army. The French marched toward a major Seneca town, Ganondagan. Before they could arrive, the Senecas burned and abandoned Ganondagan and four of their other towns and withdrew to the country of the Cayuga Haudenosaunee. The French, with no Senecas to fight and without the logistics to go further, withdrew from Seneca lands without the overwhelming victory they had sought. In the spring of 1688, the Haudenosaunee counterattacked with guns and ammunition supplied by the New York governor and laid a nearly successful siege to Montreal. The French begged the Haudenosaunee for peace and told Haudenosaunee negotiators at Montreal that they would even abandon their western Indian allies. The Haudenosaunee ambassadors asserted their independence from both France and England, but because the Mohawks and Senecas had no representatives at the meeting, a formal peace could not be made with the confederacy. Upon returning to their own country, the Haudenosaunee decided to continue their successful war.

The western Indians allied with the French were shocked to discover that the French were about to sell them out, and they pressured the French to continue the war. In the spring of 1689, the English colonists in New York struggled among themselves following a bloodless coup in England called the Glorious Revolution (1688), which replaced the pro-French James II with the anti-French William III. When the Glorious Revolution occurred, Edmund Andros was in Boston serving as governor of several other colonies clustered together as the Dominion of New England: New York, New Jersey, Pennsylvania, Connecticut, Rhode Island, Massachusetts, Maine and New Hampshire. In 1689, Andros was overthrown by colonists who identified with the revolutionary cause in England. The Haudenosaunee were particularly pleased, as they feared that Andros had planned to undercut their own war efforts by making peace with the French.

After they were assured in May 1689 of continued New York support, they planned a devastating blow against the French. On July 26, fifteen hundred Haudenosaunee attacked the French town of Lachine six miles from Montreal. In two days of battle, they killed two hundred colonists, captured at least one hundred and twenty and dealt the French the worst defeat they were to experience at the hands of any Indians. French Governor Denonville was so fearful that the Haudenosaunee would take Montreal that he recalled his troops from Fort Frontenac at the northeastern end of Lake Ontario. It was then that English and French colonial officials discovered that their respective mother countries were engaged in the War of the League of Augsburg in Europe.

Retaliation Against the Haudenosaunee and English

The overwhelming victory of the Haudenosaunee at Lachine gave them a renewed pride and unity—it also prompted many of the pro-French western nations again to reconsider their allegiance. Fearing for their empire, the French reappointed seventy-year-old Count Frontenac, who had governed from 1672 to 1682. The rugged old man was ordered to invade Haudenosaunee country and at the same time to conquer the colony of New York. Plans for such a grand conquest sounded impressive in the court of Louis XIV, but Frontenac realized limited manpower and resources made it impossible. Instead, he decided to send raiding parties against New Hampshire, Maine and Albany.

While the Haudenosaunee and English lived quietly through the late winter of 1689–1690, French raiders made their way toward Albany. Two hundred and ten men, half of them French, the other half Catholic Haudenosaunee from Caughnawaga, tramped over the snow on the long march from Montreal through the wilderness of Lake Champlain. Deciding that Albany was too strongly garrisoned, their French commander led his men instead toward Schenectady, a Dutch-English farming community that was also the closest white settlement to the Haudenosaunee. The town of Schenectady, surrounded by a log stockade, was usually guarded at night by sentries.

The night of February 8, 1690, however, was bitterly cold and the sentries foolishly went inside to keep warm and catch some sleep. Somehow the stockade's gates were left open, perhaps ajar from snowdrifts, and it was later reported that in place of the sentries someone had erected two snowmen. The French raiders stole quietly into the town and attacked. The surprise was complete. After two hours of burning and plundering, sixty inhabitants lay dead, including eleven black servants or slaves. Sixty women, children and old men were allowed to remain in the charred town, but twenty-seven, including five blacks, were taken into captivity. Despite a vigorous pursuit by Mohawk Haudenosaunee and white militiamen, the raiders returned safely to Montreal, losing only two killed at Schenectady and six wounded or killed during the pursuit.

French attacks on New Hampshire and Maine followed quickly after the Schenectady raid. Because of a smallpox epidemic, the Haudenosaunee were only able to send one hundred and twenty warriors, accompanied by twenty-nine whites, in a retaliatory raid on La Prairie on the St. Lawrence during August 1690. Six Frenchmen and fifteen cattle were killed, and the party took nineteen prisoners, two of whom the Haudenosaunee killed for being unable to keep up with the march back to Canada.

Renewing their fifty-year-old strategy, the Haudenosaunee sent war parties north of the St. Lawrence to cut off the fur trade and hence Canada's wealth.

All during the early months of 1691, the Haudenosaunee blockaded the crucial trade routes, expecting that the English would send an army to help. But no English soldiers ever came, and the Haudenosaunee finally gave up their blockade and withdrew to New York in disgust. Albany whites agreed to send a raiding party northward in the summer of 1691, but this party, while successfully raiding La Prairie, barely escaped an ambush as it made its way home. The Haudenosaunee were hardly reassured of the value of the English as allies. The English tried to reassure the Haudenosaunee, but English interaction and even intercolonial confusion belied the fine words and announced intentions the Haudenosaunee too often heard. In June 1692, at a conference in Albany with the English, an Oneida chief, Cheda, used the occasion to summarize Haudenosaunee frustration.

Far to the northeast on the Massachusetts-Maine frontier, whites under Major Benjamin Church avenged murders of white settlers by killing Abnaki women and children in an undefended Indian town. The Abnakis and other Indians along that frontier continued to raid and destroy English settlements in this and future French-English wars, and the English continued to retaliate in kind. The French Jesuits and other missionaries encouraged the raids by impressing the Indians with a decidedly French version of the gospel. Bommaseen, a chief held captive at Boston in 1696, gave the following testimony, corroborated by other Indian prisoners of war:

> He said, the *French* taught 'em, that the Lord JESUS CHRIST was of the *French Nation;* that his Mother, the Virgin *Mary*, was a *French Lady*; that they were the *English* who had Murdered him; and that whereas he rose from the Dead, and went up to the Heavens, all that would Recommend themselves unto his Favour must Revenge his Quarrel upon the *English* as far as they can. (Mather 1702 87–88, passim)

Because the Indians understood the importance of revenge for the death of a kinsman within the context of their own culture, the Abnakis and others were determined in their raids. In 1693 and again in 1696, French armies with their Indian allies invaded Haudenosaunee country. In February 1693, the French struck while the warriors were out hunting, destroying three Mohawk towns and all the Mohawks' food supplies. Three hundred Mohawks, mostly women and children, were taken captive. Although Mohawks and some bold English militiamen under wilderness fighter Peter Schuyler managed to get back most of the captives during a hot pursuit of the invaders, the Haudenosaunee were dismayed that the English were unwilling to put enough troops on the frontier to discourage such French intrusions. That concern proved well founded when in 1696 French Governor Frontenac, now seventy-six, organized an army of two thousand regular soldiers, militia and Indians and launched an invasion of Onondaga territory, the heartland of the Haudenosaunee. After burning towns and cornfields abandoned by retreating Onondagas, he ordered Oneida towns burned. Unable to face overwhelming odds without English help, the Haudenosaunee fled whenever the French appeared. The New York governor lacked the funds to send help quickly, and the Haudenosaunee soon questioned the advisability of continuing their alliance with New York and the English.

Approaching Frontenac, the Haudenosaunee offered to make peace with France but not with her Indian allies. Back in France, Louis xiv thought the offer sounded good enough, but Frontenac refused to betray his Indian allies. He told the Ottawas, who had in the past been as tempted to desert the French as the French had been to desert them, "You see that I can make peace for myself when I please. If I continue the war, it is only for your sake. I will never make a treaty without including you, and recovering your prisoners like my own" (Parkman 1877, 422).

Meanwhile, the War of the League of Augsburg ended in Europe with the Treaty of Ryswick in 1697 before the Haudenosaunee could make peace with the French and before they broke completely with the English. The Haudenosaunee learned of the peace through the governor of New York, who also informed Frontenac by express messenger. The Haudenosaunee, believing the frontier to be safe, set out to hunt beaver in Canada.

But Frontenac intended to strike at the Haudenosaunee one more time, peace or not. He sent out a war party of Adirondacks, the Adirondacks having been overwhelmed by the Haudenosaunee during the previous decades and thus eager for even the smallest revenge. These Adirondacks surprised and killed many Haudenosaunee, though they lost some of their own. In this battle, one of the Haudenosaunee leaders who was mortally wounded cried out in frustrated anguish: "Must I, who have made the whole Earth tremble before me, now die at the hands of Children?" (Colden [1747] 1958, 174). It was a cry universal to countless conquerors in all eras who find themselves suddenly brought low by lesser foes, but dead nonetheless.

The Haudenosaunee Choose Neutrality

Emerging from the war angry with the English yet still at war with the French, the Haudenosaunee adopted the wisest foreign policy they could pursue: neutrality. They had proven themselves powerful—during the war their armies were the only ones to invade Canada successfully—while New York and New England had both failed miserably. The French were therefore aware and respectful of the Haudenosaunee potential in war. In fact, the French had invaded the Haudenosaunee during the war because they had posed a greater threat to French Canada than had any of the English colonies. The Haudenosaunee correctly perceived that if they could remain neutral, neither the English nor the French would dare antagonize them for fear of pushing them into an alliance with the other side.

In 1701, the Haudenosaunee, already alarmed at the establishment of a French fort at Detroit, went to a council with the French at Montreal and stated that they would be neutral in all future wars. The Haudenosaunee hoped that their neutrality would enable them to balance the French against the English. Since neither the French nor the English could exert their own dominion in the Great Lakes without Haudenosaunee support, the Haudenosaunee hoped that their neutrality would allow the Haudenosaunee themselves to dominate Indian affairs in the Great Lakes area. The Haudenosaunee had hardly returned from this council when in 1702 France and England went to war again in Europe in the War of the Spanish Succession. The Haudenosaunee remained outside of this conflict, keeping the terrors of war both from their own towns and from those of New York. The French did not dare attack New York for fear of alienating the Haudenosaunee.

Elsewhere in the North, however, the struggle was a bloody one. The French Jesuits continued to send their Indian converts against the New England colonists, persuading the Indians that the New Englanders were enemies of God but admonishing them to baptize any children before killing them. In February 1704, for example, two hundred Abnakis and Haudenosaunee Caughnawagas (the latter descendants of the Haudenosaunee families enticed away from the league by the French) plus fifty French Canadians traveled about three hundred miles by snowshoe and approached stockaded Deerfield, Massachusetts, where frontier families had gathered for the winter. Moving in to attack two hours before dawn on February 29, the raiders discovered that the town was not guarded. Furthermore, huge snowdrifts had piled up to the very top of the eight-foot stockade on the northwestern side of the fortified town, making a ramp up and over the wall. Quickly and quietly the raiding party went up the snowdrifts, over the wall and attacked. The minister of Deerfield, John Williams, awoke to Indian war-whoops just as Caughnawaga warriors broke down his front door and rushed in. Jumping out of bed, Williams grabbed a flintlock pistol, aimed it into the chest of one of the warrior and pulled the trigger. The pistol did not go off. If it had, the others would have killed Williams immediately, for the warrior was a Caughnawaga chief. Instead, Williams was captured along with his wife and five of his children.

In the meantime, of the fifteen homes in Deerfield, only that of militia sergeant Benin Stubbiness had not been overrun by the Indians. Stebbins' house was bulletproofed by a layer of bricks between the wood planking of the outer and inner walls, and its second story jutted out over the first, making it easier to defend than other Deerfield homes. Stebbins, joined by six other men whose families had taken refuge in the house earlier that winter in fear of just such an attack, held off the Indians' numerous assaults. Although Stebbins was killed, the other defenders refused to give up. They held the house until the Indians finally left Deerfield, taking with them 111 men, women and children as prisoners. During the raid, 53 settlers had been killed and another 137 either eluded capture or were spared and left behind.

During the march back to Canada, the Indians killed the wife of the captive minister John Williams, because she was too weak to go on, having had a baby not long before. The Indians regarded this killing as merciful, for she would most certainly have died a slow death if she had been abandoned on the trail. Later, in Canada, Williams and his children, with the exception of his daughter Eunice, were exchanged as prisoners of war. Eunice grew up among the Caughnawaga Indians, adopted Catholicism and married a Caughnawaga warrior. When her father later tried to persuade her to leave her adopted nation, she refused to return to English society (Parkman 1892, 52–87; cf. Demos 1994; cf. Melvoin 1989).

The War of the Spanish Succession finally ended with the Treaty of Utrecht in 1713 and the Indian raids prompted by French Jesuits were stopped. In New York, the neutral Haudenosaunee had been courted during the war by the English. In 1710, three prominent Haudenosaunee chiefs including the Mohawk sachem Hendrick together with the chief of a neighboring subject nation, the Mahicans, traveled to London where the four "Indian kings," as they became known, had an audience with Queen Anne (Bond 1952; Garratt

1985). Shortly afterward, an Anglican mission church was built among the Mohawks at Fort Hunter in the Mohawk River valley. These events, as well as the proximity of the Haudenosaunee to the English in New York, prompted the European authors of the treaty of Utrecht to define the Haudenosaunee as subjects of England. It was not the first or the last time that European negotiators would settle statuses and boundaries of faraway peoples not represented at the negotiations.

During the decades between the end of the War of the Spanish Succession in 1713 and the beginning of the War of the Austrian Succession in 1744, the Haudenosaunee continued their policy of neutrality. When the French requested that they be allowed to establish a new trading post at Niagara, the Haudenosaunee permitted its construction in 1726. The new French post would provide a greater distribution of French goods and encourage the English to keep their prices competitive. The Senecas would also benefit because they lived closer to French trade routes, and because the English trade routes to the east and south of them were already dominated by other Haudenosaunee nations. The French, however, had something larger in mind. They built a huge, two-storied stone chateau with a massive attic enclosed by wooden-shuttered dormer windows. Behind each of the shuttered dormers was a cannon; on the inside the attic resembled the gun deck of a warship. The stone "castle" was built so that the structure could withstand the heavy jolts sure to occur whenever the cannon were fired. With an inside well, as well as barrack rooms, the stone castle was an entirely self-contained fortress. The impressive fortress at Niagara did not long go unchallenged, for in 1726–1727 the English, with Haudenosaunee permission, built their own stone fort 170 miles east of Niagara at Oswego. Because the English offered better goods and prices, Fort Oswego soon surpassed Fort Niagara in trade volume.

West of the Haudenosaunee homeland, the French continued to dominate trade; along the northern Mississippi and among the Great Lakes, French profits were heavy. The Haudenosaunee had only a tenuous hold on any of this trade, and they had to be content to hunt and trade for furs in the Great Lakes area while surrounded by pro-French nations. Between 1712 and 1732, however, the Haudenosaunee tried to disrupt French control by encouraging their Outagamie (Fox) allies to attack French-allied nations such as the Hurons and Illinois, and thus force the French to do business primarily with the Outagamies, a goal encouraged by New York. The Haudenosaunee never sent large numbers of warriors to help the Outagamies, so the French-allied Indians were able to repel the attackers by periodically gathering large armies drawn from the Potawatomies, Ottawas, Hurons, Illinois, Saginaws and other nations. With French aid these combined nations finally crushed the Outagamies by 1736, again frustrating the Haudenosaunee hope of controlling the fur trade. The surviving Outagamies were adopted into the Sac nation, to be known as Sac-Foxes.

William Johnson Arrives Among the Mohawks

In 1738, a young Irishman named William Johnson settled in the eastern Mohawk River valley to manage the extensive lands his uncle owned there. Soon Johnson bought his own land from the Mohawk Haudenosaunee he befriended and began to engage in the fur trade. Because his trade was carried on through the Mohawks and other Haudenosaunee, William Johnson came to share the Haudenosaunee dream of controlling the northwestern furs. Their efforts were faltering by the time William Johnson arrived in New York, but Johnson was not the kind of man to allow events to develop haphazardly. Eager to make his fortune, the impatient Irishman revived the idea that the Haudenosaunee could conquer the nations to the north and to the west—and defeat the French as well. Most of the Haudenosaunee rejected this, for unlike this recent white arrival they understood the lessons of the last century. But Johnson's opportunity came when France and England once again went to war in 1744 (King George's War).

Johnson convinced the Mohawks, especially Chief Hendrick, that they should fight on the side of the English. The Mohawks and the few warriors from other confederacy nations who took an active part in the war soon discovered that the English military was poorly coordinated and that the New York colonists were still quite willing to let the Mohawks do much of the fighting along the frontier. Fortunately for Johnson, King George's War ended in 1748, before the Mohawks and other sympathetic Haudenosaunee became completely disillusioned with the military abilities of Johnson's fellow colonists. Whatever the New Yorkers' failings on the battlefield, the Haudenosaunee still appreciated the excellent goods the traders of Albany offered for furs, goods that were often given to the Haudenosaunee as presents.

The military stalemate in which the war ended returned the French-English conflict to each nation's fur traders, and because of their superior goods, the English traders had the clear advantage. The French watched with growing resentment as the traders of New York, Pennsylvania, Virginia and other English colonies pushed their trade routes farther westward into territory the French had previously dominated. Watching too was William Johnson, who saw that fortunes would follow the Union Jack. After his white wife died, in about 1752 Johnson met Gonwatsijayenni, or Mary (Molly) Brant, the Mohawk granddaughter of Hendrick and a politically powerful leader among her people. Mutually attracted, the two were probably married in a Mohawk ceremony (although not in a Christian one). With Molly at his side, Johnson continued his efforts to persuade the Haudenosaunee to give up their neutrality and join the English wholeheartedly against the French in a war to determine the future of the continent. Those royal wars for empire, as Indians, English and French alike knew, would revolve around the Haudenosaunee balance of power.

Perspective

The Haudenosaunee followed a policy of neutrality in order to maintain the best trading posture between rival colonial powers. As the Outagamie Wars demonstrated, the Haudenosaunee were not above using other Indian nations' warriors to keep a white power off balance. Like the Creeks, the Haudenosaunee faced the problem of keeping whites out of their homeland. The Mohawks, and in some cases the Oneidas, did succumb to colonial expansion, granting or selling some of their lands, but many Mohawks and Oneidas, especially those influenced by various Protestant missionaries, did so because they sincerely wished to adapt to the best of white technology and agriculture. The result was that by 1750 some Mohawks and Oneidas lived in cabins or frame houses of white design, farming or trading like the whites. Nevertheless, the Mohawks and Oneidas, whether or not they had adapted some white ways, protested vigorously and often successfully throughout the first half of the eighteenth century against unjust white claims.

The Haudenosaunees' greatest success, however, was in diverting most white settlement away from their own homeland and onto lands of their subject nations. When necessary, the Haudenosaunee intimidated subject nations into accepting Haudenosaunee decisions, as was demonstrated during a crisis between the Delawares and the colony of Pennsylvania over the Walking Purchase of 1737.

The Walking Purchase resulted from a desire by Thomas and John Penn, the non-Quaker heirs of William Penn, to determine the land boundaries of a

1686 deed that the Delawares had agreed to while William Penn was founding Quaker Pennsylvania. The deed stated that the boundaries would be determined by how far a man could walk in a day and a half, and concerned lands west of the Delaware River around its fork with the Lehigh River. William Penn had walked off forty miles, but definite boundaries had not been set. A new exploratory walk was taken in 1735, and a few days before the official walk was to commence an exact trail was marked out. Three of the fastest white "walkers" in the area were hired, and even though liquor and provisions were given to these men as they briskly strode off the land, one exhausted man dropped out on the first day and another failed on the second (September 19 and 20, 1737). Although three Indians were allowed to accompany the walkers, no provisions were shared with them, and they became so fatigued that sympathetic whites watching the proceedings on horseback allowed the Indians to alternate riding the whites' horses. On the first day the leader of the three accompanying Indians, Neepaheilomon (Joe Tuneam) protested that the whites were almost running, and one of the Delaware chiefs, Lapowinsa, refused to condone the proceedings after the first day. The whites proceeded anyway, and covered sixty-six and a half miles. The Penns found themselves twelve hundred square miles richer, at least thirty-five percent more than the Delawares expected.

Both the Delaware nation and Pennsylvania appealed to the Haudenosaunee to resolve the issue, and in the meantime the Delawares living within the disputed area refused to leave their homes. At a conference in Philadelphia in July 1742, the Haudenosaunee spokesman Canasatego assured Governor George Thomas that the Haudenosaunee would make sure the Delawares removed westward (Buck 1886; Boyd 1938, 35–36).

The Haudenosaunee other business at the Philadelphia conference was to complain about white encroachments on Haudenosaunee land. Having dealt so severely with the Delawares, the Haudenosaunee found the whites agreeable to halting the encroachments. While the Haudenosaunee kept their word and forced the Delawares to move, the whites did not adhere as strictly to the termination of white expansion onto Haudenosaunee lands. Nevertheless, the basic Haudenosaunee strategy of keeping most white settlement flowing toward subject nations such as the Susquehannas, Shawnees and Delawares continued to be successful.

But such a policy angered these subject nations. Moreover, the policy subverted the equality of all Indian nations proclaimed under the Tree of Peace.

The Pueblos in the Southwest had been unable to drive out the Spanish in the late 1600s, but the claims of kings had been stalemated there. The failed Spanish-Pueblo expedition of 1720 into Nebraska exemplified how Spain was unable to take the next step and expand its colonial invasion into the Plains region. But neither could France or England occupy the Plains. During this European stalemate, the Indian nations who already made their homes on these vast lands, and those Indian nations who moved into the Plains from the East, increasingly altered their cultures to adopt the horse. Because the Spanish, French and English could not really interfere with this development, Plains Indian cultures adapted and became increasingly dependent on the horse without the distractions of a major European invasion. Had any European power been able to assert dominance over the Plains in the 1700s, those cultural evolutions might have been cut short. The Pacific coast, in the meantime, would soon attract increasing attention from Spain and other European powers, most notably Russia.

East of the Mississippi, the fur trade in the Northeast and the deerskin trade in the Southeast had undermined traditional American Indian beliefs that recognized all life forms as interdependent, spiritual equals. The colonial economy had compromised and then corrupted those beliefs. It was hardly possible to maintain a world in balance when the economics of trade became overwhelmingly important to the survival of each Indian nation. Each chose to escalate its involvement in the colonial economy in order to obtain the trade goods and guns that would ensure their survival, realizing that if they rigidly maintained their old perspectives they would be conquered. Indian nations were aware of this paradox, and in the coming decades Indian spiritual and political leaders would envision answers. But the realities of the next half-century would test the strongest Indian confederacies in both the north and south. And whether they adopted new answers, Indian decisions would not be made in a vacuum. The colonists of Spain, France, Holland and England would continue to assert the claims of kings.

CHAPTER V

Trade & Land in the Contest for Empire

Events after 1750 forever altered the major pulse of Indian history north of Mexico. For more than a thousand years before Columbus, and for two centuries afterward, American Indian history had been shaped from south to north. The great Indian civilizations of Mesoamerica had exerted their influence northward and eastward, creating wave after wave of cultural frontiers north of Mexico. Then Spanish conquistadors moving northward from occupied Mexico or from the Caribbean invaded the Southwest and the Southeast. By the middle of the eighteenth century, however, the momentum of this history had been altered. The southern frontiers remained both important and dynamic, but during the late 1600s and the early 1700s, events to the Northeast increasingly became important. After 1750 until 1890, the vast continent north of Mexico would be shaped primarily by events and decisions coming from the east.

There was, as there always is, a major exception. This influence came from the north, from Alaska, and it was Russian. In 1728, Vitus Bering, a Dane working for Czar Peter the Great, sailed eastward from Siberia and reached an island off Alaska. Captain Bering's voyage led to Russia's claim to northwestern North America, including Alaska, and further voyages followed. Russia's colonists expanded eastward into Alaska and the Pacific Northwest just as Western Europeans had expanded westward across the Atlantic. The Russians sought new areas to fish and new sources of furs. Their expansion into Alaska was a logical extension of their imperial frontier in eastern Asia.

The Russian frontier moving into North America from Alaska was important. But Russia's influence remained regional. Russia's frontier never had a continental impact such as the one imposed by Spain, France, England or the

United States. Its history, stretching over more than a century, can be briefly summarized. By 1784, the Russians had established a permanent settlement at Kodiak. In 1799, Czar Paul I officially chartered the Russian-American Company as a fur trading company. With the same arrogance that marked Spanish, French English, and U.S. claims to Indian lands, Paul I asserted Russia's claims to Native lands in Alaska and the Pacific Northwest.

Russia's expansion into Alaska led to several conflicts with the various Native peoples of Alaska and one major war from 1802 to 1804. During that war, the Tlingits captured the Russian post at Sitka, but the Russians reconquered the area. In its pattern of trade, territorial claims and warfare, Russian imperialism followed the pattern of other European nations. In addition, the Russians also accidentally introduced diseases that felled large Native populations in Alaska.

The Russian frontier reached down the Pacific Northwest coast into northern California in 1809, when the Russians established Fort Ross at Bodega Bay. Natives such as the Aleuts and the Tlingits served aboard Russian ships, just as Indians along the Atlantic coast of New England and Canada set sail as seamen and fishermen aboard French, English and U.S. vessels. Native crewmen from Alaska even sailed west to Asia with their Russian shipmates.

But Russian frontier interests in North America were never the czars' primary concerns. Furthermore, the Russians had always faced stiff competition from the Spanish moving northward and the English and the United States moving westward. Fort Ross was abandoned in 1841. In 1867, Russia chose to give up its claims to Alaska by selling them to the United States.

Russia's impact on the cultures of Alaska remained dramatic, however. Native arts and music integrated far more of Russia than the Russian empire integrated of Alaska. This was initially due in large part to the missionaries of the Russian Orthodox Church. Like missionaries from Western Europe, Orthodox missionaries made significant inroads into the spiritual ideas of Alaskan Native populations, introducing Russian theology and religious symbols to Indian communities. Converted Natives sang Russian hymns. Native artists and musicians adapted Russian ideas into their arts with spectacular results. For example, a pole topped with the cross of the Russian Orthodox Church might stand next to a wooden burial chamber beautifully painted with the traditional motifs of Native beliefs (Fitzhugh and Cowell 1988, 70–82, 236–37, passim; Pierce 1972, 21).

In 1750, the greatest impact on Indian North America was building from the East, spurred by the continually expanding frontier of English-speaking people. This frontier, begun when John Cabot voyaged to Canada in 1597, never stopped. Its overwhelming momentum, however, was not secure until the last half of the eighteenth century.

In the decades after 1750, events in the Ohio River valley and the Great Lakes region set the pace of North American history. That this area was vital was apparent at the time. But the area is also important in retrospect. The defeats and victories of the Indian nations and the European colonists who contested for these areas established a pattern of frontier expansion that lasted for the next century and a half. In part, this was because of the continuing success of the English colonies. Virginia, New York and Massachusetts, for example, all had claims and economic interests in areas north of the Ohio River, and they had increasingly large populations to back up their claims. And French Canadians had long been adroitly exerting their influences from the St. Lawrence westward. Just as importantly, southern Indian nations such as the Cherokees realized the importance of this vast area. But in the contest for this vast area, the Haudenosaunee held the balance of power.

The political savvy of the Haudenosaunee would have made these nations major factors even if the struggle for the continent's soul had remained to the south of them. But when the momentum of history clearly shifted in their direction, the Iroquois were ready, prepared by a political philosophy and centuries of experience to influence the course of events.

Vignette: European Arrogance Toward the Haudenosaunee

Despite the sophistication of the Haudenosaunee and other Indian nations, Europeans were amazingly presumptuous in their dealings with them. None exceeded the gall of Captain Pierre Joseph Céloron de Bienville, his Canadian governor the Comte de la Galissoniere and the King of France himself, Louis xv. Céloron was ordered by the governor and the king to canoe and march through western Haudenosaunee country south of Fort Niagara. Then he was to proceed down the Allegheny River among the Senecas and Delawares, continuing on to the forks of the Ohio, and then westward along the Ohio River through the lands of the Delawares and Shawnees (subject nations of the Haudenosaunee). He was then expected to move northward along the Miami

River among the Miamis (Twightwees), some of whom were also subject to the Haudenosaunee. Finally, he was to find his way home to Montreal via Fort Pontchartrain (at Detroit), Lake Erie, and Lake Ontario. As instructed, all along the way he buried little lead plates inscribed in French stating that all these lands were claimed by Louis xv (to whom they were vital to link his Louisiana and Canadian colonies and to block expanding English colonies).

Because the Haudenosaunee had conquered this land almost seventy years before, and the Haudenosaunee did not view intruders lightly, Céloron wisely did not go alone. Setting out from Montreal on June 15, 1749, Céloron was accompanied by a priest, eight officers, six cadets, two hundred soldiers and thirty Indians from Canada. He proceeded to a picturesque spot at the head of the Allegheny River where there were no Haudenosaunee at the moment, tacked to a tree a little tin sign with the arms of France stamped on it, and buried at the tree's roots one of the official leaden plates. A ceremony accompanied this act, with all the troops lined up. Céloron duly took possession of the area in the name of Louis xv and made this claim all more official and legal, at least to the French mind, by having a sheet of paper describing the proceedings signed on the spot by the expedition's own notary. Then the party pushed on, preceded by a mixed-blood interpreter named Chabert de Joncaire, who went ahead to prepare local towns for the arrival of Céloron.

Many times the townspeople simply abandoned their homes, not having enough men to challenge the two hundred troops that followed. But at the Seneca town of La Paille Coupee, Joncaire persuaded the inhabitants to wait and listen to Céloron. When he arrived, Céloron read a message to the Seneca Haudenosaunee from La Galissoniere that bluntly stated the French position. Céloron was there, Governor La Galissoniere's message explained, because English fur traders had moved into the area since the end of the last war in 1748. Calling the Seneca Haudenosaunee "my children," the governor's message declared that the land belonged to the French: "I will not endure the English on my land.... [F]ollow my advice, and the sky will always be calm and clear over your villages. I expect from you an answer worthy of true children" (Parkman [1884] 1983, 875). The surprised Senecas, outnumbered by the soldiers, agreed to drive the English traders out of the area, but only because they feared French muskets.

Céloron's expedition had revealed a new desperation on the part of the French. Unable to compete with the English in a free market because the English undersold them by fifty and even seventy-five percent, and unable to match the manpower available in the expanding English coastal colonies, the French had decided to force the issue by threatening war. Céloron continued beyond the Seneca town, traveling through a major section of the Haudenosaunee's frontier of settlement, an area also shared by many members of the various subject nations of the Haudenosaunee. Céloron reached a rock chiseled with Indian hieroglyphics and buried a plate beneath it.

Distributing presents to the Indians, Céloron left and continued down the Ohio to Wheeling Creek where he buried another of his plaques. Two more were buried later at the mouths of the Muskingum and the Great Kanawha rivers. Farther down the Ohio as the Frenchmen neared the Shawnee town of Scioto, Céloron ordered the interpreter Joncaire ahead to prepare the way, but the Shawnees shot Joncaire's flag of truce full of holes, surrounded him, and threatened to kill him. Only the intervention of a Haudenosaunee who realized Joncaire was half-Haudenosaunee prevented his murder. Céloron wisely set up camp for the night on the shore opposite Scioto. Finally some chiefs agreed to come to Céloron's tent and hold a council. Having already modified the tone of his declaration once since his first contact with the Senecas of La Paille Coupee, Céloron gave the Scioto chiefs an even looser version of the governor and king's original statement. While he warned as he had before that the English presence among the Indians meant that someday the English would seize Indian lands—certainly an accurate prophecy—Céloron did not mention that the king of France claimed the Ohio River as his own. Before Céloron and his men left Scioto, he also went through the motions of warning the English fur traders present to leave. Céloron and his men turned up the Miami River.

On the Miamis' west bank, some fifty miles north of the Ohio, lay the relatively new Miami settlement of Pique Town, or Pickawillany. The French named Pickawillany's chief, a leader of the Piankashaw band of Miamis, La Demoiselle, but to the English he was known as Old Briton. In 1747, Old Briton had moved his people to this new location sixty miles southeast of their original homes in order to be closer to the English and their cheap but high-quality trade goods. Previously tied to the French, Old Briton's people were disgusted because the French had not been able, even with their help, to defeat the English-sponsored Chickasaws who raided from the south.

The French were also unable to supply the Miamis with all necessary trade goods during King George's War (1744–1748) because of an English blockade of Canada. The Haudenosaunee, ever alert to the expansion of their own power, used these circumstances to encourage the discontented Miami faction to join the Haudenosaunee-English trading system. Accepting at least some Haudenosaunee jurisdiction, Old Briton's Miamis formally took their place in this Haudenosaunee-English plan in Pennsylvania at the Lancaster Treaty of 1748. There the three Miami-speaking representatives of Old Briton and his people delegated their speaking authority to an Oneida Haudenosaunee, Monacatoocha (also known as Scarrooyady), who was already the deputy assigned to the Shawnees by the council of the Haudenosaunee. Because of an injury suffered by Monacatoocha, the Miamis were finally represented by Andrew Montour, son of Madame Montour, a great Haudenosaunee mixed-blood interpreter who exerted influence within the confederacy in the first half of the eighteenth century. With this Haudenosaunee-Miami-English trade alliance so recently formed, it was one of Céloron's assignments in 1749 to persuade Old Briton to move closer to the French at Fort Miami. Céloron, however, failed to convince Old Briton to give up the English trade and to move. The chief was polite and thanked Céloron for the advice passed on from his French "father" Louis xv, but he promised only that he would move at a more convenient time. Céloron and his men burned their own worn canoes and trudged cross-country to Fort Miami where they replenished their supplies and, after obtaining new canoes, went back to Canada.

Céloron's mission revealed to the French just how powerful an influence the English fur traders were exerting in the formerly French-dominated territory. The Haudenosaunee had also increased their power at the expense of the French, and the Miamis had a higher standard of living now that they could trade their furs at English instead of French prices. Within the two years after Céloron's visit, for example, the Miamis were so impressed by English goods that more and more of them gave up their homes and flocked to Old Briton's Pickawillany, so that the town grew to eight times its former population. All that the French could now claim in the Ohio Valley were their lead plates, insipid symbols of the grandeur of Louis xv, buried in obscurity amid a bustling Indian-English fur trade.

The English colonists were not only expanding their influence by trading; they were also busy making treaties that enabled them to occupy Indian lands. In the Lancaster Treaty of 1744 (not to be confused with the 1748 treaty) the Haudenosaunee had given Virginia colonists the right to resettle certain lands that the whites had once occupied. These lands were primarily those of the subject nations of the Haudenosaunee, once again revealing the Haudenosaunee strategy to divert white settlement away from their homeland.

Land-Hungry English in the Ohio River Valley & Competition with the French

In 1747, a group of land speculators in Virginia, Maryland, Pennsylvania and London formed the Ohio Company. In the summer of 1752, using their political influence, the Ohio Company managed to have a council convened by colonial officials at Logstown with various Indian nations. The pretense of the officials was that they represented the Virginia government and wished to distribute a gift of trade goods from the king of England. Their real purpose was to cheat the Indians out of all their hunting lands around the forks of the Ohio, and as much of the Ohio River valley as they could get.

The Ohio Company hired Andrew Montour, the Haudenosaunee mixed-blood, to get the most he could from the Indians during the council. In return, the company promised Montour extensive lands that he could sell at an enormous profit. While the official Virginia commissioners treated the Indians royally, pretending to have their best interests at heart, Montour together with white interpreter George Croghan praised the Virginians to the Indians, subtly preparing the Indians for the shock that soon came.

On the basis of the Lancaster Treaty of 1744, the commissioners claimed the Indians had granted the whites the entire Ohio River valley and that it seemed only fair that, since the Indians accepted the king's presents of goods, the Indians take the opportunity to verify this claim. The English carefully avoided any discussion that might allow the subject of fraud to be brought up. Despite the presents, the Indians were still shocked at the claim. The Seneca Chief Tanacharisson, called the Half-King by the English because he was the representative of the Haudenosaunee to all those nations in the Ohio country who were subject to the Haudenosaunee, spoke for the assembled Indians:

> We are glad you have acquainted us with the Right to those Lands, & we assure you we are willing to confirm any Thing our Council [at Onondaga] has done in Regard to the Land, but we never understood, before you told us Yesterday, that the Lands then sold were to extend further to the Sun setting than the Hill on the other Side of the Alleghany Hill, so that we can't give you a further Answer now [before consulting the council at Onondaga]. (*Virginia Magazine of History and Biography* 1905, 168)

The land speculators finally had their way, however, because there was no way the Indians could prove the Lancaster Treaty of 1744 was otherwise, having merely heard an interpreter's version of it. More important, however, the Haudenosaunee finally gave in because they wanted to retain the English fur trade. At the moment, the Haudenosaunee especially needed the trade because they, and particularly the Senecas, were aiding the Cherokees in a war against the Creeks (each combatant Indian nation being supplied by its adjacent English colonies until the war ended late in 1753). Thus in 1752, English trade seemed of greater importance to the Haudenosaunee than worrying about the loss of some of their subjects' lands or lands on their own expanding frontier.

Because the Haudenosaunee claimed the area by right of seventeenth-century conquest, the attending Haudenosaunee sachems signed the Logstown Treaty of 1752 on the part of their subject or allied nations—the Delawares, Shawnees, Miamis and some Hurons. In exchange for seven hundred pounds of goods that were paid for by the king and not the speculators, the Ohio Company gained 200,000 acres of Indian land.

The Logstown land deal may also have been peacefully worked out among the Haudenosaunee and the Indians of the Ohio, because the presence of English settlers could have been a deterrent to French interference in the Indian-English fur trade. The French, however, decided to take swift action against the most vulnerable yet significant center of expanding Haudenosaunee and English influence: Old Briton's Miami town of Pickawillany, where as many as fifty English fur traders at a time would gather to trade at the English-built, palisaded log warehouse amid the town's bark wigwams. The Haudenosaunee-English trade expansion had so impressed the Indians living near the French fort at Detroit that many previously pro-French Indians were considering trade and even alliance with the Haudenosaunee and the English. The French suspected that even the Osages, who lived west of the Mississippi in Missouri, might join the Illinois and Miamis in a general attack on French posts scattered among them. The Ottawas, however, mindful of their century-old role as fur-trading middlemen for the French and not eager to see the French trade diminished at any point, decided as did some Ojibwas (Chippewas) to join a Frenchman, Charles Langlade, to do something about it. Gathering 250 warriors, they paddled from Michilimackinac in northern Michigan down to Detroit, where they received instructions from the French government to kill pro-English Indians and capture all English traders at Pickawillany. They set off southward, and at nine o'clock on the morning of June 21, 1752, they struck.

Miami women in the cornfields surrounding Pickawillany were the first to see the approaching raiders. Crying the alarm, they ran into the town, but there was little anyone could do, for the raiders had chosen the time of attack carefully. Recent French presents had relaxed the Miamis' vigilance, and all but a few of the warriors were out on the summer hunt. The Ottawas and Ojibwas swept through the town and charged at the palisaded warehouse of the English. There were only eight traders in the town at the time, and three were captured before they could get into the small stockade. The other five barred the gate and defended their small compound. In the meantime, fourteen Miami warriors died trying to halt the attackers. Among those slain was Old Briton himself. The five white traders held out until afternoon, when three finally surrendered and two escaped into the woods. One of the six captured traders was immediately stabbed to death because he was severely wounded and could not be taken north.

Pickawillany was burned, and the other five captives were taken to Canada and presented to the new governor, the Marquis Duquesne. Before the Ottawas and Ojibwas left Pickawillany, however, they performed a ceremony that seemed barbarous to the French and the English when they heard about it, but which among these Indians was quite an honor. The Ottawas and Ojibwas had such great respect for the slain chief Old Briton that they wished to share his qualities. They boiled and ate him.

The attack on Pickawillany came, coincidentally, only eight days after the Haudenosaunee sachems signed the Logstown Treaty. With the destruction of Pickawillany, however, the French had directly challenged the Haudenosaunee-English fur trade at a time when France and England were at peace in Europe. The French had thrown down the gauntlet, and the Haudenosaunee watched to see whether the English would pick it up. The Haudenosaunee were not likely to declare war on the French without a simultaneous declaration by the English. Haudenosaunee policy was to play the English off against the French.

The Haudenosaunee also contrived as often as possible to let other Indian nations, in this case the Miamis, bear the brunt of any violence that might evolve from either Haudenosaunee or white diplomacies. Furthermore, the Haudenosaunee were not likely to push the French out of lands they had just turned over to English jurisdiction—especially if a lack of English will to fight was a precursor of a lack of English will to maintain the trade. As for the white combatants, both the English and the French knew exactly how that issue would be decided: the eighteenth-century version of an arms race in America was tallied according to the number of forts each side possessed and where each was located.

The logical objective for both the French and the English this time was the forks of the Ohio (Pittsburgh), recently claimed by the Ohio Company in the Logstown Treaty. If the French could occupy the forts of the Ohio, they could choke off English expansion in trade and settlement. At the same time, they would be demonstrating to the Indians west of the forks that their economic future was strictly with the French trade coming down the Great Lakes from Canada. In addition, the French would be demonstrating their power to the Haudenosaunee, all six nations of which hunted in the area and had relatives living there in permanent towns that made up the Haudenosaunee's own frontier. For their part, the English had to prove their ability to fight. They did a remarkably poor job of that for most of the next six years.

The coming conflict would demonstrate the characteristics of each antagonist: the English system of freewheeling colonial enterprise in furs and land speculation resulted in impressive economic expansion, but at the same time made it difficult to bring various colonies together in a concerted effort when threatened. On the other hand, the authoritarian centralism of the French all but eliminated economic expansion in peacetime, but resulted in relatively coordinated and rapid military expansion in times of war.

A year after Pickawillany had been destroyed, the English colonies reinstated the steady flow of presents to the Miamis, Shawnees, Delawares and Haudenosaunee, which, along with the trade goods, kept the Indians from allying with the French. At first the English hoped that the Indians themselves would do the fighting and that the English would be able to stand by and profit from selling guns. Whites hoped that the Haudenosaunee would consider the attack on Pickawillany a direct affront to their own sphere of influence, and indeed for a while there were tomahawks and war belts of black wampum passed back and forth among potential Indian allies. But, as South Carolinian Edmond Atkin testified in 1755, "No people in the World understand and pursue their true National Interest better than the Indians" (Jacobs 1967, 38). The Haudenosaunee and other Indians wisely discerned that the heart of the issue was a conflict of French and English interests and that the Indians could remain aloof if they managed their affairs carefully. They knew that to go to war would ultimately benefit the whites more than the Indians. For the moment, it was better to wait and see.

English & French at War in America (French and Indian War)

The conflict that became known in American history as the French and Indian War began escalating until the French surrendered Canada in 1763. The first victories, however, went to the French, and Indians used the circumstances to each of their nations' best advantage.

The Haudenosaunee: From Neutrality to Sometime Allies of the English

In the late spring and early summer of 1753, French troops moved into the Allegheny River valley and began establishing a string of three small forts intended to stretch southward from Lake Erie (at Erie, Pennsylvania) toward the forks of the Ohio. Many Haudenosaunee living there protested vigorously, but they were told that the land belonged to the King of France. Other Haudenosaunee, as well as some Delawares and Shawnees, volunteered to help the French. The Haudenosaunee expressed their exasperation in a September 1753 council at Onondaga with an important New York trader and politician, William Johnson, complaining about the efforts of all white men to engulf them: "[W]e don't know what you Christians, English and French together, intend; we are so hemm'd in by both, that we have hardly a hunting place left" (O'Callaghan and Fernow 1855, 5:813). Johnson could do nothing, however, and among the Haudenosaunee diplomats along the Allegheny, the next hope lay in a young envoy from the colony of Virginia, twenty-one-year-old George Washington. As a major in the Virginia militia, Washington was sent by Virginia and the Ohio Land Company to warn the French to cease building their forts because the lands there did not belong to the King of France, but rather to Virginia. Because the Haudenosaunee wanted to assure the continuance of the English fur trade, they again preferred the English to the French at the moment. Tanacharisson (Half-King) and three other important Haudenosaunee accompanied Washington, his white guide Christopher Gist and six other whites as they made their way to two French forts, Venango and Le Boeuf. Tanacharisson had gone to Fort Le Boeuf in September 1753 and told the French to leave. Instead, the French commander contemptuously insulted Tanacharisson, who left in a weeping rage. Now, two months later, he was at George Washington's side. At both forts, the French attempted to conciliate Tanacharisson and beguile his associates with liquor and presents. But

Washington and Gist were alert to these bribes, and Tanacharisson continued as their guide back toward Virginia after the French had politely informed Washington that they had no intention of leaving the area. On their way back, Washington's party met some pro-French Indians, one of whose guns accidentally—it was claimed—went off while pointed in the direction of Washington and Gist, who were about thirty feet away. Washington thought it prudent not to try to punish the Indian responsible.

It was clear to the Virginians that if they were going to eject the French it would take more than words. It was also quite clear that the Indians, especially the Haudenosaunee, whose council was in close contact with Tanacharisson, were determined for the moment to remain neutral observers. The English decided to build a fort at the forks of the Ohio in the spring of 1754 in order to block further French advance. But on April 17, about five hundred French and Indians surprised the forty-one Englishmen building the fort, and obtained their surrender without a fight. All were allowed to march south, where they met George Washington, accompanied by about 120 militiamen. On May 27, Christopher Gist warned Washington that a party of French spies was somewhere ahead. Tanacharisson sent a messenger that evening from his own camp advising Washington that he thought he had found the French in a hidden glen. Washington ordered forty of his men to prepare for a night march and a surprise attack. The young Virginian and his men groped their way through a rainy black night to Tanacharisson's camp, which they reached by sunrise. Tanacharisson, the Oneida leader Monacatoocha and a few other leading warriors joined them, quickly and quietly leading Washington and his men to the very campfires of the French before they were discovered. Washington's men and the Haudenosaunee swiftly attacked, killed ten Frenchmen and captured twenty-two, allowing only one to escape. Washington's Haudenosaunee allies scalped the dead and sent the scalps to nearby Indian nations as invitations to fight the French invaders. The victory was short-lived. The French soon sent out more than five hundred of their soldiers and perhaps a hundred Canadian Indians and a few Delawares against Washington. On July 3, the young commander was forced to surrender his four hundred and fifty men after defending his hastily erected "Fort Necessity." No Indians had fought at Washington's side that day because they had always doubted the strength of Washington's fort. The French allowed Washington and his men to return to Virginia, and the Indians of the area pondered their departure carefully. They became convinced that Washington's surrender at Fort Necessity dramatized their own necessity: neutrality.

As Washington retreated, an important meeting was coming to a close in Albany, New York. Called by New York to hear complaints of the Haudenosaunee about white crimes, the meeting included twenty-three delegates from New York, Massachusetts, New Hampshire, Connecticut, Rhode Island, Pennsylvania and Maryland. These delegates hoped to persuade the Haudenosaunee to join the English in the coming war against the French, for the colonists all recognized that the Haudenosaunee were the key to the continent. Few Haudenosaunee attended, however, so distrustful had they become of the English. Chief Hendrick of the Mohawks, a friend of William Johnson, enumerated the grievances of the Haudenosaunee: lands were being taken away from them illegally; the whites traded too much rum and not enough truly valuable goods; Albany traders were selling guns and other goods to the very Frenchmen the delegates were proposing the Haudenosaunee attack. (In fact, the Albany traders had consistently and illegally always traded with French Canada. Furthermore, the Haudenosaunee, especially the Mohawks, were actively involved with the Albany traders as major players in this illegal trade, carrying and canoeing goods back and forth.) Chief Hendrick also complained that Virginia and Pennsylvania were trading, claiming and settling around the forks of the Ohio and elsewhere without the consent of the Haudenosaunee, and thus were as guilty as the French who built forts on these lands. Lieutenant Governor James DeLancey denied all these charges. Thirty wagonloads of presents and the appointment of William Johnson as Colonel of the Six Nations at the request of the Haudenosaunee and the recommendation of England's Board of Trade calmed the Haudenosaunee for the moment. They left the Congress skeptical, however, that the confederacy would ever join these corrupt Englishmen in a war. The presents bought the English only continued Haudenosaunee neutrality.

The Albany Congress had other business as well: The whites wanted to form their various colonies into a union. Benjamin Franklin of Pennsylvania had coined a catchy motto for the meeting: "Join or Die." Colonial unity seemed imperative, because it appeared that the current crisis at the forks of the Ohio might evolve into a war, and that this war would end only after either England or France dominated North America. Three years earlier, in 1751, Franklin had expressed the opinion that a colonial union loyal to the king of England could be achieved:

It would be a very strange Thing, if six Nations of ignorant Savages [the Haudenosaunee] should be capable of forming a Scheme for such

a Union, and be able to execute it in such a Manner, as that it has sub-
sisted Ages, and appears indissoluble; and yet that a like Union should
be impracticable for ten or a Dozen English Colonies, to whom it is
more necessary, and must be more advantageous; and who cannot be
supposed to want an equal Understanding of their Interests. (Labaree
1961, 118–19; cf. Lemay 1987, 444)

In referring to "ignorant Savages" Franklin drastically underestimated the
Haudenosaunee. In believing the whites could unite, he overestimated the
English. No union—political or military—was formed, for the proposals of the
Albany Congress were rejected in every one of the colonies.

In the fall of 1754, preparations were begun for an English expedition
against the new French post, Fort Duquesne. In addition to regular British
troops and Virginia militia under Major General Edward Braddock (George
Washington was an aide-de-camp), the colonial governments of Pennsylvania
and Virginia hoped to attract hundreds of Indian allies. But rivalries among
the South Carolina and Virginia governors and traders created a state of confusion. The Catawba and Cherokee Indians of the Carolinas, who were interested in joining Braddock but who had been disillusioned by the English on
numerous occasions, decided against joining the expedition. However, the
Oneida leader, Monacatoocha, with the help of Indian agents George Croghan
and Conrad Weiser, convinced numbers of Delawares, Shawnees and Iroquois
to join the British. Totaling two hundred, including women and children, with
perhaps fifty warriors among them, these Indians were quite willing allies. The
Haudenosaunee thus permitted some of their members a limited partisanship
toward the English, perhaps to test the political wind while at the same time
continuing their policy of encouraging Indians on their frontiers to take the
risks for them. Gathered at Aughwick, Pennsylvania, by September 1754, they
waited for the English to take action, but no action came. Weiser could not tell
the Indians when they would be needed, and gradually they became disgusted
with English indecision. In addition, dysentery broke out among the Indians,
and an unscrupulous mixed-blood trader plied them with liquor.

In 1755, the English finally launched their expedition against Fort
Duquesne itself. Commanded by Braddock, the Oneida scouts under
Monacatoocha scouted for the British. They reported on July 6 that they had
only seen a few Frenchmen in the fort. On that same day, Monacatoocha's son
returned to the British camp after giving chase to nearby French-allied Indian

scouts and was challenged by Virginia rangers to give the countersign. The Oneida gave the correct response—laying weapons on the ground and holding up any nearby plant or tree—but, perhaps accidentally, he was shot and killed. Braddock could have lost the other seven Indian scouts on the spot had he not understood the Indian custom in circumstances such as this, which did not require revenge or capital punishment but rather condolence gifts to the relatives. Braddock immediately bestowed the customary gifts and expressed his sorrow with such sincerity that Monacatoocha and the other Haudenosaunee intensified their feeling of loyalty to the commander. The army continued to march on with the Indians carefully scouting the way.

On July 9, shortly before three in the afternoon, the Haudenosaunee scouts and George Croghan suddenly discovered two hundred French and six hundred French-allied Indians making their way toward Braddock's column. Sufficiently warned, the advance party of British troops executed the standard maneuver of falling back to join the main army. But the main army continued to march forward into the withdrawing vanguard and chaos ensued. The French and their Indian allies had already taken the opportunity to spread out around the British flanks. Hiding behind trees and rocks and fighting wilderness style, the French and Indians had an overwhelming advantage over the more numerous British troops because Braddock tried to respond to the attack in the usual European style instead of fighting as the wilderness dictated. Braddock bravely tried to rally his troops time and time again, having a total of four horses shot from under him until he too fell mortally wounded. The British army was totally defeated and withdrew under Washington.

The scouts under Monacatoocha had fought bravely in the battle, and Pennsylvania's governor Hunter Morris commended them personally. But such commendations were not enough to convince other Indians, including the Delawares, the Shawnees and the Haudenosaunee, that the English were capable soldiers. On the other hand, the French had proved themselves and had obtained the aid of Caughnawagas, Abnakis, Hurons, Potawatomis, Ottawas and Ojibwas, as well as some Shawnees, Mingos and perhaps even Miamis who saw a new future for themselves separate from the Haudenosaunee and English.

The only English victory of any consequence in 1755 was achieved by the Haudenosaunee's supposed friend, William Johnson, whom Braddock had appointed that same year as superintendent of the Indians north of the Ohio River. Johnson defeated an army of fifteen hundred French soldiers under a German mercenary general, Baron Dieskau, on the southern shore of Lake

George on September 8, 1755. Johnson's victory was in no small part due to the sacrifice and bravery of Mohawk and other Indian allies under the Mohawk Chief Hendrick (Tiyanoga or Thoyanoguen). Hendrick, two hundred of his warriors and a contingent of a thousand white men were ordered out on a morning scout to attack the French. Hendrick warned Johnson that the force was not strong enough, and referring to his warriors and the thousand whites admonished, "If they are to be killed, they are too many; if they are to fight, they are too few" (Parkman [1884] 1983, 1052; cf. Peckham 1964, 149). But Johnson sent them out anyway, and Hendrick, seventy-five years old and too fat to lead his men on foot, mounted a horse and resolved to be at the front of the column. Most of the column walked into an ambush deep in the forest set by Dieskau, Abnakis and Canadian Haudenosaunee from Caughnawaga.

When the Canadian Haudenosaunee saw their Mohawk relatives at the head of the English column, they may have warned them of the ambush by calling out or firing a musket before the column was completely into the trap. The French troops opened fire in deadly volleys and cut down the first ranks of the Mohawks and white soldiers. Hendrick's horse was shot from under him, and as he tried to get up, a Frenchman bayoneted him to death. Hendrick's warriors and a large contingent of whites fought a brave rearguard action as the rest retreated. Back in the main camp, Johnson heard the gunfire coming closer and realized he would soon be attacked. The retreating column bought Johnson valuable time by not panicking, returning to the camp, where seventeen hundred men, including one hundred Indians, hastily threw up a small wall of felled trees and overturned boats. Finally, the retreating column reached them and streamed through the lines to at least temporary safety. The French troops, resplendent in their white uniforms, marched in perfect columns out of the pine forest and down a dirt road to make a frontal assault on Johnson. Dieskau, like Braddock, was drilled in the European combat of the open field. Johnson's men, including the Indians, fought stubbornly from behind their rough barricade and from behind trees. Johnson's four cannons raked the approaching French troops and the white-uniformed ranks reddened with blood. Dieskau reformed his men and attacked again, but when the attack faltered he went into the combat zone to review the situation. The withering fire cutting down his troops soon wounded him. Suddenly the English and Indian defenders leapt their barricades and counterattacked the failing French line. The French and their Indian allies were defeated, and the wounded Dieskau found himself a prisoner of war.

William Johnson was made a baronet for his victory, but it had cost the Indians, mostly Mohawks, too high a price: thirty-eight killed and twelve wounded. On the western frontier of the Haudenosaunee, the Braddock defeat caused the Shawnees, Delawares, and Ohio Valley Haudenosaunee (Mingos and Senecas for the most part), who at first favored the British, to reconsider their position. Many of the Ohio Haudenosaunee decided on neutrality for the rest of the war. But others joined the Delawares and Shawnees against the English. One reason was their desire to stop English settlers from encroaching on their lands. The Shawnees and the Delawares had an additional reason: the weakened English position brought about by the defeat of Braddock forced the Haudenosaunee to be less belligerent toward the French lest the French counterattack. The Mohawks reduced their aid to the British, while many Senecas favored the French. With the overall Haudenosaunee hesitant during the last half of 1755, however, the Shawnees and Delawares saw their opportunity, as did many nations further west such as the Miamis and Illinois, to break away from the subject rule of the Haudenosaunee. The Delawares and Shawnees began attacking the frontier settlements of the Pennsylvania, Maryland and Virginia whites whom they considered trespassers, and the French happily gave them the guns to do it.

The failure of the English to capture the French fort at Niagara further discouraged the Haudenosaunee, already dismayed at Braddock's defeat. The confederacy had volunteered to help the English drive the French out of their fort, and had counted on the English backing up their high-sounding plans with action. But when the English called off their expedition in October 1755, the Haudenosaunee weighed the alternatives and decided that it was too risky to continue offering help to the English. After a long series of negotiations, however, Haudenosaunee and English agreed on a common goal: ending the warfare of the Delawares and the Shawnees on the Pennsylvania-Virginia-Maryland frontier. The Haudenosaunee were anxious to take any steps that would prevent the erosion of their power. The English wanted to stop a frontier war they were losing. The Delawares and the Shawnees, who lived closest to the white frontier, were not getting the French aid they had hoped for, and so in July 1756, they had their representatives meet with the Haudenosaunee leaders and Sir William Johnson at the latter's Mohawk Valley home, Fort Johnson. The Delawares insisted that the Haudenosaunee no longer call them "women." Johnson, but not the Haudenosaunee, publicly declared the Delawares men, removing what he called "this invidious distinction," and a dance by Mohawks, Oneidas, Onondagas, Mohegans, Delawares and Shawnees celebrated their renewed unity. Many Delawares and Shawnees who lived further west were not represented at the council, however, and they continued their war (O'Callaghan and Fernow 1856, 160).

In August 1756, despite Haudenosaunee warnings to the English of an impending French attack, the Marquis de Montcalm destroyed Oswego, New York, on Lake Ontario, one of the key English-Haudenosaunee trading centers. English prestige among the Haudenosaunee sank again. In the meantime, Cherokees and Catawbas had been recruited as mercenaries by the English to fight along the Pennsylvania and Virginia frontiers from 1756 through 1758. Even though sometimes poorly paid in British goods, the warriors of these two nations became the main British army on this frontier after the defeat of Braddock, and were a major factor in causing some of the Delawares and Shawnees to make peace in July 1756 at Fort Johnson.

French-allied Indians, acting alongside French troops and undertaking their own raids as well, were keeping the English colonies and armies off balance, forcing the English to concentrate on defending their own frontiers, and preventing a land invasion of Canada. While the French benefited greatly, it is difficult to see what the Indians were winning. Those close to the English frontiers such as the Delawares and Shawnees were buffeted by counterattacks launched by colonial militia and pro-English Indians. Indians, such as the Illinois and the Ojibwas, who lived far from the English or were tied to the French trade, were losing men and yet were not receiving adequate trade goods for their nations' services, for French promises of goods were empty from Louisiana to Canada. As the pro-French Indians died, their chief Indian rivals—the Creeks in the south and the Haudenosaunee in the north—were relatively unscathed and likely to emerge from the war physically stronger.

Another factor worked against the pro-French Indians: their concept of warfare. As recently as half a century before, The Europeans widely and enthusiastically practiced the torturing of prisoners and carrying warfare to civilian populations without regard to sex or age. But these long-established European customs were currently falling out of vogue (although they would be reinstated by the end of the century). In an unusual burst of ethical and philosophical debates called "the Enlightenment," a considerable number of whites in Europe and America were determined to try to confine their incredibly destructive wars to the soldiers in their armies. While they failed miserably, the French and English—whether European or colonist—resented the fact that the

Indians weren't even contemplating a change in tactics. More important than philosophical theory was the fact that whites who had lost kin would be sure to seek revenge. The French and Indian War did much to reinforce, as had each previous war, the white colonists' belief that the Indian frontier was a border which the white man's standard of civilization had to overrun. No matter that the whites' present and past military tactics were similar: it was enough for them to maintain that they intended, someday, to change, whereas the Indians intended to remain the same.

No incident in the French and Indian War was more detrimental to the Indian's future image than that which followed the surrender of about two thousand British soldiers and militia on August 9, 1757, at Fort William Henry on the southern shore of Lake George, New York. Accepting the English capitulation was the Marquis de Montcalm, who promised the English troops that they could march southward to join their English comrades at Fort Edward on the promise they would not fight for eighteen months. Montcalm's French army of six thousand whites was augmented by about two thousand Indians, who represented almost every major Indian nation then fighting for the French: Hurons, Nipissings, Abnakis, Algonquins from Three Rivers, Micmacs and Malecites, Ottawas, Ojibwas, Mississaugas, Potawatomis, Menominees, Sauks and Foxes, Winnebagos, Miamis, Iowas and Canadian Haudenosaunee from Caughnawaga, Two Mountains, and La Presentation. These Indians already felt that Montcalm had ignored their military opinions before the fort finally surrendered, and that French officers treated them like slaves. They were frustrated over an endemic French shortage of goods and supplies. They regarded themselves as superior fighters to both the English and French. And there was the very real problem that the many warriors had language barriers both with each other and with the French—for example, not one Frenchman in the expedition could converse with the Iowas.

Immediately after the surrender, some Indians slaughtered some sick English prisoners. The following day, the sick as well as able-bodied English soldiers, together with civilians including women and children, marched out of the fort. Under the terms of their surrender, they were to be allowed to move to the safety of English-held territory to the south of them. But Indians attacked the English column. Montcalm and other French officers tried to intervene, but their efforts failed to protect their helpless foe. At least fifty English were killed and six hundred kidnapped. Four hundred of those captured were released that same day, but two hundred were carried back to Canada. Montcalm and the other French who were present never overcame their shame for failing to ensure the safety of the English who had surrendered to them. The massacre would become immortalized in American literature in the 1826 novel *The Last of the Mohicans* by James Fenimore Cooper. But Cooper, like the English colonists whose neighbors had been killed, ignored the irony of this cruel event. The massacre had been set in motion by Abnakis, whom the French had set against New England since the seventeenth century. The Abnakis were no longer representatives of a purely Indian civilization. For over fifty years they had been a part of French civilization's form of Christianity, and thus the Abnaki warriors were listed as Christians on Montcalm's rolls. Tragically, the other Indians allied with Montcalm had followed the leadership of these Christians and had taken up the slaughter. The French officers were painfully aware that Christians had started the massacre. In the meantime, the English used the massacre to rally resistance to the French. And fate had its own revenge. Some of the Indians dug up, plundered and scalped the bodies in the fort's graveyard. Indian camps were soon after swept by agony and death, for many of the fort's disinterred had been the victims of smallpox (Hamilton 1964, 172, 174–75; cf. Steele 1990, 109–85).

In July 1758, four hundred Haudenosaunee and other Indians accompanied but did not give much assistance to the English in their unsuccessful attack on French Fort Ticonderoga on the southern shore of Lake Champlain, New York. But English prestige in the north was renewed with the capture of Fort Duquesne in November 1758, a feat made possible in part by well over six hundred Cherokees, Delawares and some Haudenosaunee.

Most of the Cherokees, however, had refused to accompany the final push toward the fort, much to the confusion of the English general, John Forbes. The Cherokees' reasons were that they didn't wish to harm Shawnees with whom their leaders were independently making peace, and that the Shawnees had informed the Cherokees that the French intended to abandon the fort. The Cherokee Chief Attakullaculla, called the Little Carpenter, informed Forbes of the French intention and then headed home with most of his warriors to handle a Cherokee-Virginia crisis. Forbes had Attakullaculla seized as a deserter, stripped of his weapons and escorted out of the borders of Virginia. Attakullaculla's information proved true, however, and the French abandoned Fort Duquesne.

Renewed enthusiasm for the English cause was not lessened by the fact that the English had better trading goods and presents than the French. As many as nine hundred of the Haudenosaunee warriors fought well alongside Sir

William Johnson and 2,300 white troops in the siege and eventual capture of the French fort at Niagara on July 25, 1759. During the siege, the Haudenosaunee agreed that no French prisoner was to be harmed, and they kept their word. Johnson also decided not to allow them the spoils of war: the trade goods inside the fort. The major post of the French fur trade was now under Haudenosaunee-English control. The Haudenosaunee was again impressed when a massive English army actually captured the city of Quebec in September 1759. If the English, under the overall command of General Jeffery Amherst, could ensure that the Haudenosaunee and other Indians were treated fairly and protected from fraudulent fur traders and land speculators, English-Indian relations could only get better. Among those who recognized a winner in the English were the Haudenosaunee, those Delawares under the diplomatic, shrewd but often inebriated leadership of Teedyuscung (most of the Delawares, Shawnees, and Mingos had made peace by 1758), and many of the Indian allies of the French.

The Creek Confederacy: Neutrality to the End

During the war, the situation of the southern Indians in many ways paralleled that of those in the North, as indeed it had so often in the past. In the South as in the North, white trade goods and presents for services rendered were a key in Indian decision making. At the start of the French and Indian War, the Creek Confederacy went through the same internal indecision as to which white side to back as the Haudenosaunee had in the North. Like the Haudenosaunee, the Creeks at the war's beginning decided on neutrality as the best course, but the Creeks, unlike the Haudenosaunee, adhered to their position to the war's end. Neutrality was also still the focus of Creek policy encouraged by Creek leaders, as it had been since the days of Brims and Goa.

The Creek policy of neutrality was also encouraged by the circumstances of the war. The French were not as militarily active in the Creeks' sphere of influence as they were in the North near the Haudenosaunee. Furthermore, the Creeks saw no reason to change their policy of neutrality because there was no opportunity to increase their power or achieve a national objective by siding with their closest European trading partner, the English. Thus the Creeks' situation was in contrast to the Haudenosaunee, who saw the war as a chance to reenter the contest for empire. On November 3, 1757, at a conference at Savannah, a Creek spokesman, Stumpe, explained to Governor Henry Ellis:

Our fathers were poor [due to the Spanish occupation to the south of them], but you [through trade] have made us rich. This we often tell our young people. We desire them to hold you fast by the hand as the surest means to continue secure in their present happiness. (Corkran 1967, 190)

Despite this clear admiration for English trade, however, the Creeks refused to fight the French. They had discerned since the days of Brims earlier in the century that the policy of playing off the French and the English could work as well in war as in peace.

Not all the Creeks felt that they should remain neutral. A few aided the English in the Ohio River valley campaigns, and forty went with the English against Fort Duquesne in 1758. On the other hand, the Mortar, one of the Creeks' principal chiefs, strongly favored driving out the English because they posed the threat of continual encroachment on Creek lands, whereas the French claimed they only wanted to trade. This feeling was intensified through the effort of the Shawnees, committed in battles against the English since 1755, to create a nativist movement among all the Indians east of the Mississippi—a dream the Shawnees had proposed since 1746. In 1677, some Shawnees had been attacked by the English and their Catawba allies and had fled their South Carolina homes to join other Shawnees further north. This date, 1677, was the Shawnees' initiation as to how white colonists could swarm into the forest and build their homes as fast as they could cut down trees. The Shawnees continually tried to persuade the Creeks that all Indians must unite. By 1756, a few leaders among the Creeks, Cherokees, Chickasaws and Choctaws had discussed the danger of any single white power emerging triumphant. A pan-Indian organization was seriously discussed even while the Cherokees fought for the English and the Chickasaws and Choctaws usually fought each other on behalf of the English and the French, respectively. But all these nations, unlike the Shawnees, were very powerful. The Creeks felt that their confederacy gave them a balance of power and an opportunity for neutrality with which the Spanish, French or English could not afford to interfere. For the moment, the Creeks were right. They did not consider that someday the whites of the Southeast might conclude that Creek deerskin trade was not as valuable as Creek land.

As spokesman for the anti-English Creeks, the Mortar was also influenced by the Cherokees, whose resentment continually grew because of white encroachments on their lands, even as they aided the English. In 1758, the

Cherokees were still fond enough of English trade goods to feel they had more to lose by fighting the English than the French. By the spring of 1759, however, circumstances compelled the Cherokees to reconsider their national strategy. Traders had never ceased cheating them. Virginia frontiersmen had murdered Cherokee warriors who were serving the English. Whites were corrupting various Cherokee women, which threatened the internal social structure of the Cherokee nation. Cherokees had been killed for alleged horse stealing. And the Cherokees still chafed at English expansion onto their lands—which ironically was in part due to settlers fleeing war on the northern Virginia frontier. Some of the Cherokees went to war against the English frontiersmen. The Mortar directly influenced this decision, both because of his generally anti-English position and because his brother was married to a Cherokee woman who lost a number of relatives murdered by Virginia frontiersmen. While he was successful in adding his weight to the councils of the Cherokees, the Mortar could not convince the Creek headmen to join their northern "mountaineer" brothers, as the Cherokee were known.

Since 1756, Edmond Atkin of South Carolina had been the Superintendent of Indian Affairs for the Southern Indians, and thus was the counterpart of Sir William Johnson in the North. Atkin encouraged the Creeks to maintain their policy of neutrality by promoting the deerskin trade. The Creeks could also see that the French, their logical allies in any war against the English, could not be depended upon for supplies and ammunition. Even the Choctaws, who for half a century had usually allied with the French, had been pulled part way out of the French sphere of influence by Atkin, who, in a treaty signed in July 1759, offered them trade goods the French could not supply. Then, in the square of the Upper Creek town of Tuckabatchee, Atkin met with Creek headmen on September 28, 1759. The Mortar, still pro-French and still hoping to ally the Creeks with the Cherokees, was also there. As all sat in a circle under an arbor, the peace pipe was passed among them, but the arrogant Atkin refused to have the pipe given to the Mortar. Then Atkin announced that Cussita, a major Creek town of the Alabama branch of the confederacy, was being cut off from the English trade because of its French sympathies. At this moment Totscadeter, the Tobacco Eater, jumped up from the circle of men and swung his hatchet down on Atkin's head. Fortunately for Atkin the hatchet glanced off a log ceiling-beam before it struck him, and the wound was superficial. Atkin warded off other blows with his arms until Totscadeter was subdued by some of the other headmen.

Had Totscadeter's attack on Atkin been successful, the pro-Cherokee and pro-French Creeks would certainly have seized the opportunity to kill other Englishmen, and the Creeks would have been committed to war. Whether Totscadeter's act was part of a prearranged plot by the Mortar, or whether it was merely another furious reaction of one man incensed at the arrogance of another is not known. But on that September day war had come as close as an arbor ceiling beam.

Shortly thereafter, the peace faction among the Cherokees used the Creek refusal to join them as a chance to make peace. Raiding parties that could be reached were recalled, and on October 17 a Cherokee delegation under Oconostota, the Great Warrior of the Cherokees, arrived in Charleston. Governor William Henry Lyttelton knew their peaceful intentions and knew that the Cherokee war activities had ceased, except for war parties that could not immediately be reached. Oconostota, on October 19, explained the Cherokees' position, which like most Indian and white decisions in the eighteenth century, was partly based on trade economics:

> I am a warrior and want no war with the English.... My desire is to have the path clear and open for goods to go to the nation.... Your warriors [Virginian English, not South Carolinian English] have carried the hatchet of war against us, we have done the same against them; and both have acted like boys. I am willing to make clear weather once more and bury the hatchet of my young people. (Corkran 1962, 180)

Oconostota then placed a deerskin, a symbol of friendship, at Lyttelton's feet. Lyttelton refused to pick it up. A few days later he seized them as hostages, an action he had planned even before the peace delegation's arrival. Lyttelton took a white army and his hostages and marched toward the Cherokee country to demand that Cherokee warriors who had killed South Carolinians be arrested as murderers as a condition for ending the war. The Cherokees had thought they would offer Indian justice through retribution: each warrior would be expected to kill or capture a Frenchman for each Englishman he had killed. At Fort Prince George on December 26, 1759, Attakullaculla negotiated a treaty with Lyttelton without the necessary authority from the Cherokee capital at Chota. Securing the release of Oconostota and other important leaders, Attakullaculla, Oconostota and other leaders signed the treaty that called for the delivery of twenty-four Cherokees who had killed Carolinians. Twenty-two of the Cherokee hostages were still to be held by the English until the twenty-four were surrendered. All French emissaries were to be killed. For their part, the South Carolinians promised to renew the trade.

The majority of the Cherokees did not accept the peace that left twenty-two innocent hostages among the English. In January they began an all-out war against settlers of all ages and both sexes whom the Cherokees felt were interlopers. On February 16, 1760, Oconostota and some of his warriors went to Fort Prince George where the Cherokee hostages were held (five had already died within the fort from smallpox), lured Lieutenant Richard Coytmore, the fort's commander, into an ambush on the premise of talking peace, and mortally wounded him. The attack was Oconostota's personal revenge, for the previous fall Coytmore had been one of the whites who had lured Oconostota to Charleston on the promise of peace talks, and Oconostota had instead been made one of the early hostages. In retaliation for Coytmore's death, the soldiers inside Fort Prince George massacred the remaining hostages.

In February 1760, Superintendent Edmond Atkin tried to bring the Creeks into war against the French and the Cherokees by an open bribe: he promised to lower the trade prices if the Creeks would attack their Cherokee neighbors. Despite the fact that a few Creeks, encouraged by a Georgia scalp bounty, did attack the Cherokees, and that some other Creeks joined the Cherokees, the Creek Confederacy's headmen stubbornly held the nation to neutrality. To encourage Creek entry into the war, Georgia governor Henry Ellis worked carefully through the influential Creek Mary Bosomworth, now an old woman who had seen many crises come and go since James Oglethorpe first employed her as an interpreter. At the same time the pro-French Creek chief the Mortar and the Cherokees tried to enlist the Creeks, promising French aid and trade. But the Creeks remained neutral.

Catawbas, Chickasaws, Haudenosaunee, Delawares and Shawnees, however, aided the English against the Cherokees. Finally, in June 1761, an English army of 2,800, with one hundred Chickasaws, Catawbas, Mohawk Haudenosaunee and even Christian Stockbridge (Massachusetts) scouts marched boldly through fifteen Cherokee towns and forced their inhabitants to flee into the mountains. The army destroyed all the homes, peach trees, corn, peas, beans and other Cherokee property they found. When the English army stopped and went home, the Cherokees at first thought that it was because the whites were afraid to march farther into their country. Also, when they had served as allies of the English a few years earlier, they had seen how bogged down English armies could become. But the Cherokees soon under-stood that the English were only hoping that they had proved their point, that they could and would destroy more Cherokee towns, but were offering negoti-ated peace. The Cherokees also realized that the French were completely inca-pable of providing enough guns and supplies to any of their Indian allies. The French had made great speeches admonishing all Indians to rise against the English, but in the end it turned out that the French had faults equal to those of the English, with the additional shortcoming that the French were also losing their war with the English. Bitter toward both white powers, the Cherokees reluctantly made peace with the English on December 17, 1761. The Creeks con-tinued their neutrality and their still uninterrupted trade with the English.

Intertribal Wars in the Southeast

European conflicts continued to affect the histories of American Indian nations. In 1762, Great Britain declared war against Spain. (In 1707, "Great Britain" had been forged by the official unification of England and Scotland, symbolized by the new "Union Jack" flag—the interlocking of England's cross of St. George and Scotland's cross of St. Andrew. Wales had been officially united with England in 1535.) The Creeks found themselves skirmishing furi-ously with Spanish-allied Indians in Florida. When the European powers declared an end to their warfare in the 1763 Treaty of Paris, Spain turned Florida over to Great Britain. (Spain would regain her claims to Florida in 1783.) The Spanish feared that their Calusa Indian allies on the west coast of Florida would not fare well under British rule. Furthermore, about eighty Calusa families were devout converts to Catholicism. Interestingly, under the Spanish, the Calusas had carried on their pre-1492 tradition by sailing back and forth to Cuba in seagoing canoes to trade. Spain decided to give refuge to the eighty Calusa families. And so in 1763, these Calusa families made their way to Cuba, where they took up permanent residence.

These Calusas were fortunate. Intertribal wars continued throughout the South despite the Treaty of Paris among Great Britain, France, Spain and other European combatants. These continuing wars between Indian nations demon-strated, though tragically, that the various Indian nations had diplomatic goals and grievances of their own. Profiting most from these wars were the white traders who supplied guns and ammunition to the antagonists, and the British government, which by promoting the conflicts kept the Indians off balance.

Effects of the French & Indian War on the Haudenosaunee

Along the northern frontier, the expulsion of the French from Canada and the areas around the Great Lakes, under the terms of the 1763 Treaty of Paris, had brought triumph to two empires, not just one. Certainly the British had emerged victorious. But the Haudenosaunee, with little cost to themselves, also achieved the dream envisioned for more than a century: victory over the French and the Indian rivals of the Haudenosaunee. The Haudenosaunee had accomplished their triumph by watching the whites instead of their own men do most of the dying. However, with France out of Canada, one white nation could no longer be played off against the other in the North. The British government, on the other hand, had shown clear signs during the war that it intended to form a single colonial Indian policy instead of allowing each colony to pursue its own. A single colonial Indian policy had often been suggested by the Haudenosaunee and other Indian nations, on the assumption that Canada would always be occupied by the French. That was no longer true, as a French government ws no longer in Canada. Even though it meant that it would be harder to play off one colony against the other, the Indians hoped that a unified British policy toward them would help eliminate trade abuses and conflicting white land claims.

The Haudenosaunee were also beginning to sense, as were their old Indian rivals, that perhaps Indians should have a common policy toward the whites, and that perhaps Indians had more in common than past conflicts suggested. The whites may have observed this recognition as early as July 1759 when the Haudenosaunee and French-allied Indians negotiated unsuccessfully before fighting the battle that resulted in the British capture of Fort Niagara. The war emphasized how dependent both the pro-British and pro-French Indians were on white goods, and after 1760 when British General Jeffery Amherst ordered drastically fewer presents distributed to the Indians and initiated higher trading prices for white goods, all Indians were adversely affected. In addition, the quality of many British goods had deteriorated alarmingly.

A new kind of trade threatened the Indians as British officers were rewarded for their services with plots of Indian land near various frontier forts. Settlers began moving west, especially around the forks of the Ohio, and it seemed to the Indians that the British held forts throughout their country for the purpose of protecting present or future settlers, not merely to serve as trading posts. Worst of all, the victorious British treated all Indians alike, whether they had fought for or against Great Britain.

Pontiac's Confederacy and Seneca Efforts to Oust the British from Great Lakes Region

An Ottawa leader named Pontiac who lived near Detroit became determined by late 1762 to change all of this by capturing twelve major forts previously held by the French but now occupied by British troops and driving the British back to the eastern seaboard permanently. Pontiac already had the encouragement of the French in the Mississippi River Valley who promised to come to the Indians' aid once battles had begun. He formulated a strategy suitable to the wilderness environment and its inhabitants by organizing a loose confederation. The immediate goal was to oust the British, but no postwar goal was sought other than a return to conditions as they had been prior to the French defeat, including the reestablishment of the French trading system and the return of French power to the Great Lakes and Canada. Pontiac's call for a war by confederated Indian nations was not unique, nor was French support of such ventures. The Great Lakes nations had been united economically for well over a century through the Huron-Ottawa trading network. A confederation to repel Haudenosaunee invaders had been tried in the 1680s, and between 1712 and 1732 numerous Great Lakes Indians had been effective members of a pro-French confederation that defeated the Outagamies (Foxes). The Shawnees had been advocating an Indian military confederacy since at least 1746. Pontiac built on two more recent unification efforts with which he was very familiar: those of the Seneca Haudenosaunee and of a religious leader, Neolin, known as the Delaware Prophet.

By early 1761, the Seneca Haudenosaunee, who were in communication with the Cherokees (already at war with the British), convinced the council of the Haudenosaunee that it was time to remove the British forts and settlers from their homeland. The few British efforts to remove illegal settlers on Haudenosaunee lands in Pennsylvania failed (and would continue to fail after 1761). This clearly indicated a lack of commitment by the British to upholding the 1758 Treaty of Easton (made between Pennsylvania on the one hand and the Haudenosaunee and the Delawares on the other). The treaty forbade white settlement west of the Appalachian Mountains and in the Delaware lands of the Wyoming Valley in the Susquehanna River valley. It appeared that the British had used the opportunity of the French and Indian War to gain footholds on Haudenosaunee land, threatening both the confederacy and its imperial rights over the Delawares and the nations of the eastern Ohio River valley. Of the six nations in the Haudenosaunee, none was more interested or more involved in the expansion of the Haudenosaunee frontier than the Senecas, and so it was natural that they take the lead in organizing the war against the British. Although families of all six nations had settled southward into Pennsylvania and westward into Ohio, none had succeeded as had the more numerous Senecas. The Senecas had long maintained contact with the French at Fort Niagara, built in 1726, and their expansion into the Ohio River valley increased their French trading opportunities, making them more sympathetic to the French than were other Haudenosaunee. The Senecas' plan centered around the capture of Fort Detroit and the use of the goods stored there to conduct the rest of the war, which would engulf all the frontier forts including Niagara and Pitt and even into the Mohawk Valley. In addition, the Senecas' 1761 strategy included bringing the Cherokees into the war so that white expansion in the South would be slowed. The Senecas expected French support, which was only logical because the Indians still wanted white trade goods and weapons. Evidently, they only wished to reintroduce white competition between the English and the French (at this point in time, the French and English were still at war and one hope was that French supplies might come north from New Orleans), which in the long run would ensure their own profitable and independent position. Unfortunately, the Senecas' plan was discovered by Sir William Johnson's agents and delayed for a year.

In 1762, the Delaware Prophet revived the Seneca plan. The Delaware nation had worked closely with the Senecas as a subordinate body within the Haudenosaunee realm of conquest. Neolin had been personally instructed by the Master of Life in a code that would give the Indians dominance over their own lands once again. The Master of Life's moral directives included forsaking any manifestations of white culture such as white religions, manufactured goods and guns. His instructions called upon warriors to marry only one wife and to end promiscuity. Magic must be forsaken because it dealt with an evil spiritual force. Prayers to the Master of Life would fulfill all needs. And lastly, it would be necessary to wage a war in the name of the Master of Life against all colonial whites. The Master of Life did not support these colonists because they should live only in the lands the Master of Life had already created for them across the sea.

Pontiac tried to organize his military confederation around the Prophet's ideas, but the tenet demanding the expulsion of all whites was poorly received by Indians who wanted the Europeans' fur trade goods and were willing to put up with the French in order to get them. Whatever Pontiac's belief in 1762, by 1763 he had altered his talks to prospective allies by explaining that the Delaware Prophet's message from the Master of Life was only anti-British. Pontiac's compromise and his ability to plan strategy earned him pledges of support among many of the leading chiefs and warriors of the Ottawas, the Potawatomis, the Miamis, the Ojibwas or Chippewas, the Sauk-Foxes, the Kickapoos, the Mascoutens, the Mingos, the Delawares, and the Hurons including the Wyandots. Even the Sioux had been contacted, although most did not aid Pontiac's effort.

As events were to demonstrate, he also had some friends among the Haudenosaunee. The Haudenosaunee had a dilemma. If they expanded the full participation of Indian nations who were not Haudenosaunee into their confederacy government, their own culture and spiritual traditions would be subverted. On the other hand, there was no doubt that Pontiac, one of their archrivals had become the principal leader of the war for Indian independence. One Seneca, Kaiaghshota (also known as Guyashusta and Kiasola) perhaps advised Pontiac directly. If he did, Pontiac had an able advisor, for Kaiaghshota had been one of the originators of the 1761 Seneca strategy (Jacobs 1972, 75–97; cf. Peckham 1947, 92–111).

Red sticks and red tomahawks, symbolizing commitment to war, were passed among Indian towns during the last months of 1762 and early in 1763. Along with these symbols were wampum belts sent by the French stationed along the Mississippi pledging French military aid. French strategy in this case was consistent with past French policy: to accomplish a goal favorable to themselves, the French were willing to let Indians make most of the sacrifices. Pontiac, however, was convinced that the French planned to do some of the actual fighting. He was especially aware that without French supplies, his war would fail. By May, Pontiac was ready, and on May 5 he gathered about one hundred leaders of the Ottawas, the Hurons and the Potawatomis in the council house of a Potawatomi town not far from Detroit. These were the chiefs who would lead the first action in an Indian war for independence that they believed the Master of Life had encouraged. They had heard the talk of war, they had seen the French wampum belts and red sticks, and they had heard plans discussed. Now it was time to act. Fearing a security leak, Pontiac sent all the women and noncombatants away, and posted guards outside. Then, shortly after noon, Pontiac spoke:

It is important for us, my brothers, that we exterminate from our lands this nation which seeks only to destroy us. You see as well as I that we can no longer supply our needs, as we have done from our brothers, the French. The English sell us goods twice as dear as the French do, and their goods do not last. Scarcely have we bought a blanket or something else to cover ourselves with before we must think of getting another; and when we wish to set out for our winter camps they do not want to give us any credit as our brothers the French do.

When I go to see the English commander and say to him that some of our comrades are dead, instead of bewailing their death, as our French brothers do, he laughs at me and at you. If I ask anything for our sick, he refuses with the reply that he has no use for us. From all this you can well see that they are seeking our ruin. Therefore, my brothers, we must all swear their destruction and wait no longer. Nothing prevents us; they are few in numbers, and we can accomplish it.

All the nations who are our brothers attack them—why should not we strike too? Are we not men like them? Have I not shown you the wampum belts which I received from our Great Father, the Frenchman? He tells us to strike them. Why do we not listen to his words? What do we fear? It is time. Do we fear that our brothers, the French, who are here [near Detroit] among us will prevent us? They do not know our plans, and they could not hinder anyway, if they would. You all know as well as I that when the English came upon our lands to drive out our father, Bellestre [French commander at Detroit], they took away all the Frenchmen's guns and that they now have no arms to protect themselves with. Therefore, it is time for us to strike. If there are any French who side with them, let us strike them as well as the English. Remember what the Master of Life told our brother, the Delaware, to do. That concerns us all as well as others.

I have sent wampum belts and messengers to our brothers, the Chippewas of Saginaw, and to our brothers, the Ottawas of Michilimackinac, and to those of the Thames River [Canada] to join us. They will not be slow in coming, but while we wait let us strike anyway. There is no time to lose. When the English are defeated we shall then see what there is left to do, and we shall stop up the ways hither so that they may never come again upon our lands. (Peckham 1947, 119–20)

Most Indian nations' leaders were counselors supported voluntarily by their people, and Pontiac was in this tradition. Thus any plan could not coerce warriors (through a draft, for example) or any others into supporting a war. What followed indicates how broad the support for war was. Pontiac and the assembled leaders planned this strategy: In two days Pontiac would send the Hurons and Potawatomis to surround Fort Detroit and cut off anyone trying to get in, especially reinforcements. In the meantime, he would lead sixty carefully selected warriors inside the fort on the pretext that they had come for a council. The rest of the Ottawa men and women were to follow the first group into the fort and casually spread themselves among the buildings. All would carry concealed weapons—including sawed-off muskets prepared for the occasion—under their blankets. Pontiac, carrying a wampum belt green on one side and white on the other, together with ten counselors and a few warriors, would then enter the fort's council house to confront the commandant, Major Henry Gladwin. When Pontiac offered Gladwin the wampum belt with the green side up instead of the customary white side, the warriors were to begin the attack and the other Ottawas outside the council house were quickly to join in. All British were to be captured or killed, but Frenchmen spared. The deceptive tactic was necessary because the fort with its cannon might be too strong to storm or lay siege to. Pontiac was so confident his plan would succeed that he had already decided that Antoine Cuillerier, a Frenchman living at Detroit, would be the fort's new commander once the British were overthrown.

On May 7, Pontiac led his Ottawa warriors and women, numbering about three hundred, toward the east gate of the fort, which the British had left open as a sign of friendship. As Pontiac and his people funneled in, all but the sixty chosen warriors spread out around the fort. It was about ten o'clock in the morning. Pontiac, ten counselors and some warriors walked down a narrow dirt street toward the council house, which was the home of Captain Donald Campbell. Pontiac grew uneasy. The merchants had closed up their shops and were assembled at one of them, armed. There were twice as many sentries on the walls as usual, and every one had his bayonet fixed. The rest of the 120-man garrison was in ranks on the parade ground ready for battle. Inside the council house stood only Major Gladwin, Captain Campbell and some interpreters. The two officers were armed. The other officers, most of whom would normally have been in attendance to greet such an important chief, were with their men or poised near the open gate. It was Pontiac and the Ottawas, not the British, who were in a trap. Pontiac and his people did not lose their composure. Pontiac's associates seated themselves and then Pontiac, standing, looked at Major Gladwin and through the interpreters said:

> We are greatly surprised, brother, at this unusual step thou hast taken, to have all the soldiers under arms, and that thy young chiefs are not at council as formerly. We would be very glad to know the reason for this, for we imagine some bad bird has given thee ill news of us, which we advise thee not to believe, my brother, for there are bad birds who want to stir thee up against thy brothers, the Indians, who have been always in perfect friendship with their brothers, the English. (Peckham 1947, 131)

Major Gladwin replied with equal deviousness that he was expecting representatives from other Indian nations to visit him shortly and that he would have to have his men under arms at that time. In order not to insult these future visitors he had decided to set the precedent when the Ottawas, his great friends, visited him. Pontiac raised the wampum belt that was to be the signal for the attack. But he presented it to Gladwin with the white side up and gave a lengthy speech asking to receive condolence presents for the deaths of six chiefs. No battle began, and Major Gladwin presented the Ottawas with six suits of clothing in condolence for the six late chiefs, and gave out some bread and tobacco. The Ottawa men and women walked from the fort with their chief, some angry that the fight had not begun, some agreeing that their his leader had done well under the circumstances, but all respecting his decision.

Who had betrayed Pontiac to the British? Pontiac and his people thought that it was an Ojibwa girl named Catherine who lived among the Potawatomis and was a Catholic convert. Pontiac ordered her flogged.

Detroit was still to be taken. Pontiac tried to wait until Gladwin relaxed his vigil, even presenting Gladwin with a *calumet* or peace pipe. But Gladwin and his garrison remained alert, and Pontiac finally began open warfare on May 9, 1763, by sending out parties to cut off the fort or seize the garrison's supply of cattle on two nearby British farms. Eight British, including two women and one child, were killed, as well as a Frenchman mistaken for the enemy. On May 10, Pontiac took as hostages two Englishmen from the fort whom he had invited to come and talk peace, a betrayal of the standards of both Indian and white diplomacies. Pontiac may have taken this disreputable action because he was desperate or because he was supremely confident of an Indian victory. Whatever his reasons, Pontiac offered the British the same terms the British had offered the French during the previous war: the garrison was to lay down its arms, surrender its baggage, and be escorted eastward to the frontier settlements.

On May 11, Pontiac offered to allow the garrison, with its arms, to return to the frontier on the two vessels tied up near the fort. These terms were refused, and during the next few days Pontiac organized and committed himself to a siege that was to last through the end of October. During that time Pontiac suffered setbacks, but he was able to sustain his siege of the fort. And the other Indian nations that had decided to support Pontiac during the previous year kept their commitments even though Pontiac had yet to capture Detroit.

Of the twelve forts that formed a chain along the Great Lakes and nearby rivers, all but Detroit, Niagara and Pitt were taken. The following list indicates the rapid succession of victories for Pontiac's allies:

May 16: Fort Sandusky (Sandusky, Ohio) by Wyandots (Hurons) and some Ottawas

May 25: Fort St. Joseph (Niles, Michigan) by Potawatomis

May 27: Fort Miami (Fort Wayne, Indiana) by Miamis

June 1: Fort Ouiatenon (Lafayette, Indiana) by Weas (a Miami band), Kickapoos and Mascoutens

June 2: Fort Michilimackinac (Mackinaw City, Michigan) by Ojibwas and Sauks

June 16: Fort Venango (Franklin, Pennsylvania) by Seneca Haudenosaunee

June 18: Fort Le Boeuf (Waterford, Pennsylvania) by Seneca Haudenosaunee

June 20: Fort Presque Isle (Erie, Pennsylvania) by a Seneca Haudenosaunee expedition joined by two hundred Ottawas, Hurons and Chippewas dispatched by Pontiac from the Detroit siege. (Some or all of these two hundred allies may have also helped the Senecas at Venango and Le Boeuf.)

June 21: Fort La Baye (Green Bay, Wisconsin) not attacked, but abandoned by the British

Emissaries or war parties sent by Pontiac coordinated most of these actions. The Senecas had helped inspire at least the Miami capture of Fort Miami, for a Seneca wampum belt calling for war had been sent to the

Haudenosaunee's tributary Delawares, Shawnees and Miamis, the latter receiving the belt in March 1763. Most of the forts were taken by ruse, their tiny garrisons captured or killed. But at Ouiatenon the garrison of twenty was allowed to surrender without bloodshed. At Le Boeuf the fourteen in the garrison slipped away during the night. And at La Baye the garrison of eighteen withdrew before any attack occurred. That garrison was under the protection of some Menominees, Winnebagos, Sauks, Foxes and one Dakota (Sioux) chief, all of whom were antagonistic to the nearby Ojibwas who had allied with Pontiac. On May 29, Delawares and Mingos begun harassing Fort Pitt and by early June had been joined by Shawnees and then by Wyandots (Hurons). Frontier settlements were also attacked.

News of the many Indian victories provided vital lifts to the morale of the Indian besiegers at Fort Pitt and among Pontiac's warriors and allies at Detroit. Only Fort Niagara was not involved in battle during the summer of 1763, because the Haudenosaunee could not decide whether to join Pontiac's war for Indian independence, even though Senecas had already taken up arms. While the allies' attacks on the British posts and settlements were often cruel in the killing of some women and children and in the torture-deaths of some white men, the British retaliation was no less cruel. Certainly the retaliation caused the deaths of more Indian women and children, as well as men, than the Indians inflicted among the whites during the same period. On June 24, 1763, the acting commander at Fort Pitt, a Swiss mercenary Captain Simeon Ecuyer, was called on by a warrior and a chief of the Delawares to surrender, because so many of the other British posts had been taken. Ecuyer refused, but in line with the Indian custom on such diplomatic occasions, gave the Delawares a present. The gift was two blankets and a handkerchief, unknown to the Indians purposefully taken by Ecuyer from Fort Pitt's smallpox hospital. The Delawares, Shawnees and Mingos soon suffered a terrible smallpox epidemic. This germ warfare was later condoned and encouraged by the British commander-in-chief, Sir Jeffery Amherst (Peckham 1947, 170, 226–27; cf. Anderson 2000, 541–42, 809, fn. 11; Parkman [1870] 1991, 648–49).

In addition to the siege of Detroit, perhaps the most famous incident in the war occurred at Fort Michilimackinac on June 2, 1763. As at Detroit, the gates of the fort were left open as a sign of friendship by the British occupying forces. Stationed at the fort were thirty-five British soldiers and about sixty-five other men, including officers and both French Canadian and British fur traders. The commandant of the fort, Captain George Etherington, was warned by several of the more friendly French Canadian traders to expect trouble, but he refused to take even the slightest precaution. He even declared that the next man who uttered such ideas would be sent as a prisoner to Detroit.

For Michilimackinac's soldiers, the sultry Thursday morning of June 2, 1763 would normally have brought only the usual monotony of garrison duty, made interesting perhaps by Indians coming to trade and exchange news. But this morning, on the sand plain directly in front of the fort's land gate, the Ojibwas and the Sauks were going to play a game of *baggatiway*, or lacrosse. The rules of the game were that all Indian males who wanted to could participate, each carrying a four-foot-long lacrosse stick constructed with a small net at the end with which to catch or pass a hard ball about the size of a clenched fist. The object of the game was to pass the ball back and forth between players, each team working towards their opponent's goal, a post erected in the ground. A team scored when they struck their opponent's post with the ball. The posts of the two teams were often as much as a mile apart, and although the precise distance between the goal posts of the Ojibwas and the Sauks that day is not known, the sandy plain in front of Michilimackinac was big enough to ensure an exciting game. Hundreds of Ojibwa and Sauk warriors turned out, and the game began when the ball was dropped into the center of the field. The game was fast and chaotic. Although some of the Indian women wandered into the fort, most of them stood along the fringe of the playing area, wrapped in their blankets and carefully observing the dynamics of the game. Betting was usual at such games among both Indians and whites, so many of the whites at Michilimackinac had wagered on the outcome of the contest. Captain Etherington's bet was on the Ojibwas. As the ball was passed back and forth, the hundreds of warriors surged wherever it landed. Suddenly the ball arched loftily and sailed over the fort's stockade. The two teams rushed pell-mell after the ball and through the gates of the fort. As the warriors ran past the Indian women both outside and inside the fort, the women gave out weapons they had concealed under their blankets. The French traders calmly went indoors or merely stood and watched as twenty soldiers, one officer and one British trader were killed. Captain Etherington and the rest were made prisoners. Led by the Ojibwa war chief Matchekewis, the Ojibwas and the Sauks had effected the American Indians' Trojan horse (Henry [1809] 1971, 48–60).

Pontiac eventually lost his war, beginning with setbacks at Detroit and Fort Pitt when his warriors were too often unsuccessful in preventing the vital reinforcement and resupply of the besieged garrisons. On the night of October 29,

1763, a French courier delivered a letter to Pontiac from the French at Fort de Chartres on the Mississippi dated September 27, explaining that peace had been declared between Great Britain and France with the signing of the Treaty of Paris. The French and Indian War was now over as far as the white contestants were concerned. Because Indians allied with the French had been informed of this peace by the French courier and because Pontiac's siege at Detroit was not going well, many of his warriors returned to their towns in discouragement. Still others, in order to hunt food for their families, were forced to give up the battlefield for the forest. Pontiac decided to make peace. A French advisor transcribed the following message by Pontiac message in French, and it was delivered to Major Gladwin:

> My Brother
> The word which my father has sent me to make peace I have accepted; all my young men have buried their hatchets. I think you will forget the bad things which have taken place for some time past. Likewise I shall forget what you may have done to me, in order to think of nothing but good. I, the Chippewas, the Hurons, we are ready to go speak with you when you ask us. Give us an answer. I am sending this resolution to you in order that you may see it. If you are as kind as I, you will make me a reply. I wish you a good day.
> Pontiac

Gladwin replied that he could not make peace, and would have to await orders to do so. Gladwin wrote to commander-in-chief Amherst that since it would not be possible to punish the Indians militarily, they could be sold rum, which would

> destroy them more effectually than fire and sword. But on the contrary, if you intend to accommodate matters in the spring, which I hope you will,...it may be necessary to send up Sir William Johnson.

Peace was necessary, Gladwin continued, because otherwise the fur trade would be ruined and the Indians would withdraw westward, reinforcing

> other [Indian] nations on the Mississippi, whom they will prejudice against us and make them our enemy forever. Consequently, they will

render it extremely difficult (if not impossible) for us to possess that country, as the French have promised to supply them with every thing they want. (Peckham 1947, 238–39)

Pontiac, his peace proposal rebuffed, did not finally surrender to the king's agent, Johnson, until almost three years later on July 24, 1766, at Oswego, New York. During that time Pontiac had hoped to carry on the war in the only way possible, since French aid would not be forthcoming: by the guerrilla tactics of lightning raids on the frontier. The spirit for continuing the war had gone out of the Indians, however. One by one, beginning in 1764, the nations officially surrendered. The surrender of some nations was prompted by the fact that warriors from the Haudenosaunee, especially Mohawks, were now actively aiding the British even though some of the Seneca Haudenosaunee were still supporting Pontiac.

Perspective

Ever since Pontiac's War, the question has often been asked, How unified were Pontiac's allies? In 1763, Pontiac and his allies coordinated attacks on ten frontier forts within a month and a half. This period of time does not belie their organizational ability. Rather, it reflects the vast distances involved, which also shaped white military campaigns much the same way. While the different Indian nations defined their struggles according to individual national goals as well as common, pan-Indian agendas, British, French and Spanish military campaigns also had to coordinate European military forces with those of various colonies. Each colony, while usually sharing common imperial goals with its European sponsor, also defined its struggles according to its own objectives. Furthermore, what intangibles, such as spiritual beliefs, might be more important to a sense of unity than political or military actions? There was certainly what might be termed a "Spirit of '63" inspired by both Indian religious leaders and Indian political leaders, just as later there would be a "Spirit of '76." Finally, revolutions—including those of Pontiac and of the thirteen colonies— seldom spring to life fully developed. Instead, revolutions usually build momentum. Thus, difficulties of coordination and unity were and are circumstances that beset all those who challenge an existing system through revolution. The question of the level of unification among Pontiac's allies should be answered in the same way as how one would determine the level of unification among the thirteen colonies during the American Revolution. Other similar questions are: How unified were the Confederate States of America between 1861 and 1865? How unified were those who followed the U.S. government of Abraham Lincoln? The list of such questions is of course endless. But by applying the same standard to all events, we can discover individual definitions of how unified Pontiac's allies were, and in so doing find definitions that are meaningful to our own broader sense of history.

Pontiac's War also demonstrated how completely Indian nations east of the Mississippi had come to depend upon an alliance with a European colonial power in order to carry out their own agendas as Indian nations. This military interdependence was a logical outcome of the various Indian-European trade networks. Thus, Pontiac's War slowly collapsed when promised French aid was not forthcoming. No matter what alliances an Indian nation made with other Indian nations, the choice of a European ally and trading partner had become the primary key to success or failure, both in trade and in war. In addition to the French failure to aid Pontiac, the earlier French defeat in the French and Indian War and Canada's subsequent occupation by British troops continued to redefine Indian trade networks and Indian diplomacy until the outbreak of the American Revolution. When the American Revolution began, the choice of alliance with a non-Indian political power—either Britain or the revolutionary United States—would repeat the patterns of Pontiac's generation. In war, as in trade, there would ultimately be no "neutrals."

Despite the primary importance of Indian alliances with non-Indian powers, the pursuit of alliances among Indian nations remained significant in the diplomatic goals of Indian nations. In turn, alliances among Indian nations would continue to have dramatic impacts on the European colonies of North America. In no small measure, this was because Pontiac, despite his ultimate military failure, had inspired an Indian war for independence not soon forgotten by the British or the Indian nations. Sir William Johnson summarized both the effect of Pontiac's Indian alliances and the intertwined residue of French influence in a report to the Lords of Trade on December 26, 1764:

> That in an especial manner the French promoted the interest of
> Pontiac, whose influence is now become so considerable...that it
> extends even to the Mouth of the Mississippi, & has been ye principal

occasion of our not as yet gaining possession of the Illinois, which the French as well as the Indians are interested in preventing. (O'Callaghan and Fernow 1856, 688)

Pontiac's War was a struggle for independence, and as such it bears some remarkable similarities to the Revolutionary War fought a dozen years later by the colonial Patriots. For different reasons, both Pontiac's Indian allies and the Patriots of 1775 wanted to return to the freedoms and circumstances they had known before the French and Indian War of 1754–1763. In addition, as in the case of most previous military campaigns carried out by Europeans in North America, much of the success or failure of both Pontiac's War and the American Revolution would depend upon decisions made within the diplomatic halls of Europe, isolated from the real needs and motives of the combatants.

Another precursor of the future came just after the French had failed to provide the military aid they had promised to Pontiac and his allies. Hoping to destroy the British fur trade and desiring also to do at least something for Pontiac's confederates, the French offered to provide the Indians with a sanctuary west of the Mississippi. While most Indians chose to remain in their homelands, a few removed west voluntarily. Ironically, seventy years later, "removal" would become the official policy of the government of the United States, imposed on both northern and southern Indian nations—except that the removal carried out by the United States would not be voluntary.

In the aftermath of war, Pontiac's legacy did not disappear just because Indian nations had been temporarily defeated on the battlefield. Their extensive territories had not been conquered, and only isolated British forts were scattered throughout their national homelands. In fact, the British were eager to use those forts to reopen trade, not to renew warfare. The Indian nations were confident that renewed resistance was an option if the British did not resolve frontier tensions peacefully.

CHAPTER VI

Retrospectives: Indian Impacts on Slavery & the Roles of Women

Slavery

"Captivity narrative" is the term usually given to accounts by white men, women and children who had been captured by Indians. White colonials avidly read such narratives and used them as yet another justification for the conquest of cruel barbarians. But in colonial North America whites rarely suffered captivity. Black African slaves were an entire laboring class of captives, and were the most numerous to suffer in the continental United States. But Indians were enslaved as well, particularly in the Caribbean, Mexico and South America. If epidemic diseases had not thoroughly devastated Indian populations in the Caribbean, it is possible that the importation of Africans as slaves would have been delayed or entirely avoided. The working and living conditions of both Indians and African slaves were abominable, and African slaves— already reduced by the cruelties of the voyage from Africa (the "Middle Passage")—died under these severe conditions just as Indians did. But while there were few Indians to replace fallen Indian slaves, African leaders conspired with European traders to ensure that African victims would continue to be supplied to the European colonists.

Enslavement of Indians

The enslavement of American Indians continued into the nineteenth century, and in some areas of the Southwest continued illegally into the early years of the twentieth century. Some of these Indian slaves were prisoners of war who were enslaved by victorious whites. But other Indian slaves were sold to the whites by other Indians, making Indian slavery, like Indian history in general, far more complicated than simply a conflict of races. Furthermore, Indian nations played a role in enforcing the white institution of African slavery.

Indian slaves, particularly domestic Indian slaves, were extremely popular among French colonists in isolated fur-trading posts around the Great Lakes as well as in their settlements along the St. Lawrence and Mississippi rivers. French-allied Indians obtained other Indians in raids or wars and then sold them to the French. One Indian nation on the Eastern Plains was so often the victimized source of the French Indian slave trade in the northern areas that their tribal name became the label for Indian slaves of all tribes: Pawnee, or "Pani" as it was often spelled during the colonial period. This designation for Indian slaves was even adopted by British officials such as Sir William Johnson to designate any Indian slave. A major center of the Pani trade among the English was Oswego, New York, where Johnson reported in 1750 that Indians had sold Indian captives as slaves "every year since Oswego has been frequented by us [about 1722]. The French likewise buy them daily..." (Sullivan et al. 1921, 261). The Indians themselves used Panis as pledges of trust, as did an Algonquin Toughkamawimau spokesman living west of the Haudenosaunee, who, while he was negotiating with Sir William Johnson in 1764, made this statement as an assurance of his good intentions: "I have brought you a small Panis as a Pledge to conform my Words" (Sullivan et al., 1953, 299). These human pledges were also used as bonds in the fur trade, and a few desperate Indians would even turn over one of their own children, to say nothing of a captive child, "as pawns, or pledges" to a fur trader (O'Callaghan and Fernow 1855, 6:546).

Indian slavery had still another tragic facet. During the colonial period, all European nations frequently offered to compensate their colonial soldiers with Indian prisoners of war, including children. The soldiers could keep or sell these people. The seventeenth-century wars against the Indians in Virginia; the Pequot War and King Philip's War in New England; and wars involving Great Britain, Spain and France for the domination of North America included the enslavement of Indian prisoners of war as a method of paying the armies. During the American Revolution, the 1776 campaign against the Cherokees was partially sponsored by the Patriots through this method (Cave 1996, 158–61; Leach [1958] 1966, 125, 148, 171, 178, 197, 224–28, 231; Mooney [1891] 1982, 51, 52–53; Perdue 1979, 29).

During the colonial period, no English mainland colony had more Indian slaves than South Carolina. In 1708, South Carolina's population, excluding independent Indian peoples, consisted of 3,960 free whites, 120 indentured servants, 4,100 black slaves, and 1,400 Indian slaves. Of these 1,400 Indian slaves,

600 were women, 300 children and 500 men. These 1,400 people, numerous though they were, did not constitute the majority of South Carolina Indians who had been enslaved, for most of the Indians taken into slavery in South Carolina were not kept in the colony for fear they would run away. It was more profitable to sell Indian slaves to other colonies such as Massachusetts or colonies in the West Indies. The South Carolina government made a tidy profit on this human traffic in 1703 by approving an export duty of twenty shillings on each slave exported. In 1715, the colony provided a unique way in which Tuscarora Indians could obtain the freedom of their fellow tribesmen who had just been enslaved in the brutal Tuscarora War. South Carolina was busy fighting the Spanish and other Indians, so its legislature provided that for every free Tuscarora who died fighting on the side of South Carolina, one of their enslaved tribesmen would be freed. Furthermore, the legislature agreed that in exchange for every enemy Indian captured and turned over to South Carolina to be enslaved, one of the Tuscaroras who was already in slavery would be returned to the Tuscarora nation (Crane [1929] 1964, 112–14, 175–78, passim).

South Carolina was not unique. Every European colony had Indian slaves. In Massachusetts, hardly an issue of a newspaper came out which did not run an advertisement for an escaped Indian slave. New York and Virginia, among others, raised money for their colonial governments by levying import duties on slaves, Indian and black brought into their jurisdictions. In the 1670s during King Philip's War, Massachusetts offered freedom to any Indian slave who reported any Indian plan of war or insurrection. And in Rhode Island in 1778 during the American Revolution, following an admonition by General George Washington that slaves be enlisted into Rhode Island units, the state voted that every Indian, black, or mulatto slave who enlisted for the war's duration would be given equal pay and freedom (Quarles 1961, 55–56).

While South Carolina had the largest Indian slave population among the English mainland colonies, Massachusetts had two of the most famous Indian slaves—at least in retrospect. They were a married couple named Tituba and Indian John. Like so many Indian slaves, the couple was not native to the colony they served in. The colonists realized that Indian slaves from other locales would not have the same opportunities to escape successfully as local Indians might have because they would not know the geography of the colony as well. Furthermore, the neighboring Indian nations who were free were more likely to return slaves who were not local Indians for a reward. In the English colonies, this practice of bringing Indian slaves from other areas began with the very first English colony, Roanoke, when in 1586 Francis Drake brought to the colonies three hundred South American Indians and one hundred black slaves captured in Santo Domingo and Cartagena (Colombia). Indian John and Tituba were slaves of the Reverend Samuel Parris in Salem Village, and had been brought to Massachusetts when Parris moved there from Barbados. Indian John and Tituba may have been part black, and they may have been Indians shipped to the West Indies from a North, Central or South American mainland colony. They might have even been New England Indians or their descendants who had been sold into the West Indies after a Puritan war. Both became involved in the Salem witch hysteria. Since Tituba seems not to have drawn her husband into the turmoil, he did not suffer punishment at the hands of the Puritan authorities. But Tituba told stories of the supernatural to Salem village children and confessed to having been tempted by the Devil to sign her soul over to him. Thrown into jail, Tituba was brought before two judges on March 1, 1692, examined, and on March 7 sent to Boston where she was imprisoned for thirteen months. She was resold as a slave to pay for her prison expenses (Hill 2000, 67, 220, 227–28, 230, 232, 301; Boyer and Nissenbaum 1974, 2–3, 178).

On Slave "Suitability" and the Paucity of Black Slave Revolts

White enslavement of Indians, and for that matter Indian enslavement of other Indians, invites the question as to whether Indians were less suited to slavery than blacks. The supposed evidence that Indians were unsuitable for slavery centered around the fact that Indians died in great numbers when enslaved by whites, a fate believed caused by the Indians' great love for freedom. However, much evidence indicates that slavery was equally unsuited to all races; blacks, too, died by the thousands, perishing on the voyage across the Atlantic, wasting away as slaves, or finding death standing in solitary defiance of their masters. A major difference between Indian and black slavery was that Indians had less resistance to European diseases than did blacks. But there were also more blacks available from Africa—literally millions more—than there were Indians in North America. Thus, white prospective slave owners ran out of Indians but did not run out of blacks, and the more numerous blacks were then conveniently but illogically deemed by the whites to be more willing slaves.

Indian nations in both north and south had a complex influence on the black slaves owned by white colonists. One of the most important questions regarding the American colonial experience has been why, when there were massive black slave revolts in the Caribbean and in Central and South America, the English mainland colonies had no major slave revolt. There were instead only small and ineffectual attempts such as South Carolina's "Cato Conspiracy" in 1739. There have been many explanations. For example, whites outnumbered blacks in mainland English colonies, whereas elsewhere blacks were in the majority. The English mainland colonies' slave system was also particularly successful in crushing black people's spirit through its controlled, closed system of slavery. In this closed system, outside ideas and influences were minimized. Physical threats and harsh punishments were combined with this psychological atmosphere to reduce people's perceptions of hopeful alternatives such as escape or rebellion. The most important factor, however, was the American Indian's role in North America as compared to elsewhere in the hemisphere. More than any other persons or circumstances, the Indian nations in the English colonies helped prevent massive slave revolts. The reasons for this are complex.

In Latin America, black slave resistance often began when a few slaves escaped into the mountains and then returned to rescue other blacks until there were sufficient numbers to instigate a revolt. Escaped slaves were free to build up a resistance movement in the hinterland because the Indians who lived there had been exterminated by the whites, they abetted the blacks, or they were unable to interfere successfully. For black slaves in the English mainland colonies, however, finding refuge in the backcountry was nearly impossible. Decade after decade, Indian nations in the interior such as the Creek and the Haudenosaunee had allowed the whites to conquer and enslave many coastal tribes, and these Indians had also hunted other Indians to sell as slaves to the whites. During the 1700s, the Chickasaws and the Choctaws actually hunted each other, as Chickasaws sold Choctaws to the English while Choctaws hunted Chickasaws to sell to the French. Thus the enslavement of blacks, members of a foreign race, was hardly considered as an ethical dilemma by most Indians. Most important, however, the interior Indian nations wanted to trade with the whites for manufactured goods, and were more than willing to return escaped slaves in order to promote good business relations (Crane [1929] 1964, 17–18, 69–70, 139–40, 147; Cotterill 1954, 17–33; Usner 1992, 24, 56–59, 81–82, passim).

The whites, in addition to desiring the return of their slaves, wanted to perpetuate the immense profits that the Indian fur and deerskin trade brought and therefore befriended the large Indian nations of the interior. Rewards for the return of escaped slaves provided windfalls that were welcome supplements to the goods obtained in trade. In a few instances in the South (and perhaps in the North), Indians would return slaves, collect the reward, aid the same slaves' escape, and return the slaves again for another reward! It is true that many blacks were carried off from white settlements by raiding Indians during frontier wars. But for the most part these black captives confronted two fates: they were either sold during the wars to other whites—for example, captured slaves from English colonies would be sold to the French, the Spanish or even other English colonies—or were kept as slaves or servants within the Indian nation. If these captured slaves were returned to the white settlements, it would be because their return was as part of the negotiated terms that ended a particular war. Such circumstances prevented blacks from establishing guerrilla bases in the hinterlands from which to launch or instigate slave revolts (Crane [1929] 1964, 33; Usner 1992, 58; Littlefield 1979, 9–10, 19; Corkran 1967, 68, 71, 73, 286).

The blacks' best opportunity for revolt in any colony occurred when they were African born and could remember the dignity and culture of the homeland before slavery erased much of their cultural identities. In the English North American colonies, the greatest importation of blacks from Africa took place during the late seventeenth century and throughout the eighteenth century. This slave influx coincided with the heyday of the fur and deerskin trade when interior Indian nations were usually willing to return escaped slaves. Thus, during the blacks' greatest psychological opportunity for revolt—the period before the American Revolution when slaves had much of their African identities intact— escaped blacks were unable to create guerrilla bases in the interior.

The English colonist did not depend solely on mere friendship or good trade relations to ensure the return of escaped slaves. The whites carefully cultivated suspicion between blacks and Indians, especially by encouraging the blacks and Indians to regard each other as inferior and repulsive. The slaves' white-imposed religious and social training, exposure to the Indian wars, lack of contact with Indian communities and cultures, occasional use by the whites to track down Indians during wars, and the frequent use of Indians to hunt escaped black slaves all combined to alienate blacks from Indians. That blacks were susceptible to a common white view that regarded Indians with suspicion and fear is demonstrated most dramatically by Lucy Terry, owned by Ensign Ebenezer Wells in Deerfield, Massachusetts. This sensitive slave, carefully educated by whites, wrote the first known English-language poem by a black in the North American colonies, and she chose to describe—of all subjects possible in eighteenth-century New England—the Indian raid on Deerfield in 1746. Similar in poetic quality to white New England folk verse, Lucy Terry's poem (in Johnston Greene 1961, 242–43) reveals how black slaves could share the white masters' attitude toward Indians.

> August 'twas the twenty-fifth
> Seventeen hundred forty-six
> The Indians did in ambush lay
> Some very valiant men to slay
> The names of whom I'll not leave out
> Samuel Allen like a hero fout
> And though he was so brave and bold
> His face no more shall we behold
> Eleazer Hawks was killed outright
> Before he had time to fight
> Before he did the Indians see
> Was shot and killed immediately.
> Oliver Amsden he was slain
> Which caused his friends much grief and pain.
> Samuel Amsden they found dead
> Not many rods off from his head.
> Adonijah Gillet we do hear
> Did lose his life which was so dear.
> John Saddler fled across the water
> And so excaped the dreadful slaughter
> Eunice Allen see the Indians comeing
> And hoped to save herself by running
> And had not her petticoats stopt her
> The awful creatures had not cotched her
> And tommyhawked her on the head
> And left her on the ground for dead.
> Young Samuel Allen, Oh! lack-a-day
> Was taken and carried to Canada.

There was no reason why Lucy Terry should have identified or sympathized with Indians. If she had been captured by these Indians, the odds were against her. She might have been sold as a slave to the French in Canada, or perhaps she would have been returned to her master in exchange for French prisoners at the end of the war. Past centuries of North American history document little nonwhite interracial unity. Unless a black had a skill such as blacksmithing, or was multilingual, a slave usually would not be allowed by an Indian nation to take permanent refuge in their country. Exceptions were during times of war with the English, when a nation such as the Cherokees in 1760 would admit black refugees, welcomed because they increased an Indian nation's population. (The Seminoles, well known by the 1800s for their adoption of fugitive black slaves, were not established as a nation distinct from the Creeks until about 1763, and so did not greatly influence colonial slavery, although the Seminole impact after the American Revolution was considerable [McReynolds 1957, 23].)

Indians might refuse to admit blacks into their nations for political and economic reasons. But the white colonists encouraged them to disdain the entire black race as well. As reported by William Johnson in a letter to New York Governor George Clinton on January 22, 1749/50, one of the most effective propaganda weapons the French used to turn Indians against the English was to suggest that the English treated Indians as they treated blacks (Sullivan et al. 1921, 261). No Indian liked that equation. The Haudenosaunee ambassador Tanacharisson (Half-King), when upset at the paternalistic leadership of Indians in Pennsylvania by George Washington during the French and Indian War, complained that Washington commanded "the Indians as his slaves" (Jacobs 1966, 135). James Adair, a trader who wrote the *History of the American Indians* in 1775, reported that in 1739 South Carolina whites told the Cherokees that a smallpox epidemic that had caused a thousand deaths among them had been brought over from Africa by the blacks. This added to the Cherokees' negative image of the blacks (Adair [1775] 1973, 244). Prejudice was also overtly encouraged by the whites through using the Indians to suppress slave revolts. In South Carolina, for example, Indians helped the whites put down black slave revolts in 1739, 1744 and 1765 (Littlefield 1979, 14).

Black-Indian Intermarriage

The whites assumed that Indians who lived among whites east of the frontier would be less prejudiced against blacks because of their daily contact with them, and thus Indians who lived well within a white colony were regarded as more susceptible to conspiracy with blacks. Rumors of conspiracies joining Indian and black against white abounded in both the northern and southern colonies, but marital, rather than conspiratorial relationships seem to have been the more common reality. These Indian-black marriages within the boundaries of the white colonies were often enhanced by the common socioeconomic position of the couple—as servants, slaves or at the very least objects of white discrimination—and by factors such as disease that reduced many Indian nations' eligible singles. Indian women might seek black husbands because the tribe's Indian men had been killed while serving as mercenaries for the whites or because they had been drawn away from Indian communities to labor for white wages in coastal towns, on the frontier or on the sea as ships' crewmen. Indian men who did leave their communities and then desired to marry were not likely to find many eligible Indian women living in the towns or port cities that were their new homes. Despite the most intimate individual contact, however, prejudices between Indians and blacks in general continued.

Among the Narragansetts of Rhode Island, there was some intermarriage with blacks, but it is clear that the tribe did not look upon such intermarriage in the same way marriages with Indians were regarded. In the 1760s, members of the tribe wished to remove their sachem, Thomas Ninegrett, from office because he was selling tribal lands to whites for personal profit and to pay personal debts owed to whites. The first charge the Narragansetts brought against him, however, was not the land sale issue but that he had married a mulatto woman without the tribe's approval (Sullivan et al. 1927, 152).

The Narragansetts' subsequent experience continued to involve racial prejudice. When they and their white lawyer could not persuade white officials to stop Ninegrett's land sales, their lands were severely diminished. Finally, they joined with members of other New England tribes who were also being pressed by white colonists and appealed to the Haudenosaunee to grant them lands as a refuge.

On October 4, 1774, the Oneida Haudenosaunee, with the approval of the confederacy, agreed to provide these New England Indians—including Narragansetts, Mohegans, Montauks, Pequots, Niantics and perhaps a few from other tribes—with a portion of Oneida lands (in New York), lands that were not completely occupied by the refugees until after the American Revolution. The Oneidas made two stipulations. The first condition was that the New England Indians could hunt anything except beaver in Oneida territory. The second provision addressed the fact that blacks had intermarried or were living among these nations. This provision carefully defined the refugees' occupation of the land, "with this particular Clause, or Reservation that [the]

Same shall not be possessed by any persons, deemed of the said Tribes, who are descended from, or have intermixed with Negroes, or Mulattoes" (Sullivan et al. 1962, 684). It is probable that both the Oneidas and the English officials who approved the grant wanted this black exclusion clause inserted into the grant. The Oneidas were beset with a population decline. This fall in population was due in part to past wars, disease some Oneida migration westward to other Haudenosaunee lands, and some Oneida assimilation into white society. They wanted to increase their population through the centuries-old tradition of adopting other Indian nations into their midst. The English wanted blacks or mulattos excluded from the frontier to prevent the creation of any black-oriented nucleus beyond the whites' colonial boundaries where slave revolts might be organized.

Crispus Attucks and the Boston Massacre

An incident in Boston that preceded the American Revolution helps to demonstrate the problems in assigning a historical role to an Indian-black mulatto: In addition to a place in broad history, does the Indian-black mulatto belong in the annals of black history, Indian history or both? On Monday evening, March 5, 1770, at about nine o'clock, a gang of toughs rushed through Boston's streets. The gang was led by an Indian-black mulatto named Crispus Attucks, and he and his fellows joined a larger mob of hundreds gathered around nine British soldiers formed in front of the Custom House on King Street. As the mob taunted the Redcoats, Attucks suddenly assaulted one of the soldiers, wielding a thick piece of cordwood as a club. Angered by these provocations, the Redcoats fired randomly into the crowd. Of five colonists killed by the British bullets, Attucks was probably the first to die, the first martyr of the now famous Boston Massacre.

In the trial of the British soldiers following the confrontation, Attucks was referred to as a "mulatto," but once he was referred to as an "Indian". On the first day of the trial, lawyer Samuel Quincy asked town watchman Edward G. Langford, "Did you know the Indian that was killed?" Langford answered "No" (Trial of the British Soldiers [1770] 1824, 12). It is possible that Quincy's use of the term "Indian" implied "West Indian," as Attucks had recently been in the Bahamas. However, his last name is a Natick (Massachusetts nation) word for deer. Attucks was also a Natick Christian Indian family name dating back to the seventeenth century. There is a Framingham, Massachusetts, marriage record dated 1737 that suggests Crispus Attucks's mother could have been a

Natick Indian named Nancy Peter Attucks and that his father may have been an African, Prince Youngay, but it is more likely that Crispus was the son of a man with the name of Attucks.

Furthermore, unless Crispus Attucks was born over a decade before this marriage, or was younger than is believed, he was too old to have been Nancy Peter Attucks' son. He was more likely either the slave or the indentured servant of a white in Framingham who placed an ad in the *Boston Gazette*, October 2, 1750, regarding "a Molatto Fellow, about 27 Years of Age, named *Crispas*, 6 Feet two Inches high, short curl'd Hair, his knees nearer together than common" (Kaplan 1973, 7–8; Zobel 1971, 191, 214).

During the soldiers' trial in 1770, lawyer John Adams (later President Adams) specifically noted that Attucks was from Framingham. Being a runaway may explain why, by 1770, Attucks preferred to be known by another name, Michael Johnson. When killed in Boston, Attucks was evidently serving on a whaling ship from Nantucket, whaling being an employment often undertaken by New England Indians. Whatever Attucks' exact racial mixture of Indian and black, he was part Natick Indian. Had he been partly Indian and white, he would undoubtedly have been recognized by colonial whites, Indians, and blacks as an Indian; had he been partly black and white, he would have been termed black; but his Indian-black background placed him in a status limbo.

The Boston radicals exploited the killing of Attucks and the other four men as grist for their antiimperial propaganda mill. That they never identified Attucks's exact racial heritage is understandable, as it would not have served the cause of "liberty" to emphasize that the first martyr was either an Indian whose homelands had been stolen by these very colonists or a slave of supposedly liberty-loving people.

Ideally, history should be human, not racial. Ironically, although the exact character of Crispus Attucks is not known, the most detailed description of Attucks is also very much the most human. A colonist's autopsy gives details of how two musket balls entered his body and how the first caused his death by damaging his thorax, rib, cartilaginous extremity, sternum, diaphragm, liver, gall balder, descending aorta and spine—the examiner noted everything but his race. The issue of Crispus Attucks's identity is more than just a matter of assigning an individual to a heroes' pantheon, however. What may be called an Attucks Dilemma is shared today, as it was in the past, by many American Indians such as the Shinnecocks on Long Island in New York, Saponi people from North Carolina and Pennsylvania, and Lumbees in North Carolina. These are the people who are both Indian and black, their identity and their particular contribution to human history unsettled and often unsettling—at least to the mainstream culture that prefers tidy labels.

Indian Practices vis-à-vis Black Slaves

That Indians were not averse to having their own black slaves is clear from no less a figure than the great Ottawa leader Pontiac. At the height of his power in 1763, he offered peace to the British at besieged Detroit, but insisted that one of the conditions be the whites' delivery, as a personal gift, of a young black male slave owned by a Detroit merchant. (The whites rejected all the peace terms.) Cherokee, Creek, Choctaw and Chickasaw leaders occasionally had one or more black slaves, many of whom had been captured during wars. Although colonial laws often forbade the sale of slaves to Indians, purchased slaves were introduced into Indian communities by white traders who married into a nation and whose mixed-blood descendants continued to own slaves, influencing other tribal members to do likewise. Black slaves were often obtained by Indians to replace members of their own families. Whether these blacks would be treated as slaves, servants or full members of the Indian's family depended on the individual decision of the bereaved family; there was no mandatory custom. In 1755, William Johnson reported that the governor of Canada was giving black and Indian slaves to tribes to replace warriors killed in the French cause (perhaps as part of formal condolence ceremonies). Johnson also remarked that the Indians allied with the British expected him to do the same whenever they lost a man in battle (Peckham 1947, 140; Littlefield 1979, 15; Sullivan et al. 1922, 388).

Even an escaped slave who had been accepted into an Indian community could suddenly be surrendered to the whites if the Indian community felt that the slave's return might help end a war or encourage trade. If a black discovered through a friendly Indian that the tribe intended to turn the refugee over to the whites, the slave could try to run off, but such warnings could not be depended upon. The insecurity of blacks living as refugees in Indian communities west of the white frontier is dramatically demonstrated by the life of Sam Tony. About 1744, Tony escaped from his white master in Maryland. He lived among Indians of various nations, but twenty years later, in 1764, was living among some Haudenosaunee at Chenango (near Binghamton, New York). His high intelligence made his advice valuable to the Haudenosaunee community, at that time in the midst of debate over what their role should be in Pontiac's war against the British. Sam Tony, like many of the Haudenosaunee themselves, advocated war. The Chenango community, however, decided on continued peace with the British. No Chenango Haudenosaunee who advocated war was turned over to the British because all members of the Haudenosaunee community expected political discussion. But Tony was not an Hauden-osaunee, and some Haudenosaunee were evidently envious of his persuasive powers. Tony was turned over to Sir William Johnson as a traitor to the British. After twenty years of freedom, Tony found himself shipped to Albany and then to New York City as both a political subversive and an escaped slave. Commander-in-chief General Thomas Gage decided Tony's fate, and wrote to Johnson that "the Negro you have sent down, may easily be disposed of in the West-Indies" (Sullivan et al. 1925, 424; Sullivan et al. 1939, 174–75; Sullivan et al. 1953, 165–66). Two decades of freedom for Sam Tony evidently ended in the wretched working conditions of a West Indies plantation.

Some escaped slaves or their descendants did assimilate into Indian nations, assuming the values of their adopted society. A mixed-blood—perhaps he was even pure black—evidently became a chief of the Cayuga Haudenosaunee nation. Named "the Negro," and well known by colonial officials such as Sir William Johnson, no physical description affirms whether this man was an escaped slave, a descendant of a slave or merely a dark-skinned Haudenosaunee. Whatever his origin, he was sufficiently Haudenosaunee in culture so that the whites referred to him as an Indian.

In 1764, there were at least two mulattos living among the Genessee River Seneca Haudenosaunee, one of them serving the Senecas as a blacksmith. Both were half-Indian and half-black, and they had escaped from an unnamed southern colony. They were regarded by the Senecas as Indians, and thus were not turned over to the whites. Interestingly, during Pontiac's rebellion one of the mulattos purchased a ten-year-old white girl named Eliza Carter for £5. He bought her from a Delaware who had captured her in a raid, and treated her kindly. She was evidently returned at the end of the war (Sullivan et al. 1922, 544, 672; Sullivan et al. 1925, 495–96; Sullivan et al. 1939, 955–56).

In the nineteenth century, the route of the underground railroad from the south northward, especially through New York, was well organized by courageous blacks and whites. Its greatest success was certainly during the 1800s, but the general routes taken were already well worn long before the whites settled the areas, for blacks had made their way northward during the colonial period. Tragically, these blacks often found themselves returned to slavery by Indian nations whose white policy took precedence over its black policy.

The British encouraged Indian nations to return slaves not only by offering trade goods and rewards, but also by including fugitive slave provisions in both trade and peace treaties with Indians. For example, the 1717 Charleston, South Carolina treaty with the powerful Creeks stated that escaped slaves would be returned to the South Carolina colonists. In the London treaty of 1730, Cherokee ambassadors promised South Carolina and the British government similar terms, one of them (the Ketagustah or "Prince") perceptively noting to the British officials in phrases with possible double meanings that

> this small Rope which we shew you, is all we have to bind our [own] slaves with, and may be broken, but you have Iron Chains for yours; however, if we catch your Slaves, we shall bind them as well as we can, and deliver them to our Friends again, and have no pay for it. (Crane [1929] 1964, 300; Corkran 1967, 64)

In 1733, 1763 and 1774, similar provisions were included in treaties between the Creeks and British agents meeting in the colony of Georgia. In 1764, peace treaties were negotiated to end Pontiac's war (which finally ended in 1766 when Pontiac himself surrendered). These 1764 treaties were made with the Hurons, Ottawas, Chippewas (Ojibwas), Shawnees, Delawares and Seneca Haudeno-saunee. All included provisions that black slaves captured during the war would be returned to the whites and that in the future, whenever escaped black slaves turned up in Indian country, they too would be sent back to the whites. During Pontiac's war, as in previous conflicts, many black slaves could not be returned because they had already been sold to French traders who entered Indian country to buy this human booty. Many Indian towns refused to give up all their slaves, at least immediately, and negotiations frequently dragged on. Nevertheless, the value of Indians as deterrents to fugitive slaves was a constant in colonial history. The British names given to a few prominent eighteenth-century Cherokees speak for themselves: Slave Catcher of Chota, Slave Catcher of Kitruwa, Slave Catcher of Conutory, Slave Catcher of Tomatly, and Slave Catcher of Conasatchee.

In 1768, General Thomas Gage reported on the slave hunting of the Creeks:

The Commissioners on the part of Georgia, have been employed with the Deputys from the Creeks, in marking out the Boundary behind Georgia. And the Creeks have restored such of the Negroe Slaves, as could be taken; they were also in pursuit of others, who made their escape from the Indian Towns, when they found they were to be delivered up. The Scalp of one of those Fugitives was brought in and delivered to the Commissary, which Circumstance will break that Intercourse between the Indians and Negroes, so much to be dreaded by all the Southern Provinces. (Gage 1931, 185–86)

Southern Indian superintendent Edmond Atkin reported in 1755 that even the remnants of the coastal tribes in the south (who were not part of the large interior confederacies or nations) were useful to the whites "in hunting Game, destroying Vermin, and Beasts of Prey, and catching Runaway Slaves" (Atkin [1755] 1967, 45). While various Indian nations willingly returned black slaves as a matter of national policy toward the whites, the British saw their own policy toward the Indians as directly related to the control of black slaves within their colonies. Referring to the Indians who lived beyond the boundaries of individual colonies, General Thomas Gage explained in a letter to the Earl of Hillsborough dated November 10, 1770, that

I am of opinion, independent of the Motives of common Justice and Humanity, that the Principles of Interest and Policy should induce us rather to protect than molest them. Were they drove from their Forrests, the Peltry Trade would decrease, and [it is] not impossible that worse Savages would take Refuge in them; for they might become the Azylum of fugitive Negroes, and idle Vagabonds escaped from Justice, who in time might become formidable, and subsist by Rapine, and plundering the lower Countrys. (Gage 1931, 278)

Years later, fearing the possibility of slave revolts organized by escaped blacks gathered in the hinterland, the Patriot revolutionaries of the new United States continued British policy and included, in their very first treaty with an Indian nation, a provision for the return of escaped slaves. This September 17, 1778 treaty with the Delawares, made at Fort Pitt, Pennsylvania, stated that it is further agreed between the parties aforesaid, that neither shall entertain or give countenance to the enemies of the other, or protect in their respective states, criminal fugitives, servants or slaves, but the same to apprehend, and secure and deliver to the State or States, to which such enemies, criminals, servants or slaves respectively belong. (Kappler [1904] 1972, 4)

The whites in British North America and the Indian nations of the interior were for the most part willing to cooperate on the issue of fugitive slaves in order to continue the mutual profits of the fur or deerskin trade. They also needed each other in their wars against rivals. Therefore escaped slaves often found themselves returned to their white masters by the Indian nations west of the white frontier.

Even those slaves who did find temporary refuge in Indian towns frequently discovered that their freedom was expendable whenever their Indian hosts decided it to be so. The Indians, following their own national interests, thus eliminated the possibility of slave revolts. These revolts surely would have come in North America during the colonial period if the African-born or even American-born slave had had the chance to build a resistance movement in the hinterland.

Despite the odds, some blacks did manage to live out their lifetimes within an Indian nation as freemen. Many were adopted and shared the same socialization experiences as any of the whites who were adopted, even as other blacks were being returned into slavery. Evidence for this paradox extends from the Haudenosaunee in the North to the Creeks in the south. Blacks undoubtedly influenced both the politics and cultures of their adopted Indian nations. Even so, with few of their own race living around them, these blacks gave up much of their own cultural identities. They became Indians—Haudenosaunee, Cherokees and Creeks. Such assimilated blacks were not likely to foment slave revolts.

The Status of Indian and White Women

While Indian nations generally hindered the possibilities of freedom for black people in the colonies, they were at least partly responsible for one cornerstone in the subsequent struggle of white women to gain full equality with white men in the United States. American Indian societies usually balanced the status of women and men. Thus, Indian women offered examples of economic, political and social equality.

Another cornerstone in the struggle was practical. On the frontier, the hewn stumps in the forest were far from the protected pedestals of male-idealized womanhood, and no white frontiersmen wanted his wife on a pedestal as there was too much work for everyone to do. A white pioneer family could not survive without the strong participation of women, as well as children. White women on the frontier were a hardy lot made even stronger by the fact that they were expected to wield a musket against the Indians in defense of their homes (which were often illegally on Indian land).

Consider the experience of Hannah Dustan, who lived on the Massachusetts frontier near Haverhill in 1697. Dustan was taken captive by Maine Abenaki Indians just one week after she had given birth to her eighth child. Her husband and her other seven children were working in the fields at the time of the Indian raid and the Abenakis were able to carry off Dustan, her baby, the baby's nurse Mary Neff and a number of neighbors.

The baby was killed when a warrior tired of its crying and bashed its head against a tree. On the way north, Dustan, Mary Neff and a young boy were separated from the other prisoners and turned over to a group of twelve Indians including two warriors, three Indian women and seven Indian children. After all the Indians fell asleep around the campfire on the night of April 29, Dustan convinced Mary Neff and the boy to join her in an escape attempt. Quietly they got up, stole hatchets from the sleeping Indians, and silently tomahawked every one of them, adult and child alike, except for an old woman and a young boy who ran off into the woods in terror. Dustan and her companions removed the scalps of the two warriors, the two women and the six children and carried the ten Indian scalps home (Lincoln 1913, 263–66). The government of Massachusetts rewarded the three whites with £50 in bounty money, and Dustan returned home to her family.

The Indians' impact on women's history is more than just the role of white women as adversary. Women's history is above all the accomplishments and contributions made by women of all races. In this context, Indian women had always had a significant impact on the histories of their own nations. After 1492, they had an impact on white colonial histories as well.

When Spanish, French, British and other European men arrived anywhere in the Western Hemisphere, their first impression of Indian women was likely to be sexually oriented, an erotic factor increased by the fact that the

Europeans who initially made the long Atlantic voyage were mostly men. But these men's second impressions were of the vital political roles that Indian women played in many, though certainly not all, Indian nations.

Indian Women as Traditional Leaders and Men's Equals

There were powerful Indian women chiefs, such as the Creek (or Yuchi) chief of Cofitachique, who met the Spaniard de Soto in 1540; the woman leader known as the "Queen" of Appomattoc encountered by the Jamestown, Virginia, colonists in 1607; Weetamoo, leader of the Pocasset Wampanoags whose political role was enhanced by her duties as a wampum-maker and who joined the Indian revolt against the New England colonists in 1675; and the Queen of the Pamunkeys, who remained allied with the British in Virginia during the hostilities that began in 1675. The "Sun Woman" was the title of generation after generation of a hereditary and powerful female leader among the Natchez along the Mississippi River. The position of Sun Woman was held by the sister of the Natchez nation's hereditary ruler, the "Great Sun." Among the Cherokees, the office of "Beloved Woman" ("Gigau") was held by a woman who had proved herself brave in war. Her position was a direct contrast—or balance—of her previous role. The title of Beloved Woman carried with it the responsibility of acting as the nation's permanent, vocal and consistent advocate for peace whenever war was being debated. Goa, the wife of the Creek emperor Brims, was an influential leader of the Creeks, as was Coosapankeesa, also known as Mary Musgrove Bosomworth. There was Madame Montour, a prominent Algonquin in Pennsylvania during the early 1700s. Allaquippa, a Seneca leader in Pennsylvania, was a diplomatic representative of the confederacy of the Haudenosaunee. Allaquippa was so powerful that in 1753 a young George Washington was required to visit her as he made his way through the territory she supervised during a diplomatic mission to the French in western Pennsylvania. The Mohawk nation's Mary "Molly" Brant influenced both Haudenosaunee and British policies in the era of the American Revolution.

While Indian women proved fascinating to the Europeans, it should be recalled that Europeans had influential female leaders of their own, such as Queen Isabella of Spain who sponsored Columbus; Queen Elizabeth of England who encouraged the first British colony at Roanoke; Mary and Anne, both queens of England in the decades following the Glorious Revolution of 1688; and Maria Teresa of Austria, ruler of one of eighteenth-century Europe's greatest empires. The difference between the white and Indian women with regard to their political and social positions was that often (though not always) all the Indian women in a given community—not just the prominent women—possessed vital political power. This was enhanced whenever an Indian society was matrilineal, because this usually gave the women built-in economic power as well. Among the Hopi, Zuni, Laguna and Acoma Pueblos, for example, the women owned the homes and controlled family life because their societies were matrilineal. Thus the most influential person in any family was usually was the oldest woman, not the oldest man.

Cherokee women also had matrilineal-based power. But the arrival of the white men with their essentially discriminatory attitudes toward women evidently disrupted this power except within the home and town. Although Cherokee women were known to have participated in government and in war operations before the coming of the whites, colonial whites seldom observed women in councils or in the organization of war. Perhaps this was because the Cherokees decided that given white attitudes toward women, the Cherokees' negotiating position would only be weakened by the presence of women. Indeed, it is a moot question as to how much white discrimination against women rubbed off on the Cherokees—and other Indian nations—and to what extent Indian males used the coming of the whites to consolidate their own positions in their societies to the detriment of the women. Because the fur and deerskin trade brought European manufactured goods into Indian communities, the male hunter became more prominent as a provider of clothing, utensils and domestic luxuries than had been the case before the white trade began. But Indian women's considerable contribution to the trade—for example, their important skills in tanning the skins to their highest quality so that they could be traded—evidently was not enough to offset the increasing male dominance brought by the trade.

Among the Haudenosaunee, a matrilineal structure resulted in the women holding the responsibility of electing the confederacy's Grand Council of fifty male chiefs. When a chief died, a clan meeting to choose a replacement was held under the auspices of a respected older woman known as a clan mother. The clan mother would then report her clan's choice of the new male chief. The chief held office for life, but could be impeached by the women. The clan mothers also sat in a women's council that constantly advised the confederacy's Grand Council as to the women's political opinions. These opinions included the right to demand that the male chiefs reconsider any decision— essentially a veto. The Haudenosaunee women could veto plans for war, had the right of life and death over prisoners of war, and decided which refugees or captives would be adopted into their nations. Haudenosaunee society sought balance, and thus expected men and women to be regarded as equals even as they fulfilled different functions (Snow 1994, 60–69; Mann 2000, 115–82).

In 1783, Benjamin Franklin wrote "Remarks Concerning the Savages of North-America." Although many of his observations applied to Indian people, his focus was the Haudenosaunee. In this essay, Franklin observed the balanced political, social and economic relationships of men and women:

> The Indian Men, when young, are Hunters and Warriors; when old, Counsellors; for all their Government is by the Counsel or Advice of the Sages; there is no force, there are no Prisons, no Officers to compel Obedience, or inflict Punishment. Hence they generally study Oratory; the best Speaker having the most Influence. The Indian Women till the Ground, dress the Food, nurse and bring up the Children, and preserve and hand down to Posterity the Memory of Public Transactions. These Employments of Men and Women are accounted natural and honorable. Having few Artificial Wants, they have abundance of Leisure for Improvement by Conversation. Our laborious manner of Life compared with theirs, they esteem slavish and base; and the Learning on which we value ourselves; they regard as frivolous and useless .'.
>
> Having frequent Occasions to hold public Councils, they have acquired great Order and Decency in conducting them. The old Men sit in the foremost Ranks, the Warriors in the next, and the Women and Children in the hindmost. The Business of the Women is to take exact notice of what passes, imprint it in their Memories, for they have no Writing, and communicate it to their Children. They are the Records of the Council, and they preserve Tradition of the Stipulations in Treaties, a hundred Years back, which when we compare with our Writings we always find exact. (Franklin 1987, 969–70)

In 1751, more than three decades before Franklin wrote these words, he was confident that if the Haudenosaunee could carry out a successful government uniting their six nations in a confederation, then certainly the whites could as well. White political unity took longer than Franklin expected, and even after the formulation of the U.S. Constitution often seemed lacking. What Franklin and other male white colonists neglected or refused to admit was the fact that the confederation of the Haudenosaunee was based on the full participation of both women and men, a factor the United States chose largely to ignore until the twentieth century.

Women Captured by Indians

Some white women captured by Indians during colonial wars—Pontiac's War of 1763, for example—did not want to return to white settlements after the war even though their return was a demand made by the British in the peace terms dictated by British officials. Still other women fled to Indian communities voluntarily. The security and happiness that these women found is illustrated by a servant woman, possibly black, who had fled to live among an Haudenosaunee nation, probably the Oneida, shortly before or during the American Revolution. In 1784 at Fort Stanwix, New York, she talked with François, the Marquis de Barbé-Marbois, who was a French colleague of Lafayette. Barbé-Marbois had decided to draw her out because

> her color and bearing did not seem quite savage. I asked her in English who she was. She pretended at first not to understand. Pressed with my questions she told me that she had formerly served at the home of a planter in the State of New York, but that she had tired of the position of a servant and had fled, and that the Indians had welcomed her, and that she lived very happily among them. "The whites," she told me, "treated me harshly. I saw them take rest while they made me work without a break. I ran the risk of being beaten, or of dying of hunger, if through fatigue or laziness I refused to do what I was told. Here I have no master, I am the equal of all the women in the tribe, I do what I please without anyone's saying anything about it, I work only for myself,—I shall marry if I wish and be unmarried again when I wish. Is there a single woman as independent as I in your cities?" (François 1929, 211–12)

Mary Rowlandson

One of the most famous accounts of a white woman living among an Indian people is that of Mary Rowlandson, a Puritan whose "captivity narrative" is a significant contribution to colonial literature. Rowlandson was captured from her home in Lancaster, Massachusetts, in 1676 during King Philip's War and was held by the Wampanoag Indians for eleven weeks and six days. During and

after her capture, no Indian man ever sexually molested her. Once among
Indian families, she was placed in the company of other women, especially the
Indian leader Weetamoo. Rowlandson was finally ransomed and she returned
to her husband. In 1682 Rowlandson published her recollections, *The
Sovereignty and Goodness of God: Narrative of the Captivity of Mrs. Mary
Rowlandson.*

Mary Rowlandson's sometimes severe account is useful in understanding
white attitudes toward Indians, and despite its bias Rowlandson's account is an
interesting description of American Indian communities in New England. It is
also typical of Puritan New England, for Rowlandson believed that the major
cause of the war was God's displeasure with His chosen people, the Puritans
themselves, rather than the Puritans' policy toward the Indians. For
Rowlandson the war moved from theoretical causes to harsh reality one winter
morning:

> On the tenth of February...Came the Indians with great numbers
> upon Lancaster: Their first coming was about Sun-rising; hearing the
> noise of some Guns, we looked out; several Houses were burning, and
> the Smoke ascending to Heaven...
>
> At length they came and beset our own house, and quickly it was
> the dolefullest day that ever mine eyes saw. The House stood upon the
> edge of a hill; some of the Indians got behind the hill, others into the
> Barn, and others behind any thing that could shelter them; from all
> which places they shot against the House, so that the Bullets seemed to
> fly like hail. (Rowlandson 1913, 211–12)

The Indians killed many of the colonists (Rowlandson's husband was away in
Boston). Wounded and then captured, Rowlandson and her three children
were taken by retreating Indians into the forest where they camped.

> Now away we must go with those Barbarous Creatures, with our
> bodies wounded and bleeding, and our hearts no less than our bodies.
> ...[T]his was the dolefullest night that ever my eyes saw. Oh the
> roaring, and singing and danceing, and yelling of those black creatures
> in the night, which made the place a lively resemblance of hell.
> (Rowlandson 1913, 121)

Rowlandson, purchased from her original captor by another warrior named Quinnapin, was taken to an Indian village. Here Rowlandson's six-year-old Sarah died of a wound she had suffered while in the besieged house in Lancaster.

When I had been at my masters wigwam, I took the first opportunity I could get, to go look after my dead child: when I came I askt them what they had done with it? then they told me it was upon the hill: then they went and shewed me where it was, where I saw the ground was newly digged, and there they told me they had buried it: There I left that Child in the Wilderness, and must commit it, and my self also in this Wilderness-condition, to him who is above all. God having taken away this dear Child, I went to see my daughter Mary, who was at this same Indian Town, at a Wigwam not very far off, though we had little liberty or opportunity to see one another. She was about ten years old, and taken from the door at first by a Praying Ind and afterward sold for a gun. When I came in sight, she would fall a weeping; at which they were provoked, and would not let me come near her, but bade me be gone; which was a heart-cutting word to me. I had one Child dead, another in the Wilderness, I knew not where, the third they would not let me come near to: *Me* (as he said) *have ye bereaved of my Children, Joseph is not, and Simeon is not, and ye will take Benjamin also, all these things are against me.* I could not sit still in this condition, but kept walking from one place to another. And as I was going along, my heart was even overwhelm'd with the thoughts of my condition, and that I should have Children, and a Nation which I knew not ruled over them. Whereupon I earnestly entreated the Lord, that he would consider my low estate, and shew me a token for good, and if it were his blessed will, some sign and hope of some relief. And indeed quickly the Lord answered, in some measure, my poor prayers: for as I was going up and down mourning and lamenting my condition, my Son came to me, and asked me how I did; I had not seen him before, since the destruction of the Town, and I knew not where he was, till I was informed by himself, that he was amongst a smaller percel of Indians, whose place was about six miles off.... One of the Indians that came from Medfield fight, had brought some plunder, came to me, and askd me, if I would have a Bible, he had got one in his Basket. I was glad of it, and asked him, whether he thought the Indians would let me read? he answered, yes: So I took the

Bible, and in that melancholy time, it came into my mind to read first the 28. Chap. of Deut., which I did.... (Rowlandson 1913, 126–27)

The Indians moved from their village to a new camp, and then moved again. It was now March.

The occasion (as I thought) of their moving at this time, was, the English Army, it being near and following them: For they went, as if they had gone for their lives, for some considerable way, and then they made a stop, and chose some of their stoutest men, and sent them back to hold the English Army in place whilst the rest escaped: And then, like Jehu, they marched on furiously, with their old, and with their young: some carried their old decrepit mothers, some carried one, and some another. Four of them carried a great Indian upon a Bier; but going through a thick Wood with him, they were hindered, and could make no haste; whereupon they took him upon their backs, and carried him, one at a time, till they came to Bacquaug River. Upon a Friday, a little after noon we came to this River. When all the company was come up, and were gathered together, I thought to count the number of them, but they were so many, and being somewhat in motion, it was beyond my skil. In this travel, because of my wound, I was somewhat favoured in my load; I carried only my knitting work and two quarts of parched meal: Being very faint I asked my mistriss to give me one spoonful of the meal, but she would not give me a taste. They quickly fell to cutting dry trees, to make Rafts to carry them over the river; and soon my turn came to go over: By the advantage of some brush which they had laid upon the Raft to sit upon, I did not wet my foot (which many of themselves at the other end were mid-leg deep) which cannot but be acknowledged as a favour of God to my weakened body, it being a very cold time. I was not before acquainted with such kind of doings or dangers. *When thou passeth through the waters I will be with thee, and through the Rivers they shall not overflow thee*, Isai. 43. 2. A certain number of us got over the River that night, but it was the night after the Sabbath before all the company was got over. On the Saturday they boyled an old Horses leg which they had got, and so we drank of the broth, as soon as they thought it was ready, and when it was almost gone, they filled it up again.

The first week of my being among them, I hardly ate any thing; the second week, I found my stomach grow very faint for want of something; and yet it was very hard to get down their filthy trash: but the third week, though I could think how formerly my stomach would turn against this or that, and I could starve and dy before I could eat such things, yet they were sweet and savoury to my taste. I was at this time knitting a pair of white cotton stockins for my mistriss; and had not yet wrought upon a Sabbath day; when the Sabbath came they bade me go to work; I told them it was the Sabbath-day, and desired them to let me rest, and told them I would do as much more to morrow; to which they answered me, they would break my face. And here I cannot but take notice of the strange providence of God in preserving the heathen: They were many hundreds, old and young, some sick, and some lame, many had Papooses at their backs, the greatest number at this time with us, were Squaws, and they travelled with all they had, bag and baggage, and yet they got over this River aforesaid; and on Munday they set their Wigwams on fire, and away they went: On that very day came the English Army after them to this River, and saw the smoak of their Wigwams, and yet this River put a stop to them. God did not give them [the English] courage or activity to go over after us; we were not ready for so great a mercy as victory and deliverance; if we had been, God would have found out a way for the English to have passed this River, as well as for the Indians with their Squaws and Children, and all their Luggage. *Oh that my People had hearkened to me, and Israel had walked in my ways, I should soon have subdued their Enemies, and turned my hand against their Adversaries*, Psal. 81: 13. 14. (Rowlandson 1913, 130–31)

Still moving to avoid the British armies, the Indians again changed their location and entered Vermont, where Rowlandson met the great Wampanoag leader Philip.

We travelled on till night; and in the morning, we must go over the River to Philip's Crew. When I was in the Cannoo, I could not but be amazed at the numerous crew of Pagans that were on the Bank on the other side. When I came ashore, they gathered all about me, I sitting alone in the midst: I observed they asked one another questions, and laughed, and rejoyced over their Gains and Victories. Then my heart began to fail: and I fell a weeping which was the first time to my remembrance, that I wept before them. Although I had met with so much Affliction, and my heart was many times ready to break, yet could I not shed one tear in their sight: but rather had been all this while in a maze, and like one astonished: but now I may say as, Psal. 137. 1. *By the Rivers of Babylon, there we sate down: yea, we wept when we remembered Zion.* There one of them asked me, why I wept, I could hardly tell what to say: yet I answered, they would kill me: No, said he, none will hurt you. Then came one of them and gave me two spoon-fulls of Meal to comfort me, and another gave me half a pint of Pease; which was more worth than many Bushels at another time. Then I went to see King Philip, he bade me come in and sit down, and asked me whether I woold smoke it (a usual Complement nowadayes amongst Saints and Sinners) but this no way suited me. For though I had formerly used Tobacco, yet I had left it ever since I was first taken. It seems to be a Bait, the Devil layes to make men loose their precious time: I remember with shame, how formerly, when I had taken two or three pipes, I was presently ready for another, such a bewitching thing it is: But I thank God, he has now given me power over it; surely there are many who may be better imployed than to ly sucking a stinking Tobacco-pipe.

Now the Indians gather their Forces to go against North-Hampton: over-night one went about yelling and hooting to give notice of the design. Whereupon they fell to boyling of Ground-nuts, and parching of Corn (as many as had it) for their Provision: and in the morning away they went. During my abode in this place, Philip spake to me to make a shirt for his boy, which I did, for which he gave me a shilling: I offered the mony to my master, but he bade me keep it: and with it I bought a piece of Horse flesh. Afterwards he [Philip] asked me to make a Cap for his boy, for which he invited me to Dinner. I went, and he gave me a Pancake, about as big as two fingers; it was made of parched wheat, beaten, and fryed in Bears grease, but I thought I never tasted pleasanter meat in my life. There was a Squaw who spake to me to make a shirt for her *Sannup* [husband], for which she gave me a piece of Bear. Another asked me to knit a pair of Stockins, for which she gave me a quart of Pease: I boyled my Pease and Bear together, and invited my master and mistress to dinner, but the proud

Gossip [the woman], because I served them both in one Dish, would eat nothing, except one bit that he [her husband] gave her upon the point of his knife...

The Indians returning from North-Hampton, brought with them some Horses, and Sheep, and other things which they had taken: I desired them, that they would carry me to Albany, upon one of those Horses, and sell me for Powder: for so they had sometimes discoursed. I was utterly hopeless of getting home on foot, the way that I came...

But in stead of going either to Albany or homeward, we must go five miles up the River, and then go over it. Here we abode for a while...

One bitter cold day, I could find no room to sit down before the fire: I went out, and could not tell what to do, but I went in to another Wigwam, where they were also sitting round the fire, but the Squaw laid a skin for me, and bid me sit down, and gave me some Ground-nuts, and bade me come again: and told me they would buy me, if they were able, and yet these were strangers to me that I never saw before. (Rowlandson 1913, 134–37)

After several other removes to new camps, Mary Rowlandson's narrative described a tragic encounter:

I went to see an English Youth in this place, one John Gilberd of Springfield. I found him lying without dores [out of doors], upon the ground; I asked him how he did? he told me he was very sick of a flux, with eating so much blood: They had turned him out of the Wigwam, and with him an Indian Papoos, almost dead, (whose Parents had been killed) in a bitter cold day, without fire or clothes: the young man himself had nothing on, but his shirt and wastcoat. This sight was enough to melt a heart of flint. There they lay quivering in the Cold, the youth round like a dog; the Papoos stretcht out, with his eyes and nose and mouth full of dirt, and yet alive, and groaning. (Rowlandson 1913, 143)

Rowlandson persuaded the sick young man to seek out a campfire, but evidently she left the child to die—Mary Rowlandson could not oppose the Indians' decision to give up the orphaned, sick child to fate, Spartan-like. Then, at this same camp, my Mistresses Papoos was sick, and it died that night, and there was one benefit in it, that there was more room. I went to a Wigwam, and they bade me come in, and gave me a skin to ly upon, and a mess of Venson and Ground-nuts, which was a choice Dish among them. On the morrow they buried the Papoos, and afterward, both morning and evening, there came a company to mourn and howle with her: though I confess, I could not much condole with them. Many sorrowfull dayes I had in this place. . . . (Rowlandson 1913, 144–45)

Rowlandson went with the Indians when they moved again. Her "master," the warrior Quinnapin, had been away in battle for some time, and she had not fared as well in his absence.

Going along, having indeed my life, but little spirit, Philip, who was in the Company, came up and took me by the hand, and said, Two weeks more and you shal be Mistress [of Quinnapin] again. I asked him, if he spake true? he answered, Yes, and quickly you shal come to your master again; who had been gone from us three weeks. After many weary steps we came to Wachuset, where he was: and glad I was to see him. He asked me, When I washt me? I told him not this month, then he fetcht me some water himself, and bid me wash, and gave me the Glass to see how I lookt; and bid his Squaw give me something to eat: so she gave me a mess of Beans and meat, and a little Ground-nut Cake. I was wonderfully revived with this favour shewed me, Psal. 106. 46, *He made them also to be pittied, of all those that carried them Captives.*

My master had three Squaws, living sometimes with one, and sometimes with another one, this old Squaw, at whose Wigwam I was, and with whom my Master had been those three weeks. Another was Wattimore [Weetamoo, the female chief of the Pocasset Wampanoags], with whom I had lived and served all this while: A severe and proud Dame she was, bestowing every day in dressing her self neat as much time as any of the Gentry of the land: powdering her hair, and painting her face, going with Neck-laces, with Jewels in her ears, and Bracelets upon her hands: When she had dressed her self, her work was to make Girdles of Wampom [wampum] and Beads [an extremely important duty]. (Rowlandson 1913, 150)

Still more removes followed, but finally the message came that Rowlandson would be ransomed. Two Christian Indians, Tom Dublet and Peter Conway, had conducted the negotiations between the two sides. Mary Rowlandson recorded her encounter with the two Christian men:

> Though they were Indians, I gat them by the hand, and burst out into tears; my heart was so full that I could not speak to them; but roux recovering my self, I asked them how my husband did, and all my friends and acquaintance? they said, They are all very well but melancholy. (Rowlandson 1913, 151)

After still one more move, Rowlandson and eventually her two children were returned to the Puritans. Rowlandson, having been a captive for eighty-three days (February 10 through May 2, 1676), noted that

> if trouble from smaller matters begin to arise in me, I have something at hand to check my self with, and say, why am I troubled? It was but the other day that if I had had the world, I would have given it for my freedom, or to have been a Servant to a Christian. I have learned to look beyond present and smaller troubles, and to be quieted under them, as Moses said, Exod. 14. 13. *Stand still and see the salvation of the Lord.* (Rowlandson 1913, 167)

Mary Jemison

Eight decades after Mary Rowlandson's capture during King Philip's War in Massachusetts, another white woman, Mary Jemison, began a life among American Indians that she also recorded. Unlike Rowlandson, she would not be exchanged and would happily live out her life with the Indian people who adopted her. She left a detailed account of this life.

In 1758, Mary Jemison, about fifteen years of age, was captured during the French and Indian War by Shawnees while living with her family on the Pennsylvania frontier. After capture, her mother, father, two brothers and a sister were killed. Mary was taken to the French Fort Duquesne, now Pittsburgh. There she was traded or given to two Seneca Haudenosaunee women. By canoe she was taken down the Ohio River to a small Seneca village. In 1762, the Senecas adopted her, she married, survived one Delaware and one Seneca husband, raised a family, and finally dictated a narrative of her life in

1824. The white author who recorded Jemison's account, James E. Seaver, embellished some accounts of Indian battles and incidents of the torture of enemies. He also used other sources such as Jemison's cousin, George Jemison, who is acknowledged in the book as having been recommended by the aged narrator. Most of the book, however, is clearly the recollection of Mary Jemsion. Her account remains an excellent record of the Haudenosaunee people during the last half of the eighteenth century and during the first decades of the 1800s.

At night we arrived at a small Seneca Indian town...where the two squaws to whom I belonged resided. There we landed....

Having made fast to the shore, the Squaws left me in the canoe while they went to their wigwam or house in the town, and returned with a suit of Indian clothing, all new, and very clean and nice. My clothes, though whole and good when I was taken, were now torn in pieces, so that I was almost naked. They first undressed me and threw my rags into the river; then washed me clean and dressed me in the new suit they had just brought, in complete Indian style; and then led me home and seated me in the center of their wigwam.

I had been in that situation but a few minutes, before all the Squaws in the town came in to see me. I was soon surrounded by them, and they immediately set up a most dismal howling, crying bitterly, and wringing their hands in all the agonies of grief for a deceased relative.

Their tears flowed freely, and they exhibited all the signs of real mourning. At the commencement of this scene, one of their number began, in a voice somewhat between speaking and singing, to recite some words to the following purport, and continued the recitation till the ceremony was ended; the company at the same time varying the appearance of their countenances, gestures and tone of voice, so as to correspond with the sentiments expressed by their leader:

"Oh our brother! Alas! He is dead—he has gone; he will never return! Friendless he died on the field of the slain, where his bones are yet lying unburied! Oh, who will not mourn his sad fate? No tears dropped around him; oh, no! No tears of his sisters were there! He fell in his prime, when his arm was most needed to keep us from danger! Alas! he has gone! and left us in sorrow, his loss to bewail: Oh where is his spirit? His spirit went naked, and hungry it wanders, and thirsty and wounded it groans to return! Oh helpless and wretched, our brother has gone!...But well we remember his deeds!—The deer he could take on the chase! The panther shrunk back at the sight of his strength! His enemies fell at his feet! He was brave and courageous in war! As the fawn he was harmless: his friendship was ardent: his temper was gentle: his pity was great!...Though he fell on the field of the slain, with glory he fell, and his spirit went up to the land of his fathers in war! Then why do we mourn? With transports of joy they received him, and fed him, and clothed him, and welcomed him there! Oh friends, he is happy; then dry up your tears! His spirit has seen our distress, and sent us a helper whom with pleasure we greet. Dickewamis [meaning a pretty, handsome girl] has come: then let us receive her with joy! She is handsome and pleasant! Oh! she is our sister, and gladly we welcome her here. In the place of our brother she stands in our tribe. With care we will guard her from trouble; and may she be happy till her spirit shall leave us."

In the course of that ceremony, from mourning they became serene—joy sparkled in their countenances, and they seemed to rejoice over me as over a lost child. I was made welcome amongst them as a sister....(Seaver [1824] 1963, 35–38)

Jemison was confident that

No people can live more happy than the Indians did in times of peace, before the introduction of spirituous liquors amongst them. Their lives were a continual round of pleasures. Their wants were few, and easily satisfied; and their cares were only for to-day; the bounds of their calculations for future comfort not extending to the incalculable uncertainties of to-morrow. If peace ever dwelt with men, it was in former times, in the recesses from war, amongst what are now termed barbarians. The moral character of the Indians was (if I may be allowed the expression) uncontaminated. Their fidelity was perfect, and became proverbial; they were strictly honest; they despised deception and falsehood; and chastity was held in high veneration, and a violation of it was considered sacrilege. They were temperate in their desires, moderate in their passions, and candid and honorable in the expression of their sentiments on every subject of importance (Seaver [1824] 1963, 64).

While enamored with the Haudenosaunee lifestyle in peace, Jemison was not blind to their war practices such as torture, which she regarded with dismay. But she also saw the horrors that white armies could wreak against Indians. For Haudenosaunee communities, however, the horrors of battle seldom included women and children because the Haudenosaunee warriors went to every effort to get their families away from combat zones. To save their families, Indian societies and the Haudenosaunee in particular were willing to let an enemy destroy their material possessions, including their homes and towns. This stood in marked contrast to the white pioneer tradition of involving families in the perils of combat. This was reflected in their frontier architecture: white pioneer men placed their families in fortified houses and stockades because they were determined to hold their land and their material possessions at the risk of their wives and children.

One particular passage is suggestive of the many facets of life—including the presence of escaped black slaves—among the Senecas in the midst of the American Revolution. In 1779, with her husband Hiokatoo away at war, she and five of her children fled the Patriot army of General John Sullivan. Sullivan's army destroyed their corn,

> burnt our houses, killed what few cattle and horses they could find [that had not been led to safety by the Senecas], destroyed our fruit trees, and left nothing but the bare soil and timber. (Seaver [1824] 1963, 73)

Finally, feeling confident that Sullivan's army would not return, the Senecas returned to their lands along the Genesee River (western New York) but were unable to take up life again in their destroyed towns because

> we found that there was not a mouthful of any kind of sustenance left, not even enough to keep a child one day from perishing with hunger.
>
> The weather by this time had become cold and stormy; and as we were destitute of houses and food too, I immediately resolved to take my children and look out for myself, without delay. With this intention I took two of my little ones on my back, bade the other three follow, and the same night arrived on the Gardow flats [on the Genesee River], where I have ever since resided.
>
> At that time, two negroes, who had run away from their masters somtime before, were the only inhabitants of those flats. They lived in

a small cabin and had planted and raised a large field of corn, which they had not yet harvested. As they were in want of help to secure their crop, I hired to them to husk corn till the whole was harvested.

I have laughed a thousand times to myself when I have thought of the good old negro, who hired me, who fearing that I should get taken or injured by the Indians, stood by me constantly when I was husking, with a loaded gun in his hand, in order to keep off the enemy, and thereby lost as much labor of his own as he received from me, by paying good wages. I, however, was not displeased with his attention; for I knew that I should need all the corn that I could earn, even if I should husk the whole. I husked enough for them, to gain for myself, at every tenth string, one hundred strings of ears, which were equal to twenty-five bushels of shelled corn. This seasonable supply made my family comfortable for samp and cakes through the succeeding winter, which was the most severe that I have witnessed since my remembrance. The snow fell about five feet deep, and remained so for a long time, and the weather was extremely cold; so much so indeed, that almost all the game upon which the Indians depended for subsistence, perished, and reduced them almost to a state of starvation through that and three or four succeeding years. When the snow melted in the spring, deer were found dead upon the ground in vast numbers; and other animals, of every description, perished from the cold also, and were found dead, in multitudes. Many of our people barely escaped with their lives, and some actually died of hunger and freezing. . . .

The negroes continued on my flats two or three years after this, and then left them for a place that they expected would suit them much better. But as that land became my own in a few years, by virtue of a deed from the Chiefs of the Six Nations, I have lived there from that to the present time. (Seaver [1824] 1963, 74–76)

A proud Seneca grandmother, Mary Jemison died in 1833, ninety years of age, on the Buffalo Creek Reservation in New York.

Perspective

Some of the best qualities of American Indian national cultures are exemplified by Mary Jemison's account of her life as an adopted member of the Seneca

Nation and her description of the two blacks who lived freely among the Senecas and who had befriended her. In contrast, the return of black slaves by Indian nations to European colonies is an example of how the moral inclinations of Indian cultures could be turned by profit or political necessity. However noble or ignoble, the attitudes described in this chapter were aspects of American Indian cultures that were on the defensive or even in decline. Thus, Indian attitudes towards blacks and Europeans were shaped when Indian nations and their cultures were strained to their limits by generations of war and epidemics.

The two blacks who befriended Mary Jemison may have been the two blacks reported in 1764 and briefly noted earlier in this chapter. They were "2 Molattoes...half Indians who came several years ago from the Southward" whom the Senecas "look upon as Inds. [Indians]" (Sullivan et al. 1925, 495–96, 500). One of them was a blacksmith. Blacksmiths were highly regarded among Indian nations for their general skills and specifically for their abilities to repair guns. Eighteenth-century records also suggest the possibility that at least one black woman lived with or near them in the 1760s, but that any black women among them had evidently been returned under a peace treaty, moved elsewhere or died by the time the 1779 Sullivan campaign devastated the towns of the Seneca nation.

Of course, the status of the two black friends of Mary Jemison contrasts with the status of those blacks who were not regarded as adopted as full members of an Indian nation. They were living precariously among American Indian nations during a time when British policy required a return to slavery of all slaves who had escaped or been captured in war. Not surprisingly, blacks resisted being returned. In 1765, for example, at least one black living among the Senecas "fled to the Southward" (Sullivan et al. 1953, 812) upon learning that he would be returned to colonial slavery as a requirement of a peace treaty between the British and those Senecas who had supported Pontiac.

Like the blacks, white prisoners were also supposed to be returned under terms of peace treaties. Some prisoners, such as Mary Jemison, were able to remain among their adopted families. Of course, many white prisoners were happy to return to the colonies. But as noted in this chapter, not all white prisoners were willing to return, and both they and their adopted Indian families grieved when they were forced to part. A famous account of this circumstance was written as Pontiac's War drew to a close. In November 1764, along the Muskingham River in Ohio, Indian representatives of the Caughnawaga Mohawks, Senecas, Delawares, Mingos and Shawnees who had sided with

Pontiac sought peace with the British. A major condition expected by the British military commander Colonel Henry Bouquet was that the Indians return prisoners. Dr. William Smith, the provost of the College of Philadelphia, wrote an account that reflected the papers and recollections of a British officer who had been present when 206 prisoners (81 men and 125 "Females & Children") were returned. In a book published the year after the prisoners' return, Dr. Smith ([1765] 1966, 27) noted how the Indians

> delivered up their beloved captives with the utmost reluctance; shed torrents of tears over them, recommending them to the care and protection of the commanding officer. Their regard to them continued all the time they remained in camp. They visited them from day to day; and brought them what corn, skins, horses and other matters, they had bestowed on them, while in their families; accompanied with other presents, and all the marks of the most sincere and tender affection. Nay, they did not stop here, but, when the army marched, some of the Indians sollicited and obtained permission to accompany their former captives all the way to Fort-Pitt, and employed themselves in hunting and bringing provisions for them on the road. A young Mingo carried this still further, and gave an instance of love which would make a figure even in romance. A young woman of Virginia was among the captives, to whom he had form'd so strong an attachment, as to call her his wife. Against all remonstrances of the imminent danger to which he exposed himself by approaching to the frontiers, he persisted in following her, at the risk of being killed by the surviving relations of many unfortunate persons, who had been captivated or scalped by those of his nation.

Smith reluctantly admired the treatment given to those whites who had been adopted, maintaining that Indian culture and religion, not race, was what prevented them from being "fit subjects of cultivation," that is, civilized by the whites. He also reported that none of the women captives had been raped, and that slavery as defined in the colonies had not yet taken hold among American Indians:

> Those qualities in savages challenge our just esteem. They should make us charitably consider their barbarities as the effects of wrong education, and false notions of bravery and heroism; while we should look on their virtues as sure marks that nature has made them fit subjects of

cultivation as well as us; and that we are called by our superior advantages to yield them all the helps we can in this way. Cruel and unmer-
ciful as they are, by habit and long example, in war, yet whenever they
come to give way to the native dictates of humanity, they exercise
virtues which Christians need not blush to imitate. When they once
determine to give life, they give every thing with it, which, in their
apprehension, belongs to it. From every inquiry that has been made, it
appears—that no woman thus saved is preserved from base motives
[i.e., because of an Indian male's sexual motives], or need fear the violation of her honor. No child is otherwise treated by the persons
adopting it than the children of their own body. The perpetual slavery
of those captivated in war, is a notion which even their barbarity has
not yet suggested to them. Every captive whom their affection, their
caprice, or whatever else, leads them to save, is soon incorporated with
them, and fares alike with themselves. (Smith [1765] 1966, 27–28)

Smith also noted how some of the prisoners did not want to leave the Indian
families that had adopted them.

Among the children who had been carried off young, and had long
lived with the Indians, it is not to be expected that any marks of joy
would appear on being restored to their parents or relatives. Having
been accustomed to look upon the Indians as the only connexions they
had, having been tenderly treated by them, and speaking their language, it is no wonder that they considered their new state in the light
of a captivity, and parted from the savages with tears.

But it must not be denied that there were even some grown persons
who shewed an unwillingness to return. The Shawnees were obliged to
bind several of their prisoners and force them along to the camp; and
some women, who had been delivered up, afterwards found means to
escape and run back to the Indian towns. Some, who could not make
their escape, clung to their savage acquaintance at parting, and continued many days in bitter lamentations, even refusing sustenance
(Smith [1765] 1966, 29).

Smith's descriptions of whites unwilling to leave their adopted Indian families and of Indians unwilling to part with adopted children, spouses, and sib-

lings were dramatically visualized in a stunning drawing by an American colonial artist working in London, Benjamin West. In 1766, a London edition of Smith's work included an engraving of West's poignant drawing, along with another engraving by West that portrayed Indians and whites negotiating for peace (Uhry Abrams 1985, 176–77, 179). At that time, Europe and its colonies were in the midst of the "Enlightenment" era. Smith's narrative, together with West's art, were counterpoints and challenges to anyone who believed that eighteenth-century Europe monopolized the ethical heights of human philosophies. How ironic that in both eighteenth-century Europe and North America, the noblest manifestations of the human spirit existed simultaneously with warfare and slavery—as they so often have.

CHAPTER VII

Betrayal "Christians Only Were Capable Of"

The so-called era of the American Revolution, 1763–1783, was actually an era of two parallel revolutions. The better-known one is that of the colonists who went to war against each other in their war for independence. Paralleling that war were the revolutions and civil wars among American Indian nations such as the Cherokees and the Haudenosaunee. By the 1760s, the dilemma among both Natives and colonists was how to effectively coordinate society. There were traditionalists and revolutionaries among both races, and while the stakes were as different as the cultures were, their respective dilemmas were remarkably similar. How much change could the establishment safely concede, and how much change could the revolutionary thinkers push upon the old system before open warfare broke the societies apart? Like their colonial neighbors, the American Indian nations finally divided into factions. The differences and the similarities soon became mixed into a single continental cauldron.

After Pontiac's War, a few bands among some Indian nations who fought for Pontiac accepted the 1763 French offer to move west of the Mississippi River where they could continue their contacts with French traders. Here both the Indians and French were under the jurisdiction of the area's new rulers, the Spanish, allies of the French to whom France had ceded claims west of the Mississippi as compensation for Spain's war losses to Britain. Various migrations in every direction had always been part of Indian history. But in the century preceding 1763, eastern Indian migration across the Mississippi had sparked especially dramatic cultural changes and conflicts with Indian nations already living on these lands, resulting in a violent Indian-versus-Indian frontier that preceded the white frontier. After 1670, for example, some of the Dakotas (Sioux) of the western Great Lakes were pushed south and then west, toward the Plains, by better-armed Crees, Assiniboins, Ojibwas, Kickapoos and others who traded extensively with the French or English. The retreating Lakotas in turn fought for room to live by attacking nations such as the Omahas, Iowas, Pawnees and Arikaras—some of whom were themselves recent arrivals.

A similar series of pressures forced the Osage out of the western Ohio River valley and west of the Mississippi, where by the mid-1700s they dominated major areas along the Arkansas River. In the first half of the 1700s, the contesting Indian nations began hunting and fighting on horseback, riding mounts obtained by trade or war with Indians living to the south and the west. While many old traditions continued, the overall result was a new Plains culture based on the horse.

After 1763, Indian bands invited west by the French intensified the cultural and political transition going on west of the Mississippi. This Indian-versus-Indian frontier, gripped in the chaos of certain change, was both dangerous and exciting for the nations involved. The major changes that began about 1670 culminated between 1820 and 1860. In those decades, the newest stage of chaos was imposed by the new United States, as tens of thousands of Indians east of the Mississippi were forced westward by white governments. They, in turn, usually came into conflict with the Indian nations that had been forced westward a century earlier. The outcome of this long struggle on the Indian-Indian frontier was the weakening of all Indian nations' abilities to resist the ever-advancing white invaders.

Westward migration was not the only attraction or necessity for various Indians living east of the Mississippi. Beginning in 1765, for example, the Chickasaws spread out to the east along the Tennessee River in northern Alabama. In 1769, a Cherokee army challenged this eastward expansion, but the Chickasaws emerged victorious. Concurrently, the Haudenosaunee continued to expand their influence north of the St. Lawrence River. The Haudenosaunee realized that while their southern frontier was almost hopelessly strangled by whites, their northern frontier—Canada—was thinly settled by Europeans and open to Haudenosaunee expansion. At the same time, the Haudenosaunee continued to expand westward, refusing to concede that opportunity to the exclusive exploitation of the British. Strong nations such as the Haudenosaunee and the Chickasaws continued another kind of expansion by adopting weaker nations. For example, just before the outbreak of the American Revolution and during the period immediately thereafter, the Oneida Haudenosaunee admitted Stockbridge (Massachusetts) Christian Indians onto their lands. Between 1730 and 1775, the Chickasaws adopted the

Natchez, Quinipissas (Napissas), Taposas, Ibitoupas and Chakchiumas. And all Indian nations after 1763 experienced the rise of what had previously been a relatively small group within their peoples: white-Indian mixed-bloods. These mixed-bloods would become especially influential during and after the American Revolution. Especially in the South, there were also an increasing number of black-Indian unions.

Like the white colonies near them, Indian nations in the 1760s were undergoing dramatic changes. They accelerated their adoption of those aspects of white technology and material culture that they believed aided them—cattle, horses and fruit orchards were now commonplace in Indian towns from the North to the South—and they pursued diplomacies that would continue their prosperity.

One Indian group even emerged as a new nation: the Seminoles. By 1763, the Seminoles regarded themselves and were perceived by most whites as a nation separate from the Creek Confederacy, although the Creeks themselves considered the Seminoles part of the confederacy throughout most of the rest of the eighteenth century. The Seminoles, who usually saw their political role as coordinate with the Creeks, were made up of Creek frontiersmen and Creek outlaws from many of the confederacy's member nations, as well as remnants of the Apalachees, Apalachiolas, Timucuas, Mayucas, Ays and Tegestas. An increasing number of escaped black slaves, as well as white traders and adventurers, added to the nation's heterogeneity.

The Creek policy of neutrality had almost entirely spared the Creek people from the debilitations of the French and Indian War and Pontiac's War. In 1763, the Creeks tried to preserve their nation through diplomacy by granting Georgia lands that were greatly envied by the whites and in some cases already illegally settled. In the Treaty of Augusta on November 10, 1763, the conciliatory Creeks gave up a little in order to keep the rest of their lands. As in the past, the whites promised a more strict regulation of traders and pledged to respect Indian lives and property, including lands. This time, however, the Creeks and indeed all Indian nations east of the Mississippi who negotiated with the British in 1763 or thereafter saw signs that the whites really meant their promises and could enforce them. In this way, the Indians were benefiting from the sacrifices of Pontiac and his allies. Until Pontiac laid siege to Detroit in 1763, British efforts to curb squatters and curtail trade abuses were ineffectual. On October 30, 1761, for example, Colonel Henry Bouquet at Fort Pitt issued a proclamation to enforce the 1758 Treaty of Easton with the Haudenosaunee and the

Pennsylvania Delawares banning white settlement west of the Allegheny Mountains, but to no avail. Even Bouquet's burning of a few settlers' cabins failed to halt the tide. But in 1763, Pontiac's allies not only drove out these illegal settlers, they inspired the British government to increase centralized action.

Consequences of British Failure to Reform Indian Affairs

In London, the cabinet officials of King George III were already planning to reorder Indian affairs even before they learned of the outbreak of Pontiac's War. In the eighteenth century, news did not travel fast across the Atlantic. Even the fastest ship took at least six weeks to sail from North America to Great Britain. Thus, even though Pontiac had already laid siege to Fort Detroit on May 7, the King's ministers were still unaware of the war when they met in June. On June 8, 1763, the ministers decided to stop expansion west of the Appalachian Mountains and the Alleghenies except along the upper Ohio River. When they received news of Pontiac's War, the ministers quickly withdrew permission for the Ohio River settlement. They established the Appalachians and the Alleghenies as the white boundary. The ministers also declared that land deals with the Indians had to be negotiated by official rather than private individuals, and they declared that British-Indian obligations would be enforced by the military. The ministers hurried these new policies through government channels and had them signed by King George III on October 7, creating the Proclamation of 1763. Still confronted with Pontiac's War, the ministers hoped to avoid future confrontations by developing a series of guidelines which became known as the "Plan for the Future Management of Indian Affairs" or the "Plan of 1764."

Under the Plan of 1764, which was based on reports by white officials in the colonies, responsibility and control over all aspects of Indian relations were given to the commander-in-chief of all British forces in North America. All traders were to be licensed by the colonial governors to specific and limited locations; in the North, the trade would be carried on only at certain posts and in the South only at Indian towns. These trade locations were to be under the scrutiny of commissaries appointed by the Indian superintendents. No military personnel were to deal with Indians except through Indian Department officials. Prices were to be fixed and then adhered to, and no credit above fifty shillings was to be given to any Indian; larger debts were void. An interpreter and a gunsmith were to be at each post to serve Indian visitors. Neither rum nor rifles were to be sold to the Indians (although the sale of smoothbore muskets was permitted). A deputy Indian superintendent was to inspect proceedings at each trade location at least once a year. The Plan of 1764 also called for the redrawing of the boundary set by the Proclamation of 1763, because the hastily declared 1763 line had been intended as a temporary expediency in the hope of halting white expansion and placating the Indians. While redrawing the line would more than likely benefit white land speculators, it was necessary because the officials who drew the line in London did not realize that the Haudenosaunee, the Cherokees and the Creeks all owned land *east* of the 1763 line. These lands would either have to be guaranteed to the respective Indian nations or purchased by the whites, and so the 1763 line had to be altered by treaties.

British efforts to secure peaceful relations in the South resulted in a treaty with the Choctaws at Mobile, Alabama, on April 1, 1765. At the treaty council, an eighty-year-old Choctaw leader, Alibamon Mingo, raised the following issue:

There was one thing I would mention tho' it cannot concern myself, and that is the Behavior of the traders towards our Women, I was told of old by the Creeks and Cherokees, wherever the English went they cause disturbances for they lived under no Government and paid no respect either to Wisdom or Station. I hoped for better things, that those Old Talks had no truth in them. One thing I must report which has happened within my own knowledge, that often when the Traders sent for a Basket of Bread and the Generous Indian sent his own wife to Supply their wants instead of taking the Bread out of the Basket they put their hand upon the Breast of the Wives which was not to be admitted, for the first maxim in our Language is that Death is preferable to Disgrace. (Usner 1992, 125)

The British chose to conduct Indian affairs largely (although not completely) under the control of the British military by having the Indian superintendents report to North America's commander-in-chief. This was not a reflection on the Indians so much as it was upon the colonists. Only the British military had the physical power to enforce imperial law on a frontier inhabited by lawless settlers, unethical traders and representatives of scofflaw land speculators. Unfortunately, a few officers at the frontier posts became involved in civilian land deals, undermining the military's value as law enforcer.

Britain had a second rationale for requiring the superintendents to report to the British commander-in-chief: Indian nations were still being wooed as allies in international politics. In fact, in 1755 the original superintendent positions had been established as military adjuncts, during the French and Indian War. In wartime, Indian allies were a necessity, making the superintendents' positions as military adjuncts a logical arrangement. This tie with the military, however, further reinforced the white perception of Indian affairs more as a matter of military strategy than national diplomacy. This tradition would be carried on by the United States, which placed Indian affairs with the Secretary of War, not the Secretary of Defense, until 1849, when Indian affairs would be transferred to the Department of the Interior.

In 1763, the perceived link between Indian affairs and the military may have been narrow, but it was not unwarranted. The French had unconcealed hopes of retrieving their lost empire in a future war. French traders who remained in Canada after 1763 traveled as far as the western Great Lakes region and were in continual contact with other French traders working the Mississippi River Valley from Spanish-occupied New Orleans. General Thomas Gage, commander-in-chief of all British troops in North America from 1763 to 1773, lived with the fear that the French traders residing in British-claimed territory would become the fifth column of a new French conquest whenever the next war broke out. The situation was even more alarming because most Indians got along better with the French traders than with the British ones. Especially in 1768 and 1771, rumors of war with France or Spain made Gage eager to keep the Indians tied closely to the British.

As commander-in-chief of Britain's military establishment in North America, General Gage was in charge of two military districts, north and south, which coincided administratively and geographically with two Indian districts. The superintendent for the Indians living to the south of the Ohio River was John Stuart, while Superintendent Sir William Johnson represented British interests in dealing with Indians north of the Ohio. Both men reported directly to Gage, who in turn reported to Whitehall Palace in London, but the British government failed to define the exact role of the military in Indian affairs. Whitehall's directives lacked consistency in all but one area: orders to cut expenses. This, in turn, undermined the Plan of 1764.

The Plan of 1764 lacked operational funds because Parliament originally intended to levy a tax on goods used in the Indian trade to pay for the policy. But Parliament soon learned that the colonists opposed this and other taxes to raise revenue unless the measures were passed by their own colonial legislatures. The colonial protest, "No taxation without representation!" applied to taxes on the Indian trade just as surely as it did to stamp or tea taxes. In this way, the colonial protests against taxation, so well known as a cause of the American Revolution, were also intertwined with Britain's ability to carry out its Indian policy. In refusing to pay taxes on goods used in the Indian trade, the colonists benefited threefold. They made their point of "no taxation without representation." They also undermined an imperial Indian policy that would have thwarted unbridled colonial expansion into Indian lands. Finally, when the frontier erupted in warfare again, because Indian nations resented Britain's lack of a just frontier policy, the self-righteous colonists could blame the Indians for the violence while pretending that they had nothing to do with its origins.

Instead of actually enforcing the Plan of 1764, which might have brought justice to the frontier, the British reverted to their earlier practices: They made promises to Indian nations that they could not keep. The British also distributed engraved medals to be worn around the necks of loyal Indian leaders. In the meantime, during the mid-1760s, colonial land speculators planned future acquisitions of Indian territories, often working closely with well-placed British officials. And traders continued to make their profits, seldom at official trading posts and all too often through shady practices. The governors of Virginia, South Carolina and Georgia refused to allow courts to prosecute offending traders. British officials in London failed to evolve a consistent and workable Indian policy, and the Plan of 1764 withered for lack of funds.

Role of Intertribal Wars

Indian nations weakened their own ability to withstand white expansion by warring against each other. Notable in these conflicts were the wars of the Creeks versus the Choctaws and the Chickasaws; and the Cherokees versus the Delawares, Shawnees and some Haudenosaunee.

The wars among Indian nations were often encouraged by the British in order to keep the Indians from creating a pan-Indian movement. When Indians tried to make their own peace without British approval, British agents often blocked the effort, as Indian Superintendent John Stuart did in 1768 when the Creeks sought peace with the Choctaws and Chickasaws. The Indians' intertribal wars were also being fought, however, for the same reasons Europeans fought wars: for territory, economics and nationalism. Territory involved agricultural and hunting grounds extensive enough to supply meat to feed the nation and skins for trade to the whites. The Haudenosaunee in the north were also attempting to counter British colonial strength by maintaining and expanding an orderly pan-Indian empire. Similar attempts by the Creeks in the south were less successful than the efforts of the Haudenosaunee. The Haudenosaunee, like the British, were confronted with both the problems and the opportunities created in 1763 by a frontier suddenly devoid of official French occupation and influence. Both the Haudenosaunee and the British were attempting to enforce centralized laws and policies. Both were faced with the problems of distance and the fact that subject populations and their local councils had their own agendas.

Factions within the Haudenosaunee, especially the westernmost nation, the Senecas, had in the past often divided the Haudenosaunee. The Senecas had recently shaken the confederacy during Pontiac's War by allying with the anti-British Indians while the vast majority of Haudenosaunee remained neutral or loyal to the British. In addition, subject nations such as the Delawares and the Shawnees had tried to break away during the French and Indian War, and during the 1760s the Haudenosaunee found it imperative to bring these nations back into line. As the Haudenosaunee recovered from their latest political divisions and adjusted to a white frontier dominated in the north solely by the British, they also faced a grave economic situation. Centered in New York, the Haudenosaunee had long controlled the British fur trade in the northern colonies. But after 1763, Canada became another base for British traders in direct competition with New York, and New York soon lost its dominant position. Despite further Haudenosaunee expansion in Canada, the Mohawk Haudenosaunee—who lived along the Mohawk River surrounded by white independent and tenant farmers friendly to Sir William Johnson—found themselves especially tied to the declining fortunes of New York's fur distribution centers. The fur trade itself moved its marketplace westward from Oswego and Niagara to Fort Michilimackinac on the straits between Lakes Michigan and Huron. In fact, the quest for furs was reported to have led traders and Indians even farther west by as much as five hundred leagues (about fifteen hundred miles). This would mean that some traders, including both Indians and whites, were reaching the Rocky Mountains. Attempting to adapt to these circumstances, the Haudenosaunee pursued two courses: Some packed up each spring to follow the trade ever farther west, while others turned increasingly toward the white man's way of living. By 1775, Daniel Claus, an able assistant to Superintendent Sir William Johnson, predicted that within fifty years many of the Haudenosaunee would be completely absorbed into white society because they were enthusiastically adopting the white man's way of life.

White Frontiersmen: Beyond the Rule of Law

As Indian nations, individual colonies and British officials each tried to establish their own ideas of order and rights, it was the white frontiersmen who caused them to chafe against each other. If the land speculators and illegal settlers had not been permitted to operate, Indian nations might have peacefully resolved their futures by themselves or with the colonies and British government. But the frontiersmen were unwilling to follow the rule of any law, British or Indian. While most Indian people respected white boundaries and sincerely made every effort to negotiate conflicts of interest with white powers, the frontiersmen made their own laws, pushing onto Indian lands and killing Indians at will. In October 1767, General Gage admitted that between 1764 and 1767 only one white—a man in New Jersey—had been found guilty by a local jury for the murder of an Indian. "It is a Fact," Gage reported in a letter to the Earl of Shelburne, "that all the People of the Frontiers from Pennsylvania to Virginia inclusive, openly avow, that they will never find a Man guilty of Murder, for killing an Indian" (Carter 1931, 152). Even as Gage wrote, most white colonists expected an Indian war to break out at any time. Land speculators even planned their claims and purchases accordingly, for they knew that a war with the Indians could only be averted if a permanent boundary replaced the tentative 1763 line. Such a line, when redrawn, would hopefully quiet Indian complaints with a firm definition of territory and with the payment of goods in exchange for any ceded land. In setting a western boundary, the British planned to negotiate primarily with the Creeks and the Cherokees in the South and the Haudenosaunee in the North. The Cherokees were in the worst diplomatic position because they had recently been at war with the Haudenosaunee and the British, while the Creeks were in the best position because they had remained neutral in the recent wars. The boundary councils held with all three nations followed official British cancellation of the Plan of 1764 in March 1768. The Indian superintendents continued to act as political liaisons between the British government and the Indian nations. However, the supervision and cost of the trade were returned to the individual colonies.

The Plan of 1764 had intended to restrict the business of fur trade to frontier posts where fair prices and other ethical business practices could be enforced. The British never allocated sufficient funds to enforce the prohibition against traders going directly to Indian towns, in part because the colonists refused to be taxed to pay for the enforcement. Thus the British traders had never stopped going directly into the Indian towns, and neither had French and Spanish competitors from the Mississippi River valley. These illegal traders obtained the best skins and furs, making trade at the forts second-rate. Furthermore, the Indians also found that it was inconvenient to have their trade restricted to the posts—hence their cooperation with the illegal traders. Capitulating to all these circumstances, the British no longer restricted trade to specific posts or locations after March 1768.

Boundary Negotiations

The new boundary negotiations were left in the hands of the two superintendents, Sir William Johnson and John Stuart, who began calling councils. The Indian nations wanted these councils because white trespassers on their lands—hunters as well as farmers—were destroying their food supply. They were also driving away or killing the fur-bearing animals upon which the Indian trade economies rested. To complicate matters, the Creeks, Cherokees and Haudenosaunee were all in possession of lands that lay to the east of the 1763 line (as noted earlier). Because the 1763 line had been drawn in London, these Indian lands had been accidentally included within the territory white colonists were supposedly permitted to settle. Thus from the Indians' perspective, the land boundary councils were an opportunity to stabilize each nation's territorial boundaries. There was also the added inducement that the whites could be expected to present manufactured goods as gifts and as payment for any land ceded. Preliminary boundary negotiations had dragged on for years, but in the fall of 1768 the Creeks, Cherokees and Haudenosaunee reached accord with the British. On October 14, 1768, at the Treaty of Hard Labor (South Carolina), the Cherokees were guaranteed possession of some of the lands that lay on their eastern border. These had previously been east of the Proclamation Line of 1763. In exchange for these lands, the Cherokees willingly ceded, in return for manufactured goods, their claims to extensive lands on their northeastern boundary that originally had been west of the 1763 line. On November 5, 1768, at the Treaty of Fort Stanwix (New York), the Haudenosaunee were guaranteed some of their lands in south central New York and north central Pennsylvania that had fallen east of the Proclamation Line of 1763. But the Haudenosaunee gave up, in return for relatively little compensation (£10,460) extensive lands along the Susquehanna River in northeastern Pennsylvania and a vast territory south of the Ohio River including southwestern Pennsylvania and most of West Virginia and Kentucky. The Haudenosaunee were economically sophisticated when it came to the profits and benefits of the fur trade, but perhaps they did not yet realize the true value of land in the white marketplace. Sir William Johnson, who as Indian superintendent could have informed them about land values, was speculating in some of the lands being ceded, so giving honest advice to the Haudenosaunee would not have been to his advantage. There was more to the negotiations than these factors, however.

Throughout the 1700s the Haudenosaunee had determined, whenever possible, to direct the negative impacts of white-Indian contacts toward Indian nations subject to the Haudenosaunee. At Fort Stanwix, the Haudenosaunee continued this policy by satisfying white land greed primarily with lands of the Delawares in both eastern and western Pennsylvania and of the Shawnees south of the Ohio. Although the Haudenosaunee themselves hunted in and occasionally occupied these areas, the Haudenosaunee saw their empire's future north of the Ohio River and north of the Great Lakes. Shawnee lands north of the Ohio still lay within the Haudenosaunee empire. But by ceding the Shawnees' lands south of the Ohio, as well as some of the Delawares' eastern land, the Haudenosaunee protected cherished lands of their own in New York and Pennsylvania. These were lands that otherwise might have been demanded by the British as a penalty against the Seneca Haudenosaunee for their participation in Pontiac's War. The Delawares and the Shawnees were present at Fort Stanwix in 1768, having already agreed in 1765 to give up lands as a consequence of their alliance with Pontiac. By forcing acceptance of this agreement upon the Delawares and Shawnees at Fort Stanwix, the Haudenosaunee were able to discipline their wayward subjects and consolidate their empire within what the Haudenosaunee hoped would be a more orderly and easily administered area. The consolidation of the Haudenosaunee was perhaps also the result of their declining confederacy population due to European diseases, to losses sustained during their military aid to the British, and to their wars with other Indian nations. Lest anyone doubt which Indian nation was in charge at Fort Stanwix, the Haudenosaunee kept most of the British payment in goods. This further angered the Delawares and Shawnees, who already felt manipulated by the British and the Haudenosaunee.

The Creeks in the meantime were negotiating that same month (November 1768) with the British at Pensacola, Florida. The Creek Confederacy had ceded some lands in 1763, but the British monarch, George

III, had almost simultaneously set a boundary line (Proclamation of 1763) that designated an extensive area of unceded Creek lands—amounting to about one-third of Georgia—for possible future white settlement. The Creeks wanted the erroneous line redrawn and their lands guaranteed, and in November 1768, after ceding only a tiny piece of land, the Creeks were guaranteed all the lands west of the Ogeechee River, well over eighty percent of Georgia. Having also accommodated the British with strips of land in Florida, the Creeks felt their boundaries were now secure.

The year 1768, then, should have finally provided a demarcation between Indian and white that each group could then enforce among its own people. But white pioneers and land speculators were unsatisfied, and just as they troubled British officials, so the Delawares and Shawnees chafed at Haudenosaunee discipline and order. Moreover, the Cherokees resented the Haudenosaunee claim that the confederacy could cede Kentucky to the British, for the Cherokees' own claim there was as strong. The Kentucky issue was even more complicated because in obtaining the cession of the Haudenosaunee at Fort Stanwix, Sir William had exceeded the orders given to him by the British government. Sir William was expected to obtain only the land westward to the junction of the Great Kanawha River with the Ohio River (western West Virginia) because the British government feared Indian complaints if a line were drawn farther west. The Cherokees at the Treaty of Hard Labor (1768) had agreed to a line drawn to this point from the south. But Sir William Johnson and other land speculators pressured southern Indian superintendent Stuart. As a result, Stuart renegotiated the Treaty of Hard Labor boundary with the Cherokees. On October 18, 1770, at the Treaty of Lochaber (South Carolina), the Cherokees ceded nine thousand square miles (mostly in West Virginia) for goods worth £2,500. In addition to the goods, the Cherokees were guaranteed possession of all their other lands. On May 27, 1771, a party of whites led by John Donelson and accompanied by a few Cherokees including Attakullaculla set out on what was to be a five-month survey of this grand cession. Along the way, Donelson promised the Cherokee nation an additional five hundred pounds sterling if he were allowed to alter the line westward in the whites' favor. The accompanying Cherokees agreed, but most probably did not anticipate the extent of Donelson's convenient alteration: Going up the Kentucky River, he added eighteen thousand square miles to the nine thousand ceded at Lochaber. The Cherokees were never paid the promised five hundred pounds sterling, but the whites nevertheless hunted and settled upon the lands.

Pontiac's Assassination

During the years that these treaties were made, 1768 through 1771, there was a constant fear among British officials, traders and land speculators that there would be another pan-Indian war for independence such as the one inspired by Pontiac in 1763. Was it coincidence, then, that the respected symbol of pan-Indian independence, Pontiac, was assassinated on April 20, 1769? Pontiac was not killed by a white, but by a Peoria Indian who clubbed him from behind and then stabbed him just after he left a trading store in Cahokia, Illinois. The Kickapoo Indians, who had made peace with the British back in 1765 because Pontiac advised them to, swore revenge on all Illinois Indians and for months carried on a war that spread to British settlers in southern Illinois. A few warriors from other nations joined in these retributions, which continued until 1771. Pontiac's assassination was avenged, but not against the real culprits. Pontiac, still capable of inspiring a united Indian effort against the British, had been killed leaving a very special store. It was owned by the trading company of Baynton, Wharton and Morgan. Both Pontiac's Indian allies and the Peorias claimed that one of the firm's traders, perhaps Alexander Williamson, arranged the assassination. Baynton, Wharton and Morgan were not only managing a trading company, but were also land speculators who happened to have, as partners in various land schemes, some very influential friends including Benjamin Franklin (Peckham 1947, 309–16).

Land Grabs Continue Unabated

The assassination of Pontiac, the encouragement of intertribal warfare, and the land cession treaties were all part of a complicated and confusing era in which white government officials and businessmen both in Britain and in the colonies cooperated or competed with one another to undercut Indian land rights. Speculators and settlers alike regarded the boundary lines set up by treaties as launching points, not limits, of their expansion. For example, in 1767 George Washington cynically described the boundary line of 1763 "as a temporary expedient to quiet the minds of the Indians." Washington added, "Any person, therefore, who neglects the present opportunity of hunting out good lands [beyond the boundary lines] . . . will never regain it." (Ford 1889, 200–22).

Bumbling errors, lack of coordination and impractical schemes were frequent among the speculators, but these were matched by audacious successes that perpetuated Indian land grabs by business interests over the next two centuries. Monarchs, noblemen, churchmen, governors and soldiers of fortune had dominated the exploitation of Indian lands in the 1500s. During the 1600s, these elements shared the quest for Indian land with businesses such as the Virginia and Massachusetts Bay companies. But during the 1760s, the Indian trade became increasingly less profitable for most whites. In turn, land speculation became more rewarding, and private business interests came to dominate the usurpation of Indian lands. Government was used by these business interests as a tool. The subordination of government to business in efforts to obtain Indian land continued throughout the nineteenth and twentieth centuries, and continues in the twenty-first.

The economic conditions that encouraged the land grabs accentuated a pattern established among the English colonies in the seventeenth century. In that century, whenever coastal whites in a particular area or colony shifted emphasis from trade to a land-based economy, the Indians were left economically stranded, for as white trade diminished or became more costly, the foundations of their native economies slipped out from under them. Simultaneously pressed by land speculators, the Indians often sold their lands in lieu of their deerskins or furs to obtain the manufactured goods. For many whites, on the other hand, land was an important investment, especially in the mid-eighteenth century. By the time the American Revolution began, well-known figures such as George Washington, Benjamin Franklin, Thomas Jefferson and Patrick Henry had had considerable experience in the business, while frontiersmen such as Daniel Boone served to carry out the speculators' aims. The schemes launched by these men were possible because the British government was in constant turmoil at home. Changes in ruling cliques and alterations in imperial philosophies negated any possibility of consistently avoiding the mistakes of previous centuries in enforcing a just Indian policy upon the white citizenry. The Indian nations matched Britain in their continually fragmented politics, giving further advantage to white speculators.

In addition to old or altered theories pertaining to Indian-white relations, new interpretations compounded the imperial confusion. For example, in 1757 Britain's attorney general, Charles Pratt (later the Earl of Camden), and Britain's solicitor general, Charles Yorke, issued a legal opinion on British ownership of land in India. Known as the Camden-Yorke opinion, it stated that private individuals could obtain land in India directly from princes or other East Indian officials without authorization from the British Crown. The premise of this decision was that the leaders of India had every right to dispense with their subjects' lands as they saw fit. By 1772, Camden was active as a land speculator in North America, and he and his cohorts tried diligently but unsuccessfully to have his principle applied to American Indian lands, causing great debate and confusion between speculators and officials charged with protecting the integrity of Indian territory. Since American Indian leaders did not in most cases possess the degree of authority over their people enjoyed by princes in India, successful application of the theory would have been disastrous to Indian people. Unscrupulous whites could almost always find an equally unscrupulous Indian who would claim to be some sort of chief and sell out his people. Had the theory of the Camden-Yorke opinion been applied over a long period of time, the Indian superintendents—the Crown's representatives—would have been unable to prevent fraud. Before the situation could be resolved, however, the American Revolution ended the fine points of the legal debate.

Simultaneous with the decline in profits from Indian trade and increased efforts by white colonials to concentrate on land speculation was an accelerating population increase among non-Indians. From 434,600 colonists in 1715, the non-Indian population grew to 1,485,634 by 1754 and to 2,600,000 or more by 1774, bringing on a demand for more farmland. At the same time, the Indian population generally remained static, with most nations barely able to recover war losses. In 1774 when the white colonists numbered at least two million and the black slaves about half a million, perhaps only 130,000 to 200,000 Indians—at most 40,000 warriors—lived east of the Mississippi and south of the Great Lakes and St. Lawrence River.

Shawnee Again Propose Pan-Indian Alliance

There were efforts on the part of Indian nations to take action against the white threats and overcome the major obstacle to effective Indian action: fragmentation. In the summer and fall of 1769, the Shawnees still dreamed of a successful pan-Indian movement, as they had since at least 1746. The Shawnees and other Indian nations north of the Ohio River—including Miamis, Ottawas and Delawares—began organizing a confederation. Because the confederation was anti-British, it was encouraged by the French who lived along the Mississippi. The Indians opposed white expansion, especially onto their lands ceded by the Haudenosaunee and the Cherokees in treaties the year before. Because the Shawnees' efforts were aimed not only at defying the British but also the imperial authority of the Haudenosaunee, the Haudenosaunee opposed the pan-Indian movement unless they could take over its leadership. War against the whites was a possibility considered by the Haudenosaunee, and during the summer of 1769 they received wampum belts of friendship from the western nations, although the Haudenosaunee council of such chiefs was still generally opposed to such a war.

The Shawnees were challenging the Cherokees' right to cede land to the whites that was also claimed by the Shawnees. But the Shawnees also hoped that the Cherokees would see the injustice and join their movement. The Cherokees, however, chose to approach the Haudenosaunce in the hope of gaining an ally against a Cherokee nemesis, the Choctaw nation. In the fall of 1769, Cherokee ambassadors traveled to the Haudenosaunee capital at Onondaga. The Haudenosaunee sachems were under pressure from Sir William Johnson to uphold the recent land cessions made at Fort Stanwix in 1768 and they were well aware that their confederacy's economy was intertwined with that of the British. The sachems put off a discussion of the confederacy's possible role in a pan-Indian movement. They decided for the present only to aid the Cherokees in their current war with the Choctaws, who were allied with some of the Miamis eager to cast off their political ties to the Haudenosaunee. Reacting to the decision of the Haudenosaunee, Shawnee emissaries arrived in the Creek nation in January 1770 and asked the Creeks to join the pan-Indian movement, an idea the Creeks debated seriously.

In the midst of all these Indian to Indian diplomatic efforts, the British government decided that any Indian unity, no matter what nations were involved—and no matter how justified—was detrimental to British interests, especially since it might lead to an Indian war. The British had kept the Indians off balance in the past by encouraging them to fight one another. On April 14, 1770, the Earl of Hillsborough wrote to General Thomas Gage, stating officially an attitude suggested by Sir William Johnson and Gage:

> The uniting [of] the Savages in one common Interest is a Measure which, abstractedly considered, appears to be founded in Principles of Justice and humanity; but if such Union is to be accompanied with the hazard of their turning their Arms against us, and thereby endangering the Tranquillity of Our Frontiers, good Policy certainly points out a different System of conduct towards them, and Self-preservation will justify what Humanity might otherwise condemn. (Carter 1933, 100)

In July 1770, the Haudenosaunee and the Cherokees met with Sir William Johnson at German Flats on the Mohawk River. Although most of the Haudenosaunee sachems, many under Johnson's influence, wanted peace, the Haudenosaunee warriors and their leaders wanted to gain British military support for a war against the Shawnees and all other nations who opposed the Haudenosaunee's and the Cherokees' right to grant the recent land cessions. Johnson, operating under the British desire to avoid giving strength to any Indian movement that would give Indians greater power, convinced the Haudenosaunee to send only a strong warning to the western nations, threatening war if Haudenosaunee wishes were opposed.

In a conference on the Scioto River (Ohio), the western nations, offered help by the French and French-allied Indians of the Illinois, Missouri and Arkansas rivers, responded by offering to end their wars with the Cherokees and all other southern Indians. It was either an attempt to entice the Cherokees away from the Haudenosaunee or an attempt to promote a complete pan-Indian movement. A pan-Indian motive would have meant that past rivalries would have to be put aside. Whatever the real motive, the Cherokees and the Haudenosaunee both responded negatively, the Haudenosaunee sending warriors south to the Cherokees in order to reaffirm Haudenosaunee willingness to fight alongside them against western enemies.

British Cut Military Expenditures on the Frontier

In March 1772, General Gage abandoned some interior forts in order to decrease military expenditures. He then agreed with the officials in London that two more forts—Fort Chartres, on the east bank of the Mississippi River in Illinois, and Fort Pitt—would be destroyed. This would leave only Niagara, Detroit and Michilimackinac as British posts in the west. It was clearly an abdication of British responsibility to enforce law and order on the frontier, where whites too often killed or cheated Indians. This policy also exposed many colonists to attack in case of an Indian war. Gage's rationalization was that

> If the Colonists will afterwards force the Savages into Quarrels by using them ill, let them feel the Consequences, we shall be out of the Scrape. The Sums are vast that have been expended in Indian Affairs since the King took the Management of them, and the Colonies will take no Step to assist in putting them on the best Footing (Carter 1993, 601).

The pullback of troops began in the summer of 1772 when Fort Chartres was destroyed and abandoned. In the late fall, Fort Pitt was vacated but left partially intact.

On October 7, 1772, Gage wrote to the Earl of Hillsborough that the Indians in both the North and the South

> say that as the white People have advanced from the Coast, the Original Natives have been destroyed, and of the Numerous Nations which formerly inhabited the Country possessed by the English, not one is now existing, that we are drawing nearer and nearer to them, and they see it must be soon their turn also to be exterminated. These are truths too manifest to be contradicted, and I have little doubt that it is from their inability alone to carry on a war, that they don't all unite against us. They see and dread our Power, and that it is from the English only they can now draw conveniently the [trade] Articles they are in need of, and all that is Necessary either for war or hunting. (Carter 1931, 335)

Nearly a year later Sir William Johnson noted:

> The Indians Justly observe that we have not half settled the Country near the Sea, and that those [whites] who go back [onto the frontier] are a Banditti, who disregard our Laws. (Haldimand Transcripts 1773, B.10, 119)

Increasingly disregarded by the British military and pressed by settlers, the Indians' day-to-day confrontations with trespassing hunters and unscrupulous traders multiplied. Because the traders made high profits in arms sales, the traders also encouraged intertribal wars such as the one renewed in January 1771 between the Creeks and the Choctaws.

The traders became so manipulative that they could influence and even control some internal tribal politics. Among the Chickasaws, for example, traders maneuvered their own candidate, Mingo Ouma, into office as the Chickasaws' principal chief. The appointment was nullified in January 1772 through the efforts of Indian Superintendent John Stuart, and the traditional leader Paya Mattaha was installed instead. Nevertheless, among the Chickasaws as among all Indian nations, the traders' influences continued to be powerful.

Debt Used to Extract Land from Indians

Trading interests with the Indians also gave whites opportunities to extract land from the Indians. Beginning in 1764, wealthy, powerful traders such as George Croghan and the firm of Baynton, Wharton and Morgan declared that they had sustained severe losses during Pontiac's War and, banding together with men such as Sir William Johnson and Benjamin Franklin, asked the British government for Indian lands as recompense. These so-called "suffering traders" had begun by manipulating a handsome grant of 1,800,000 acres from the Haudenosaunee at the Fort Stanwix treaty negotiations in 1768. But the British government continually refused to recognize the legality of the grant.

The speculators broadened their support by recruiting officials in the British government and their political rivals at home (including George Washington). The speculators never gave up hopes of obtaining confirmation of their claim. They even lobbied the British government for larger grants of land.

The outbreak of the American Revolution seemed a setback at first, but soon many of the fortune-seekers realized that they could continue their land pursuits by shifting their pressures from the British government to the new government of the United States. In the meantime, however, Governor James Wright of Georgia and those traders who dealt with the Cherokees and the Creeks evolved a land scheme of their own. When the Plan of 1764 was repealed in 1768, a slackening of traders' licensing procedures led to a terrific increase in the number of traders. Unbridled competition among these numerous traders lowered prices and resulted in smaller profits.

Profits were even more elusive because the termination of the Plan of 1764 also ended the London-imposed, fifty-shilling credit limit to the Indians. Wright and his friends decided to collect debts by asking for Indian land. The Cherokees and the Creeks, victimized by the easy credit terms, signed the Treaty of Augusta (Georgia) on August 3, 1773, turning over 2,100,000 acres in order to settle their current debts.

The various traders' schemes demonstrated how willing the land-hungry colonists were to take advantage of the ethical vacuum left by British refusal to take responsibility for a just Indian policy. These traders' schemes also added another dimension to trade abuse—an unfortunate occurrence, as trade was the only major Indian-white institution that was even somewhat mutually beneficial. The British had intertwined offers of trade with demands for Indian land concessions since the early 1600s. But this combined strategy had been used against smaller coastal nations, not—at least on a large scale—against the major Indian nations of the interior. Certainly trade had always involved fraud and certain political and economic pressures. But the Indians nevertheless sought out the trade for the economic adaptations that they believed improved their ways of life. The Indians had even used trade to play off competing European and colonial powers in order to maintain Indian independence. But now the trade had become potentially as dangerous to the Indians as outright white land greed, religious missionizing, colonial politics and international warfare.

Despite provocations by traders, squatters, and other frontier whites, the major Indian powers refrained from hostilities against the whites because they sincerely wanted peace and the trade that only peace could insure. Without the major nations' support, lesser Indian nations held back their warriors. The only bloodshed was caused either by whites or by individual warriors who did not adhere to their nations' desires. After 1770, the Haudenosaunee, more than any other nation, were trying to refrain from intertribal warfare as fostered by the British because of the long-held belief of the Haudenosaunee that except when victory seemed a certainty, others should do the fighting. In 1773, Sir William Johnson wanted the Haudenosaunee to go to war against the Miamis and some Indians farther to the west. The confederacy claimed sovereignty over these nations, but their ties had weakened. If the Haudenosaunee could regain control, those nations would be unable to go to war against the British. They could then be persuaded to abandon their trade with the French and Spanish along the Mississippi and instead make firm trading commitments to the British. The Haudenosaunee refused unless the British agreed to do most of the fighting. It was an independent decision similar to that of 1752 when, after the French massacre of pro-British Miamis at Pickawillany, Ohio, the British had also mistakenly expected the Haudenosaunee to go to war without British help.

Lord Dunmore's War

In 1774, no Indian nation wanted war with the British. Grand plans of unity had fallen into confusion because of the subversive and divisive tactics ably employed by the British. However, the Indian economies were threatened. White hunters and squatters such as Daniel Boone not only illegally scouted out lands for speculators; they also depleted the Indians' hunting grounds of animal skins. These frontiersmen were so unscrupulous that they stole from one another as well as from the Indians. It was in lands south of the Ohio River that the real crisis lay, because here the hunters and squatters were joined by agents of speculators. George Washington and Patrick Henry, among others, sponsored surveys of Shawnee land that the Haudenosaunee—willingly selling out the Shawnees—had granted to the whites at Fort Stanwix in 1768. The governor of Virginia, Lord Dunmore, was determined to seize land for his speculating friends and disregard both the claims of the Shawnees and the colony of Pennsylvania. He appointed frontier officials who were aggressively anti-Indian. Whites indiscriminately murdered Shawnees, Delawares and Mingos, but still the Indians hoped for peace. They also intended to hold onto their lands, which they still believed the Haudenosaunee had unjustly ceded. The Shawnees, especially, made it clear that they would defend their lands by force if necessary.

Then on April 30, 1774, eight or more Mingos, including women and children, were murdered by whites when they came to trade as they had many times before at a farm-trading post ("Baker's Cabin") on the south bank of the Ohio River in what is now West Virginia. The Mingo chief Logan, or Tachnechdorus, whose sister was one of the slain, sought revenge, as did many other Mingos. The Shawnees protected the white traders among them and still intended to avoid war if possible. As for the traders, they believed as the Indians did—that frontiersmen and not Indians were to blame for all the recent tensions and incidents. The Haudenosaunee ordered the Delawares to remove from Shawnee country immediately rather than risk involvement in any hostilities. The majority of Shawnees, even though whites had murdered some of their people recently, still hoped for peace. Logan led a few Mingos and Shawnees out to revenge a total of thirteen Indian deaths, and called off their war by mid-June after killing thirteen white Virginians. They had carefully avoided harming Pennsylvania families, as they knew that Virginians had begun the war. But the Virginians chose to escalate the conflict.

The Haudenosaunee, whose power and empire were being eroded by marauding whites, grew impatient and demanded that the British officials do something. In a great conference at Sir William Johnson's estate in the Mohawk River valley in July, Johnson tried to quiet the Haudenosaunee, many of whom were now proposing to aid the Shawnees. Johnson's major speech on July 11 was a success, but the day was hot and Johnson had been severely ill. Immediately after his speech, the sixty-year-old superintendent collapsed, and he died that evening. His nephew Guy Johnson became the new superintendent. The Haudenosaunee, moved by the dramatic death of a man they considered their friend, agreed to make efforts for peace, sincerely believing promises that the

British would soon initiate a just Indian policy and an effective Indian Department. Early in August, the Shawnees were visited by a Haudenosaunee ambassador, Guyasuta, a Seneca. The Senecas had been strongly pro-Shawnee during debates about the war, and the Shawnees hoped that the Haudenosaunee would help form an alliance already planned to include the Haudenosaunee, Shawnees, Delawares, Mingos, Potawatomis, Ottawas, Cherokees, Creeks and other nations, including some in Canada. The Shawnees asked Guyasuta for official permission to go to war as a nation, for until now they had only gone out to battle as bands of individual warriors. But Guyasuta refused and told them that such permission could not be given until the Haudenosaunee council at Onondaga, which had called a special autumn meeting with other nations, debated the issue. In the meantime, he pressured the Mingos to halt their war, and some responded. The Wyandots and the Ottawas were also somewhat successfully pressured by the Haudenosaunee to remain aloof. But then Virginia declared war against the Indians, with the Shawnees as their special target. The war was aptly titled "Lord Dunmore's War" after the Virginia governor who sponsored it. By mid-August, Virginia troops destroyed one Shawnee and six Mingo towns. On September 8, 1774, Guy Johnson reported to General Gage that the Shawnees had told the Haudenosaunee, whose own lands were not entirely free of manipulating speculators, what Gage himself must have only too painfully known: "[E]ven those Nations who are most faithfull to the British are treated with Injustice" (Thomas Gage Papers 1774).

The Shawnees counterattacked in the fall of 1774. On October 10, 1774, eight hundred Shawnees and a few Mingos and Delawares challenged nine hundred whites at the Battle of Point Pleasant (West Virginia). The Indians were defeated and sued for peace. After extended negotiations in late October at the Treaty of Camp Charlotte, the Shawnees agreed to give up their claims south of the Ohio River. In exchange, they were guaranteed their lands north of the Ohio. Logan, the Mingo leader who had lost his sister and other relatives in the April 30 massacre that began the war, refused to attend the treaty proceedings because he felt it was the whites, not the Indians, who had been wrong. Nevertheless, he wanted to give his support to peace and so he met with a Virginia negotiator, General John Gibson, near a Mingo camp in October 1774. Gibson was related to Logan through marriage, and Logan freely wept in the grief and bitterness of the moment as the two men—and two cultures—faced each other in the forest. Then Logan spoke, in his own tongue, and Gibson delivered the message later, in translation, to Dunmore:

I appeal to any white man to say, if ever he entered Logan's cabin hungry, and he gave him not meat: if ever he came cold and naked, and he cloathed him not. During the course of the last long and bloody war [Pontiac's War] Logan remained idle in his cabin, an advocate for peace. Such was my love for the whites, that my countrymen pointed as they passed, and said, "Logan is the friend of white men." I had even thought to have lived with you, but for the injuries of one man. Colonel [Michael] Cresap, the last spring, in cold blood, and unprovoked, murdered all the relations of Logan, not even sparing my women and children. There runs not a drop of my blood in the veins of any living creature. This called on me for revenge. I have sought it: I have killed many: I have fully glutted my vengeance: for my country I rejoice at the beams of peace. But do not harbor a thought that mine is the joy of fear. Logan never felt fear. He will not turn on his heel to save his life. Who is there to mourn for Logan?—Not one. (Jefferson 1801, 95–96)

The Shawnees' defeat in Lord Dunmore's War was bitter. Their nation had originally hoped for peace, but during the war they had become the leaders of their Indian allies. In large measure, the Shawnees had been defeated because the Haudenosaunee pressured most of the Shawnees' potential allies to stay out of the war. The Haudenosaunee in turn were beguiled by the British and believed promises that the British intended to remedy the Indians' white problem. The French continued to meddle—as usual, the French were long on encouragement and short on active support. The French believed that although the Haudenosaunee had not supported the Shawnees' war to defend lands south of the Ohio River, the Haudenosaunee had no intention of ever allowing the whites to settle on any lands north of the Ohio. In this, the French were correct. But the Haudenosaunee still hoped that the diplomatic maneuvering at Fort Stanwix in 1768 would divert white settlement away from the Haudenosaunee homelands and into lands south of the Ohio River. Haudenosaunee claims to these lands were weaker, and the confederacy's warriors could not as easily defend these lands.

The Treaty of Camp Charlotte, ending Lord Dunmore's War, forced the Shawnees to accept the Haudenosaunee's cession in 1768 to lands south of the Ohio River. Now white expansion into Kentucky was blocked by only one nation, the Cherokees. In 1775, the Cherokees were interested in obtaining the manufactured goods that would come with any land sale, but they were also in dire need of muskets and ammunition for their periodic war with the Chickasaws.

Now that the Shawnees had abandoned their Kentucky lands, speculator and former judge Richard Henderson of North Carolina realized that if he acted quickly, he could take advantage, especially if the Cherokees could also be persuaded to cede their Kentucky lands. Henderson knew that the British-Cherokee Articles of Agreement of 1730 and the Proclamation of 1763 provided that only agents of the British Crown could legally purchase Indian lands and thus that private land purchases from the Cherokees were specifically forbidden. He nevertheless felt that he and his partners could take advantage of the confusion caused by an escalating confrontation between the British imperial government and a newly formed radical intercolonial rights organization called the Continental Congress.

On March 17, 1775, at Sycamore Shoals (Tennessee), Cherokee leaders including Oconostota and ninety-year-old Attakullaculla sold their lands in Kentucky and Tennessee that were south of the Ohio River between the Kentucky River in the east and the southern edge of the watershed of the Cumberland River to the west and south. They also sold their lands through the Cumberland Gap and lands in the Watauga River Valley. All this was ceded for only £10,000 in trade goods. Dragging Canoe (Chincohacina) and a few other important leaders among the Cherokees opposed the sale vehemently, but to no avail.

The outbreak of the American Revolution one month later prevented Indian Superintendent John Stuart from taking any action to nullify the illegal treaty, and Henderson had already moved swiftly to occupy the lands. On March 10, before negotiations with the Cherokees had even begun, he had sent Daniel Boone, a longtime employee of his, with ax-men to blaze a road into Kentucky. On March 20 Henderson followed with forty riflemen and some black slaves.

On April 2, 1775, Daniel Boone founded Boonesborough but the settlers were so busy staking out claims they refused to build a fort until some time later. Actually there was no need for a fort because the Cherokees were friendly. During the summer, Henderson's dreams of reaping a fortune selling lands to pioneers were shattered by an influx of frontier families who were no more respectful of white land rights than of Indian ones. They also believed that since Henderson had obtained the land illegally they could do the same. By the next year, June 1776, anti-Henderson settlers found a leader in a twenty-four-year-old Virginian named George Rogers Clark. Clark dreamed of using the escalating American Revolutionary War as an opportunity for white frontiersmen. With British authority and resources diverted to the East Coast, these frontiersmen could break Indian treaties and expand north of the Ohio River onto Indian homelands.

American Revolutionary War Begins

The American Revolutionary War between British authority and a colonial minority known as the Patriots went from political protest to armed violence on April 19, 1775. On that day, British soldiers and colonial dissidents opened fire on each other at Lexington, Massachusetts. The American Revolution was a civil war fought between those who supported and those who denied the authority of Great Britain. When the war began, most Indians on the British colonial frontier intended to remain neutral. Certainly the Indians owed the British no debt of gratitude: after 1763, no consistent trade policy was enforced and Indian lands were whittled away through various schemes hatched both by colonists and British officials. British imperial laws were not enforced upon marauding white hunters and squatters who illegally settled on Indian lands and who killed innocent Indian men, women and children. The royal governor of Virginia, Lord Dunmore, who had so recently been at war with the Indians along the Virginia frontier, was now, due to his imperial position, one of the major leaders of the British forces.

From north to south all along the frontier, there were many pro-British squatters and frontier settlers who had antagonized the Indians in the past and would not cease their illegal actions simply because they were loyal to King George III. Land speculators were often Loyalists. Clearly, being a Loyalist did not automatically mean law abiding, at least from an Indian point of view. Nor did being a Patriot necessarily alienate Indian people. Many highly regarded traders were Patriots, such as George Galphin, who dealt with the Creeks. Thus, neutrality was the logical choice for the vast majority of Indian nations.

During the first year of the war, every Indian nation was involved in internal debates similar to those conducted among the whites. In each of these many Indian nations, every town had a strong neutral faction, some adamant Loyalists, a number of dedicated Patriots, and a large number of apathetic families—not so very different from virtually every colonial community caught up in the early years of the Revolution. The apathetic Indians would eventually be drawn along by circumstance rather than by commitment, just as occurred in the colonial communities. In the Indian debates, however, the Indian nations were not as violent as their white neighbors were. These white frontiersmen were often fond of vigilante intimidation against anyone adhering to minority opinions.

The failure of British Indian policy from 1763 to 1775 can be viewed as a microcosm of the breakdown of the entire British imperial structure in the thirteen North American colonies. Some of the major failures of British policy that antagonized Indians had parallels that prompted Patriot dissent. For example, the failure to define laws that were equitably applied throughout the empire was exemplified by the inconsistently enforced Plan of 1764. For many colonists, on the other hand, the revenue acts proposed or passed by Parliament after 1765, which would have supported imperial policies such as the Plan of 1764, seemed ill-conceived and certain to erode the rights of the colonists and their colonial legislatures.

Both Indians and colonists were also affected by ill-advised boundary decisions that only increased tensions: for Indians, the Proclamation Line of 1763; for Patriots, the Quebec Act of 1774. The inability of the British to define and enforce an equitable and consistent economic and legal order caused the crises of both Indians and white colonials during the period 1763 to 1775. Indians and colonists were both treated as appendages to the British empire when in fact they were members of many sophisticated political units with goals quite apart from the empire's. British failure to centralize control in the midst of these diverse peoples caused both Indians and colonists (who were themselves of many nationalities) to resent the London government. The British solution to both Indian and colonial discontent ultimately ignored the causes of the problems and concentrated only on suppressing their symptoms.

The Indians thus had as much reason to rebel against the British as the Patriots did, but since the Indians saw no more merit in the land-hungry men who frequented Patriot circles than they did in those who advocated the British cause, the Indians' best course was neutrality.

Most Indians, however, ended up fighting for the British. While it is true that the Indians were not inevitable allies of the British, their decision was not made independently. Their economies were too intertwined with white trade, and it was trade that largely dictated their final political decisions. The Patriots offered trade in exchange for neutrality, but after 1775 the British offered trade only in exchange for promises of alliance. Because the British had more trade to offer, Indian nation after Indian nation was drawn into the vortex of the British counterrevolution.

When the American Revolution began, the determination of many Indian nations to remain neutral was exemplified by a Creek statement on September 7, 1775. Tese [Jesse] Mico of the Lower Creeks , defined the Creek position and sent it to the British and Patriots alike:

> [W]e are determined to lye quiet and not meddle with the Quarrel... [W]e wish all the white People well...as you are all one Mother's Children we hope that the great man above will soon make Peace between you. (Sir Henry Clinton Papers 1775)

Tese Mico, in giving this talk, noted three times that he hoped trade would continue with all whites. British Indian Superintendent John Stuart told the Creeks that he would accept their neutrality for the moment. (Stuart knew that the British were not yet able to integrate the Indians into their military strategy.) On September 29, five Creek chiefs stated their case for neutrality and trade. They emphasized that the Patriots had also agreed to support the Creeks' neutrality (in the awkward language of the white translator, not the Creeks'):

> We have heard your talk, and we Like it, and See its the Same as all the beloved men in Georgia [Patriots] Sent us some time past, you are all one people...we hear there is Some Difference Between the white people, and we are all Sorry to hear it....We are all glad to hear you Desire us to keep in friendship with all white men our friends as we Don't want to Concern [ourselves] in the matter But Leave you to Settle the matter your Selves, and will Be glad to hear the Difference Settled and all at peace again.... [W]e all Desire our Old white [i.e., peaceful] trading Road Still to be kept white and Clear after matters is Settled. (Sir Henry Clinton Papers 1775)

A British attempt to capture Charleston, South Carolina, during June 1776 threatened to force the Creeks onto the British side because Charleston was a major center of their trade with the Patriots, and Creek neutrality depended on being able to trade with both the British and the Patriots. Because the Patriot defense forces in Charleston held, however, the Creeks continued to trade with both sides and maintained their neutrality.

South: Land Grabs Under Various Guises

Just to the north of the Creeks, the Cherokees had a reason to go to war and yet strove for peace instead. Settlers of both Loyalist and Patriot persuasion, not satisfied even with the lands the Cherokees had ceded in 1775 at Sycamore Shoals, were settling on the Cherokees' northeastern lands and were refusing to move even at the direction of various British officials. In May 1776, the Cherokees received a delegation of Shawnees, Delawares, Nanticokes, Ottawas and some Haudenosaunee (who were acting without the sanction of the Haudenosaunee's council). The emissaries, under the Shawnee Cornstalk, urged the Cherokees to use the opportunity of the white man's war to reconquer lands south of the Ohio. They were clearly counting on the British being victorious on the Southeast coast to draw off Patriot strength. Most Cherokees, including Attakullaculla, Oconostota and a woman chief (Beloved Woman) named Nancy Ward, opposed going to war. But one leader, Dragging Canoe, finally decided that peaceful pleas, which included a warning to illegally settled whites to leave Cherokee lands, were no longer enough. Perhaps Dragging Canoe intended only to strike at those squatters on Cherokee lands when he led bands of Cherokees to the attack on July 20, 1776, but the war soon spread to enflame the entire Cherokee-white frontier.

Many—perhaps most—of the Cherokees were still opposed to war. The Cherokees' Beloved Woman even warned the whites of Dragging Canoe's first attack, which the whites were then able to defeat decisively. During September and October 1776, Loyalist and Patriot frontiersmen united and invaded the Cherokee country. The whites destroyed Cherokee towns. But they only killed a few Cherokees because most fled, their retreat protected by the warriors. (Tragically, at the time of the attack, many if not most of the Cherokees had still considered themselves at peace with the whites.) In March 1777, those Cherokees still enthusiastic for war and under the leadership of Dragging Canoe seceded from the Cherokee nation. These Cherokees left their burned-out homes to build towns farther west (near Chattanooga, Tennessee) on Chickamauga Creek. Here they became known as Chickamaugas. (They rejoined the Cherokee nation in 1788). The rest of the Cherokee nation was forced by the whites to pay a severe price to the Patriots of Georgia, South Carolina and Virginia: 5,000,264 acres ceded in two treaties, at DeWitt's Corner on May 20 and at the Long Island of the Holston on July 20, 1777. Many Cherokees were disgusted with these cessions and went to join the Cherokee secessionists on Chickamauga Creek. These Chickamaugas continued their war, and soon they had another reason to maintain their struggle. White settlers were not satisfied with the more than five million acres just ceded by the Chickamaugas' conciliating Cherokee kinsmen, and they began squatting on even more Cherokee lands.

The British in the meantime were bringing trade pressures upon the Creeks to force them to join the war against the Patriots. The Creeks were unsure that the British could supply them with the trade goods they were now buying from the Patriots in exchange for deerskins and other commodities. The Creeks, however, were weary of a war they were having with the Choctaws, and the British used this to their own advantage. On October 26, 1776, southern Indian Superintendent John Stuart at Pensacola, Florida, brought about a peace between the Creeks and the Choctaws on the condition that the Creeks join the British and aid the Cherokees. Pro-British Creeks were ready to go to war by February 1777, but by then the Cherokees had been defeated. Although there were some angry Creek raids against squatters on Creek lands and a number of engagements with Patriot forces, as the summer of 1777 approached, a Patriot Indian agent, George Galphin, still hoped to persuade the Creeks to return to neutrality. Most Creeks were hesitant about a full commitment to the British unless the British would coordinate white troop support to help the Creeks. The Creeks were especially wary, as they knew how thoroughly the Patriots had devastated the Cherokee homeland. The possibility of the Creeks returning to neutrality centered on whether the Patriots could send enough trade goods to the Creeks to allow them to avoid a permanent British alliance. In September 1777, the neutral party among the Creeks drove British agents from their midst and anticipated a brisk business with Patriot traders. Although many Creeks continued to raid the frontier, the Patriots sent out trade goods in November 1777, an action which greatly impressed the nation. At least one Creek war party, however, continued to fight. Then the Patriot trade slowed to a trickle, and Patriot traders were often able to offer only a promise of goods in exchange for Creek skins. In March 1778, British Indian Superintendent John Stuart launched a trading counteroffensive, sending traders and goods to all Creek towns. The Creek nation debated, a few Creeks went out against the Patriots in June, and the neutral faction waited for Patriot trade. The Patriots failed to supply the Creeks' needs, and during July and August 1778 many of the Creek warriors went to war as allies of the British. The British capture of Savannah on December 29, 1778, strengthened the position of the Creek war faction so that by March 1779 the Creek neutral party diminished to ineffectuality.

West of the Creeks, the Choctaws and the Chickasaws kept the southern Mississippi River Valley secure for the British despite the poor strategy and erroneous deployment ordered by Superintendent John Stuart. To the south, the Seminoles ably protected Florida from Patriot invasion. But the Creeks' northern neighbors, the Chickamaugas, faced new peril. In January 1779, Governor Patrick Henry of Virginia ordered an expedition launched against the Chickamaugas, and in April six hundred whites burned and looted eleven towns with ease: Most of the warriors were attacking the Georgia and South Carolina frontiers, and the women and children escaped into the forest. The Chickamaugas rebuilt a few of their towns but also accepted the Creeks' invitation to move southward onto their lands in southern Tennessee and northern Alabama. Beginning that same year, however, both the Chickamauga secessionists and the Cherokee nation proper suffered a more terrible scourge than any white army could inflict, as a smallpox epidemic broke out and eventually killed at least twenty-five hundred.

In April 1780, on the eastern bank of the Mississippi below the mouth of the Ohio, a Patriot post, Fort Jefferson, was erected and almost immediately besieged by Chickasaws. After a sporadic siege of one year, the Chickasaws forced the fort's abandonment, keeping their own and the British claims to the area intact. Farther east, a few Cherokees tried to drive off whites illegally settled on their lands, but most Cherokees were not willing to risk a war. Suddenly, in December 1780, a Patriot army ordered to attack the Chickamaugas surprised and attacked these Cherokees instead, and many of their towns were wantonly destroyed. The stunned Cherokees surrendered more land at the second Treaty of Long Island on July 26, 1781.

Early in 1781, the Choctaws unceremoniously dropped out of the war when their British supply base at Pensacola fell to the Spanish. The British disaster at Yorktown (October 19, 1781) did not drastically affect the goals of the Creeks or the Chickamaugas (nor of the few Cherokees who were still in the war). They had already learned that the British and Loyalists could not be depended upon for direct or coordinated troop assistance. The goal of their war now was almost solely to stop white expansion, and this cause would know no setback unless the Patriots could actually defeat the Indians. The Indians did depend upon the British for supplies, however, and by the winter of 1781–1782 the Creeks were desperate. In January 1782, they tried to get ninety-three horses packed with deerskins through the Patriot lines surrounding British-held Savannah. The packhorse caravan was captured, and the Creek people learned that their great leader Emistesigo had been killed in battle as he led one hundred fifty Creeks against the Patriot lines. By June 1783, it was clear to both the Creeks and the Chickamauga Cherokees that the British had abandoned them. (Preliminary terms ending the whites' war were signed by the Patriots and the British on November 5, 1782, and January 20, 1783.) The leaders of the Creeks and Chickamauga Cherokees protested, but they were ignored by the British, as was a Creek demand that the British assign them new lands where they could live apart from the hated, land-hungry Patriots. On November 1, 1783, a minority of Creeks ceded eight hundred square miles of land to the Patriots in a council in Augusta, Georgia. Opposed by the majority of the Creeks, the question of land cessions as a price of peace—a question for all Indians still at war with the Patriots—remained largely unresolved within the Indian nations. However, quick treaties and white legislation were manipulated by southern states eager to wrench greater land cessions from the Creeks, Chickamaugas, Cherokees and other southern Indian nations.

The American Revolution in the North

For the Indian nations in the North, the American Revolution began in 1775 while Indian nations were still awaiting the promised changes in British Indian policy that were supposed to guarantee to them their lands north of the Ohio and west of the 1768 Treaty of Fort Stanwix line. At the start of the American Revolution, both the British and the Patriots realized that if they could carry out a consistent and honest policy, the Indians would be obliged to them. The Patriots originally desired only what the Indians wanted—Indian neutrality. In September and October 1775, Patriot agents met with Haudenosaunee, Delawares, Shawnees, Wyandots and Ottawas to sign the Treaty of Pittsburgh. The provisions of the treaty were intended to strengthen the Haudenosaunee at the expense of the other Indian nations. The terms made it clear that those Indians defeated in Lord Dunmore's War recognized the 1768 Fort Stanwix cession by the Haudenosaunee of the lands south of the Ohio River to the whites. In exchange, the Patriots guaranteed that the lands north of the Ohio River would remain in Indian possession. All Indian nations present also promised to remain neutral. The Delawares took the opportunity to declare once again that they were not "women" despite the Hauden-osaunees' continued labeling of their Delaware subjects.

During the spring and summer of 1776, however, about eighty Mingo warriors, together with a few Shawnees, Delawares and other Indians, began devastating raids into the Virginia frontier intending to help the Cherokees retake Kentucky from frontiersmen such as Daniel Boone. By the end of 1776 the warring Indians had forced most Kentucky pioneers to huddle in three stockaded towns: Harrodsburg, St. Asaph's, and Boonesborough. Pressures by the Haudenosaunee and fear of a disastrous repeat of Lord Dunmore's War kept the vast majority of Shawnees, Delawares and Wyandots in line with the official policy of neutrality. In the fall of 1776, the Haudenosaunee realized that the American Revolution threatened the survival of their empire just as surely as it did that of the British. The Haudenosaunee increased their diplomatic pressures to bring the Mingos back to neutrality. At one point, the Haudenosaunee even hoped to remove the Mingos from the confederacy's frontier and bring them into the Haudenosaunee heartland to live among the Senecas. At the same time, most Ojibwas, Ottawas, Miamis and other Great Lakes nations watched the white man's war to see if and when any advantage could be gained by aiding one side or the other.

As in the South, however, Indian diplomatic efforts to maintain neutrality in the North could continue only if the Indians could obtain, in exchange for pelts or as outright gifts, enough trade goods from the Patriots. The British trade increasingly came tied with requests for military alliance. Furthermore, on May 25, 1776, the Continental Congress in Philadelphia approved Patriot recruitment of Indians to counteract British efforts in the contest for allies, and this further undermined the Indians' chances of remaining neutral. A scarcity of British goods due to a Patriot blockade of the St. Lawrence River ended with the Patriot withdrawal from Canada in July 1776, and by January 1777 British goods grew more plentiful as the availability of Patriot goods diminished. The Haudenosaunee soon despaired of obtaining enough trade goods from the Patriots and leaned more and more toward supporting the British, though no decision was made. The politically powerful and influential Haudenosaunee women seemed especially reluctant to undertake war. Increasing debate within the confederacy weakened the Haudenosaunee's leadership of their subject nations, and in February 1777 these nations took advantage of the indecision of the Haudenosaunee. Many of the Shawnees, Delawares, Mingos and Wyandots who had not previously joined their brothers in the battle for Kentucky did so now. White squatters on lands guaranteed to the Indians by the Patriots further aggravated the situation.

Although hostile acts were carried out by both Patriots and Indians, the majority of the Haudenosaunee, the Shawnees and the Delawares still hoped to be able to maintain neutrality. During the summer of 1777, the Haudenosaunee factions became involved in their own civil war with a majority of the warriors eventually fighting alongside the British. The Shawnees and Delawares were for the most part still neutral, however. As a mark of good faith and with the hope of success through negotiation, Cornstalk, the Shawnees' war leader during Lord Dunmore's War, approached the Patriots. With one other warrior, Cornstalk came to Port Randolph at the mouth of the Great Kanawha River at the Ohio River, because he had heard that the Patriots intended to invade his country. Cornstalk was convinced that a Patriot invasion of his homeland would force neutral Shawnees into war against the Patriots. Intent on peace, he and his friend were nevertheless seized as hostages. When Cornstalk's son Elinipsico came to inquire about his father's whereabouts, he too was taken. On November 10, 1777, one of a group of Patriot hunters was killed by unidentified Indians. Seeking revenge, the Patriots returned to the fort and murdered Cornstalk, his son and their companion in cold blood. It was later learned that Mingos, not Shawnees, had shot the white hunter. Governor Patrick Henry of Virginia ordered Cornstalk's murderers tried, but they were acquitted because no witnesses came forward to accuse them.

As the Revolutionary War continued, more and more warriors from the Indian nations north of the Ohio River joined the British. The Patriots realized that if they were to hold Kentucky and win the frontier war in the West, the British posts north of the Ohio River, especially Detroit, had to be captured so that the Indians would be deprived of their trade goods and war supplies. Such a military occupation would also benefit whites eager for new lands to speculate in or settle. Moving suddenly, July 4, 1778, a Patriot army under George Rogers Clark surprised and captured Kaskaskia (Illinois) on the Kaskaskia River near its junction with the Mississippi. A French priest, friendly to Clark because France had allied with the Patriots earlier that year, traveled eastward to Vincennes (Indiana) in July and persuaded the French townsmen to ally with Clark.

Both Kaskaskia and Vincennes were more valuable as bases for future white land speculation and settlement than they were for blocking Indian attacks, because those Indians who supported the British were supplied primarily from Detroit, far to the northeast. The swiftness of the Patriot takeover of the Illinois frontier impressed the local Indians, however, and beginning in August 1778, bands of Illinois, Ojibwas, Ottawas, Potawatomis, Missisaugas,

Winnebagos, Sauks, Foxes, Osages, Iowas and Miamis came to make their peace with George Rogers Clark.

On December 17, 1778, however, a British and Indian force from Detroit under captain Henry Hamilton retook Vincennes, using presents to regain some of the Indians' friendship. Clark still held Kaskaskia and he had an important ally at Vincennes: a Piankashaw Miami chief, Tobacco's Son, who had told the British he would always be on the Patriots' side. In addition, the French inhabitants at Vincennes were still sympathetic to the Patriot cause. Moving eastward from Kaskaskia across flooded and near-frozen lands, a small army under Clark surprised and recaptured Vincennes on February 24, 1779. Keys to Clark's surprise were that Tobacco's Son's Piankashaw Miamis did not allow one word of alarm to reach the British, and that some Kickapoo warriors aiding Clark convinced Kickapoos helping Hamilton to join them. The major Indian supply base at Detroit, however, remained in British hands, and British Detroit continued to be the real center of power north of the Ohio River.

In the meantime, at Fort Pitt on September 17, 1778, the self-declared independent United States made its first treaty with an Indian nation. Signed with the Delawares, most of whom had remained neutral, the treaty ended any mutual hostilities. This first U.S. treaty with Indian people included limited Delaware military assistance to the United States in a projected attack on Detroit (a provision the Delawares may not have understood, as it was poorly translated, perhaps purposefully). The treaty also permitted Patriot forces to travel across Delaware lands in order to attack British forts and pro-British Indian nations. In exchange, the United States promised to respect Delaware land rights, to ensure an honest trade, and to erect a fort for the Indians' protection. The treaty also included a truly revolutionary idea: a state within the United States inhabited solely by Indians.

> And it is further agreed on between the contracting parties should it for the future be found conducive for the mutual interest of both parties to invite any other nations who have been friends to the interest of the United States, to join the present confederation, and to form a state whereof the Delaware nation shall be the head, and have a representation in Congress: Provided, nothing contained in this article to be considered as conclusive until it meets with the approbation of Congress. (Kappler [1904] 1972, 5)

Congress never approved.

A chronic shortage of Patriot trade goods increasingly alienated most Indians friendly to the United States in 1779. A few Delawares rebelled in early 1779 against the Patriots because the treaty of 1778 had been vaguely translated, leaving the Delawares confused as to its exact terms; because the promised trade was not sufficient; and because squatters were invading lands north of the Ohio. But most Delawares continued their neutrality. Farther west in Illinois, George Rogers Clark had promised the Kickapoos that none of their lands would be taken by white settlers, yet by late 1779 grants of land were frequently distributed as payment for Patriot military service.

In 1780, the Kickapoos looked for help to the British in Detroit. Despite the increasing number of squatters, the Patriot military presence north of the Ohio River was largely ineffective, and if the British armies had been successful in the East the Indians would easily, with increased British supplies, have overwhelmed the northern white frontier. The French, allies of the United States, sponsored a small army of sixty French and Indians under Augustine Mottin de La Balme who marched from Vincennes in October 1780 intending to capture Detroit. A Miami chief named Little Turtle, with the help of two pro-British French traders, organized a resistance and overwhelmed the French invaders. The Indian victory ended French hope of wielding power north of the Ohio. Just as significantly, the victory brought prominence to Little Turtle, a man who would lead his people courageously for the next three decades.

Until 1781, the majority of Delawares had remained friendly to the United States despite the fact that Delaware leaders and people were murdered by whites, Delaware lands were invaded by white squatters, and the Delaware nation suffered from a lack of trade goods promised by the Patriots. Without adequate trade goods, the Delawares were forced to turn to the British for supplies. The Patriots, believing that the Delawares were going to strike in the spring of 1781, decided to attack first and in April destroyed two Delaware towns. The whites murdered fifteen Delaware prisoners of war and a Delaware peace emissary, and carried off livestock and furs belonging to the Delawares valued at 80,000 pounds sterling. The Delawares went to war in retaliation. George Rogers Clark launched a major expedition against Detroit, hoping to end this British post's Indian operations north of the Ohio River. One hundred of Clark's men under Colonel Archibald Lochry, who were attempting to catch up with the main army, were trapped in an ambush by ninety warriors under Mohawk Haudenosaunee Joseph Brant (Thayendanegea, or Bundle of Sticks) and defeated on August 24, 1781. A lack of supplies and discouragement resulting partly from the army's lack of faith in his abilities forced Clark to give up his plan of capturing Detroit.

Despite the British surrender at Yorktown on October 19, 1781, the Indians north of the Ohio—like their southern counterparts—would not give up their homelands unless actually conquered. Those Delawares and other Indians north of the Ohio who were still undecided about which cause to support were shocked into action by the wanton slaughter of about ninety pacifist Moravian Christian Delawares. The innocent victims included twenty-seven women and thirty-four children. The massacre occurred on March 8, 1782, and three hundred Patriots carried it out at the praying Indians' town of Gnadenhutten (Ohio).

The Patriots were filled with hate because non-Christian Indians were raiding the frontier and killing white families. They also mistakenly thought the Moravian Delawares had given shelter to the raiders. The Patriot soldiers herded their Christian victims into two of the Indians' log cabins, men in one and women and children in the other, and as the pacifist Indians sang and prayed, killed them two by two. Among the many ironies of the slaughter was that the praying Indians had been among the Indian refugees fleeing the Paxton Boys' attacks in 1763. They were at Gnadenhutten because they had been removed from Pennsylvania in 1772 to protect them from white frontiersmen.

On June 4 and 5, 1782, five hundred Wyandots, Mingos, Shawnees and Delawares gained revenge by defeating an equal number of Patriots under Colonel William Crawford. Crawford was taken prisoner and tortured to death in revenge for the deaths of the Christian Delawares because, as an Indian explained to Crawford before his execution, he had allowed the murderers to join his army. Crawford was well known to the Indians who killed him. Before the Revolution, William Crawford had come among them and made many friends, some of whom were among his executioners. It is possible that the Indians would have killed Crawford before the war if they had realized why he had come among them earlier. Crawford's mission was to survey Indian lands for a land speculator, so that the land speculator would have an advantage over other speculators in knowing the locations of the most attractive lands. That these lands were still protected by treaty did not bother Crawford's employer, because the speculator believed that the treaty line was just a temporary line meant to buy the Indians' temporary friendship. The speculator who had employed William Crawford to conduct illegal surveys was George Washington.

In August 1782, between 240 and 300 warriors from various Indian nations, together with white Loyalists including Simon Girty, struck south of the Ohio. Feigning retreat after unsuccessfully besieging a Patriot fort, they turned at the Lower Blue Licks on the Licking River (Kentucky) and on August 19 ambushed two hundred pursuing Kentucky militiamen whose officers included Colonel Daniel Boone, the expert frontiersman whose advice of caution had gone unheeded by his men.

After five minutes of fighting, the Patriots fled in a rout. Seventy Patriots were killed. The triumphant Indians and Loyalists counted only seven of their own dead. In November 1782, George Rogers Clark led a surprise Patriot coun-terattack into Ohio and dealt the Shawnees a severe blow by destroying six of their towns. But because the Shawnee warriors escorted their families to safety, the whites killed very few Indians. Despite Clark's expedition, the white Kentucky frontier was still on the defensive by the end of the American Revolution. The Indians, on the other hand, had won most of their recent bat-tles and had protected their families. At best, the Indians had defeated the Patriots in the war by preventing the capture of their supply base at British-held Detroit despite repeated Patriot attempts, and at worst the Indians had stale-mated the Patriots. Nevertheless, the Indians lost jurisdiction over their lands north of the Ohio River at the Treaty of Paris in 1783 when the British gave the United States political sovereignty over the area without consulting a single Indian ally. One of the Patriot diplomats in Paris who negotiated what his Patriot friends could not win on the battlefield was an old hand at trying to manipulate the Indians out of their homelands: Benjamin Franklin.

The Haudenosaunee: A Microcosm of Indian Experiences during the American Revolution

More than any other Indian nation during the American Revolution, one proved itself to be militarily and diplomatically preeminent: the Haudenosaunee. The Haudenosaunee had more than a thousand warriors and their homelands were strategically located west of the Hudson River and south of Lake Ontario. Because the Haudenosaunee could contribute significant mil-itary and geographic advantages to either the British or the Patriot side, the Haudenosaunee held the balance of power during the American Revolution. Like most Indians, in the early years of the white revolutionary conflict the confederacy's members had hoped to remain neutral, but neutrality proved an impossible course. The American Revolution became the Haudenosaunee's last military defense of an independent homeland and of their own empire.

The Haudenosaunee war for independence, a civil war, was just as strongly fought as the whites'. Its results were just as revolutionary. Haudenosaunee war leaders openly disobeyed many of the confederacy's official political leaders (sachems), defiant actions that paralleled the white Patriots' defiance and breakdown of traditional British colonial government. Because the confederacy could not agree on how the defense could be accomplished, some of its warriors joined each side. Although the confederacy politically maintained neutrality, the national identity of the warriors fighting for one side or the other led both the British and the patriots to identify the six nations of the Haudenosaunee individually as either British or Patriot allies.

Those Haudenosaunee who fought on the Patriot side, mostly Oneidas with some Tuscaroras, provided invaluable service to the Patriot armies. For example, 150 Oneidas and Tuscaroras helped the Patriots defeat General John Burgoyne at the decisive battles of Saratoga in 1777. About fifty Oneidas endured the suffering at Valley Forge along with their non-Indian compatriots. These Oneidas scouted for Washington on daring forays toward the British lines. And on March 20, 1778, at Barren Hill, Pennsylvania, they fought off an attack of British cavalry and thus helped save the retreating Marquis de Lafayette and one-third of Washington's entire Valley Forge army. They were the last Patriot unit in Lafayette's army to withdraw from the field that day.

Most Haudenosaunee warriors, however, fought for the British. Despite their bravery, they could not reverse overall British defeat. Moreover, their treatment during the war by their British allies was indicative of the callous disregard the British often showed for their Indian allies. Like the other Indians who fought for the British, they too were finally betrayed. The British sold Haudenosaunee interests to the United States in exchange for a white man's peace.

The events that led to the betrayal of the Haudenosaunee by the British evolved slowly. Some of these events were beyond the control of the Haudenosaunee, while other events were the consequences of decisionsby the Haudenosaunee. During the fall of 1774, more than seven months before Patriot protest evolved into military confrontation with British soldiers at Lexington, Massachusetts, some of the Patriots, primarily from New England, attempted to entice the Haudenosaunee and other Indians away from the Crown. This faction of Patriots preferred an agreement of alliance or neutrality with the Indians to an alliance with the white frontiersmen, whom they considered lawless and beyond the concern of the Patriot movement. They approached the Indians not primarily because of altruism, which a few sincerely felt, but because they saw Indian friendship as politically valuable. These Patriots told the Indians that the King had abandoned them to the ravages of crude frontiersmen, and therefore that the Indians and the New Englanders shared the common grievance of having been deserted by the King. British Indian Superintendent Guy Johnson, frustrated because he knew that this Patriot propaganda had some truth to it, wrote on November 10, 1774, to his superior, General Thomas Gage, that

> Indians should have no knowledge of Internal disputes, as they Lessen their Ideas of Government, [and] inspire them with Contempt for our Constitution. (Sullivan et al. 1962, 691)

Nevertheless, the Haudenosaunee debated colonial politics at a November council held at the confederacy capital, Onondaga. Fortunately for the British, they made no final judgment with regard to the king's intentions. Much to Guy Johnson's relief, they also decided to remain out of Virginia's war with the Shawnees (Lord Dunmore's War), which the Shawnees had by then virtually lost.

The growing crisis of potential revolution between Patriot colonists and Great Britain provided Gage and Guy Johnson with the excuse to avoid resolving British abuses of Indians and instead to reinstate the policy of recruiting Indians as military allies. If they could turn the Indians against the colonists before the Indians turned against the Crown, positive steps to remedy the Indians' grievances would be unnecessary.

On September 4, 1774, Gage sent word to Guy Carleton, the governor of Canada, asking him to raise a force of Indians and Canadians for possible use in Massachusetts if large-scale violence erupted there. When Gage told Guy Johnson in a letter of December 28, 1774, to secure the Indians' friendship, he stated simply that the Haudenosaunee and other Indians should "be taught to look upon the King as their firm Friend" (Thomas Gage Papers 1774). He did not offer the Indians the protection of their lands or guarantees of an honest fur trade because he did not have to. The Indians depended upon trade goods—cloth shirts, blankets, utensils, muskets, gunpowder—and therefore were easily manipulated by Gage. His power was demonstrated from December 1774 through spring 1775. The Haudenosaunee and other Indians threatened to attack British forts in the West because British officials still had done nothing to arbitrate the land disputes and war between the Virginians and the Shawnees. Gage could not attempt to stop the war, for that would involve the kind of careful diplomacy and measured action of which he was simply not capable. Instead, he ordered the commander at Fort Niagara to instruct the Indians to fight the Virginians if they so desired but not to attack the British forts or their trade goods would be cut off. If the Indians did as they were told they would continue to receive supplies at the posts. No British forts were attacked.

During the winter of 1774–1775, Gage's superintendents lined up many of the Haudenosaunee on the side of the Crown. On May 10, 1775, less than a month after Lexington and Concord, Gage sent secret orders to Guy Johnson asking that the Haudenosaunee and other Indians be mobilized in case the revolt in Massachusetts spread to other colonies. Despite the fact that he had been planning to use the Indians months before Lexington, Gage found it convenient to blame the Patriots for the first actual use of Indians in battle. In a letter to Dartmouth dated June 12, 1775, Gage wrote:

> [W]e need not be tender of calling upon the Savages, as the Rebels have shewn us the Example by bringing as many Indians down against us here [in Boston] as they could collect (Carter 1931, 404).

Gage neglected to mention that these rebel Indians were "praying Indians" from Massachusetts's Christian Indian farming communities such as Stockbridge.

The Patriots, of course, suspected that the British would employ the Indians. Both of Gage's superintendents were pressured by local Patriots during May and June 1775, to guarantee that the Indians would not be used. Unwilling and unable to make such guarantees, each superintendent decided to reestablish his headquarters in an area more securely British. Guy Johnson left the Mohawk Valley for Montreal and John Stuart withdrew from Charleston to Saint Augustine. In their new headquarters, Johnson and Stuart went about consolidating support for the British among the Indians through further conferences.

There was still hope that hostilities with the Patriots could be settled without a war, and in order to prevent an expansion of the conflict, young warriors eager for battle were temporarily restrained from attacking settlements by their leading men and women. While many young Haudenosaunee were quite ready to go into battle, the Haudenosaunee as a nation remained in their towns, assuring Guy Johnson of their loyalty to the King at a conference in Oswego in July 1775, but carefully watching the developing crisis between the rebels and the British. At conferences in Albany during September and at Fort Pitt in October, Haudenosaunee delegates assured Patriot commissioners that they would remain neutral. For the moment, most Haudenosaunee chose to see the conflict as the Continental Congress viewed it, a "family quarrel" in which they had no real interest.

The King's cause among the Haudenosaunee was continually subverted by various Patriots, especially by missionaries trained in New England who had sown political as well as spiritual seeds. In addition, after Lexington many citizens of Montreal told Indians who had come to trade that they hoped the Patriots would drive the British from Canada. When the Patriot armies of Richard Montgomery and Benedict Arnold invaded Canada in August and September 1775, the Haudenosaunee chose to remain aloof from the conflict. Although the Patriots failed to take Canada during the winter of 1775–1776, a British counterattack under Guy Carleton in the summer and fall of 1776 also failed. Noting this, most Haudenosaunee continued to avoid participation in the war during the second winter of revolution, 1776–1777. Yet in the early months of 1777, the British abruptly secured most of the Haudenosaunee firmly to their side.

The influences of specific white men played an important part in this decision of the Haudenosaunee. The British obtained the support of the majority of the Haudenosaunee warriors—the Mohawks, the Cayugas, the Onondagas and the Senecas—partly because the members of the northern Indian Department remained loyal to the Crown. Guy Johnson, Sir John Johnson, John Butler and Daniel Claus all had earned the respect of the Haudenosaunee after years and even decades of personal contact along the frontier.

In contrast, most of the Oneida and Tuscarora Haudenosaunee remained neutral or actually aided the Patriots during the war in part because of the Reverend Samuel Kirkland. He had been a missionary among the Oneidas since 1765. Kirkland mixed the Gospel with political lessons on how Britain oppressed the colonists. Kirkland and his fellow Patriots expected his teaching to counteract the overtures made by the Loyalist Indian Department. On June 28, 1775, Patriot farmers told a group of Oneidas and Tuscaroras at German Flats on the banks of the Mohawk River that "we looks to you perticuler to be men of more understanding than others by the benifitt you have Recevd in Larning" ("Speech," June 28, 1775). Kirkland was so valuable to the Patriot cause that he became a paid agent of the Continental Congress in July 1775.

Personalities, however, were not the determining factor in the Haudenosaunee decision. Most Haudenosaunee, in spite of their hopes of neutrality, were forced into the British alliance by the trade goods and presents that had long made them dependent upon the white man for much of their clothing and utensils, and their guns and ammunition for hunting. The Continental Congress was aware that trade articles and presents could determine the alliance of the Haudenosaunee, and they made an attempt to compete with the British. Faced with a lack of funds, Congress hoped throughout 1775 that enough goods would be brought in by private merchants from France and the French West Indies to supply the Haudenosaunee, but other than distributing presents Congress made no effort of its own to provide goods. In January 1776, however, Congress received reports that many Haudenosaunee were suffering through a hard winter because of the lack of clothing and supplies. On January 27, 1776, Congress resolved to buy the needed supplies with money raised selling some colonial products in foreign markets. Despite this effort the Haudenosaunee were still not receiving enough. They did not break their neutrality, though, because the British were not having any greater success supplying them. British goods could not be shipped to the Haudenosaunee distribution point, Fort Niagara, because the Patriot armies of Montgomery and Arnold occupied the St. Lawrence River valley, the main supply route to Lake Ontario.

During the summer of 1776, after the Patriot armies had been driven from the St. Lawrence, the Haudenosaunee still did not receive enough supplies from the British because most British ships coming to Canada brought only military reinforcements. The Patriots could not adequately supply the Haudenosaunee because the Continental Congress was still very short of funds. The Haudenosaunee were soon placed in an even worse position when General Sir William Howe captured New York City, the major port of entry for the Haudenosaunee trade route, in September 1776. During the winter of 1776–1777, the situation of the Haudenosaunee became desperate. They needed clothing, and they needed food because they had no powder and lead for hunting. The British found themselves in an excellent position to use trade and presents to bring the Haudenosaunee to their side. By now they completely controlled the St. Lawrence route to the Haudenosaunee from Quebec to Fort Niagara. In addition, many Mohawk Haudenosaunee were already committed to the British and proved to be useful persuaders. Early in 1777 the British were able to distribute a few articles to the Haudenosaunee by appropriating some of the military supplies brought over to help secure Canada. These supplies were not sufficient to fill the Indians' needs, but because the Patriots were able to offer even less, the British consignment was enough to retain the desperate Haudenosaunee. The British also promised future deliveries of blankets and guns. In exchange they did not ask for furs; they requested military assistance. Unable to face another year without sufficient manufactures, the Haudenosaunee warriors early in 1777 gave up their role as fur traders and became mercenaries.

Had the Haudenosaunee been economically independent of the whites, the appeal of the Continental Congress to remain neutral would have been a better option for them than a military alliance with the British, who were short of manpower and could not afford to request Haudenosaunee neutrality. The Continental Congress, on the other hand, did not ask for military aid. Asking only that the Haudenosaunee remain neutral, Congress promised to bring justice to the frontier by preventing dishonest trade and protecting Haudenosaunee lands. Significantly, the Patriots were willing as early as the fall of 1774 to alienate the frontiersmen in exchange for this neutrality. The British had failed to implement these very pledges for more than fourteen years, and the Haudenosaunee might have continued to remain neutral, waiting to see whether the Continental Congress could any better.

On the other hand, if the Haudenosaunee had not chosen to become entangled in the fur trade and the acquisition of white trade goods, they would have contravened their long history of adaptation. This theme in their history began long before the arrival of the Europeans. During the colonial period, the Haudenosaunee might have attempted to reverse this long tradition by trying to remain aloof from the fur trade and the colonial wars of the French, the Dutch and the British. However, had they done so, they would undoubtedly have been eliminated as a political power by both Indian and European rivals long before 1700. They certainly would not have been a major factor in North American history by the time of the American Revolution.

The Haudenosaunee example, paralleled by the efforts of southern Indian nations such as the Creeks, raises the question of options. The Haudenosaunee and the Creeks were practical, responding to existing economic factors and adhering to treaty promises they had received from the British. Neutrality in any civil war (which the Revolution was) is nearly an impossible course for any people to follow. In every era during the colonial period, the impulse among one or more American Indian nations to cut off all of their economic and political ties to Europeans and their trade goods was raised as an idealistic alternative, and often inspired by spiritual messages. That isolationist appeal would be powerful again among many Indian nations during the century after the American Revolution. But such idealistic hopes never matched the realities of history. Against overwhelming odds of population and economics, American Indian nations would be fortunate just to survive the Revolution. Haudenosaunee leaders were determined to see that their ancient confederacy would indeed survive.

1777: Turning Points

In 1775 and 1776, the war escalated among the whites. It became increasingly clear that the intended neutrality of the Haudenosaunee was already undermined by their own treaties and their economic alliance with the British through the Covenant Chain, the symbolic representation of the links of trade and diplomacy. Evoking these ties, British officials sought to bring the Haudenosaunee into the war, just as British officials had done in every previous colonial war. Indian Superintendent Guy Johnson spent the winter of 1775–1776 in London learning how the Privy Council expected him to make use of any Indian allies he might obtain. With him was one of the most important Haudenosaunee leaders, Joseph Brant, who was white-educated, articulate in both Mohawk and British, and a Mason. Brant and Johnson were told to utilize Indians only in formal military expeditions. The first opportunity to use the Haudenosaunee came during the summer of 1777. In order to capture all of New York and split the colonies, an army led by General John Burgoyne marched south from Canada to capture Albany. The Haudenosaunee and other northern Indians such as the Canadian Missisaugas committed a total of more than fourteen hundred warriors to the campaign.

A thousand Haudenosaunee and Missisaugas were not assigned to Burgoyne's army. Instead, they became part of a separate army marching on Albany from the west, down the Mohawk Valley. These Haudenosaunee and Missisaugas, as well as a few from other Canadian Indian nations, were led by Joseph Brant and by John Butler, an experienced Indian Department officer. They joined Colonel Barry St. Leger's army of seven hundred regulars, German mercenaries and Loyalists at Oswego. Their first objective was Fort Stanwix, the major Patriot defense guarding the western approach to the Mohawk

Valley (and ironically the site of the 1768 treaty that drew a supposedly firm boundary line between colonists and Haudenosaunee). During the ensuing siege, the Haudenosaunee were well disciplined by their chiefs and white officers. The Haudenosaunee were determined, after decades of experience, to fight only alongside white armies. In such circumstances, they could avoid taking most of the risks and casualties. On this expedition, some of the Haudenosaunee believed that they would serve mainly as scouts, and as spectators to a great British victory brought about by the whites and their artillery. Then, on August 5, three days after the siege began, a Patriot relief column of eight hundred militia under General Nicholas Herkimer was reported marching toward the fort. Herkimer's Patriots were accompanied by about sixty Oneida Haudenosaunee scouts.

The Oneida Haudenosaunee's presence on the Patriot side, and the formidable number of other Haudenosaunee on the British side, were clear declarations that conflicting debates within the confederacy had transformed into conflicting choices. The messengers bearing the warning of the approaching Patriots had been sent from the white settlements by Brant's sister Molly (Mary). She resided at Canajoharie near the Patriot farmers in a comfortable frame farmhouse given to her by her late consort, Sir William Johnson. The Indian allies of the British, together with some white troops, were assigned to attack the approaching Patriots.

On August 6, 1777, executing a near-perfect ambush, the whites and Indians might have wiped out the relief force had the trapped Patriots not been stubborn and courageous fighters. The ensuing Battle of Oriskany ended in an exhausted stalemate, with both sites retreating from the battle site. But the Haudenosaunee and their white allies had accomplished their objective of preventing the Patriot army from reaching the fort. The Haudenosaunee had not expected such stout resistance and though the Patriots suffered higher casualties—at least two hundred killed—the Haudenosaunee's own losses of about one hundred, including some favorite warriors and chiefs, were severe. Added to this were about fifty Loyalist troops dead. Discouraged by these losses, the Haudenosaunee refused to continue the siege of Fort Stanwix when they learned that another Patriot relief column, this one under Benedict Arnold, was approaching the fort. The Indians withdrew westward toward Lake Ontario. The British commander, St. Leger, was forced to retreat with them because his seven hundred white troops were not sufficient to continue the siege and face the relief column at the same time.

Because the Battle of Oriskany and the retreat from Fort Stanwix eliminated his western support, Burgoyne cited them later as two principal reasons for his army's surrender at Saratoga on October 17, 1777. But the Battle
of Oriskany had an even greater effect on the Haudenosaunee. It initiated
them into the British cause with a bloody baptism that demanded revenge.
Oriskany had a similar effect on frontier New York Patriots, who now hated
the pro-British Haudenosaunee without reserve. Both Patriots and
Haudenosaunee remembered Oriskany with vendetta fervor, and
Haudenosaunee and Patriots alike would excuse themselves for many an
atrocity in the future by explaining they were taking revenge for Oriskany.

Sixty of the Oneidas served with the Patriots as scouts at Oriskany and
then, together with some Tuscaroras, fought alongside the Patriots at
Saratoga. By the end of 1777 the Oneidas were completely committed to the
Patriot cause. The Patriot position taken by the Oneidas, shared to some
extent by the Tuscaroras, divided the Haudenosaunee Confederacy even more
severely than during the Indian war of 1763. A number of Onondagas worried
British officials by abruptly switching their allegiance to the Patriots, and after
the fall of 1777 the Onondagas were divided into three factions: pro-British,
pro-Patriot and neutral.

As for the Mohawks, Cayugas and Senecas, their fear of a retaliatory Patriot
attack on their towns brought 2,700 Indians, including 1,200 warriors,
swarming to Fort Niagara for protection during the fall and winter of 1777.
When the Patriot Indian commissioner Philip Schuyler asked the
Haudenosaunee to a council, however, a spokesman turned him down, "saying
the Wounds of his Warriors Killed at Fort Stanwix [Oriskany] were still
bleeding" (Colonel Mason Bolton to Sir Guy Carleton, 31 January, Haldimand
Transcripts 1778 B.100, 11). The British, to encourage continued Haudenosaunee friendship, distributed the presents and food they knew to be such an
effective lever of policy.

Some of the Haudenosaunee finally did agree to a council with Schuyler,
however, and in March 1778 met at Johnstown, New York. Although Oneidas,
Tuscaroras and Onondagas made up most of the more than seven hundred
Haudenosaunee assembled, the Mohawks and the Cayugas were also repre-
sented. Only the Senecas failed to send a representative. After listening to
Schuyler demand Haudenosaunee neutrality or face Patriot punishment, an
Onondaga named Tenhoghskweaghta explained that extreme confusion
existed within the Haudenosaunee league.

Your Belt [a wampum belt given to the Iroquois by Schuyler as a record of his message] is of great Importance, the Answer is attended with many Difficulties for even my Nation [the Onondagas] are divided in Sentiment as well as [i.e., as are] white people respecting your Quarrel. Some retain their Friendship for America our common Island. As for the Senecas they have long since forsaken our Council Fire. Many Times have we sent for them without any Effect. But be assured we shall once more exert ourselves to rekindle our ancient Council Fire at Onondaga [to discuss Schuyler's speech] ...

It is very true you have some Friends to our common Island among the six Nations and you have some Enemies. It [internal division] is perhaps [as] much with us as it is with you white people. We have some Indians [Oneidas and Tuscaroras] that are so unwise as to throw off their Affection and turn Enemies to their native Land. We could wish there were none such on this Island our common Dwelling place.

Tenhoghskweaghta then noted the breakdown of authority that had occurred throughout the confederacy, a problem that had occurred before but never to this extreme extent:

Times are altered with us Indians. Formerly the warriors were governed by the wisdom of their Uncles the Sachems but now they take their own way & dispose of themselves without consulting their Uncles the Sachems. While we [sachems] wish for peace and they are for war, Brothers they must take the Consequences. (Schyler Papers 1778)

In the campaign of 1777, the British intended to use the Haudenosaunee only as allies operating as a part of a larger British army. Haudenosaunee war leaders also wanted their warriors to work with larger British armies. By fighting alongside a white army, the Haudenosaunee felt that they would be provided with better supplies—for nearly a century the Haudenosaunee had felt that the British continually failed to provide Haudenosaunee armies with adequate supplies and weapons. But more importantly, the Haudenosaunee leaders realized that a part of the American Revolution was a war of propaganda.

Knowing how the British colonists had made villains out of French-allied Indians during previous colonial wars, the Haudenosaunee leaders wished to avoid the stereotypes of forest warriors fighting a guerilla war. But when the first British-Haudenosaunee campaign ended in failure at Oriskany and Fort Stanwix, the Haudenosaunee had no choice but to fight a guerilla war because the British refused to assign a white army to fight alongside them. The Haudenosaunee had turned to guerrilla warfare as their primary method of attack after Champlain fired the first European musket balls into their massed ranks back in 1609. European epidemics had further reduced their ability to assemble large armies. Thus both the lessons of past combat with the Europeans and their own diminished population forced the Haudenosaunee to conduct the very style of warfare their war leaders had hoped to avoid.

Strikes and Counterstrikes

Having committed the Haudenosaunee to war, the British now failed to order that war limited to battles with Patriot military units. In fact, after 1777 the British encouraged the Haudenosaunee to conduct raids on civilian areas with the justification that the civilians produced foodstuffs that fed Patriot troops. While the British authorized Haudenosaunee raids against civilians, the Patriots were also ready, if not quite able, to destroy Haudenosaunee civilian areas on the New York frontier. The March 1778 speech given by Patriot commissioner Philip Schuyler to the Haudenosaunee at Johnstown, which warned that the Patriots would avenge any future hostilities by attacking in Hauden-osaunee country, was authorized by the Continental Congress. After the council, Schuyler wrote to the president of the Continental Congress, Henry Laurens, on March 15, 1778. He suggested that in order to prevent Indian raids on Patriot settlements, the Patriots should strike first, attacking Haudeno-saunee towns. He believed that this first strike would not require any more troops than would otherwise be necessary to defend the frontier settlements.

But in 1778, the Haudenosaunee were able to carry out their plans before the Patriots. Patriot raids, when they were finally launched, thus took on the appearance of justified retaliation, when actually the Patriots would have been just as willing to have initiated such warfare. The British made a sincere attempt to prevent Haudenosaunee raiders from killing unarmed Patriot civilians by authorizing the organization of a corps of white rangers under Colonel John Butler to work with the Indians. The rangers were recruited from among agents in the Indian Department who had long experience with the Indians. Haudenosaunee leaders also intended to do their best to prevent civilian casualties during planned raids. Intent on destroying a major Patriot wheat crop, four hundred Haudenosaunee and one hundred Loyalist rangers swept down on Wyoming, Pennsylvania, in July 1778.

The Patriots were waiting, and expected to ambush and annihilate the Haudenosaunee attackers. The Patriot plan was discovered, and the Haudenosaunee emerged victorious against their overconfident foes. While only six warriors and two rangers were killed, the Haudenosaunee slew more than three hundred Patriot regulars and militiamen in battle, taking only five prisoners. A few other Patriot soldiers captured in battle were evidently tortured to death in revenge for Haudenosaunee lives lost at Oriskany. In four days, the raiders destroyed eight forts, one thousand dwellings and all the mills in the area. Despite this destruction, not one civilian was killed. In fact, entire garrisons chose to surrender and were allowed by the Haudenosaunee to return unharmed to their homes once they promised never to fight in the war again. The surrendered forts were burned.

Battle of Cherry Valley

Then, on November 11, 1778, the Haudenosaunee and their allies attacked the last target of that long year: Cherry Valley, New York. The fighting spirit of the Haudenosaunee was on edge. They approached Cherry Valley already angry because some of the Wyoming Patriot soldiers whom they had allowed to surrender and return to their homes had in the meantime taken up arms again and some had actually attacked Indian towns. Thus the Haudenosaunee were not inclined to show Patriot soldiers any future mercy. Furthermore, the Haudenosaunee had learned that fantastic, fictional stories had been invented about Haudenosaunee atrocities against civilians at Wyoming, when in fact during all their major raids the Haudenosaunee carefully protected, with very few exceptions, the lives of enemy noncombatants. As many as 470 Haudenosaunee, 300 Loyalist volunteers, 150 rangers and 50 British regulars were led by John Butler's son Walter and by Joseph Brant. Among other Haudenosaunee leaders present was the Seneca war chief Cornplanter (Gayentwahga). During the march toward Cherry Valley, Walter Butler insulted Brant by attempting to usurp his leadership among the Indians and the three hundred white volunteers loyal to him. The Mohawk chief was persuaded by his warriors to forget the insult for the moment and concentrate on the expedition, but ninety of the white volunteers left in disgust, refusing to serve with the arrogant Walter Butler. Other whites as well as Indians may have also left at this time. Because of the incident, Brant and Butler did not work closely during the raid. Butler separated the white and Indian forces, attaching only fifty-three rangers to the Indians. Brant, although he did his best, was unable to prevent some warriors from scattering across the countryside. These warriors slaughtered at least thirty men, women and children without mercy. In a letter to Colonel Mason Bolton dated November 17, 1778, Walter Butler claimed he had taken precautions against the killing of noncombatants, and reported that

> the Death of the Women & Children upon this occasion may I believe be truly ascribed to the Rebels having falsely Accused the Indians of Cruelty at Wyoming; this had much exasperated them, and they were still more incensed at finding the Colonel [Nathan Dennison] and those men who had there [at Wyoming] laid down their Arms, Soon After, marching into their Country intending to Destroy their Villages, & they declared they would no more be falsely accused, or fight the enemy twice; meaning that they would not in future give Quarters. (Haldimand Transcripts B.100, 86)

Whites in Europe and in the Americas had long debated whether it was "moral" to ally with Indians during any war. Although thousands of civilians died horribly in Europe every time the great powers went to war, there was something unacceptable about white civilians dying at the hands of nonwhites. Even after Cherry Valley, however, British officials in charge of the war, such as Lord George Germain, seemed convinced that the frontier warfare in America was being kept within acceptable moral boundaries. The Patriots, of course, disagreed, adding the terrible reality of Cherry Valley to the abundant rumors and few concrete examples they already had to form an image of the Haudenosaunee as mass murderers. As for the Haudenosaunee, their leaders continued to attempt to confine their warriors to military objectives, although with less success. No single generalization may be made about the style of Indian warfare during the American Revolution, except perhaps that the whites recognized that Indians did not rape white women, a claim whites could not make regarding their own treatment of Indian women. (Indian rape of white women occurred primarily in the nineteenth century, west of the Mississippi.) Throughout the war, many other Indian nations and some Haudenosaunee included attacks on civilians as necessary targets, particularly when these white civilians were illegally settled on Indian lands. In addition, white pioneer women and all but the youngest children could and did wield weapons as readily as any white male. This made the identification of a non-combatant on the frontier often impossible. Finally, Indians had their own images of the whites. The whites' reputation for slaughter and cruelty, including their failure to take Indians alive as prisoners of war—unless it was to sell them into slavery—was well established and ongoing (as events the next year, 1779, would prove).

Sullivan Campaign of 1779

The Haudenosaunee successes of 1778 disturbed Patriot commander-in-chief George Washington, who saw morale on the frontier weakened and the wheat crops needed to feed his soldiers destroyed. In 1779, he ordered expeditions, under the overall command of General John Sullivan, to march into the Haudenosaunee country of western New York, terminate Haudenosaunee participation in the war, and if possible capture Fort Niagara. During this year the Haudenosaunee women began to see how selfishly the British were using their people, and they asked their warriors to make peace with the Patriots. But the Haudenosaunee warriors refused. They had committed themselves to the British cause and fought for two years in the bloodiest theater of the war, the frontier. It was time, they thought, for the British to provide the reciprocal aid so often promised, in the form of a British army to protect Haudenosaunee families and towns. British promises of protection to the Haudenosaunee proved as shallow as similar promises to the Shawnees in 1775, and no British army ever came. In April 1779, a part of General James Clinton's army prepared for their cooperation with Sullivan by marching westward from the Mohawk River and destroying most of the Onondaga Haudenosaunee communities. To the dismay of the Patriot commanders, this small army also raped and butchered Onondaga women.

Then the major army of General Sullivan, together with much of Clinton's army and aided by Oneida and Tuscarora scouts, marched north along the Susquehanna River. The Patriots defeated a futile Haudenosaunee and Delaware resistance at Newtown (Elmira), New York, on August 29, 1779. Then they swept through the Haudenosaunee heartland, destroying forty towns evacuated by the Senecas and Cayugas. Sullivan did not attempt to attack Niagara and in fact turned back in the middle of September because of the lateness of the season. In the meantime, another Patriot army under Colonel David Brodhead marched north from Pittsburgh and burned Haudenosaunee towns along the Allegheny River. The Haudenosaunee were furious with their so-called allies for their failure to provide assistance. By mid-September 1779 the commander at Fort Niagara, Colonel Mason Bolton, believed there was every possibility the Haudenosaunee would quit the British alliance. This would be disastrous, for only the Haudenosaunee prevented the Patriots from invading otherwise poorly defended Canada. What Bolton apparently did not realize was that Britain's failure to protect its allies actually made the Haudenosaunee even more dependent on the British. With their homes and food supplies destroyed, they had no recourse but to accept what Britain would give them. More than five thousand Haudenosaunee arrived at Fort Niagara during the last two weeks of September, seeking food, clothing and the protection of the fort. This was at least a quarter and possibly even a third of the total Haudenosaunee population. Sullivan's army failed to accomplish its military objectives of defeating the Haudenosaunee and capturing Fort Niagara. However, the army had destroyed much of the Haudenosaunee way of life—especially the economic base of the Haudenosaunee women. Towns of log cabins and a few frame or stone houses, as well as fields and orchards of apple, pear and peach trees represented more than a century of adaptation. The houses, fields and orchards were primarily the property of the women. All this was destroyed in a month.

Sullivan's soldiers were surprised to find that the Haudenosaunee towns were as prosperous if not more so than white frontier settlements, and the land-hungry soldiers remembered after the war how beautiful and rich the countryside was. The Haudenosaunee, for their part, remained allied with the British not solely because they were dependent upon British goods but also because they sought revenge for Sullivan's acts. This replaced even the memory of Oriskany in their minds. During the expeditions, Sullivan's Patriots had proved on a number of occasions that atrocities in war were hardly racially exclusive. One of the most notorious instances occurred when Patriot soldiers skinned two dead Haudenosaunee "from their hips down for boot legs; one pair for the Major [Daniel Piatt] the other for myself," as Lieutenant William Barton wrote in his journal (Cook 1887, 8).

However, nothing burned so deep in the Haudenosaunee memory as the rapes and murders at Onondaga in April, during the first Patriot thrust of the campaign. During a council in Niagara on December 11, 1782, an Onondaga chief recalled the incident:

When They came to the Onondaga Town (of which I was one of the principal Chiefs) They put to death all the Women and Children, excepting some of the young Women that they carried away for the use of their Soldiers, and were put to death in a more shameful and Scandalous manner; Yet these Rebels calls themselves Christians. (Haldimand Transcripts 1782 B.119, 172)

Governor Haldimand in Quebec, having failed to give the Haudenosaunee sufficient military aid during Sullivan's invasion, quickly ordered the distribution of food and supplies he hoped would keep the Haudenosaunee loyal. He suggested that the Haudenosaunee set up winter camps on the Genesee River, close enough to Fort Niagara to obtain provisions. The provisions proved inadequate, and during the unusually severe winter of 1779–1780, a number of Haudenosaunee men, women and children starved to death. The Haudenosaunee warriors had a long winter in which to plan and dream of vengeance. In February 1780, four emissaries acting on behalf of the Continental Congress arrived at Fort Niagara, offering the Haudenosaunee peace and the status of neutrality for the rest of the war. The emissaries were two Oneida Haudenosaunee (including Skenandon, in his early seventies) and two Mohawk Haudenosaunee. Their fellow Haudenosaunee rejected the peace with disdain, but were shocked when Indian Superintendent Guy Johnson threw the four emissaries into a windowless, heatless dungeon for five months. Pleas of the Haudenosaunee finally forced the British to let the four out of the dungeon and turn them over to the Loyalist Haudenosaunee. The Haudenosaunee remained allied with the British because the Patriots could not even furnish as many goods as the miserly British; because the Haudenosaunee justifiably continued to mistrust the land-hungry Patriots; and because the war perpetuated itself as a cumulative vendetta over previous battles.

A few raids were conducted in the spring of 1780, but a thorough revenge for Sullivan's campaign could not be taken until the Loyalist soldiers' families still living in the Mohawk Valley were brought to safety. Unless they were removed to Canada, these families might be captured by the Patriots and held as hostages. In May, Sir John Johnson led a brilliant foray into Johnstown, New York, where many Loyalist families lived. Without the loss of one of his two hundred Haudenosaunee and four hundred Loyalist troops, Johnson rescued almost every man, woman and child vulnerable to the Patriots. Now the Haudenosaunee and Loyalists began their campaign of revenge, choosing as their first target the fifteen hundred Patriot-allied Oneida Haudenosaunee, expecting by a show of force to persuade the Oneidas to join the British. An Onondaga chief came to the Oneidas in June 1780 to warn his friends to leave, and later that month a Mohawk raiding party met with the Oneidas in council and received an Oneida pledge that their nation would soon join the British. However, the Oneidas had already told their Patriot allies that an attack was expected. The other Haudenosaunee soon realized that the Oneidas intended to remain allies of the Patriots, and so in July, despite a shortage of supplies and equipment, raiders led by Joseph Brant struck at the Oneida and Tuscarora towns. A few Oneidas and Tuscaroras joined the British, but hundreds of others scurried to the safety of nearby Fort Stanwix while their vengeful Haudenosaunee brothers burned their log and frame houses to the ground. The raiders must have taken particular delight in burning one building: the chapel of the Oneidas' Patriot missionary, Samuel Kirkland.

The Patriots had failed to protect the Oneidas just as the British failed to protect the Haudenosaunee from Sullivan. And, as the other Haudenosaunee had fled from Sullivan to the safety of Niagara in 1779, so now the Oneidas removed to Schenectady, New York, where they kept their families for the rest of the war. Joseph Brant and his warriors, together with some Loyalists and Haudenosaunee reinforcements including the great Seneca war leader Cornplanter, turned their attention next to Canajoharie, New York. Before the war the Mohawk Haudenosaunee had lived there in fine log and even frame or stone houses. They had farmed extensively as well as hunted, but they had left their homes to fight for the King. Patriots had seized their cattle and other property or had moved onto their farms, and Brant was determined that they would not remain. Swiftly the raiders attacked these and other farms, killing sixteen people and destroying ripe grain fields, livestock and fifty-three homes. Then they withdrew toward the west.

In October 1780, Sir John Johnson, the Mohawk leader Joseph Brant, and Seneca leaders Sayenqueraghta and Cornplanter set out with six hundred Loyalists, German mercenaries and regulars, plus at least five hundred Haudenosaunee warriors. Their specific purpose was to take revenge for the Sullivan expedition. Within four days the raiders burned homes and fields at Schoharie, Stone Arabia and other settlements in the center of the Mohawk Valley. Finally, fifteen hundred Patriot militiamen and a few Oneida scouts challenged the raiders at Klock's Field on the north bank of the Mohawk and after a furious battle the invaders were forced to retreat. But the Haudenosaunee and their allies left the Mohawk Valley frontier knowing they had almost completely destroyed the farming capability of every settlement there. The next year, 1781, lack of supplies forced the Haudenosaunee to restrict themselves to small-scale raids in the Mohawk Valley. Because the Haudenosaunee nation was short of food as well as materiel, the raiders came away with droves of cattle, but accomplished little else. The valley farmlands were largely deserted and the population huddled in strong forts that would succumb only to a much larger expedition equipped with cannon. The Haudenosaunee and Loyalists looked forward to launching that larger expedition, their greatest effort since 1777, during the fall, but again no supplies from the British were forthcoming. Disappointed, the Haudenosaunee and their Loyalist allies began to view the war as a futile stalemate.

The British had concentrated their major efforts in other theaters every year since 1777. Now, in 1781, most supplies were going to General Cornwallis, whom Britain hoped would deal the Patriots the death-blow in the South. The Haudenosaunee could foresee no significant victories, only never-ending piecemeal raids. Guy Johnson had warned the British in 1777 that raids during a prolonged white man's war would frustrate the Indians and demoralize them. The warning came true as the Haudenosaunee prepared for the last raid of 1781. Loyalist officers who intended to go with the Haudenosaunee on the raid were also frustrated. The war on the Haudenosaunee frontier, in which the Loyalists often fought their former neighbors, had degenerated into a contest of hate. The Loyalists had already sensed this hate in 1780 when they felt compelled to bring their families from Patriot-held territory. On October 1, 1781, John Butler and other ranger officers made a significant request to the governor of Canada, Frederick Haldimand. They asked for new commissions which left out the words "to serve with the Indians" because the Patriots were mistreating rangers captured with these words in their commissions. The rangers intended to continue fighting alongside the Indians and felt it was their duty, but fearing the consequences if captured, admitted the "uneasiness of mind they labour under" (Haldimand Transcripts B.214, 272–73).

Before the governor could cancel the worrisome phrase from the Loyalists' commissions, seven hundred Haudenosaunee, Loyalists and regulars set out from Fort Niagara and headed toward Johnstown in the Mohawk Valley. The raiders were led by a regular British officer, Major John Ross, and by Loyalist Walter Butler. Butler had never been fully accepted by the Haudenosaunee, partly because his insult to Joseph Brant during the Cherry Valley campaign four years earlier had never been settled. Brant, whose leadership would have been helpful during this mission, had been sent to Detroit where he was successfully coordinating western Indians against George Rogers Clark. To these factors was added a general demoralization. When Ross's seven hundred raiders reached Johnstown on October 25, Patriot troops vigorously counterattacked. The Haudenosaunee and their allies fell back after a day's battle, but the Patriots pursued them for two days. On October 27, Walter Butler was commanding the rear guard as the raiders retreated toward West Canada Creek. Unable to keep up an effective rearguard action any longer, he hurried his men across the creek. As he reached the other side, he was shot and killed by an Oneida scout serving with the Patriots. Suddenly the Haudenosaunee dispersed into the forest, perhaps expecting the Loyalists and regulars to do the same, for Indian warfare dictated that in a retreat each man would fend for himself and the band would regroup later. But the white troops did not understand the Indians' maneuver. Without Haudenosaunee support, they were routed. Alone or in small groups they struggled back to Fort Niagara. The action of the Haudenosaunee was understandable in terms of their own style of warfare, and since the British had encouraged them to fight battles in their own way it was only reasonable that they would someday retreat in their own way. Yet after the battle the Haudenosaunee came to realize that they had let their allies down, and this hurt their sense of honor and marked the nadir of their morale. They reprimanded the two chiefs they considered responsible.

The news soon arrived that Washington had defeated Cornwallis at Yorktown. This meant that the Patriots were likely to turn their attention to Canada. Since there were not enough regulars to defend Canada, the Haudenosaunee were indispensable to the British. The Haudenosaunee remained unsettled, however, over the meaningless war they were fighting on behalf of their British allies. During the winter of 1781–1782, the British were never without fear that the Patriots would subvert the allegiance of the Haudenosaunee. Patriot emissaries, often Oneida Haudenosaunee, were constantly among them. The British countered these attempts with presents and persuasive speeches, but this was not enough. In the summer of 1782 the British called for the Haudenosaunee to mobilize again. Five years before, in 1777, the Haudenosaunee had contributed well over a thousand warriors to the British effort. In summer 1782, however, no more than six hundred could be convinced to fight. Fortunately for the British, no Patriot army invaded Canada. The Haudenosaunee's disastrous Ross-Butler raid of October 1781 proved to be their last organized action of the war.

Toward Peace

Unknown to the Haudenosaunee, the British had decided to draw out the war until peace terms acceptable to London could be made. To encourage favorable negotiations, no Haudenosaunee raids were to be permitted for fear of further antagonizing the Patriots. Even the fighting begun in 1774 between the Shawnees and settlers along the Virginia-Pennsylvania frontier subsided and during the summer of 1782 there was a genuine lull. The whites who had fought the Shawnees, however, could not contain their desire for Indian land. During the fall of 1782 the war between whites and Shawnees broke out again. The Haudenosaunee watched uneasily. They noted that the British were doing nothing to protect the Shawnees. Would the Haudenosaunee be ignored in a similar manner if whites invaded Haudenosaunee lands? Without informing any white man, the Haudenosaunee held a secret council in December 1782 at the Mohawk town near Fort Niagara. They decided to go to war to help the Shawnees, but because they knew they would need British guns and supplies, they told the commander at Fort Niagara about their council's decision and asked for British aid. The Haudenosaunee felt they had an excellent reason to fight: "[T]he Fate they [the Shawnees] have met with, may be ours next, if we do not go to War to prevent it" (General Allan Maclean to General Frederick Haldimand, December 16, 1782, in Haldimand Transcripts B.102, 249). The Haudenosaunee were angry also that the Patriots usually killed Haudenosaunee prisoners of war, whereas the Haudenosaunee spared most British and Loyalist prisoners. On April 2, 1783, again at Niagara, the aged Seneca Sayenqueraghta summarized the Haudenosaunee viewpoint of a war that had become admittedly cruel for both sides, noting that the Patriots had given the Haudenosaunee

> great Reason to be revenged on them for their Cruelties to us and our Friends [i.e., Indians on other frontiers], and if we had the means of publishing to the World the many Acts of Treachery & Cruelty committed by them on our Women & Children, it would appear that the title of Savages would with much greater justice be applied to them than to us. (Haldimand Transcripts B.104, 42)

Governor Haldimand in Canada, however, was under orders from London to prevent the Haudenosaunee from continuing the war, and the commander at Fort Niagara had received an appeal from George Washington to keep the Haudenosaunee out of combat. The Haudenosaunee were told that they would not be given the guns and supplies necessary to fight and that they were not permitted to go to war. With no British supplies, the Haudenosaunee had no choice but to comply. On May 4, 1783, the commander at Niagara assured George Washington in a letter that the Haudenosaunee would not fight.

The Haudenosaunee became justifiably suspicious that the British might abandon them. The British had not protected the Haudenosaunee towns from Sullivan's army in 1779; they seldom provided the Haudenosaunee with enough food or supplies; they expected Haudenosaunee warriors to expend their lives on a never-ending series of offensives while British efforts concentrated in other theaters of the war. These were indicative of the British attitude of expecting maximum Haudenosaunee cooperation in return for minimum British aid. This British attitude was not only significant in shaping Haudenosaunee suspicions toward the end of the war, but also in retrospect had been an important factor in determining the pattern of Haudenosaunee warfare during the entire conflict.

Food Supplies: A Major Problem

In fact, Haudenosaunee problems with the British, while they differed in specifics, were typical of some of the problems faced by the other Indians allied with the British along the entire North American frontier. The British expected the Haudenosaunee to conduct only raids primarily because the British did not have enough regulars to accompany them on formal expeditions. A second reason the Haudenosaunee went out on raids, however, was because the British consistently failed to supply them with enough food, and so it had to be seized from prosperous frontier farms. During the first year of Haudenosaunee commitment, 1777, the food problem was not great because well-supplied British armies used Canada to launch the Burgoyne and St. Leger expeditions and could be counted on to share their food. The first real shortage came in 1778. The Haudenosaunee raided the Wyoming settlement in Pennsylvania and brought back a substantial amount of grain and a few cattle. But this was not adequately supplemented by the British, who expected the Haudenosaunee to supply more for themselves. Faced with this situation, the Haudenosaunee attacked Cherry Valley in November specifically to obtain the corn and cattle there.

An attack by such a large force may not have been launched so late in the season had there not been an urgent need for food. The British had promised them food for their families if they fought during the summer instead of attending to their families' needs. But then the British informed the Haudenosaunee that the promised food would not arrive. Desperate to feed their families, the warriors set off knowing that if they failed, their families would starve.

While the Haudenosaunee' conduct cannot be excused, the primary responsibility for the massacre at Cherry Valley must be placed with the British. During the next year, 1779, raids in New York such as those on Schoharie and on Minisink were again conducted for two purposes: harassment of the Patriots and food for the Haudenosaunee, who were still inadequately supplied by the British. The Haudenosaunee did have fields and cattle of their own, but as long as the warriors fought for the British they had no time to help the Haudenosaunee women in these fields. And because they were away on campaigns, the men could not hunt to provide meat, or to obtain the skins and beaver pelts so vital to the Indian trade economy. The British did not consider these factors, nor did they look upon the Haudenosaunee as anything but mercenaries who owed complete submission to British direction. During the summer of 1779, when the Haudenosaunee refused to sell some of their cattle to the commander at Fort Niagara at a low price, Canada's Governor Haldimand demanded they accept it anyway. In a letter to Colonel Mason Bolton dated August 9, 1779, Haldimand insisted that the Haudenosaunee "should be taught to expect every Benefit immediately from the Hand of Government, to place their sole dependence on it" (Haldimand Transcripts B.104, 42).

Sullivan's invasion of the Haudenosaunee country during the fall of 1779 destroyed much of the Haudenosaunee's own food supplies. Governor Haldimand was unable to distribute enough food to sustain the Haudenosaunee during that winter, but the following spring he began cutting corners even further. Flour had been issued regularly to the Haudenosaunee, and quite often the Indians would request that it be baked into bread in the ovens of the forts they lived near. When Haldimand discovered early in 1780 that the Haudenosaunee were not aware that seven pounds of flour yielded nine pounds of bread, he ordered that the Haudenosaunee be given bread in exchange for their flour "pound for pound." Haldimand conceived this larcenous measure while Haudenosaunee towns and fields lay in ruin and the Indians were in the direst need of food.

The Haudenosaunee complained often of the shortage of food, but without result. Haldimand knew the Indians could not do without the guns, clothing and utensils he supplied. On September 29, 1780, having failed to protect the Haudenosaunee from Sullivan the previous year and having recently implemented his flour swindle, Haldimand ordered that Colonel Bolton, the commander at Fort Niagara, send every "useless mouth" away from the fort (Haldimand Transcripts B.102, 266). These "useless" mouths were the Haudenosaunee women and children who had fled the previous year from Sullivan, and whose warrior husbands were unable to help rebuild their homes because they were fighting Patriots. Less than two weeks later Haldimand informed Niagara's commander that the fort would receive even less than the meager supplies granted in the past. Philip Schuyler, the Patriot Indian commissioner, soon learned of Haldimand's flour policy and the food shortage through a network of spies. In November and December 1780 he sent Patriot emissaries—primarily Oneidas and other Haudenosaunee who had remained neutral or had become pro-Patriot—among the Haudenosaunee calling upon them to end their British alliance and make peace. Governor Haldimand, however, still could offer more presents and trade goods than the Patriots. This was enough to prevent the Haudenosaunee from accepting the Patriots' offer. During 1781, a caterpillar blight wiped out much of the Canadian farmers' wheat, leaving Haldimand with even less food to send to the Haudenosaunee. The wheat grown around Fort Niagara by the Haudenosaunee and Loyalists was not enough to make up the shortage, which continued during the last two years of the war.

The continual failure of the British to supply the Haudenosaunee adequately with muskets and other goods also shaped the participation of the Haudenosaunees in the war. During the campaign of 1777, there were not enough muskets, ammunition or clothing for the one thousand Haudenosaunee and Missisaugas with St. Leger's expedition. This was perhaps a factor in the Haudenosaunee failure to overwhelm the Patriots in the ambush at Oriskany, and in their withdrawal from the siege of Fort Stanwix soon after; both incidents in turn contributed to the defeat of Burgoyne at Saratoga. In 1778, the problem was inferior goods or goods damaged in transit from Great Britain. Inadequate supplies hindered the Haudenosaunee from launching major campaigns throughout the war, and, with each new year, Governor Haldimand reduced allotments further.

The reason for the perpetual supply shortage was a simple one: the Indian Department was part of the military establishment, and the regular army always took preference. Even the other mercenaries—the Germans—took precedence over the Haudenosaunee. In May 1779, for example, when the German artillerists at Fort Niagara needed clothing, garments were commandeered from the Haudenosaunee allotment. In July 1782, the Haudenosaunee were given leftover powder that proved to be of very poor quality. In December 1782, an absurd supply mix-up occurred: The Haudenosaunee were allotted far too many kettles and garters but absolutely no leggings for the cold winter. They received only one-sixth of the calico they needed and not one yard of warm serge. There were not enough blankets. But the crowning confusion was the allotment to the Haudenosaunee of two large trunk loads of sponges, about which General Allan Maclean, the commander at Niagara remarked in a letter on December 24, 1782 to Governor (General) Frederick Haldimand, "what use they are intended for, no man here can tell" (Haldimand Transcripts B.102, 266).

These problems might all have been avoided if the Indian Department, which dealt with Indian families as well as warriors, had been separate from the military. Governor Haldimand finally did order the separation of the two establishments—on May 26, 1783, at the end of the war. British leadership of the Haudenosaunee alliance was sadly deficient during the war. At the top, Governor Haldimand expected the Haudenosaunee to sacrifice their lives while he did nothing to protect their lands from Patriot invasion and provided only the sparest supplies of food, presents and goods. Prominent Loyalists responsible for advising the Haudenosaunee were split into quarrelsome factions from the very beginning of the war. Their self-serving antics continually confused the Haudenosaunee. For example, Daniel Claus, one of the late Sir William Johnson's most valued assistants, disliked Guy Johnson and John Butler because they excluded him from major policy decisions after Sir William's death in 1774. Sir John Johnson disliked Walter Butler and later John Butler. By the end of the war, John Butler mistrusted Guy Johnson. And at one time or another during the war, Walter Butler, John Butler and Guy Johnson all clashed with the most prominent Haudenosaunee leader, Joseph Brant.

But the most shocking and disappointing failure among the white advisors of the Haudenosaunee came in the fall of 1781. At that time, the commander at Fort Niagara discovered that Indian Superintendent Guy Johnson had been embezzling funds from the Indian Department for at least fifteen months. Guy Johnson's embezzlement had been carried out through the cooperation of two merchant suppliers at the fort. Guy Johnson had set himself up at Fort Niagara in baronial style. He built a large house and surrounded himself with ten or twelve Patriot prisoners whom he used as servants. Under the pretext that he needed sumptuous surroundings to impress visiting chiefs, Guy Johnson drank the best white wines and had raisins, almonds and prunes on his table twice a day, quite a luxury in the wilderness of Fort Niagara. While Haudenosaunee families went hungry, he had an abundance of brown sugar, rum, tea, fresh beef, port, chocolates, vinegar, butter and soap. To conceal this he turned in accounts stating that the wine was used to treat sick Indians, and that the rest of the luxuries were distributed as presents to visiting chiefs.

In addition to obtaining goods for his own use, Guy Johnson embezzled funds by claiming on his accounts two to five times as much beef, rum, wine and other supplies as he had actually distributed to the Indians. He also tampered with the pay records of the men in the Indian Department. A sergeant, for example, was paid seven pounds sterling, but Johnson, with the help of his accountants, inserted a four before the seven in the departmental account book and reported the pay as forty-seven pounds sterling. Reimbursed by an unsuspecting Governor Haldimand for these fabricated expenses, he made an impressive profit.

One expense finally brought Guy Johnson's graft into the open—the bill he submitted for butter supposedly allotted to the Haudenosaunee: 170 pounds of butter per month for fifteen months. Yet butter was seldom distributed and absolutely none had been issued during the last five of these fifteen months—the Haudenosaunee didn't like the taste (Haldimand Transcripts 1782–83 B.102, 145; B.103, 166–71; B. 104, 268–71, 303–304).

Guy Johnson was relieved of his position as Indian superintendent, and on March 14, 1782, King George III commissioned in his place Sir John Johnson, Sir William's son and Guy's brother-in-law. Sir John proved to be honest and well intentioned if somewhat unimaginative. Guy Johnson went to London and contested the accusations against him until his death in 1788. But there remains no doubt of his guilt. He made his profits and lived in relative luxury while the Haudenosaunee, whom he was supposed to serve, received low quality goods and insufficient food.

An Uneasy Wait for Peace

It is quite understandable why by the end of 1782 the Haudenosaunee were suspicious of their British allies. Adding to the Haudenosaunee uneasiness were frequent rumors of a treaty between the British and the Patriots, made with no regard for the confederacy's rights. Recognizing the opportunity to subvert the allegiance of the Haudenosaunee, the Patriots worked hard to convince them to turn on the British, in the hope that the war could be ended with Canada in the hands of the Continental Congress. Because the Haudenosaunee distrusted the Patriots even more than they did the British, they remained in the British alliance.

By spring 1783, the question was whether the British would remain the allies of the Haudenosaunee. Loyalists and British at Fort Niagara learned of the actual terms of the Peace of Paris on April 23, 1783, when four Loyalist rangers returned with the news from a winter-long spying mission during which they had been within eighteen miles of George Washington's camp in the Hudson Highlands. Corroboration of these terms came during the first days in May when other spies brought in copies of Philadelphia newspapers. The newspapers confirmed that the treaty turned over the entire Haudenosaunee country to the Continental Cong-ress. The Haudenosaunee had never been consulted, and there was no guarantee that the Patriots could not continue the war with the Haudenosaunee despite formal peace with the British. Loyalist and British officers concealed these terms from the Haudenosaunee, and instead assured them that the British would protect them with military support if the Patriots ever invaded their country. Despite these assurances by the white officers, the Haudenosaunee were suspicious and kept inquiring about the terms of peace. The officers put them off continuously for two and a half months, saying that Sir John Johnson, their new Indian superintendent, would tell them all they desired to know as soon as he arrived from Quebec. In the meantime the white officers kept the lid on Haudenosaunee frustration through the increased use of one of the white frontier's oldest weapons: rum.

Even as early as the spring of 1778, rum was being used in excessive quantities at Fort Niagara and in the Haudenosaunee towns to keep the Indians firmly allied. The commander at Fort Niagara opposed the extensive use of liquor but Guy Johnson and John Butler had always refused to listen to his objections. Maintenance of the Haudenosaunee alliance was their responsibility and they could not fulfill it without rum. Because Sir John Johnson remained in Quebec during the first tense months of 1783, the actual handling of Haudenosaunee affairs was left to John Butler. Butler used so much rum in keeping the Haudenosaunee from thinking about the peace terms that Fort Niagara almost ran dry. By June the use of rum was openly recognized by the white officers as the only effective persuasion they could offer the Haudenosaunee. At least one Haudenosaunee, Joseph Brant, was capable of seeing through this ruse. By May 1783, Brant had heard rumors of peace, had bluntly told the commander at Fort Niagara that "England had sold the Indians to Congress" (General Allan Maclean, May 13, 1783, to General Frederick Haldimand, Haldimand Transcripts, B.103, 157), and had gone to

Quebec to protest the treaty's violation of his people's rights and lands. The British officers at Quebec, including General Haldimand, knew that Brant would stir up the Haudenosaunee if he were allowed to return to Niagara, and it became a kind of game among them to stall Brant and keep him in the city. He was called to frequent meetings and entertainments, and was told of nonexistent Patriot plots against his people and against Canada. The officers managed to keep Brant in Quebec for two months. They also convinced him that the British had no intention of betraying the Haudenosaunee.

Brant returned to Niagara on July 5 and assured his people that the British would protect their every interest. The officers were relieved, having feared that the Haudenosaunee might turn on them in order to ingratiate themselves with the Continental Congress. Thirteen days after Brant's arrival, the new superintendent, Sir John Johnson, appeared at the fort and requested that his first council with the Haudenosaunee be laced with ample issues of rum. Brant apparently did not suspect Johnson's motive. The Haudenosaunee were told that the war was over, but they were not given the specific terms of the treaty. Johnson and the British officers knew it was unlikely the Americans would reveal the peace terms to the Haudenosaunee because the Patriots feared the Haudenosaunee might start an Indian war like Pontiac's of 1763. Sir John also discouraged the Haudenosaunee from forming a general confederacy of the Indians north of the Ohio River. Throughout 1783, no official definition of the peace terms came to the Haudenosaunee. In January 1784 a group of Mohawk Haudenosaunee gathered outside Montreal and angrily demanded to know exactly what the peace terms were. By spring, they and most of the rest of the Haudenosaunee knew: Their lands and all other Indian lands east of the Mississippi, south of Canada, and north of Florida were now under the jurisdiction of their enemy, the United States. It was too late to protest or fight. The Americans had had almost a full year of official peace and were now in a better position to resist any Haudenosaunee or other Indian attack along the frontier. A united Indian war similar to Pontiac's effort twenty years before might have been successful while the Patriots were still involved in ending the war with Britain. But the British had kept the peace provisions secret in order to protect their own tenure in Canada and to ensure the safety of their western garrisons. These garrisons probably would have been attacked had the Haudenosaunee learned the peace terms earlier. The Haudenosaunee vainly protested to their former allies on January 8, 1784 that "we don't consider ourselves conquered" (Mohawks' address to Daniel Claus, January 8, 1784, Claus Papers). But it was no use. The British peacemakers viewed the Haudenosaunee as subjects who had no separate rights and therefore no independent claim to the lands they lived on.

During a May 1783 meeting with the commander at Niagara, a Mohawk chief, Aaron Hill (Kanonraron), had expressed amazement that the British could even think of breaking their honor and the 1768 Treaty of Fort Stanwix by giving the lands of the Haudenosaunee over to Patriot jurisdiction. As reported on May 18, 1783, by the British commander Allan Maclean to Governor Haldimand "exactly as translated":

> [T]hey told me they never could believe that our King could pretend to Cede to America What was not his own to give, or that the Americans would accept from Him, What he had no right to grant. That...in the Year 1768...a Line had been drawn from the Head of Canada Creek (near Fort Stanwix) to the Ohio, that the Boundaries then Settled were agreeable to the Indians & the Colonies.... That the Indians were a free People Subject to no Power upon Earth, that they were faithful Allies of the King of England, but not his Subjects.... They added, that Many Years ago, their ancestors had granted permission to the French King to build trading Houses, or small Forts...in the Heart of their Country for the Convenience of *Trade Only* without granting One Inch of Land, but What these forts Stood upon, and that at the End of the last War, they granted leave to Sir William Johnson to hold these forts for their Ally the King of England, but that it was impossible from that Circumstance only to imagine, that the King of England Should pretend to grant to the Americans, all the Whole Country of the Indians Lying between the Lakes and the fixed Boundaries, as settled in 1768 between the Colonies and the Indians.... That if it was really true that the English had basely betrayed them by pretending to give up their Country to the Americans Without their Consent, or Consulting them, it was an act of Cruelty and injustice that Christians *only* were capable of doing, that the Indians were incapable of acting So . . . to friends & Allies, but that they did believe We had Sold & betrayed them. (Haldimand Transcripts B. 103, 177–79)

The unfortunate truth was that the Haudenosaunee, like most Indians east of the Mississippi, were eager for manufactured goods and had become too dependent upon these "Christians." When the British turned over the entire

Haudenosaunee nation and empire to U.S. jurisdiction, most Haudenosaunee had no choice but to accept it. About sixteen hundred men, women and children, however, did move to Canada. Four hundred and fifty, including Joseph Brant, were Mohawks who had lived in the Mohawk River valley and could not go home for fear of Patriot reprisals. The refugees settled along the Grand River (Ontario), part of the northern frontier of their own Haudenosaunee empire. They built frame houses, cleared fields and tried to rebuild the prosperity they had once known.

During the decades following the American Revolution, the Haudenosaunee who had not fled to Canada faced continuous encroachment by American frontiersmen who claimed the lands by right of conquest during the revolution, by right of treaty and by various legitimate or unscrupulous land purchases. Significantly, the few Haudenosaunce in Canada experienced a pattern of events similar to that encountered by the Haudenosaunee majority in the United States. Whites, both with permission and without, moved onto their Grand River lands. The result was an undermining of Haudenosaunee identity, and by 1789 one group of Haudenosaunee decided to move away from the main body in protest of Joseph Brant's policy of permitting certain whites to live among them.

The problems that had occurred under British rule in the thirteen colonies continued in Canada because while the location had changed, British Indian policy had not. The British demonstrated they had learned little about Indian affairs from the American Revolution. Even the same family—the Johnsons—controlled the Indian Department before and after the war. Sir John Johnson, who remained Indian superintendent until 1828, continued to send presents and rum to the Indians and to discourage any unification movement with other nations in Canada and the United States. British policy viewed the Indians simply as wards to be kept divided and therefore harmless.

The American Revolution brought an end to the confederacy's national and imperial power. But the culture of the Haudenosaunee, well-honed diplomatic skills and will to survive remained. Today, the confederacy of the Haudenosaunee continues to be a vibrant political and spiritual entity.

Perspective

The impact of the American Revolution was the most important event in Indian history north of Mexico since the droughts of the 1200s. The impact of the Revolution was as "revolutionary" in its long-term effects as the centuries of impact wrought by Mesoamerican cultures on the areas north of Mexico. The reduction of the powers of the Cherokees, the Creek Confederacy and the confederacy of the Haudenosaunee affected every Indian nation in North America for at least the next two centuries, down to the present day. The American Revolution put in place a new nation that would eventually reach to the Pacific and even dominate Alaska. The Cherokees, the Creek Confederacy and the Haudenosaunee had provided a buffer between the English-speaking whites and the Indians to the west. This had now been breached. In the early 1700s, the Spanish had been unable to break through eastward onto the Plains from the Southwest and Mexico. Furthermore, in the Southwest, the buffer of the Pueblo people, even during Spanish occupation, proved resilient and the Spanish had to compromise with the Pueblo people. In the East, however, Euroamericans finally broke through from east to west.

Thus it is significant that the only major penetration by white settlers into Indian lands between 1763 and 1775 was westward from Virginia and Pennsylvania, an area populated by neither the Haudenosaunee nor the Cherokees or Creeks. In 1774, the Haudenosaunee realized the necessity of closing that gap. But the Haudenosaunee were still debating alternatives when the American Revolution broke out among their colonial neighbors in 1775.

Of the three Indian buffer states, the Haudenosaunee had been the most powerful and far-reaching. Had the Haudenosaunee survived the Revolution with their economic and diplomatic power intact, Indians to the west might have been able to develop behind the buffer and adjust their cultures suffi-ciently to survive if or when the tide of U.S. settlers reached them. But as history evolved, only a little more than a century—from 1783 to 1890—passed before all the Indians of North America had been overwhelmed.

A century after the American Revolution, in 1879, the United States and New York state celebrated the centennial of the Sullivan Campaign. What was said during this celebration is revealing of the attitudes that all too often remain widely held by non-Indians in the Americas. At one of the celebratory events General William Tecumseh Sherman gave a commemorative speech at the Newtown battlefield site near Elmira, New York. During the Civil War, General Sherman had marched his Union Army through Georgia in 1864, destroying homes and crops and burning the city of Atlanta. At the time Sherman spoke, wars with Indian nations west of the Mississippi were still being fought. Three years before, in 1876, the Lakotas and Cheyennes had been victorious in their battle with George Armstrong Custer at the Little Big Horn. Sherman's speech was recorded and included in a commemorative history book published for the occasion as follows:

> Battles are not measured by their death-roll [list of fatalities], but by their results, and it makes no difference whether one man was killed or five hundred, if the same result followed. This valley was opened to civilization; it came on the heels of General Sullivan's army, and has gone on, and gone on until to-day. The same battle is raging upon the Yellow Stone. The same men, endowed by the same feelings that General Sullivan's army had, to-day are contending with the same causes and the same races, two thousand miles west of here; not for the purpose of killing, not for the purpose of shedding blood, not for the purpose of doing wrong at all; but to prepare the way for that civilization which must go along wherever yonder flag floats...
>
> I know it is a very common, and too common a practice, to accuse General Sullivan of having destroyed peach trees and cornfields, and all that nonsense. He had to do it, and he did do it. Why does the Almighty strike down the tree with lightning? Why does He bring forth the thunder storm? To purify the air, so that the summer time may come, and the harvest and the fruits. And so with war. When all things ought to be peaceful, war comes and purifies the atmosphere. So it was with our Civil war; that purified the atmosphere; we are better for it; you are better for it; we are all better for it. Wherever men raise up their hands to oppose this great advancing tide of civilization, they must be swept aside, peacefully if possible, forcibly if we must....
>
> We are a people united by bonds of love and of law; and that we are determined to carry on what our forefathers began; and that years will only bring renewed honors and renewed population.
>
> And wherever that flag floats, whether in New York State or on the Mississippi, or in the Rocky Mountains, justice and liberty and law must prevail; and all men, be they what color they may, Indians or negroes or white men, no better, no worse than we are, shall be free to live the appointed time. (Cook 1887, 439–40)

Sherman could speak nobly about liberty, but the price of liberty was always Indian land. Sherman, like George Washington before him, found noble justifications for imperialism. More than warfare conquered Indian America. Peacetime was as perilous a time for Indian nations as war. As in the colonial period, the invaders regarded each treaty line and each treaty promise as temporary expedients—pauses rather than resolutions to conflicts. Today, old promises remain unfulfilled and new promises are continually broken—and as in the colonial period, legislation is as effective as warfare. Thus what is perhaps most tragic regarding the conquest of Indian America is not the wars, but the unwillingness of the United States to maintain peace.

The justifications for all these broken promises and all these wars were—and still are—always nobly stated and legally defined. Indian nations were unable to resist, and they barely survived. They continue to fight for survival today. There is no real peace, but rather, from the Native American perspective, only a pause before the next broken promise. And thus no single moral logic has yet emerged from this crowded wilderness.

References

Adair, James. [1775] 1973. *History of the American Indians.* Edited by Samuel Cole Williams. New York: Promontory Press.

Akwesasne Notes. 1978. *Basic Call to Consciousness.* Mohawk Nation, via Rooseveltown, N.Y.: Akwesasne Notes.

Anderson, Fred. 2000. *Crucible of War: The Seven Years' War and the Fate of Empire in British North America, 1754–1766.* New York: Alfred A. Knopf.

Andrews, Charles M., ed. 1915. *Narratives of the Insurrections.* New York: Charles Scribner's Sons.

Anonymous. 1846. "The Early Records of Charleston." In *Chronicles of the First Planters of the Colony of Massachusetts Bay, from 1623 to 1636.* Edited by Alexander Young. Boston: Charles C. Little and James Brown.

Biggar, H.P., ed. 1924. *The Voyages of Jacques Cartier.* No. 11. Ottawa: Publications of the Public Archives of Canada.

Blair, William M. 1971. "Indians Clash with U.S. Guards," *New York Times,* 23 September.

Bolton, Herbert E. 1921. *The Spanish Borderlands.* New Haven, Conn.: Yale University Press.

Bond, Richmond P. 1952. *Queen Anne's American Kings.* Oxford: Oxford University Press.

Boyd, Julian P., ed. 1938. *Indian Treaties Printed By Benjamin Franklin, 1736–1762.* Philadelphia: Historical Society of Pennsylvania.

Boyer, Paul, and Stephen Nissenbaum. 1974. *Salem Possessed: The Social Origins of Witchcraft.* Cambridge, Mass.: Harvard University Press.

Bradford, William. 1952. *Of Plymouth Plantation.* Edited by Samuel Eliot Morison. New York: Random House.

[Bradford, William, and Edward Winslow?]. [1622] 1966. *Journall of the English Plantation at Plimoth.* Ann Arbor, Mich.: Readex Microprint.

_____. [1622] 1865. *Mourt's Relation or Journal of the Plantation at Plymouth.* Boston: John Kimball Wiggin.

Buck, William J. 1886. *History of The Indian Walk Performed for the Proprietaries of Pennsylvania in 1737; to Which is Appended a Life of Edward Marshall.* Philadelphia: Edwin S. Stuart.

Cappon, Lester J., et al. 1976. *Atlas of Early American History: The Revolutionary Era, 1760–1790.* Princeton, N.J.: Princeton University Press.

Carter, Clarence Edwin, ed. 1931. *The Correspondence of General Thomas Gage.* Vol. 1. New Haven, Conn.: Yale University Press.

_____. 1933. *The Correspondence of General Thomas Gage.* Vol. 2. New Haven, Conn.: Yale University Press.

Cave, Alfred A. 1996. *The Pequot War.* Amherst: University of Massachusetts Press.

Champlain, Samuel de. 1907. *Voyages of Samuel de Champlain, 1604–1618.* Edited by W.L. Grant. New York: Charles Scribner's Sons.

Claus Papers. Indian and Northern Affairs. Manuscript Group 19. Ottawa: The Public Archives of Canada.

Clayton, Lawrence A., Vernon James Knight, Jr. and Edward C. Moore, eds. 1993. *The De Soto Chronicles*. Vol. 1. Tuscaloosa: University of Alabama Press.

Coe, Michael, Dean Snow and Elizabeth Benson. 1986. *Atlas of Ancient America*. New York: Facts on File.

Colden, Cadwallader. [1747] 1958. *The History of the Five Indian Nations Depending on the Province of New-York in America*. Ithaca, N.Y.: Cornell University Press.

Cook, Frederick, ed. 1887. *Journals of the Military Expedition of Major General John Sullivan against the Six Nations of Indians*. Auburn, N.Y.: Knapp, Peck & Thomson.

Corkran, David H. 1962. *The Cherokee Frontier: Conflict and Survival, 1740–62*. Norman: University of Oklahoma Press.

———. 1967. *The Creek Frontier, 1540–1783*. Norman: University of Oklahoma Press.

Cotterill, R. S. 1954. *The Southern Indians: The Story of the Civilized Tribes Before Removal*. Norman: University of Oklahoma Press.

Cotton, John. [1630] 1964. "God's Promise to His Plantations." In *The Indian and the White Man*, edited by Wilcomb E. Washburn. New York: Doubleday & Company.

Crane, Verner W. [1929] 1964. *The Southern Frontier, 1670–1732*. Ann Arbor: University of Michigan.

Deloria, Vine, Jr. 1991. "Reflection and Revelation: Knowing Land, Places, and Ourselves." In *The Power of Place: Sacred Ground in Natural and Human Environments*. Wheaton, Ill.: Quest Books.

Deloria, Vine, Jr., and Raymond J. DeMallie. 1999. *Documents of American Indian Diplomacy*. Vol. 1. Norman: University of Oklahoma Press.

Deloria, Vine, Jr., and Clifford M. Lytle. 1998. *The Nations Within: The Past and Future of American Indian Sovereignty*. 2d ed. Austin: University of Texas Press.

Demos, John. 1994. *The Unredeemed Captive: A Family Story from Early America*. New York: Alfred A. Knopf.

Dixon, E. James. 1993. *Quest for the Origins of the First Americans*. Albuquerque: University of New Mexico Press.

Dobyns, Henry F. 1983. *Their Numbers Become Thinned: Native American Population Dynamics in Eastern North America*. Knoxville: University of Tennessee Press.

Downing, Emmanuel. [1645] 1947. Letter to John Winthrop, c. August 1645. In *Winthrop Papers*. Vol. 1. Boston: Massachusetts Historical Society.

Drake, Sir Francis. [1628] 1854. *The World Encompassed*. London: Hakluyt Society.

Emerson, Thomas E. 1997. *Cahokia and the Archaeology of Power*. Tuscaloosa: University of Alabama Press.

Fenton, William N. 1998. *The Great Law and The Longhouse*. Norman: University of Oklahoma Press.

Fitzhugh, William W., and Aron Cowell, eds. 1988. *Crossroads of Continents: Cultures of Siberia and Alaska*. Washington, D.C.: Smithsonian Institution.

Ford, Worthington Chauncey, ed. 1889. *The Writings of George Washington*. Vol. 2. New York: G.P. Putnam's Sons.

François, Marquis de Barbé-Marbois. 1929. *Our Revolutionary Forefathers: The Letters of François, Marquis de Barbé-Marbois.* Edited by Eugene Parker Chase. New York: Duffield & Co.

Franklin, Benjamin. 1987. *Writings.* Edited by J.A. Leo Lemay. New York: Library of America.

Gage, General Thomas. 1931. *The Correspondence of General Thomas Gage.* Vol. 1. Edited by Clarence Edwin Carter. New Haven, Conn.: Yale University Press.

Garratt, John G. 1985. *The Four Indian Kings.* Ottawa: Public Archives of Canada.

George-Kanentiio, Doug. 2000. *Iroquois Culture & Commentary.* Santa Fe, N.M.: Clear Light Publishers.

Gibson, Charles. 1966. *Spain in America.* New York: Harper & Row.

_____, ed. 1968. *The Spanish Tradition in America.* New York: Harper & Row.

Gray, Robert. 1609. *A Good Speed to Virginia.* London: Felix Kyngston for William Welbie.

Hackett, Charles Wilson, ed. 1942. *Revolt of the Pueblo Indians of New Mexico and Otermín's Attempted Reconquest, 1680–1682.* Trans. Charmion Clair Shelby. Vol. 1. Albuquerque: University of New Mexico Press.

Hakluyt, Richard. 1609. *Virginia Richly Valued, By the Description of the Maine Land of Florida, Her Next Neighbor.* London: Felix Kyngston for Matthew Lownes.

_____. [1582] 1850. *Divers Voyages Touching the Discovery of America and the Islands Adjacent.* Edited by John Winter Jones. London: Hakluyt Society.

Haldimand Transcripts. Manuscript Series B. Ottawa: The Public Archives of Canada.

Hamilton, Edward P., trans. and ed. 1964. *Adventure in the Wilderness: The American Journals of Louis Antoine de Bougainville, 1756–1760.* Norman: University of Oklahoma Press.

Hammond, George P., and Agapito Rey, eds. 1953. *Don Juan de Oñate: Colonizer of New Mexico, 1595–1628.* 2 vols. Albuquerque: University of New Mexico Press.

Hanke, Lewis. 1951. *Bartolomé de las Casas: An Interpretation of His Life and Writings.* The Hague (the Netherlands): Martinus Nijhoff.

_____. 1959. *Aristotle and the Indians.* Bloomington: Indiana University Press.

_____. 1974. *All Mankind Is One.* DeKalb: Northern Illinois University Press.

Hariot, Thomas. [1588] 1955. "A Briefe and True Report." In *The Roanoke Voyages, 1584–1590,* edited by David Beers Quinn. Vol. 1. London: Hakluyt Society.

Harris, William. [1676] 1963. *A Rhode Islander Reports on King Philip's War: The Second William Harris Letter of August, 1676.* Edited by Douglas E. Leach. Providence: Rhode Island Historical Society.

Hauptman, Laurence M., and James D. Wherry, eds. 1990. *The Pequots in Southern New England: The Fall and Rise of an American Indian Nation.* Norman: University of Oklahoma.

Hayden, Dolores. 1997. *The Power of Place: Urban Landscapes as Public History.* Cambridge, Mass.: M.I.T Press.

Henry, Alexander. [1809] 1971. *Attack at Michilimackinac.* Edited by David A. Armour. Mackinac Island, Mich.: Mackinac Island State Park Commission.

Hesseltine, William B. 1930. *Civil War Prisons: A Study in War Psychology.* Columbus: Ohio State University Press.

Hill, Frances. 2000. *The Salem Witch Trials Reader*. New York: Da Capo Press.

Hodge, Frederick W., and Theodore Lewis, eds. 1907. *Spanish Explorers in the Southern United States, 1528–1543*. New York: Charles Scribner's Sons.

Horigan, Michael. 2002. *Elmira: Death Camp of the North*. Mechanicsburg, Penn.: Stackpole Books.

Hotz, Gottfried. 1970. *Indian Skin Paintings from the American Southwest: Two Representations of Border Conflicts between Mexico and the Missouri in the Early Eighteenth Century*. Trans. Johannes Malthaner. Norman: University of Oklahoma Press.

Hudson, Charles. 1997. *Knights of Spain, Warriors of the Sun: Hernando de Soto and the South's Ancient Chiefdoms*. Athens: University of Georgia Press.

Hunt, George T. 1940. *The Wars of the Iroquois*. Madison: University of Wisconsin Press.

Jacobs, Wilbur R. 1966. *Wilderness Politics and Indian Gifts*. Lincoln: University of Nebraska Press.

_____, ed. 1967. *The Appalachian Indian Frontier: The Edmond Atkin Report and Plan of 1755*. Lincoln: University of Nebraska Press.

_____. 1972. *Dispossessing the American Indian*. New York: Charles Scribner's Sons.

Jefferson, Thomas. 1801. *Notes on the State of Virginia*. New York: M.L. & W.A. Davis for Furman & Loudon.

Jemison, G. Peter, and Anna M. Schein, eds. 2000. *Treaty of Canandaigua 1794*. Santa Fe, N.M.: Clear Light Publishers.

Jennings, Francis. 1975. *The Invasion of America: Indians, Colonialism, and the Cant of Conquest*. Chapel Hill: University of North Carolina Press.

Johnston Greene, Lorenzo. 1971. *The Negro in Colonial New England*. New York: Atheneum.

Kaplan, Sidney. 1973. *The Black Presence in the Era of the American Revolution, 1770–1800*. Washington, D.C.: Smithsonian Institution Press.

Kappler, Charles J., ed. [1904] 1972. *Indian Treaties, 1778–1883*. New York: Interland Publishing.

Labaree, Leonard W., ed. 1961. *The Papers of Benjamin Franklin*. Vol. 4. New Haven, Conn.: Yale University Press.

Lane, Ralph. 1955. "Discourse on the First Colony, 17 August 1585–18 June 1586." In *The Roanoke Voyages, 1584–1590*, edited by David Beers Quinn. Vol. 1. London: Hakluyt Society.

Lanning, John Tate. 1935. *The Spanish Missions of Georgia*. Chapel Hill: University of North Carolina Press.

Lauber, Almon Wheeler. 1913. *Indian Slavery in Colonial Times within the Present Limits of the United States*. Studies in History, Economics and Public Law No. 134. New York: Columbia University.

Leach, Douglas E. [1958] 1966. *Flintlock and Tomahawk: New England in King Philip's War*. New York: W.W. Norton.

Leder, Lawrence H., ed. 1956. *The Livingston Indian Records, 1666–1723*. Gettysburg: Pennsylvania Historical Association.

Lemay, J.A. Leo, ed. 1987. *Benjamin Franklin, Writings*. New York: Library of America.

Leon-Portillo, Miguel, ed. 1962. *The Broken Spears: The Aztec Account of the Conquest of Mexico*. Boston: Beacon Press.

Lepore, Jill. 1998. *The Name of War: King Philip's War and the Origins of American Identity*. New York: Alfred A. Knopf.

Lincoln, Charles H., ed. 1913. *Narratives of the Indian Wars, 1675–1699*. New York: Charles Scribner's Sons.

Littlefield, Daniel F. 1979. *Africans and Creeks from the Colonial Period to the Civil War*. Westport, Conn.: Greenwood Press.

London Council [The]. [1606] 1969. "Instructions Given by Way of Advice." In *The Jamestown Voyages under the First Charter, 1606–1609*, edited by Philip L. Barbour. Vol. 1. Cambridge: Cambridge University Press.

Madore, James T. 1994. "Gambling Deals Oneida Nation a Better Hand: Once Poverty-Stricken Tribe Undergoes Renaissance with New Turning Stone Casino." *Buffalo (N.Y.) News*, 10 July.

Mann, Barbara A., and Jerry L. Fields. 1997. "A Sign in the Sky: Dating the League of the Haudenosaunee." *American Indian Culture and Research Journal* 21, No. 2: 105–63.

Mann, Barbara Alice. 2000. *Iroquoian Women: The Gantowisas*. New York: Peter Lang.

Marsalis, Wynton. 1997. *Blood on the Fields*. New York: Columbia/Sony Music. Three compact discs.

Mather, Cotton. 1702. *Magnalia Christi Americana: Or, The Ecclesiastical History of New-England From Its First Planting in the Year 1620 Unto the Year of our LORD, 1698*. Vol. 7. London: Thomas Parkhurst.

McNeill, William H. 1976. *Plagues and Peoples*. New York: Doubleday.

McReynolds, Edwin C. 1957. *The Seminoles*. Norman: University of Oklahoma Press.

[Melyn, Cornelis]. 1857. "Broad Advice, Or Dialogue About the Trade of the West India Company, Etc." Trans. Henry C. Murphy. In *Collections of the New-York Historical Society*. Vol. 3, second series. New York: D. Appleton and Company.

Melvoin, Richard I. 1989. *New England Outpost: War and Society in Colonial Deerfield*. New York: W.W. Norton.

Meyer, Roy W. 1993. *History of the Santee Sioux: United States Indian Policy on Trial*. 2d ed. Lincoln: University of Nebraska Press.

Milanich, Jerald T. 1995. *Florida Indians and the Invasion from Europe*. Gainesville: University Press of Florida.

Minge, Ward Alan. 1991. *Ácoma: Pueblo in the Sky*. Rev. ed. Albuquerque: University of New Mexico Press.

Mohawk, John C. 2000. *Utopian Legacies: A History of Conquest and Oppression in the Western World*. Santa Fe, N.MM.: Clear Light Publishers.

Montaigne, Michel de. 1958. *Essays*. Trans. J.M. Cohen. Harmondsworth, England: Penguin.

Mooney, James. [1891/1900] 1982. *Myths of the Cherokees and Sacred Formulas of the Cherokees*. Nashville, Tenn.: Charles and Randy Elder, Booksellers-Publishers.

Morgan, William N. 1980. *Prehistoric Architecture in the Eastern United States*. Cambridge, Mass.: M.I.T Press.

Morison, Samuel Eliot. 1971. *The European Discovery of America: The Northern Voyages*. New York: Oxford University Press.

Morris, Richard B. 1965. *Government and Labor in Early America*. New York: Harper Torchbooks.

Morton, Richard L. 1960. *Colonial Virginia*. Vol. 1. Chapel Hill: University of North Carolina Press.

Newport, Christopher. [1607] 1907. "The Description of the Now-Discovered River and Country of Virginia." *Virginia Magazine of History and Biography*. Vol. 14.

O'Callaghan, E.B., and B. Fernow, eds. 1855. *Documents Relative to the Colonial History of the State of New York*. Vols. 5 and 6. Albany: Weed, Parsons and Company.

_____. 1856. *Documents Relative to the Colonial History of the State of New York*. Vol. 7. Albany: Weed, Parsons and Company.

Orr, Charles, ed. 1897. *History of the Pequot War: The Contemporary Accounts of Mason, Underhill, Vincent and Gardener*. Cleveland, Ohio: Helman-Taylor Company.

Parkman, Francis. 1877. *Count Frontenac and New France under Louis XIV*. Boston: Little, Brown & Company.

_____. 1892. *A Half Century of Conflict*. Vol. 1. Boston: Little, Brown, and Company.

_____. [1884] 1983. *France and England in North America*. Vol. 2. New York: The Library of America.

_____. [1870] 1991. *The Oregon Trail and the Conspiracy of Pontiac*. New York: The Library of America.

Peckham, Howard H. 1947. *Pontiac and the Indian Uprising*. Princeton, N.J.: Princeton University Press.

_____. 1964. *The Colonial Wars, 1689–1762*. Chicago: University of Chicago Press.

Peirson, George Wilson. [1938] 1996. *Tocqueville in America*. Baltimore: Johns Hopkins University Press.

Penney, David W., and George C. Longfish. 1994. *Native American Art*. Detroit: Hugh Lauter Levin Associates.

Perdue, Theda. 1979. *Slavery and the Evolution of Cherokee Society*. Knoxville: University of Tennessee Press.

Peterson, Iver. 1997. "20 Pulitzer Prizes Are Announced with a Theme of Personal Impact on Lives." *The New York Times*, April 8.

Pierce, Richard A. 1972. "Alaska's Russian Governors: Ivan Kupreianov." *Alaska Journal* 2, no. 1: 21–24.

Quarles, Benjamin. 1961. *The Negro in the American Revolution*. Chapel Hill: University of North Carolina Press.

Quesenberry, Stephen V. 1999. "Recent United Nations Initiatives Concerning the Rights of Indigenous Peoples." In *Contemporary Native American Political Issues*, edited by Troy Johnson. Walnut Creek, Calif.: Alta Mira Press.

Ramenofsky, Ann F. 1987. *Vectors of Death: The Archaeology of European Contact*. Albuquerque: University of New Mexico Press.

Rowlandson, Mary. 1913. *Narrative of the Captivity of Mrs. Mary Rowlandson*. In *Narratives of the Indian Wars*. Edited by Charles H. Lincoln. New York: Charles Scribner's Sons.

Ruskin, John. [1851–1853] 2001. *The Stones of Venice*. Edited with an introduction by Jan Morris. London: Folio Society.

Sando, Joe S. 1998. *Pueblo Profiles: Cultural Identity through Centuries of Change.* Santa Fe, N.M.: Clear Light Publishers.

Sauer, Carl Ortwin. 1971. *Sixteenth Century North America: The Land and the People As Seen by the Europeans.* Berkeley: University of California Press.

Schoolcraft, Henry R. [1846] 1975. *Notes on the Iroquois: Or, Contributions to the Statistics, Aboriginal History, Antiquities and General Ethnology of Western New York.* Millwood, N.Y.: Kraus Reprint Co.

Schuyler Papers. New York Public Library, New York, N.Y.

Seaver, James E. [1824] 1963. *A Narrative of the Life of Mrs. Mary Jemison.* New York: American Scenic and Historic Preservation Society.

Silko, Leslie Marmon. 1991. "Writing: Cultural Preservation/Cultural Liberation." Lecture presented at "Voices from Native North America" series, 7 February, Alfred University, Alfred, N.Y.

Simmonds, William. [1612] 1907. "The Proceedings of the English Colonies in Virginia." In *Narratives of Early Virginia, 1606–1625,* edited by Lyon Gardiner Tyler. New York: Charles Scribner's Sons.

Sir Henry Clinton Papers. The William L. Clements Library, University of Michigan, Ann Arbor, Mich.

Smith, Buckingham, trans. 1866. *Narratives of the Career of Hernando de Soto in the Conquest of Florida As Told By A Knight of Elvas and In A Relation by Luys Hernandez de Biedma Factor of the Expedition.* New York: Bradford Club.

———. 1871. *Relation of Alvar Núñez Cabeça de Vaca.* Albany, N.Y.: J. Munsell for H.C. Murphy.

Smith, John. [1612] 1910. *Travels and Works of Captain John Smith.* Edited by Edward Arber. Vol. 1. Edinburgh, Scotland: John Grant.

———. [1624] 1910. *Travels and Works of Captain John Smith.* Edited by Edward Arber. Vol. 2. Edinburgh, Scotland: John Grant.

Smith, William. [1765] 1966. *An Historical Account of the Expedition Against the Ohio Indians, in the Year 1764.* Ann Arbor, Mich.: Readex Microprint.

Snow, Dean R. 1994. *The Iroquois.* Cambridge, Mass.: Blackwell Publishers.

"A Speech from the People of German Flats to the Onidas & Tuscororas." 1775 [28 June]. Tryon County 1775 MSS. New York Historical Society, N.Y.

Steele, Ian K. 1990. *Betrayals: Fort William Henry and the "Massacre."* New York: Oxford University Press.

Strachey, William. [1618] 1849. *The Historie of Travaile into Virginia Britannia.* Edited by R.H. Major. London: Hakluyt Society.

Sullivan, James, et al., eds. 1921. *The Papers of Sir William Johnson.* Vol. 1. Albany: University of the State of New York.

———. 1922. *The Papers of Sir William Johnson.* Vol. 2. Albany: University of the State of New York.

———. 1925. *The Papers of Sir William Johnson.* Vol. 4. Albany.: University of the State of New York.

———. 1927. *The Papers of Sir William Johnson.* Vol. 5. Albany: University of the State of New York.

Sullivan, James, et al., eds. *The Papers of Sir William Johnson*. Vol. 9. Albany: University of the State of New York.

———. 1953. *The Papers of Sir William Johnson*. Vol. 11. Albany: University of the State of New York.

———. 1962. *The Papers of Sir William Johnson*. Vol. 13. Albany: University of the State of New York.

Swanton, John R. 1922. "Early History of the Creek Indians and Their Neighbors." *Smithsonian Institution Bureau of American Ethnology*. Bulletin 73. Washington, D.C.: U.S. Government Printing Office.

Swanton, John Reed. 1911. Indian Tribes of the Lower Mississippi Valley and Adjacent Coast of the Gulf of Mexico. *Smithsonian Institution Bureau of American Ethnology Bulletin*. 43. Washington, D.C.: Smithsonian Institution.

Thomas, David Hurst. 1994. *Exploring Ancient Native America: An Archaeological Guide*. New York: Macmillan.

Thomas Gage Papers. American Series. The William L. Clements Library, University of Michigan, Ann Arbor.

Thornton, Russell. 1987. *American Indian Holocaust and Survival: A Population History Since 1492*. Norman: University of Oklahoma Press.

Thwaites, Reuben G., ed. 1899. *The Jesuit Relations and Allied Documents*. Vol. 41. Cleveland: Burrows Brothers.

Tiller, Veronica E. Velarde, ed. 1996. *American Indian Reservations and Trust Areas*. Washington, D.C.: U.S. Department of Commerce, Economic Development Administration.

[The] Trial of the British Soldiers. [1770] 1824. Transcript. Boston: William Emmons, November.

Trumbull, Charles P., ed. 2002. *2002 Britannica Book of the Year*. Chicago: Encyclopedia Britannica.

Uhry Abrams, Ann. 1985. *The Valiant Hero: Benjamin West and the Grand-Style History Painting*. Washington, D.C.: Smithsonian Institution Press.

Underhill, John. [1638] n.d. *Newes From America; Or, A New and Experimentall Discoverie of New England; Containing, A True Relation of Their War-like proceedings these two years last past, with a Figure of the Indian Fort, or Palizado*. New York: Underhill Society of America.

Usner, Daniel H., Jr. 1992. *Indians, Settlers, & Slaves in a Frontier Exchange Economy: The Lower Mississippi Valley before 1783*. Chapel Hill: University of North Carolina Press.

Vaughan, Alden T. 1965. *New England Frontier: Puritans and Indians, 1620–1675*. Boston: Little, Brown, and Company.

Velarde Tiller, Veronica E., ed. 1996. *American Indian Reservations and Trust Areas*. Washington, D.C.: U.S. Department of Commerce.

Verano, John W., and Douglas H. Ubelaker, eds. 1992. *Disease and Demography in the Americas*. Washington, D.C.: Smithsonian Institution.

Villagrá, Gaspar Pérez de. [1610] 1933. *History of New Mexico*. Trans. Gilberto Espinosa. Los Angeles: Quivira Society.

Virginia Magazine of History and Biography. 1905. "The Treaty of Logg's Town, 1752." *The Virginia Magazine of History and Biography*. Vol. 13. Richmond: Virginia Historical Society.

Vries, David de. [1655] 1909. "Short Historical and Journal-Notes." In *Narratives of New Netherland, 1609–1664*, Edited by J. Franklin Jameson. New York: Charles Scribner's Sons.

Wallace, Paul A.W. 1946. *The White Roots of Peace*. Philadelphia: University of Pennsylvania Press.

Whiting Young, Biloine, and Melvin L. Fowler. 2000. *Cahokia: The Great Native American Metropolis*. Urbana: University of Illinois Press.

Wilford, John Noble. 1998. "In Peru, Evidence of an Early Human Maritime Culture." *The New York Times*, 22 September.

_____. 2000. "The New World's Earliest People." *New York Times*, April 11.

Winslow, Edward. [1624] 1897. "Good Newes from New England." In *The Story of the Pilgrim Fathers, 1606–1623 A.D.; as told by Themselves, Their Friends, and Their Enemies*, edited by Edward Arber. London: Ward and Downey, Ltd.

Winthrop Papers. 1938. *Winthrop Papers*. Vol. 2. Boston: Massachusetts Historical Society.

_____. 1943. *Winthrop Papers*. Vol. 3. Boston: Massachusetts Historical Society.

Wissler, Clark. 1966. *Indians of the United States*. Rev. ed. Garden City, N.Y.: Doubleday & Company.

Young, Alexander. [1731] 1846. *Chronicles of the First Planters of the Colony of Massachusetts Bay, from 1623 to 1636*. Boston: Charles C. Little and James Brown.

Zobel, Hiller B. 1971. *The Boston Massacre*. New York: W.W. Norton.

Index

A

Abnakis (Tarrantines), 78–79, 156, 158
Acolapissa Indians, 126
Acoma Pueblo, 43, 45–48
Adair, James, 212
Adirondack Indians, 157
Alaska, 165–66
Albany Congress, 177–78
Albany Treaty, 151
Aleut Indians, 166
Algonquin Indians, 37–42, 138–41
American Revolutionary War, 266–310
    Cherry Valley, 290–92
    food supplies, 299–303
    Indian experiences, 278–85
    in the North, 272–78
    perspective, 307–10
    Southern land grabs, 269–72
    strikes, 289–90
    Sullivan campaign, 292–97
    toward peace, 298–99
    turning points, 285–89
    waiting for peace, 303–7
Anasazi, 36, 119
Andros, Govenor Edmund, 110–11, 149–50, 154
Apache Indians, 44, 115, 119–23
Apalachee Indians, 124–25, 127, 130
Aquaseogoc Indians, 57–58
Archbishop of Canterbury, 133
Aristotle, 23
Arnold, Benedict, 282–83
arrow-rattlesnake bundle, 80
Atkin, Edmund, 58, 174, 187–88
Attucks, Crispus, 214–16
Awashonk Indians, 105
Ayllón, Lucas Vásquez de, 9–11, 15, 22, 32
Aztec Empire, 7–8

B

"Bakers Cabin," 262
Barbé-Marbois, François Marquis de, 225
Battle of Oriskany, 286–87
Bayton, Wharton and Morgan, 260–61
Beloved Woman, 269
Bering, Vitus, 165
Bimini, 8
Bishop of Darien, 21
black-Indian intermarriage, 212–14
Black Mesa, 121

Black Minquas, 145
black slaves, 22, 73, 208–12
    compared to Indian slaves, 208–12
    Indian relations with, 216–20
    rebellion, 10–11
Block Island Indians, 93
Boone, Daniel, 261, 265, 278
Boonesborough, 265, 273
Bosomworth, Mary Musgrove. *See* Goa.
Boston Massacre, 214–16
Braddock, Edward, 178–81
Bradford, William (Govenor), 80–81
Brant, Joseph, 276–77, 285, 290–91, 295, 304–5
Brant, Molly (Mary), 286
Brims, 126–27, 129–30
British
    American Revolutionary War, 266–310
    failure to reform Indian affairs, 245–67
    against pan-Indian unity, 257–58
Bua, Nicolas, 116
Butler, John, 285, 304
Butler, Walter, 290–91, 296–97, 302

C

Cabeza de Vaca, Alvar Núñez, 11–13
Cabot, John, 167
Caddoan Indians, 126
Cahokia Indians, 126
California, 166
California Indians, 56
Calusa Indians, 8–9, 189
Camp Charlotte, 264
Canada, 29–31, 147–48, 153–55, 307
Canasatego, 163
cannibalism, 12, 65
Canonicus, 80, 90
Cape Fear River, 10
captivity narrative, 205
Caribbean islands, 31
Carib Indians, 9
Carignan-Sallieres Regiment, 147
Carleton, Guy, 282
Cartier, Jacques, 29–30
Carver, Govenor John, 78
Catawba Indians, 126
Catholicism, 20–25, 49–54
Caughnawaga (Kahnawake), 147
Cavelier, René Robert, 121, 151–52
Cayuga Indians, 153, 287

Céloron de Bienville, Pierre Joseph, 167–70
Champlain, Samuel de, 38–43
Chanco, 83
Charles I (King of England), 90–91, 102
Charles River, 98
Charles Town. *See* Charleston, S.C.
Charles v (King of Spain), 9–10, 23
Charleston, S.C., 123, 125, 127, 268
Chatot Indians, 123
Chawasha Indians, 126
Cherokee Indians, 308
    and Creeks, 123, 125–29, 132–34, 172
    in American Revolution, 269–72, 308
    in French and Indian War, 184, 186–90
    Treaty of Hard Labor, 251
    women, 223
Cherry Valley, New York, 290–92, 300
Chesapeake Bay, 49, 59–60, 64, 147
Chichumecoe Indians, 123
Chickamauga Indians, 271–72
Chickasaw Indians, 17, 126, 129, 131, 209, 271
Chicorana, Francisco, 9–10, 30
Chigelley, 127, 134–35
Chippewa Indians, 151
Choctaw Indians, 125–26, 131, 209, 271
"Christ our victory," 59
Christian Indians, 97–98, 103–4, 111–13, 277, 281
Christianity, conversion to, 5–8, 97–98, 108
Church, Benjamin, 156
Clark, George Rogers, 274–78, 296
Claus, Daniel, 302
clergy, Spanish reliance on, 49–54
Clinton, James, 292–97
Cofitachique, 14
College for Indians, 71–72, 81–84
colonial
    expansion, 32
    Indian policy, 191
colonists dependence on Indians, 82, 85–86
colonization
    justification of, 70
Columbus, Don Diego (Spanish Govenor of
        Hispaniola), 9
Comanche Indians, 122
confederacies, 36
Confederation of New England, 96
Congaree Indians, 126
Connecticut, 91
conquest of the Americas, 2
conquista, 55
Continental Congress, 283–84, 305
Cooper, James Fenimore, 184

Coosa, 15, 26
Coosaponakeesa. *See* Musgrove, Mary.
Corbitant, 79–80
corn, 32–33
Cornplanter, 290, 295
Cornstalk, 269, 274
Cornwallis, General, 296–97
Coronado, Francisco Vázquez de, 18–21
Corpa, Father Pedro, 52
Cortés, Fernando (Hernando), 7, 32
Covenant Chain, 285
Coweta, 126
Crawford, William, 277
creation, nature of, 1
Creek Confederacy, 13–15, 36
    in American Revolution, 268–72, 308
    in French and Indian War, 185–90
    neutrality, 124–37
    slave hunting, 218–19
    Treaty of Hard Labor, 251–53
    women leaders, 222
Creole Indians, 51
Croatoan Indians, 60–62
Croghan, George, 171, 178–79
Cusabo Indians, 9–10, 27, 49–55
Custer, George Armstrong, 309
Cutshamekin, Chief, 98

D

Dale, Sir Thomas, 68
Dare, Virginia, 62
Dasemunkepeuc, 59–61
Dasemunkepeuc Indians, 60–61
Deerfield, Massachusetts, 158–59
Deganawidah, 37, 43
Deleware Indians, 163, 272–77
Deleware Prophet, 192–94
Deleware River, 162
democracy, initial step of, 73
Denonville, French Govenor, 154
Detroit, 168, 275–77
the Devil, 49
Divine Providence, 8
Doegs, 103, 149
Domagaia, 29–30
domination, 113
Dominicans, 49–50
Don Francisco, 52–53
Dongan, Govenor Thomas, 153
Donnacona, Chief, 29–30
Dorantes, Stephen. *See* Estevanico.
Dragging Canoe, 269

Drake, Sir Francis, 56, 59–60
Dunmore, Lord, 261–66, 272–73
Dunmore's War, 261–66
Dustan, Hannah, 221
Dutch, 98–105, 147–49
    and Northeast fur trade, 137–40, 147

E

Elinipsico, 274
Elliott, John, 89–90, 97–98
Ellis, Henry, 189
empires in the Northeast, 152
encomienda, 6–7
Endecott, John, 93
endowment for Indian education, 71–72
English. *See also* British.
    at Roanoke, 57–63
    competition with French, 171–90
    in the Georgia Colony, 131–35
    in Jamestown, 63–73
    pilgrims, 74–113
enslavement of Indians, 5–7, 106, 112–13
    of Acomas, 47–48
    Charles V's position on, 10
    French Indian slave trade, 206
    laws against, 22
    Philip II's position on, 55
    pope's position on, 21
    slaves sold by Indians, 205–8
    unsuitability for slavery, 208–12
epidemics, 49–50, 72, 78–79, 88–89
    impact of, 33–35
Erie Indians, 143
Erie, Lake, 143
Eskimos. *See* Inuits.
Esopus Wars, 101–2
Essays, 55
Estevanico (Stephen Dorantes), 12–13
ethical debates, 20–25, 54–56, 90
extermination, wars of, 102–5

F

Ferdinand II, 4–7, 21
fisherman, 30–31
Five Nations. *See* Iroquois Confederacy.
Florida, 8–13, 25–29, 122, 125, 189
food supplies for Haudenosaunee, 299–303
forced labor, 6–7
    policy of, 68
Fort
    Caroline, 28
    Chartres, 258

Detroit, 196–98, 200
Duquesne, 178
Jefferson, 271
La Baye, 198–200
Le Boeuf, 198–200
Miami, 198–99
Michilimackinac, 198–200
Nassau, 40
Necessity, 176
Niagara, 160, 167, 191, 198, 283, 292–94
Orange (Albany), 138
Oswego, 160
Ouiatenon, 198–99
Pitt, 198–200, 258, 275
Pontchartrain, 168
Presque Isle, 198–200
Ross, 166
St. Joseph, 198–99
St. Louis, 153
Sandusky, 198–99
Toulouse, 127, 134–35
Venango, 198–200
fountain of youth, 8
four hundred year's war, 3
Franciscans, 49, 51, 115
Franklin, Benjamin, 177–78, 224–25, 260, 278
French, 27–31
    and Indian War, 175–202
    in American Revolution, 275–76
    in Haudenosaunee nations, 167–70
    Indian allies, 153–57
    Indian slave trade, 206
    Natchez war, 131
    Northeast fur trade, 142–48
French Mississippi Company, 131
Frobisher, Martin, 56
Frontenac, Count, 154–55, 157
frontiersmen, 250–51, 261–62
fur trade, 107–9, 113, 173–74
    and Indian slavery, 206–10
    and traditional beliefs, 164
    Northeast, 137–47, 151–52, 155–56, 161–62
    Russian-American Company, 166

G

Gage, Thomas (General), 218–19, 250, 257–59,
    263, 280–81
Gallop, John, 92–93
Galveston Bay, Texas, 12
Ganondagan, 153
Gayentwahga. *See* Cornplanter.
the Genesis pyramid, 1

"The Gentleman of Elvas," 14
George III, 245
Georgia, 53, 122, 131–35
Germain, Lord George, 291
Gibson, John (General), 263–64
Girty, Simon, 278
Gladwin, Henry, 196–97, 201–2
Glorious Revolution, 154
Goa, 222
God's Chosen, 88–91
God's will, 88–89
Gorton, Samuel, 90
grave robberies, 75–77
Gray, Reverend Robert, 68–69
Great Kanawha River, 169
Great Sun, 131
Great Tree of Peace, 152
Grenville, Sir Richard, 57–58, 60, 62–63
Griffin, 152
Guale Indians, 28–29, 50–55, 122–24
Guyashusta. *See* Kaiaghshota.

H

Hakluyt, Richard, 63, 76
Haldimand, Govenor, 294, 300–302, 306
Hall Island (Resolution Island), 56
Hamilton, Henry, 275–76
Hariot, Thomas, 56–57, 60
Harrodsburg, 273
Harvard College, 104–5
Haudenosaunee, 2–3, 26
  Confederacy, 2, 26, 37–43
  European arrogance toward, 167–70
  French & Indian War, 175–85, 191–202
  in American Revolution, 272–74, 278–308
  matrilineal-based, 223–25
  neutrality, 158–64
  offensive diplomacy, 137–57
  Treaty of Hard Labor, 251–52
Havana, Cuba, 50
headright system, 72–73
Henderson, Richard, 265
Hendrick, Chief, 180
Herkimer, Nicholas, 286
Herrera, Antonio de, 54
Hiawatha, 37
Hill, Aaron, 306
Hispaniola, 3–8
Historie of Travaile into Virginia Britannia,
  69–70
History of the American Indians, 212
Hobomock, 80–81

Hochelaga, 29–30
Hopis, 48
horses, 164
House of Burgesses, 73
Howe, Sir William, 283
Hudson River Valley, 40, 91, 102, 137–38
Huguenots, 27, 32, 60
humane treatment of Indians, 68–69
  sermon on, 21–22
Huron Indians
  and Mohawks, 38–42
  Northeast fur trade, 138–42, 151
Huron (Lake), 141

I

"ignorant savages," 177–78
Illinois Indians, 152–53
In Defense of the Indians, 23
Indian John, 207–8
Indian Policy
  legal codes, 105–17
  rights of land, 90–91
Indian(s). *See also* Christian Indians. *see also*
    Christian Indians; "praying Indians."
  adaption of, 81–82, 108–9, 114
  black slave relations, 216–20
  in European Literature, 75–76
  unity, 110
  woman, 220–25
inequality of laws, 105–17
intermarriage, black-Indian, 212–15
intertribal conflict, 91–95, 122–24, 248–50
Inuits, 56
Iroquois Confederacy (Five Nations), 2, 26, 37.
    See also Haudenosaunee.
Isabella I, 4–7
Isleta del Sur, 120
Isletas, 119

J

James I, 83
James River, 81–83
Jamestown, 63–73, 81–83, 102
Jemez Pueblo, 115–18
Jemison, Mary, 233–38
Jesuits, 49–50, 138, 143–46, 151, 158
Jigonhsasee, 37
Johnson, Guy, 262–63, 280, 282, 285, 302–3
Johnson, Robert, 67
Johnson, Sir John, 295, 303–4, 307
Johnson, William, 161–62, 179–81, 184–85, 206,
    212, 251, 253, 257, 259–61

"Join or Die," 177–78
Joliet, Louis, 151–52
Joncaire, Chabert de, 168–69
Journall of the English Plantation at Plimoth, 76
Juanillo, 52–53
Juanillo Revolt, 54

K

Kahnawake. *See* Caughnawaga.
Kaiaghshota, 194
Kanonraron, 306
Kaskaskia (Illinois), 274–75
Kere Indians, 115, 118
Keres Pueblos, 44
Kiasola. *See* Kaiaghshota.
Kickapoo Indians, 275–76
Kieft, William, 98–101
King Philip's War, 103–5, 110–11, 149
Kiotsaeton, 140
Kirkland, Samuel, 282–83, 294–95
kivas, 44
Klock's Field, 295
Kodiak, 166
Kussos, 123

L

La Balme, Augustine Mottin de, 276
La Demoisele, 169
Lafayette, Marquis de, 279
La Galissoniere, Comte de, 167
Lancaster Treaty of 1744, 170–72
Lancaster Treaty of 1748, 170
Land in America, 90–91
Lane, Ralph, 57–59, 62–63
Langlade, Charles, 172–73
La Paille Coupee, 168
Lapowinsa, 163
La Salle, Sieur de, 121, 153
Las Casas, Bartolemé de, 21–25, 31–33, 57, 75
The Last of the Mohicans, 184
legal codes, 105–17
Leon-Portillo, 7–8
Lesser Antilles, 9
Little Big Horn, 309
Little Turtle, 276
Lochry, Archibald, 276–77
Logstown Treaty of 1752, 172–73
London Company, 65, 67–69, 72, 81, 83
longhouse. *See* Haudenosaunee.
Long Island, 102
Louis xv, 167–68
"loving nature," 56

Luis, 49
Luna y Arellano, Tristán de, 26

M

Machiavelli, Nicolo, 20
Maclean, Allan, 306
Mahican Indians, 38, 40, 147
Major, John, 5
Mamusse Wunneetupanatamwe Up-Biblum God, 97
Manhattan Island. *See* New Amsterdam.
Manifest Destiny, 8
Manteo, 56–59, 61
Marquette, Pere Jacques, 151–52
Martha's Vineyard, 80
Martinez, Fray Alonso, 47
Maryland, 148–49
Massachusetts, 74, 207
Massachusetts Bay Colony, 88–89, 91–98, 111
Massachusetts Indians, 85–87, 98
Massasoit Indians, 78–80, 86–88
Master of Life, 43, 144–45, 193–94
Mathew, Thomas, 103
matrilineal-based power, 223–24
Mauilla, 16–17
Mayhew, Jr., Thomas, 90
Mesoamerican architecture, 2
Miami Indians, 167, 170, 173
Miami River, 169
Miantonomo, 96
Michicans, 138
Mico, Tese (Jesse), 268
Mingo Indians, 262–63, 272–74, 277
minorities, 98
missionaries, 97–98, 108
　Russian Orthodox, 166
Missisauga Indians, 285
Mississippi, 125
Mississippi Mound Builders, 131
Mobile, 15–16
Mohawk Indians, 39, 101, 103, 141, 156, 162, 180, 283–84, 287
Mohawk Valley, 286–86, 295–96
Mohegan Indians, 40, 90, 94–95
Moho. *See* Tiguex Puebos.
Monacatoocha, 178–79
Montaigne, Michel de, 55
Montcalm, Marquis de, 182–83
Montesinos, Andonio de, 5, 21, 68
Montgomery, Richard, 282–83
Montour, Andrew, 171
Montreal, 29–30, 146

moral
    directive, 21–25
    issues, 4–8
More, Sir Thomas, 20, 70
the Mortar, 186–87
Mourt's Relation, 76
Musgrove, Mary, 132
Muskingum River, 169

N

Nanagoucy, 153
Napochies, 26
Narragansett Indians, 78–81, 85, 90 98, 104–5,
        213
Narváez, Panfilo de, 11–12
Nashob, 103
Natchez, 130–31
Natick, 103
Nauset Indians, 75–80, 86
Navajo Indians, 115, 119
Neepaheilomon, 162
Neolin. *See* Delaware Prophet.
Neutrals (Attiwandaronks), 139, 143
New Amsterdam, 98–105
New England Confederation, 96
New Jersey, 99
New Mexico
    Spanish colony, 48
New Netherlands, 98–105
Newport, Captain Christopher, 65
Newtown (Elmira), New York, 292
Nicomachean Ethics, 23
North Carolina, 56–57
Norton, Walter (Captain), 91
Nova Britannia, 67–68

O

Oaxaca Indians, 32
Oconostota, 188–89
Oglethorpe, James, 132–34
Ohio Company, 171–74
Ohio River valley, 167, 171–74
Ohke, 44–45
Ojibwas, 172–73
Old Briton, 169–70, 172–73
Oldham, John ("Mad Jack"), 92–93
"On Cannibals," 55
Onandaga Indians, 143–45, 157
Oñate, Juan de, 44–45, 47–48
Oneida Indians, 147, 162, 213–14, 279, 282, 286,
        292, 294–95
Onondaga (castle), 43

Onondaga Indians, 42, 287
Onondaga (town), 40–43, 64
Ontario Lake, 40, 141, 153
Opechancanough, 72, 81–85, 102
Orista Cusabo nation, 28–29
Oswego, New York, 206, 285
Otermín, Antonio de, 117–20
Ottawa Indians, 151, 153, 172–73, 192 202,
        272–73
Outagamie Wars, 162
Ovando, Nicolas de, 5

P

Pacific Northwest, 165–66
pacificación, 55
Pamlico River, 57
Pani, 206
pan-Indian unity, 135–37, 256–58
Parris, the Rev. Samuel, 208
Paspaheghs, 66
Patuxet, 79
Paul I (Czar), 166
Pauset Indians, 86
Pavonia, 99
Pawnee Indians, 152, 206. *See also* Pani.
Peace of Paris, 304
Peach War, 101
Peckham, Sir George, 70
Pecos pueblo, 44
Penn, John, 162–63
Penn, Thomas, 162–63
Pennsylvania, 147
Pensacola, 26, 271
People of the Longhouse. *See* Haudenosaunee.
Pequot Indians, 91–95
Peter the Great (Czar), 165
Petun Indians, 139, 142
Pickawillany (Pique Town), 169, 172–74
Picuri Indians, 118
Pilgrims, 74–81, 85–91
Piro Indians, 119–20
Pittsburgh, 174
Plains Indians, 164
"Plan for the Future Management of Indian
        Affairs." *See* Plan of 1764.
Plan of 1764, 245–48, 250–51, 260
Plymouth, 87
Pocahontas, 71
Pocasset Indians, 105
Pocumtuck Indians, 105
political exclusion of Indians, 73
Ponce de León, Juan, 8–9

Pontiac, 142, 254
Pontiac's War, 83, 192–204
Pope Paul III, 21
Popé's rebellion, 116–21
Potawatomi Indians, 196
Potomac River, 84
Powhatan, 71, 73
Powhatan's Confederacy, 36, 63–68, 81, 102
"praying Indians," 97–98, 103–4, 111–12, 277, 281
prejudice, 85, 212
The Prince, 20
Privy Council, 285
Proclamation of 1763, 251–53
protective wars, 20–21
Puaray Pueblo, 45
Pueblos, 308
   Acoma, 43–45
   communities, 36–37, 43–48
   reconquest of, 121–22
   unification of, 116–21
   uprisings, 115–16
Puritan Revolt, 91
Puritans, 88–98, 103, 105–17

Q

Quakers, 106
Quebec, 29–30, 142
Quebec Act of 1774, 267

R

racism, 84–85
Raleigh, Sir Walter, 56–57, 63
Ramirez, Father Juan, 48
Randolph, Edward, 111
Reformation, 23
religious beliefs, traditional, 116
"Remarks Concerning the Savages of North-
   America," 224–25
Requerimiento, 6, 13
resistance to European invaders, 36–73
Rhode Island, 90, 106, 207
Ribaut, Jean, 27–28, 60
right of discovery, 90–91
Roanoke colony, 57–68, 208
Roanoke Indians, 58, 61
Rogel, Juan, 49–50
Rolfe, John, 71
Ross, John, 296–97
Rowlandson, Mary, 225–33
Russia, 165–66
Russian-American Company, 166

S

Sac-Forces, 161
Saguenay, 29–30
St. Augustine, Florida, 28, 50, 53, 127
St. Jean, 142
St. Lawrence, Gulf of, 29–31
St. Lawrence River, 29–31
St. Leger, Barry, 285–86
Sakonnet Indians, 105
Salem Village, 208
Samoset, 78–81
San Juan Pueblo, 116
San Miguel de Guadalupe, 10
Sando, Joe S., 116–17
Santa Elena, 50–51
Santee Indians, 126
Sassacus, 94–95
Sassamon, John, 104
Savannah, Georgia, 132
Savannah Indians. *See* Shawnees.
Savannah River, South Carolina, 14
Sayenqueraghta, 295
Schuyler, Philip, 287, 289, 301
Scioto, 169
Secotan, 58, 60
Seminole Indians, 244, 271
Seneca Indians, 141, 147, 153, 167–68, 171–72,
   192–202, 287
Sepúlveda, Juan Ginés de, 22–25
Shawnee Indians, 123, 126, 135–37, 167
   in American Revolution, 272–74, 277
   Dunmore's War, 262–65
   propose pan-Indian alliance, 256–58
Shenandoah, Leon (Chief), 2
Sherman, William Tecumseh, 308–10
silver cup, 58
Sioux Indians, 3, 102–3
Sky City. *See* Acoma Pueblo.
slavery. *See* black slaves; enslavement of Indians.
smallpox, 4, 88–89
Smith, John (Captain), 65–68, 71, 84
Smith, William, 239–41
Soto, Hernando de, 13–18, 21, 26
South Carolina, 53, 123, 126
The Soverignty and Goodness of God, 226–33
Spanish, 2–26, 43–54, 115–24
The Spanish Colonie, 57
Spanish-Pueblo expedition of 1720, 164
spirituality, 44, 113
   underminded by fur trade, 164
Squanto, 78–81
Stadacona, 29–30

Standish, Myles, 80, 87
starvation, as war strategy, 102
"starving time," 65
Stone, John (Captain), 91–93
Strachey, William, 69–70
Stuart, John, 248, 251, 253
Stumpe, 185–86
Stuyvesant, Peter, 101
Sublimus Deus, 21
"suffering traders," 260–61
Sullivan Campaign of 1779, 292–97
Sullivan, John, 292–94, 309
Sun Woman, 222
Susquehanna Confederacy, 147–49
Susquehanna Indians, 38, 40–43, 102–3
Sycamore Shoals (Tennessee), 265

T
Tadadaho, 2
Taignoagny, 29–30
Taino Indians, 3
Tampa Bay, Florida, 13
Tanacharisson, 171, 175–76
Taos, 118
Tarrantines. *See* Abnakis.
Tascalusa, 15–16
tenacity of American Indian nations, 3–4
Tenhoghskweagha, 287–88
Terry, Lucy, 210–12
Tesuque Pueblo, 117
Tewa Pueblos, 44
Thanksgiving
    celebration, 80–81
    the myth, 74–75
Thanksgiving's children, 74
Thayendanegea. *See* Brant, Joseph.
Thomas, GovenorGeorge, 163
Thorpe, Captain George, 71–72, 81, 83
Three Rivers, 140
Tiguex Pueblos, 18–19, 44
Timucua Indians, 28, 50–51
Timucuas, 126
Tituba, 207–8
Tiwas, 115
Tlaxcalans, 7
Tlingits, 166
Toa, 14
tobacco, 69, 71–72, 81
Tobacco's Son, 275
Tockamahamon, 80
Tomochichi, 132–33
Tony, Sam, 216–17

trade, 136
    abuse, 260–61
    goods, 71–72, 81, 86, 107–9
    paradox of, 31
    political impact during American
        Revolution, 267–68, 270–72, 283–84,
        299–303
Trade Plan of 1764, 245–48
traders, 259–61
Treaty of Agusta, 260
Treaty of Fort Stanwix, 251
Treaty of Hard labor, 251–53
Treaty of Long Island, 271
Treaty of Paris, 190–91, 201, 278
treaty of peace, 78–79
Treaty of Pittsburgh, 272
Tree of Peace, 163
Tuneam, Joe. *See* Neepaheilomon.
Tuscarora Indians, 125, 279, 282, 292
Twightwees. *See* Miami Indians.

U
Unca Indians, 94–96
underground railroad, 217–18
Underhill, Captain John, 94–95, 101
unification of Pueblos, 116–21
United Colonies, 96
United States, first Indian treaty, 275–76
University of Salamanca, 20
Utopia, 20, 70

V
Valley Forge, 279
Vargas Zapapa y Lujan, Diego de, 121
*Very Brief Account of the Destruction of the
    Indies*, 57
Vincennes (Indiana), 274–175
Virginia, 56, 69, 72, 81–85
Virginia Richly Valued, 76
Vitoria, Francisco de, 20, 70
Vries, David de, 99–100

W
Waban, Chief, 98
Wahunsonacock. *See* Powhatan.
Walking Purchase, 162–63
Wamesit, 103
Wampanoag alliance, 105
Wampanoag Indians, 74, 78–80, 86, 103–5
Wampanoag-Pilgrim alliance, 80
wampum, 92, 109–10

Wanchese Indians, 56–60
Wappinger Confederacy, 99
War of the League of Augsburg, 154, 157
War of the Spanish Succession, 124
Washington, George, 176–77, 207, 212, 260, 277
Wesley, John, 133
Wessagusett colony, 85–88
Westo Indians. *See* Chichumecoes.
westward migration, 242–45
"Where was God?" 8
White, John, 57–58, 61–62
Williams, John, 159
Williams, Roger, 89–90, 96–97
Wingina (chief of the Roanoacs), 59–60
Winthrop, John, 88–89
Witawamet, 87
women
    captured by Indians, 225–37
    Indians and, 220–25
"work it out together," 2
Wounded Knee, 3
Wright, James, 260
Wyandot Indians, 146, 272–73, 277

Y

Yamacraw Indians, 132
Yamasee Indians, 123, 125–27, 129–30
Yeardley (govenor of Virginia), 72
York River, 102
Yorktown, 271, 277, 297
Yuchi Indians, 123

Z

Zaldivar, Juan de, 45–46
Zaldivar, Vicente de, 46–48
Zuni Indians, 48
Zutancalpo, 45, 47
Zutucapan, 45, 47